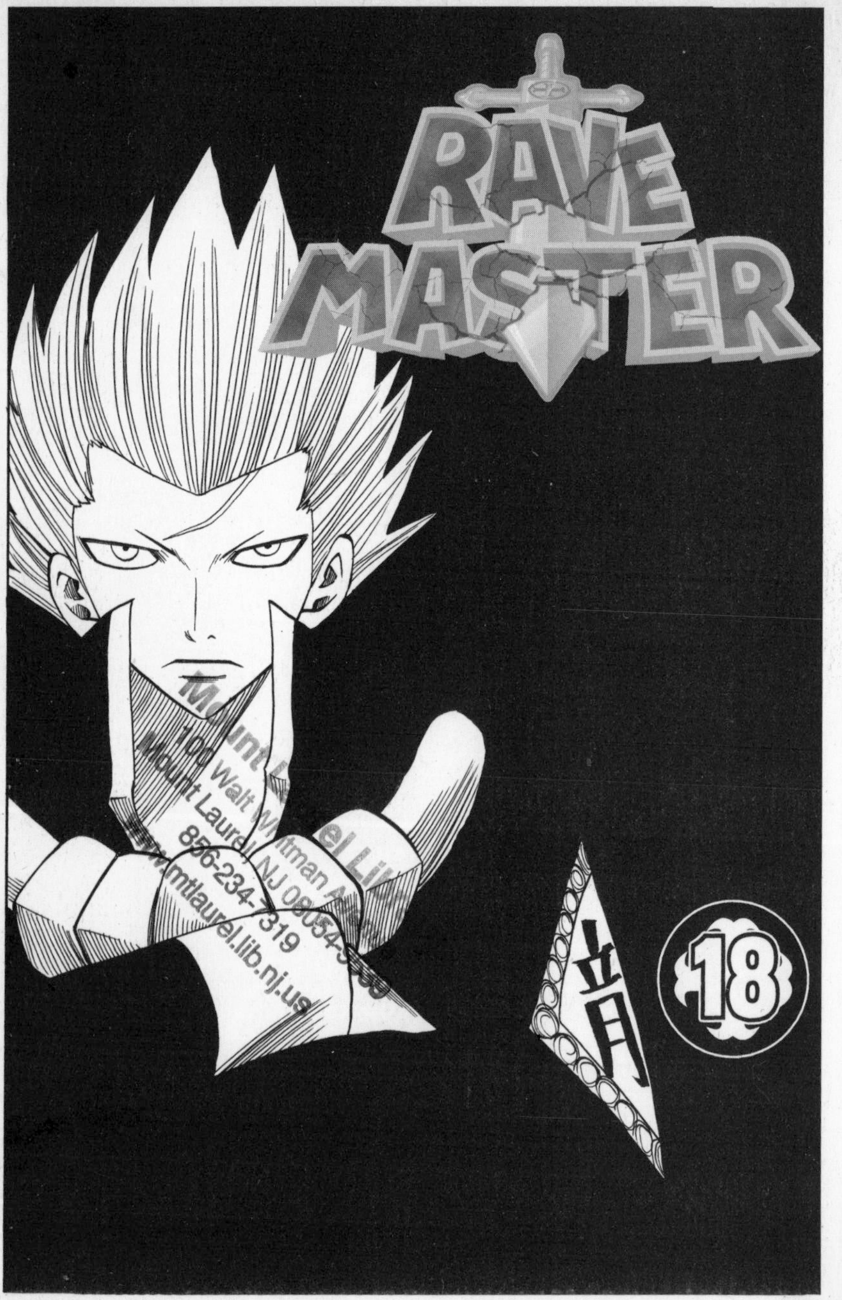
RAVE MASTER
18

Rave Master Vol. 18
Created by Hiro Mashima

Translation - Jeremiah Bourque
English Adaptation - Jake Forbes
Retouch and Lettering - Rafael Najarian
Production Artist - Rafael Najarian
Cover Design - Al-Insan Lashley

Editor - Troy Lewter
Digital Imaging Manager - Chris Buford
Production Managers - Jennifer Miller and Mutsumi Miyazaki
Managing Editor - Lindsey Johnston
VP of Production - Ron Klamert
Publisher and E.I.C. - Mike Kiley
President and C.O.O. - John Parker
C.E.O. - Stuart Levy

A  Manga

TOKYOPOP Inc.
5900 Wilshire Blvd. Suite 2000
Los Angeles, CA 90036

E-mail: info@TOKYOPOP.com
Come visit us online at www.TOKYOPOP.com

ISBN: 1-59532-023-7

First TOKYOPOP printing: December 2005
10 9 8 7 6 5 4 3 2 1
Printed in the USA

VOLUME 18

Story and Art by

HIRO MASHIMA

HAMBURG // LONDON // LOS ANGELES // TOKYO

THE STORY SO FAR...

Of the many obstacles **Haru** has faced to obtain the fourth **Rave Stone,** this latest one has proven to be the most perilous. Haru, still injured after his first battle with **Doryu,** confronted him again—only this time, he had his friends by his side. During the ensuing battle, Doryu reveals his backstory, in which he was a creature of light and good, but was imprisoned by humans simply because he was a different species (**a sentinoid**). After his story, **Lilith** arrives to assist Doryu, revealing that he is in fact **King** of the **Mystic Realm.** However, Haru and his friends' pleas for Doryu to come back to the side of good fall on deaf ears, and after he kills Lilith, Doryu resumes his assault on them. In the end, Haru finally kills him...but then Haru, having expended massive amounts of energy to defeat Doryu, begins to fade from existence...

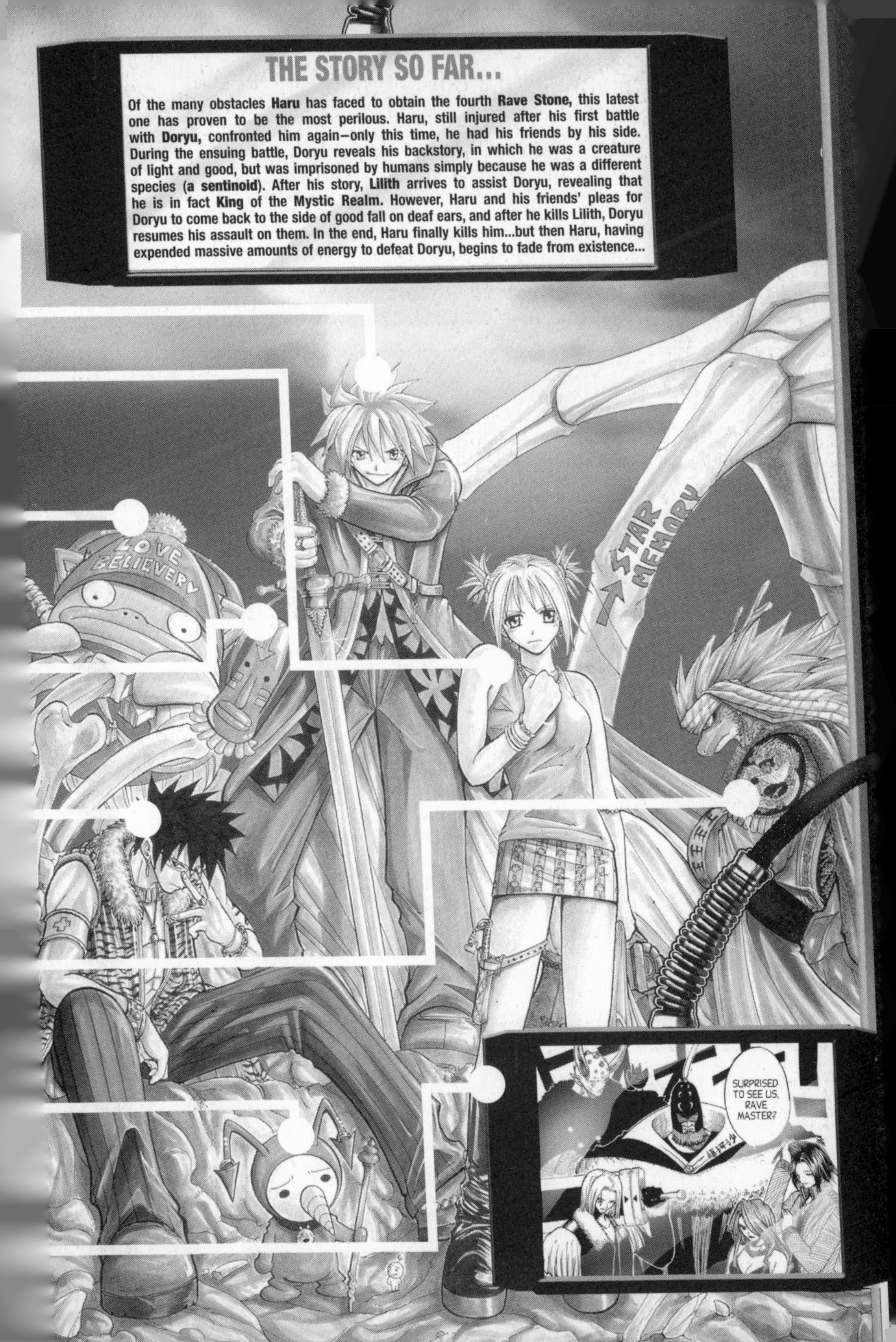
LOVE BELIEVER
STAR MEMORY
SURPRISED TO SEE US, RAVE MASTER?

THE RAVE MASTER CREW

HARU GLORY

A small-town boy turned savior of the world. As the **Rave Master** (the only one capable of using the holy weapon RAVE), Haru set forth to find the missing Rave Stones and defeat **Demon Card**. He fights with the **Ten Powers Sword**, a weapon that takes on different forms at his command. With Demon Card seemingly out of the way, Haru now seeks the remaining two Rave Stones in order to open the way to Star Memory.

ELIE

The girl without memories. Elie joined Haru on his quest when he promised to help her find out about her past. She's cute, spunky and loves gambling and shopping in equal measure. Locked inside of her is the power of **Etherion**.

RUBY

A "penguin-type" sentenoid, Ruby loves rare and unusual items. After Haru saved him from Pumpkin Doryu's gang, Ruby agreed to sponsor Haru's team in their search for the ultimate rare treasures: the Rave Stones!

GRIFFON KATO (GRIFF)

Griff is a loyal friend, even if he is a bit of a coward. His rubbery body can stretch and change shape as needed. Griff's two greatest pleasures in life are mapmaking and peeping on Elie.

MUSICA

A "Silverclaimer" (an alchemist who can shape silver at will) and a former street punk who made good. He joined Haru for the adventure, but now that Demon Card is defeated, does he have any reason to stick around?

LET

A member of the **Dragon Race**, he was formerly a member of the Demon Card's Five Palace Guardians. He was so impressed by Haru's fighting skills and pureness of heart that he made a truce with the Rave Master. After passing his Dragon Trial, he gained a human body, but his blood is still Dragon Race.

PLUE

The **Rave Bearer**, Plue is the faithful companion to the Rave Master. In addition to being Haru's guide, Plue also has powers of his own. When he's not getting Haru into or out of trouble, Plue can be found enjoying a sucker, his favorite treat.

THE ORACION SIX

Demon Card's six generals. Haru defeated **Shuda** after finding the Rave of Wisdom. The other five generals were presumed dead after King destroyed Demon Card Headquarters.

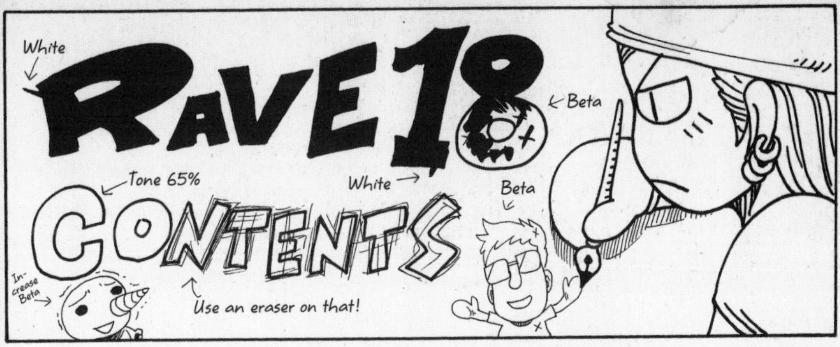
White
RAVE 18
Beta
Tone 65%
White
Beta
CONTENTS
In-crease Beta
Use an eraser on that!

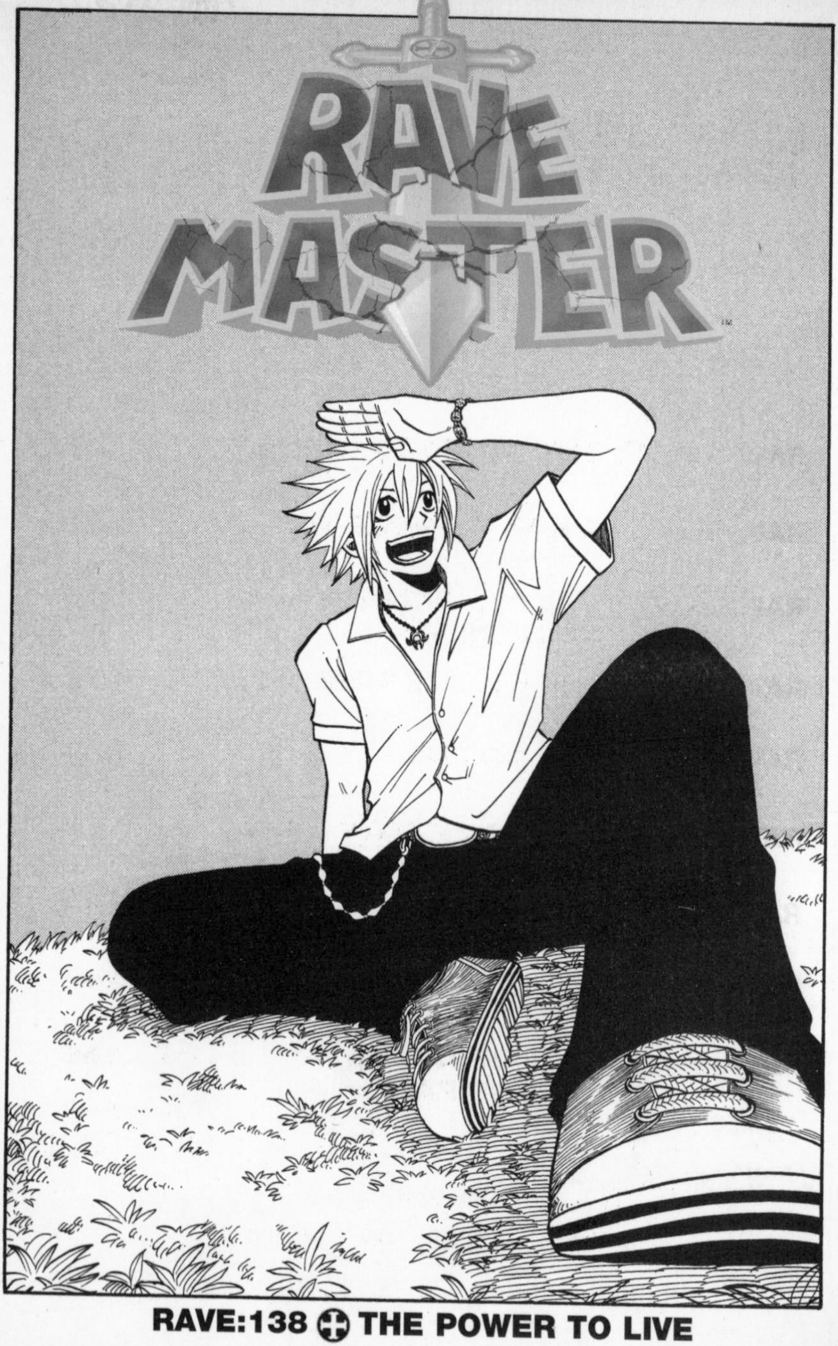
RAVE MASTER

RAVE:138 THE POWER TO LIVE

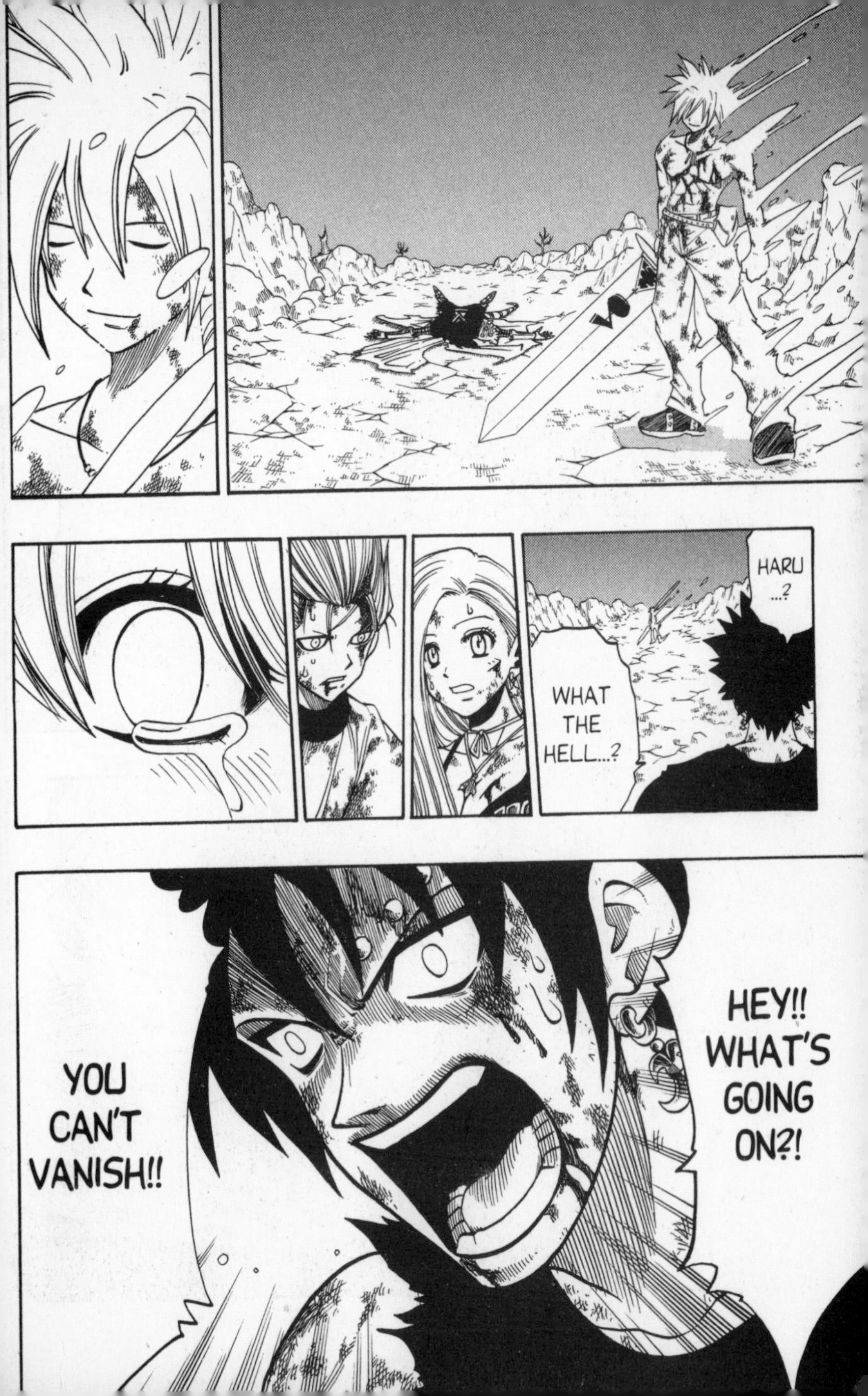
HARU ...?
WHAT THE HELL...?
HEY!! WHAT'S GOING ON?!
YOU CAN'T VANISH!!

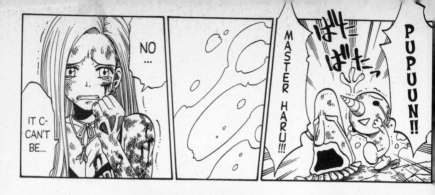

PUPUUN!!
MASTER HARU!!!
NO ...
IT C- CAN'T BE...
. . . . . .
"I DON'T KNOW THAT I'LL..."
"...SURVIVE THIS FIGHT."
LIAR.
"SO, YOU CAN'T FORGET THE NAME I'M ABOUT TO TELL YOU."
"YOU MUST REMEMBER, BECAUSE HE'LL BE THE THIRD RAVE MASTER."

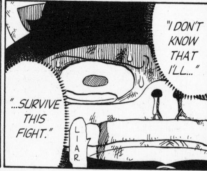

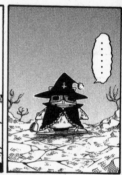

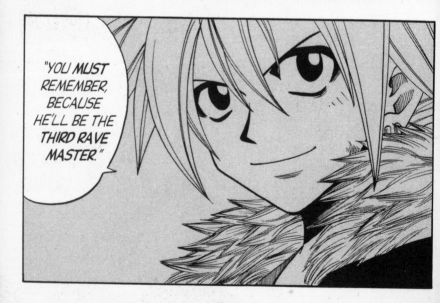

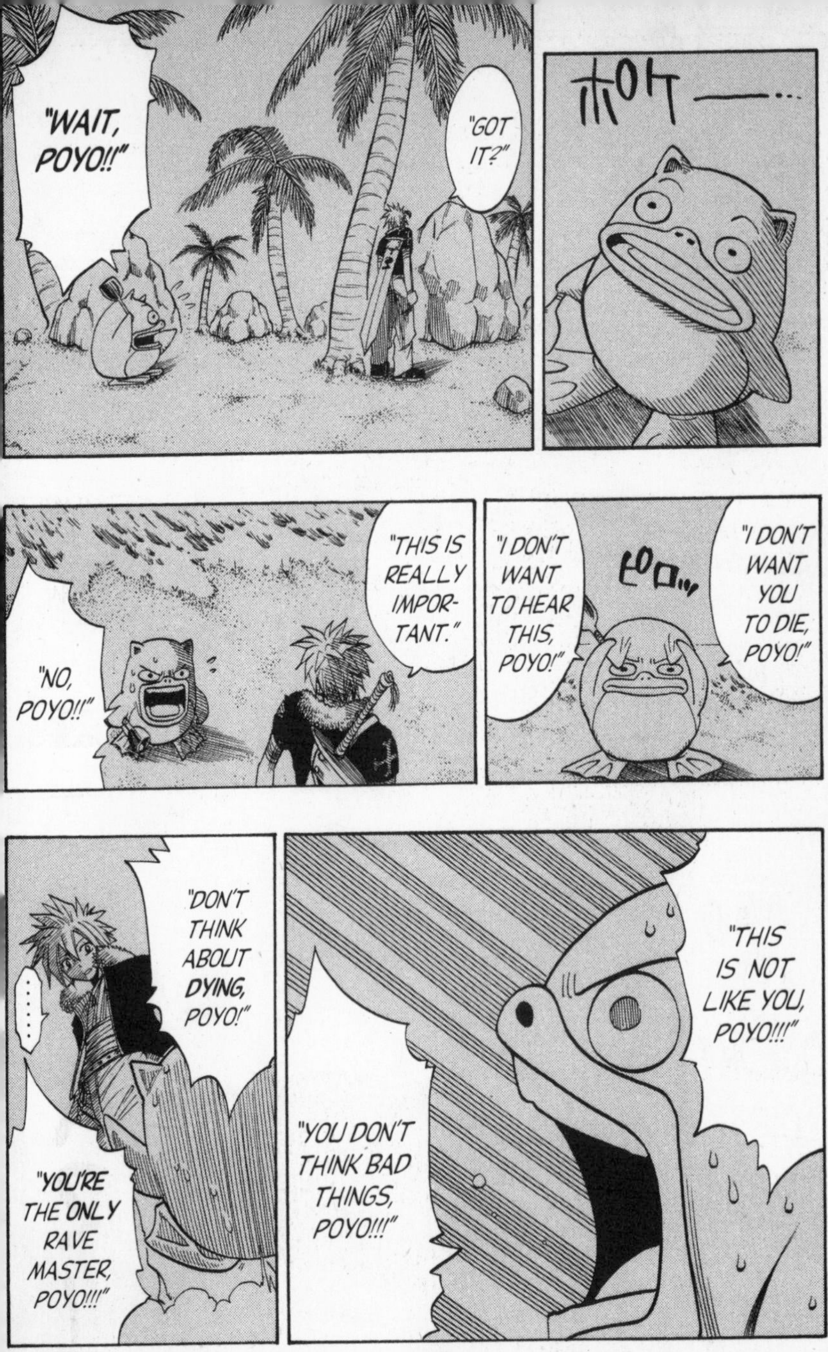
"GOT IT?"
"WAIT, POYO!!"
"I DON'T WANT YOU TO DIE, POYO!"
"I DON'T WANT TO HEAR THIS, POYO!"
"THIS IS REALLY IMPOR-TANT."
"NO, POYO!!"
"THIS IS NOT LIKE YOU, POYO!!!"
"YOU DON'T THINK BAD THINGS, POYO!!!"
"DON'T THINK ABOUT DYING, POYO!"
……
"YOU'RE THE ONLY RAVE MASTER, POYO!!!"

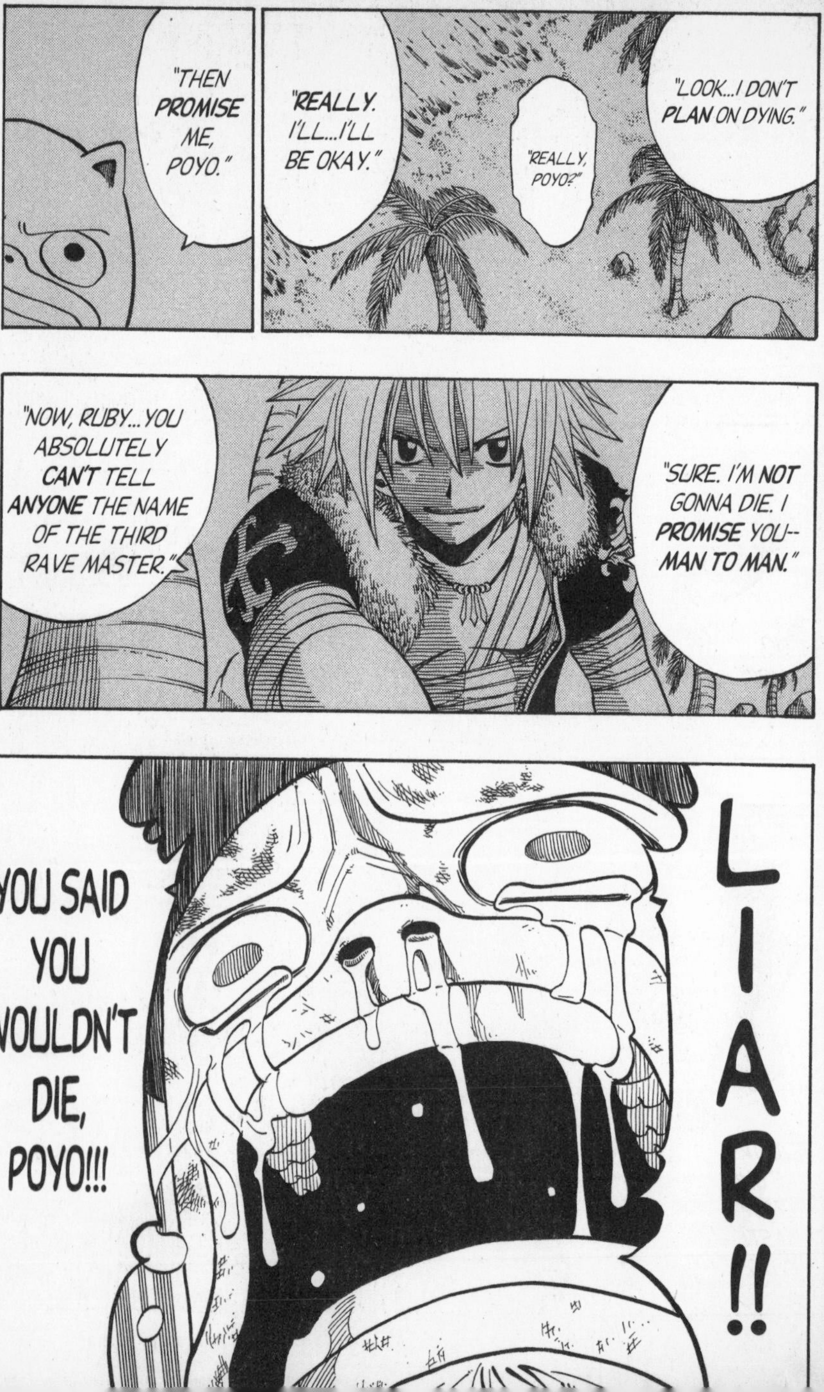
"LOOK...I DON'T PLAN ON DYING."
"REALLY, POYO?"
"REALLY. I'LL...I'LL BE OKAY."
"THEN PROMISE ME, POYO."
"SURE. I'M NOT GONNA DIE. I PROMISE YOU--MAN TO MAN."
"NOW, RUBY...YOU ABSOLUTELY CAN'T TELL ANYONE THE NAME OF THE THIRD RAVE MASTER."
LIAR!!
YOU SAID YOU WOULDN'T DIE, POYO!!!

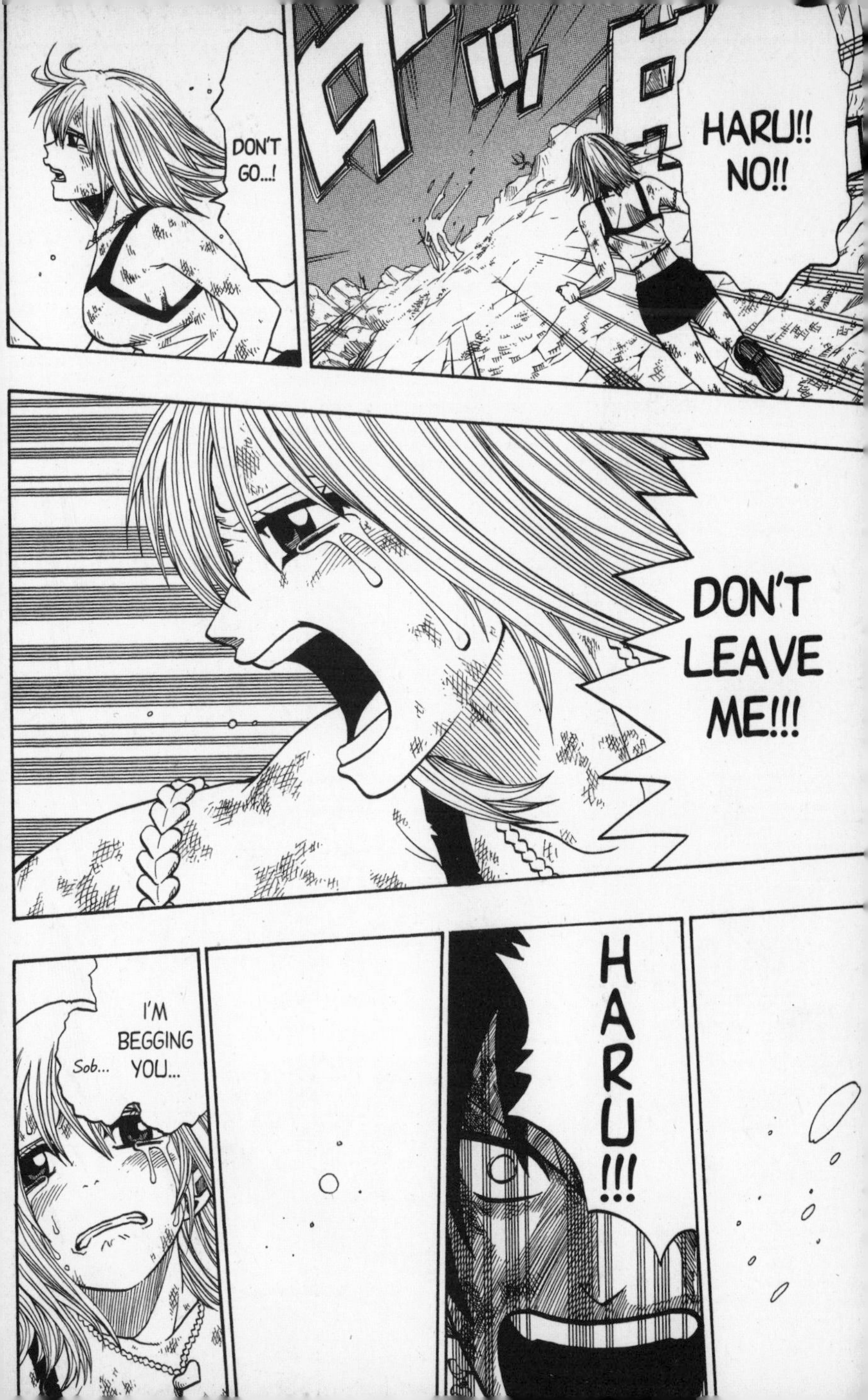
HARU!! NO!!
DON'T GO...!
DON'T LEAVE ME!!!
HARU!!!
I'M BEGGING YOU...
Sob...

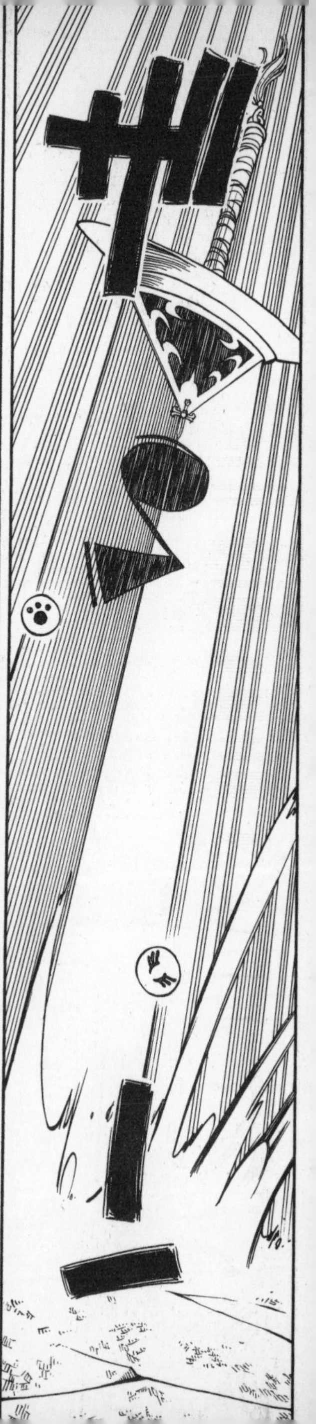
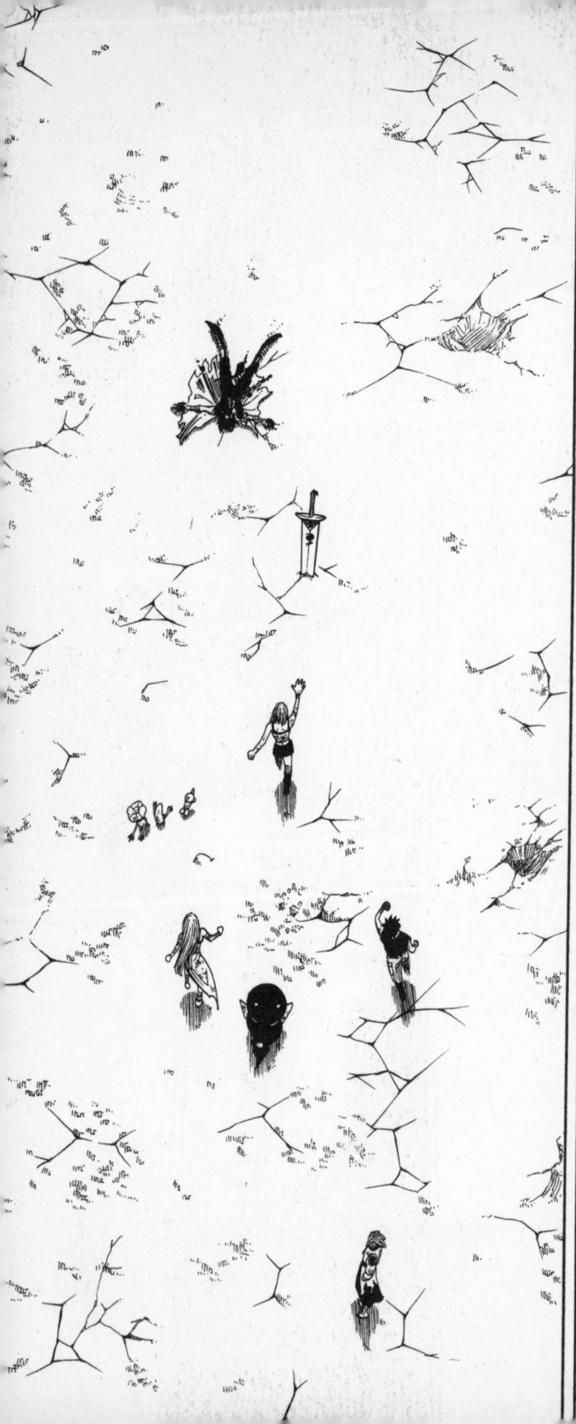

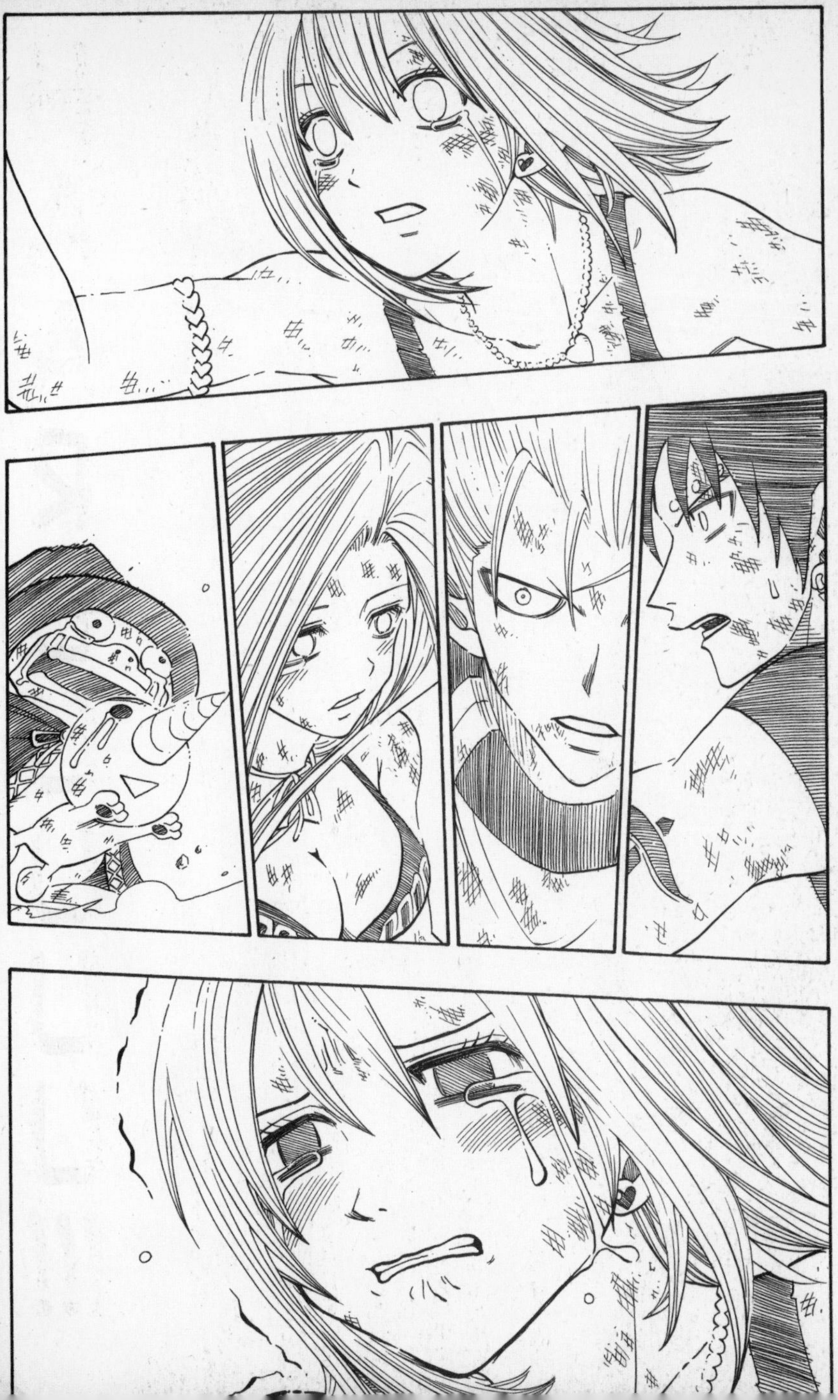

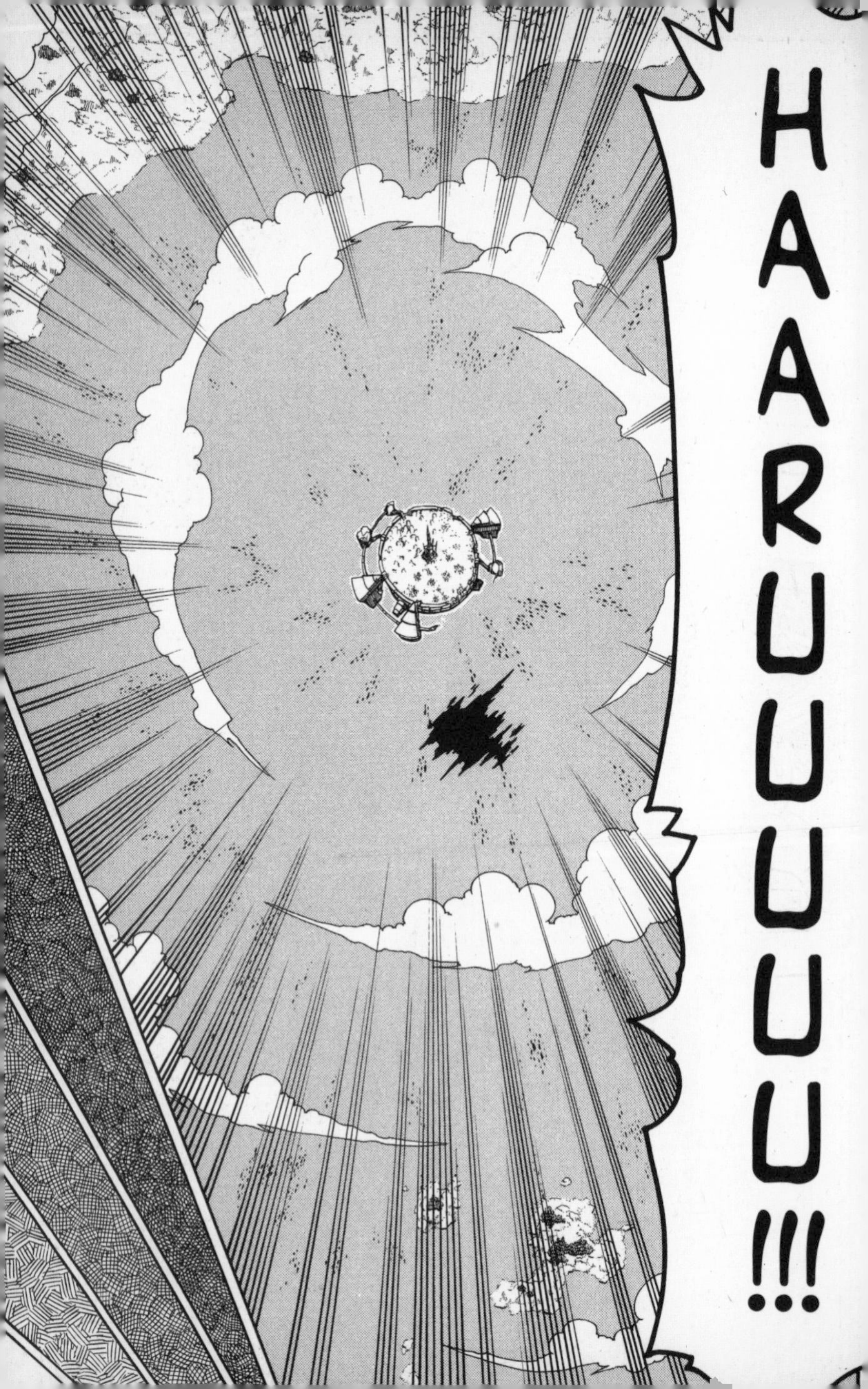
HAARUUUU!!!

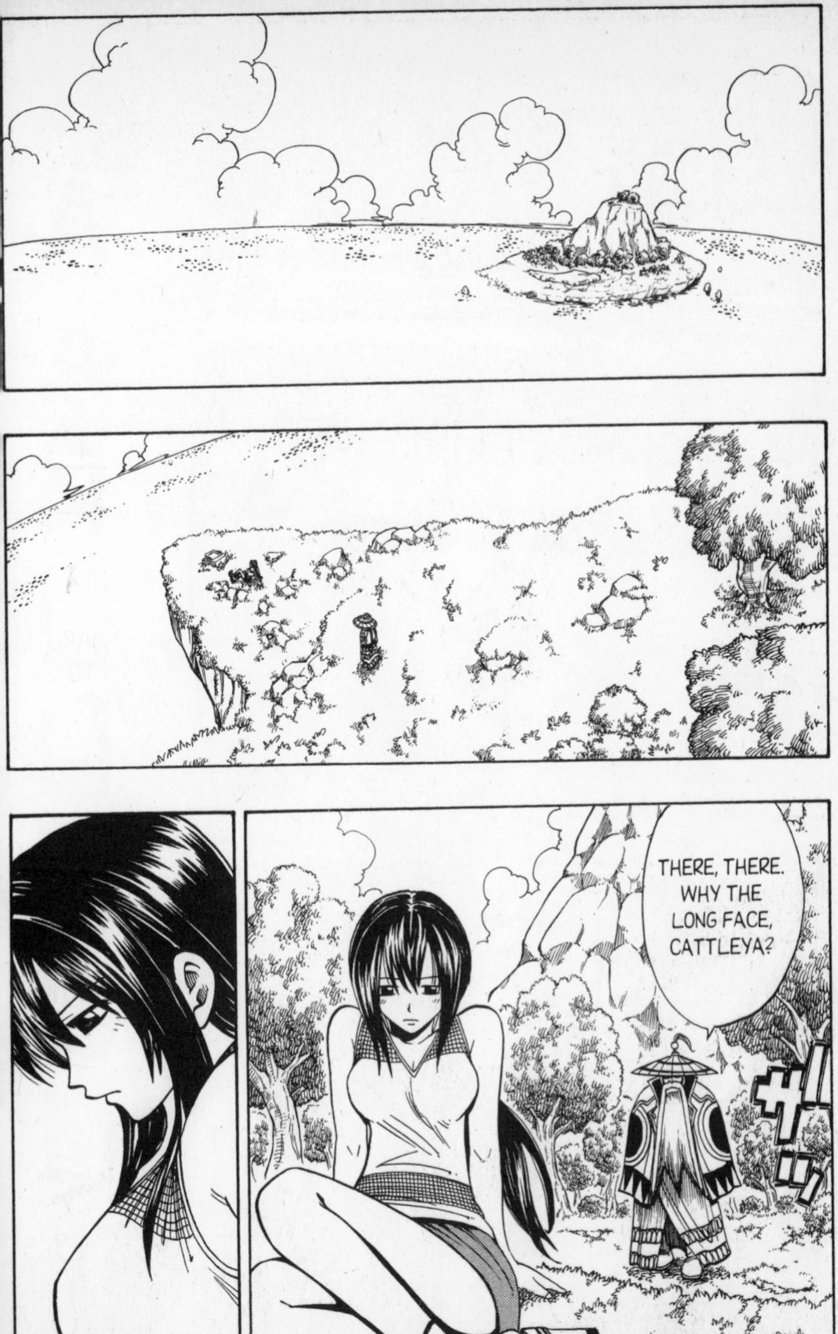
THERE, THERE. WHY THE LONG FACE, CATTLEYA?

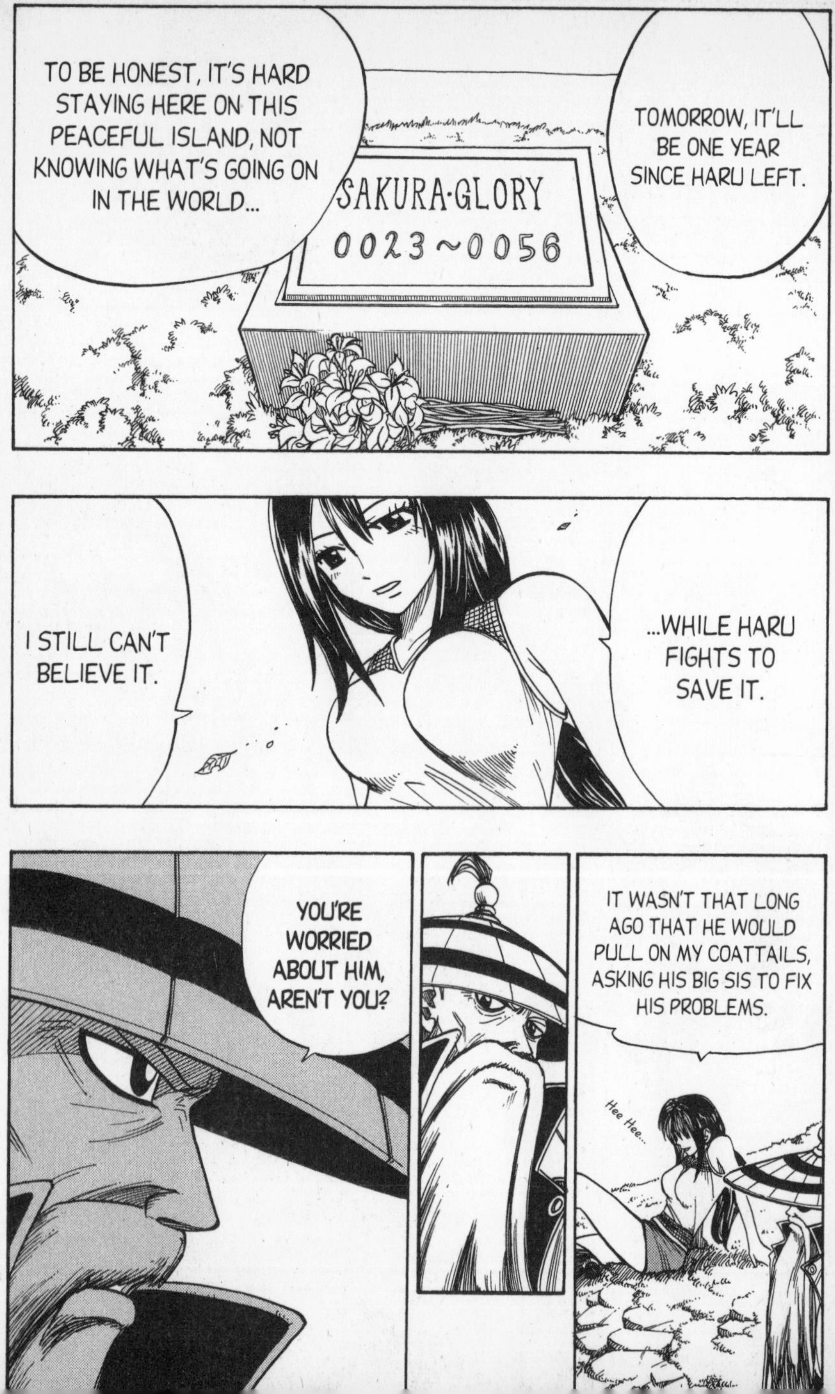
TOMORROW, IT'LL BE ONE YEAR SINCE HARU LEFT.
SAKURA·GLORY
0023~0056
TO BE HONEST, IT'S HARD STAYING HERE ON THIS PEACEFUL ISLAND, NOT KNOWING WHAT'S GOING ON IN THE WORLD...
...WHILE HARU FIGHTS TO SAVE IT.
I STILL CAN'T BELIEVE IT.
IT WASN'T THAT LONG AGO THAT HE WOULD PULL ON MY COATTAILS, ASKING HIS BIG SIS TO FIX HIS PROBLEMS.
Hee Hee...
YOU'RE WORRIED ABOUT HIM, AREN'T YOU?

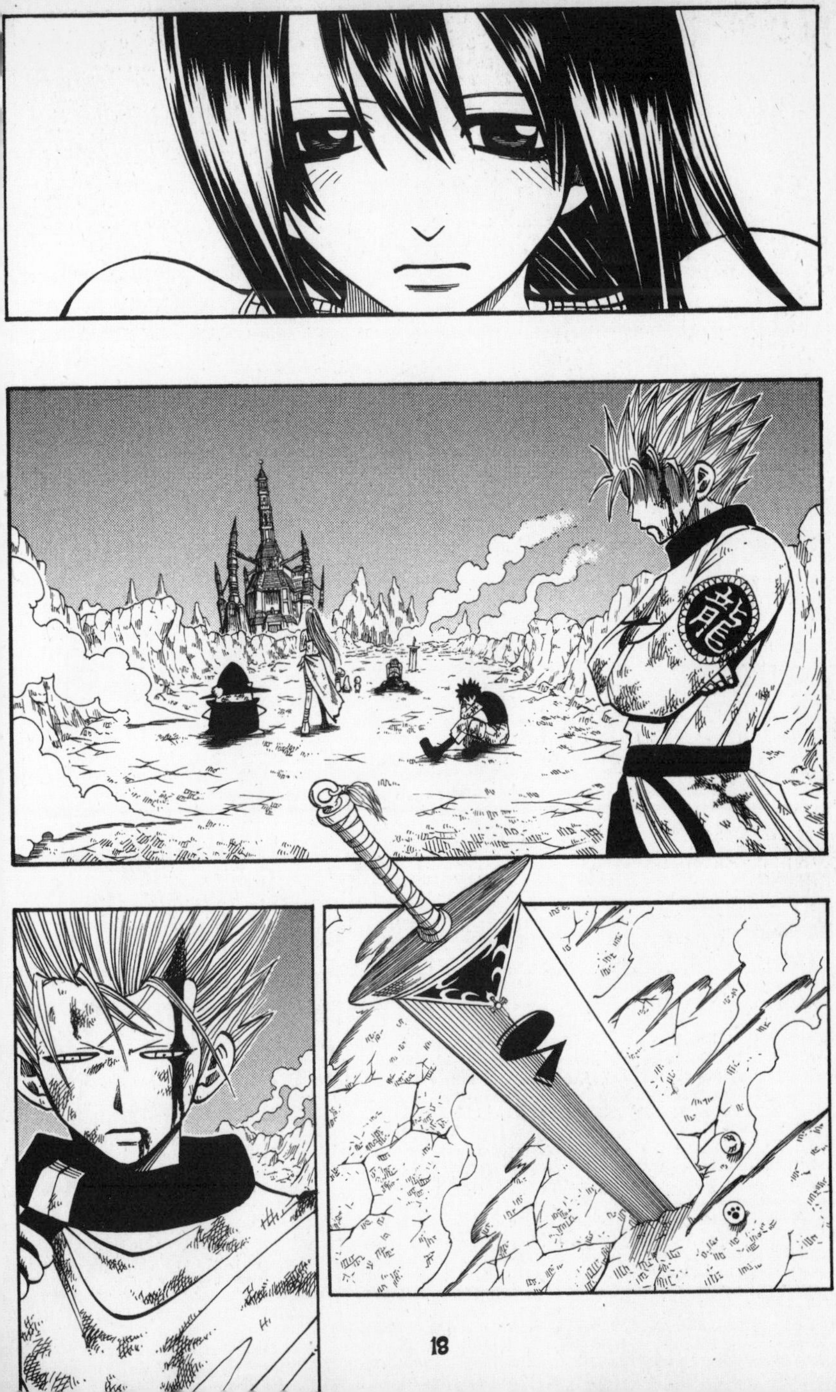
龍

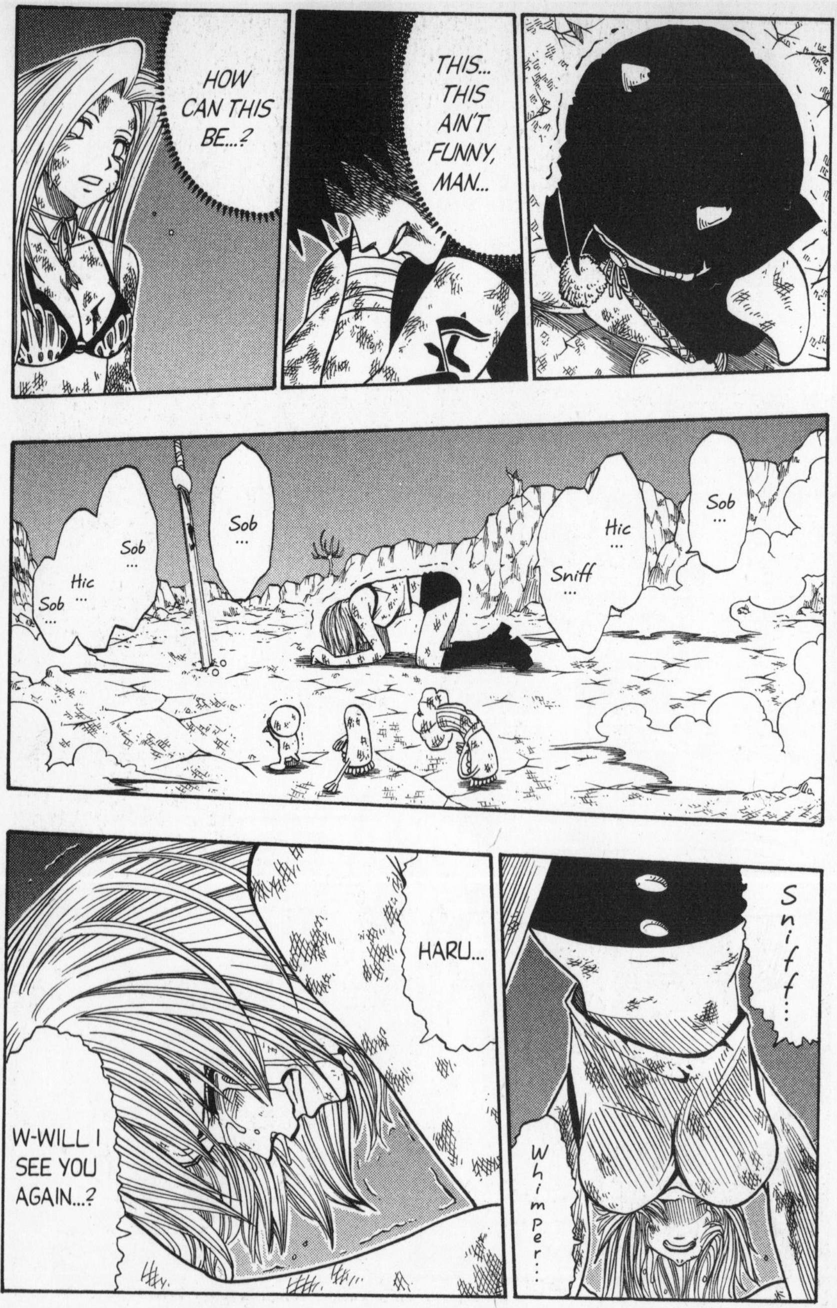

THIS... THIS AIN'T FUNNY, MAN...
HOW CAN THIS BE...?
Sob ...
Hic ...
Sniff ...
Sob ...
Sob ...
Hic ...
Sob ...
Sniff...
Whimper...
HARU...
W-WILL I SEE YOU AGAIN...?

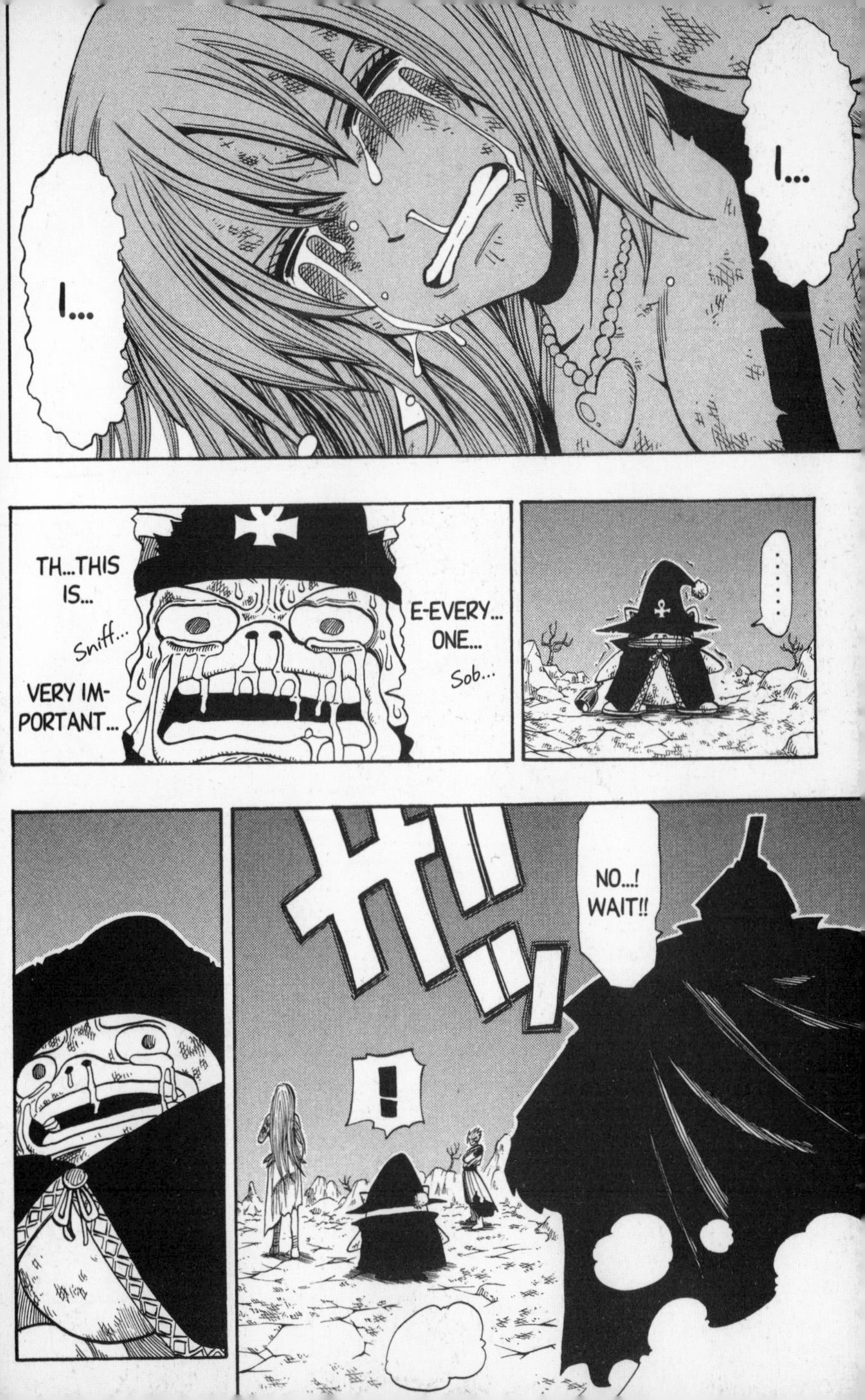
I...
I...
......
TH...THIS IS...
Sniff...
VERY IM-PORTANT...
E-EVERY... ONE...
Sob...
ガッ
NO...! WAIT!!
!

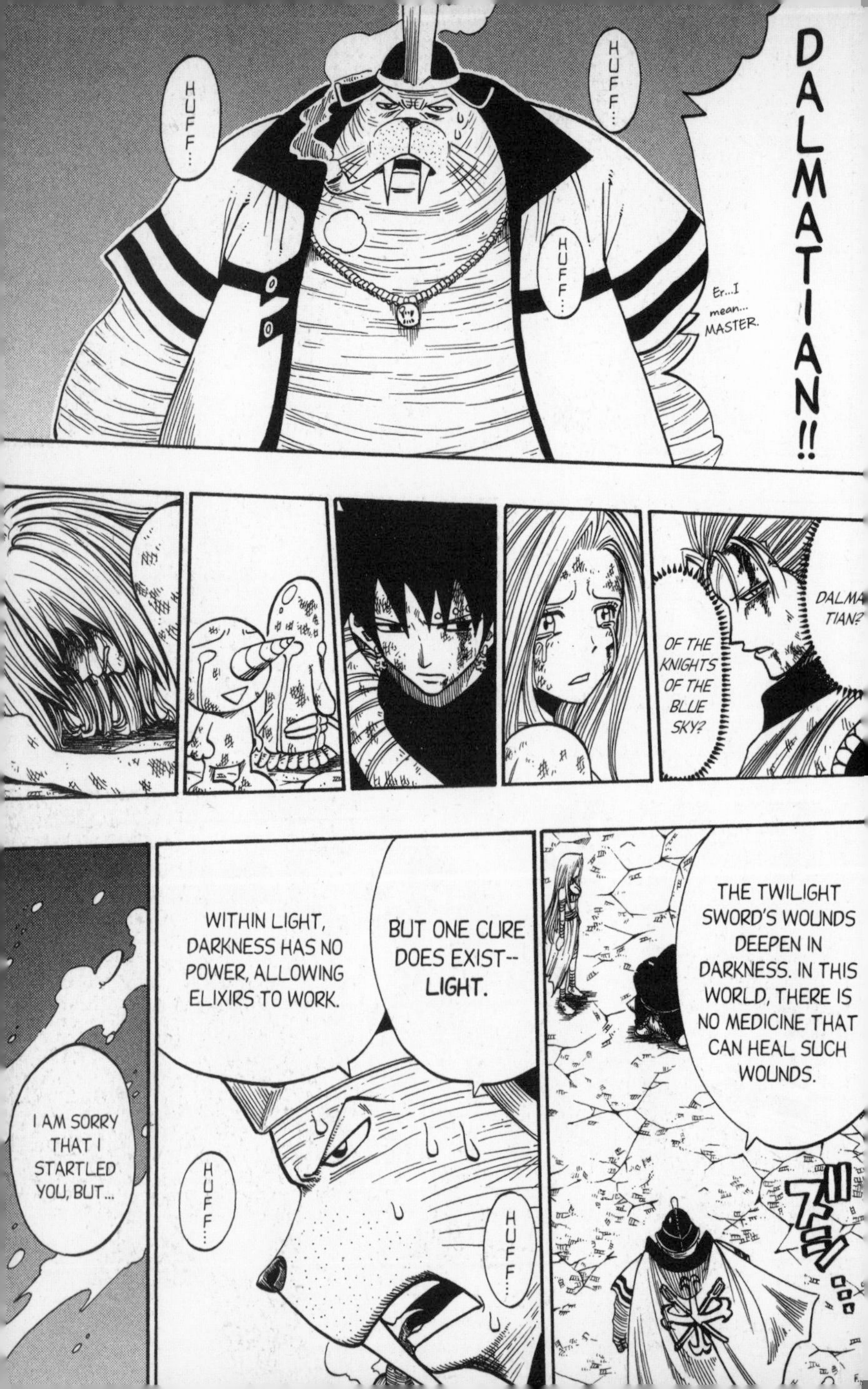
DALMATIAN!!
HUFF...
HUFF...
Er...I mean... MASTER.
HUFF...
DALMATIAN?
OF THE KNIGHTS OF THE BLUE SKY?
THE TWILIGHT SWORD'S WOUNDS DEEPEN IN DARKNESS. IN THIS WORLD, THERE IS NO MEDICINE THAT CAN HEAL SUCH WOUNDS.
BUT ONE CURE DOES EXIST-- LIGHT.
WITHIN LIGHT, DARKNESS HAS NO POWER, ALLOWING ELIXIRS TO WORK.
HUFF...
HUFF...
I AM SORRY THAT I STARTLED YOU, BUT...

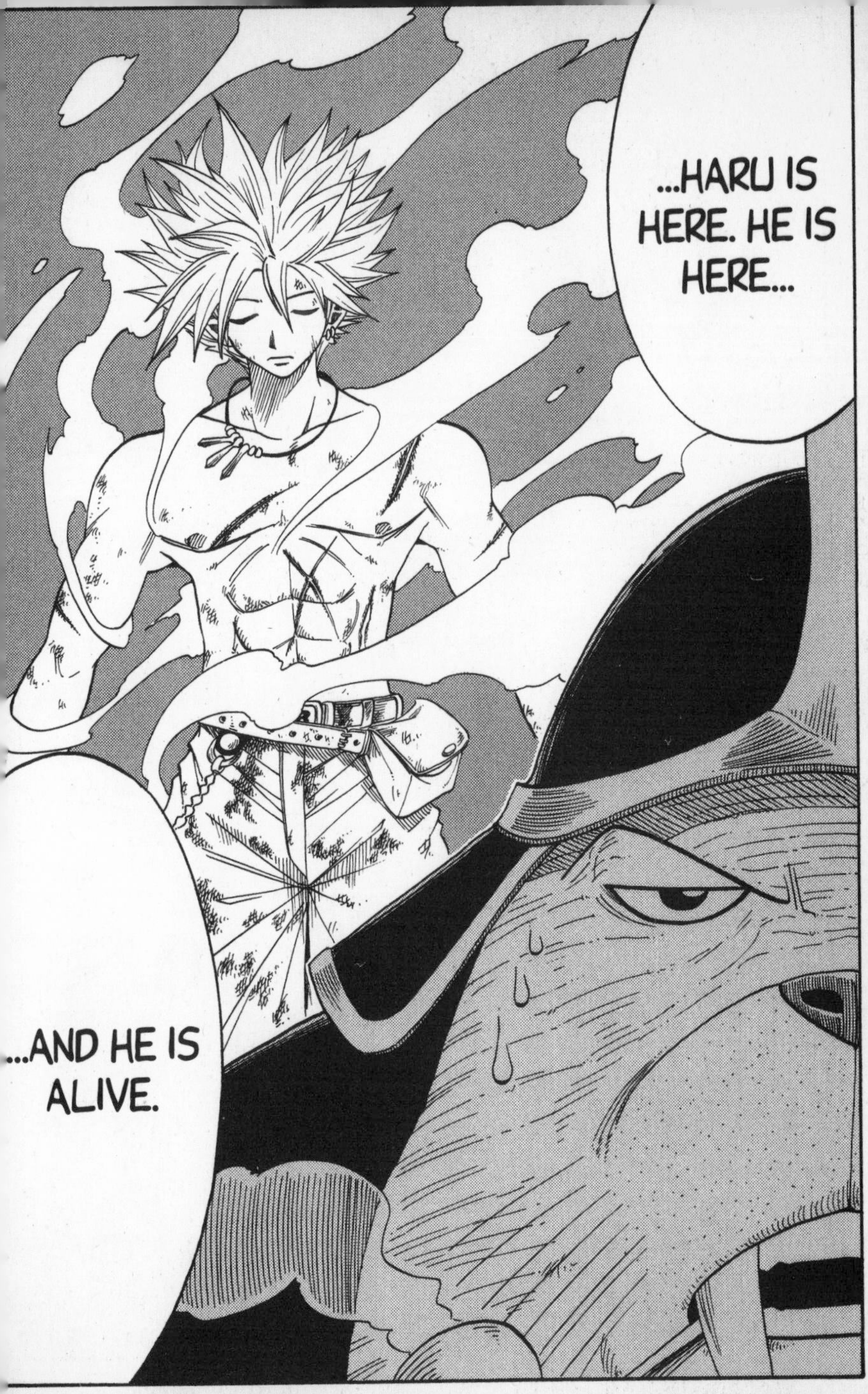
...HARU IS HERE. HE IS HERE...
...AND HE IS ALIVE.

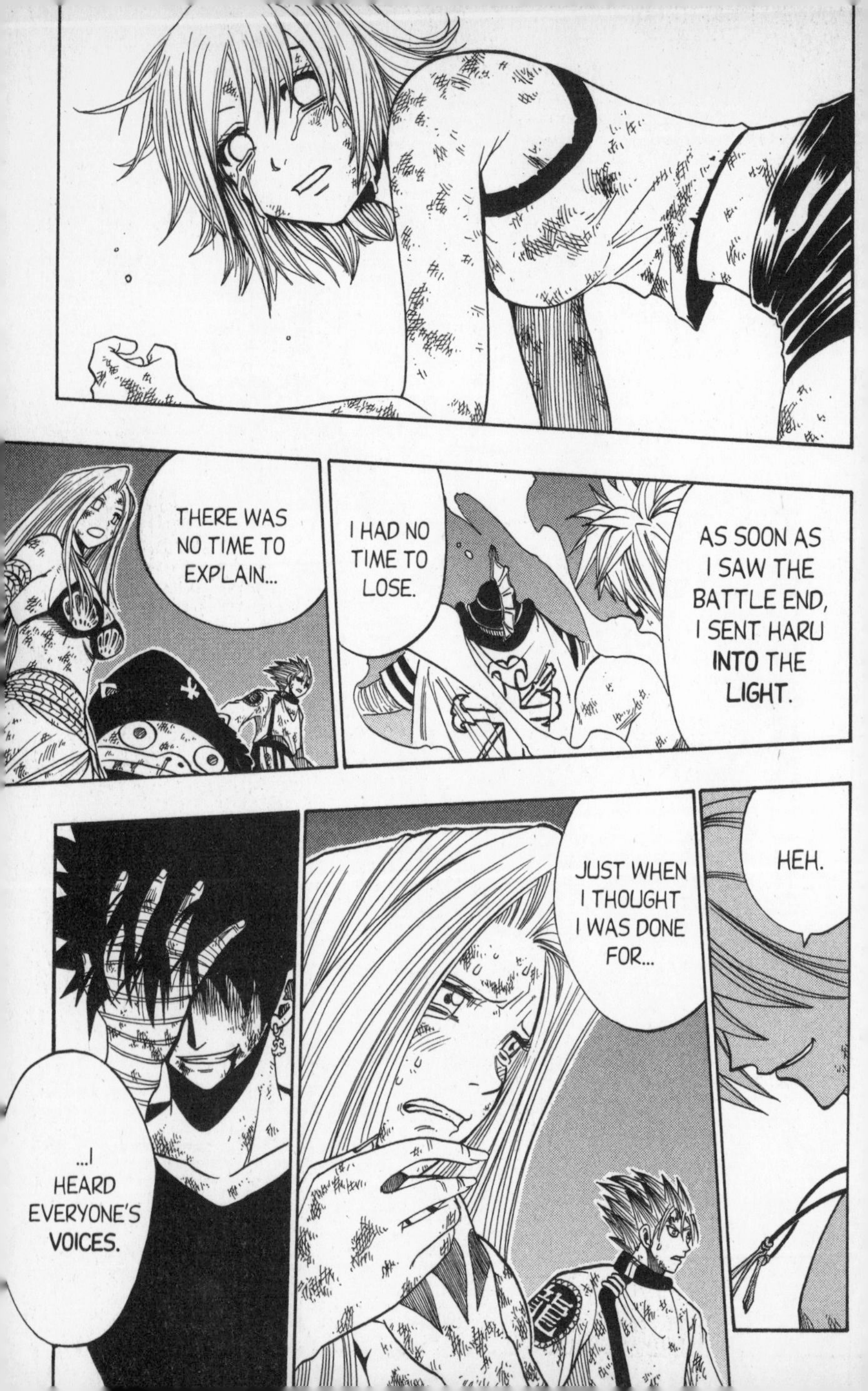
AS SOON AS I SAW THE BATTLE END, I SENT HARU **INTO THE LIGHT.**
I HAD NO TIME TO LOSE.
THERE WAS NO TIME TO EXPLAIN...
HEH.
JUST WHEN I THOUGHT I WAS DONE FOR...
...I HEARD EVERYONE'S **VOICES.**

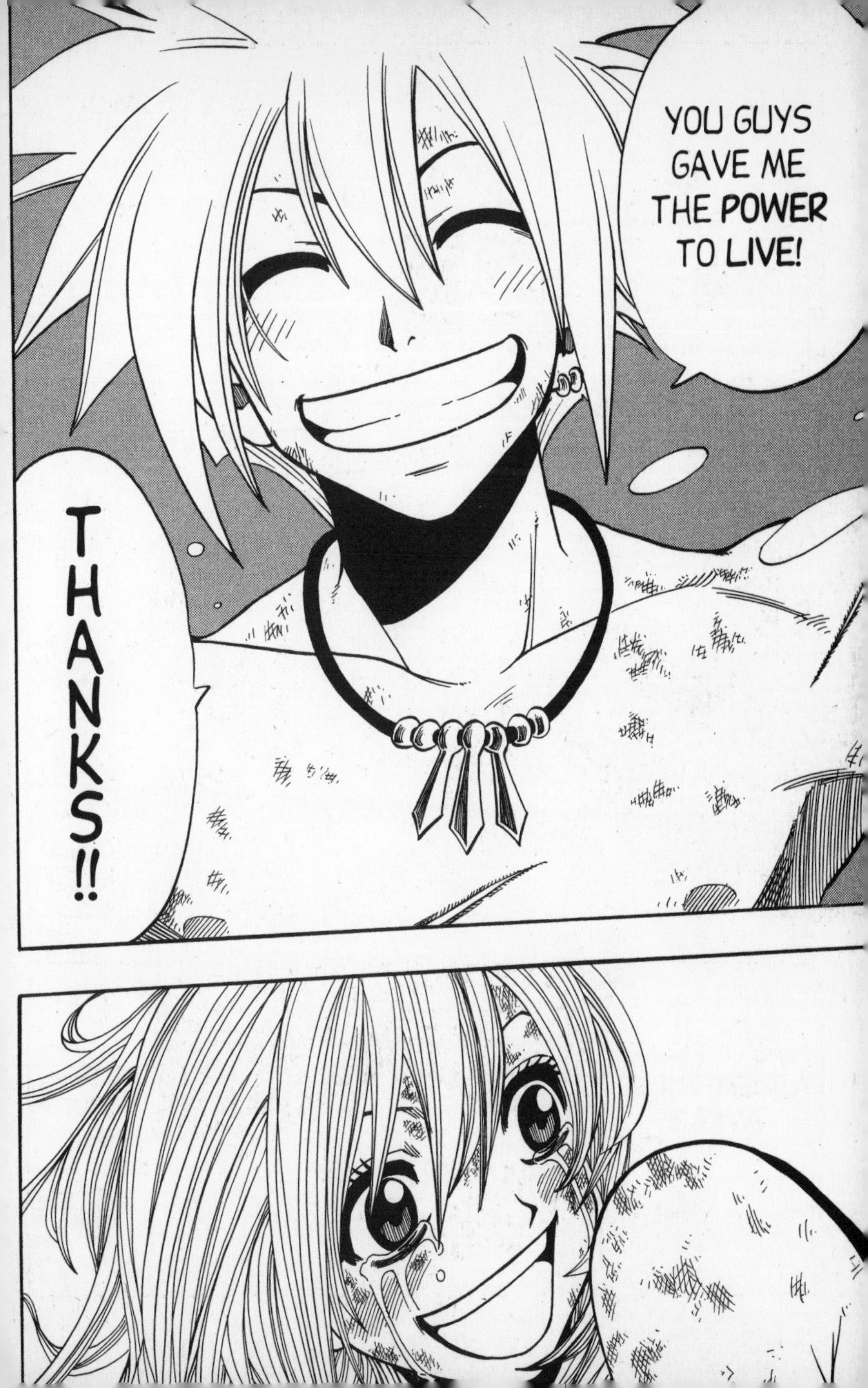
YOU GUYS GAVE ME THE POWER TO LIVE!
THANKS!!

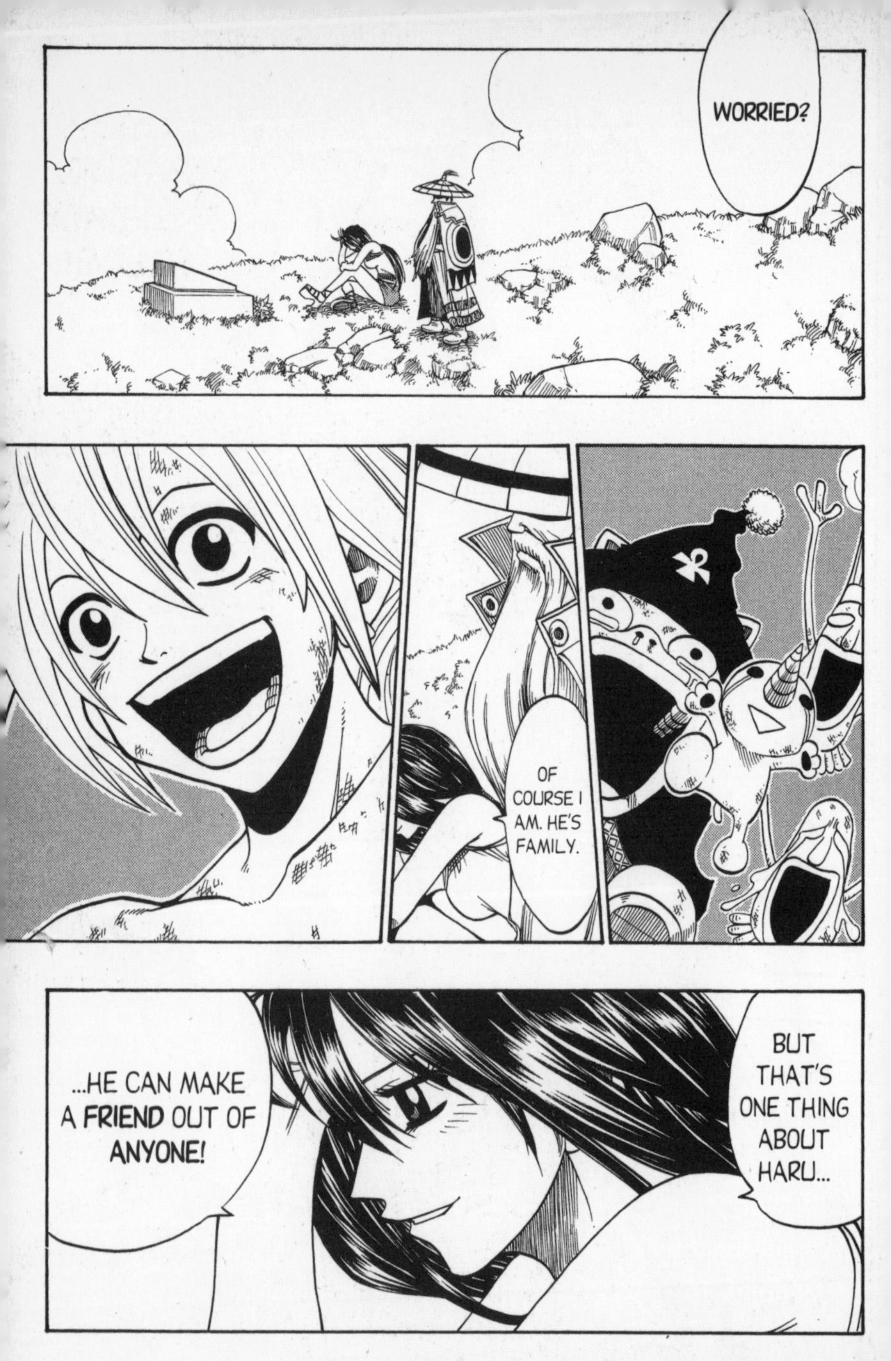
WORRIED?
OF COURSE I AM. HE'S FAMILY.
BUT THAT'S ONE THING ABOUT HARU...
...HE CAN MAKE A **FRIEND** OUT OF **ANYONE!**

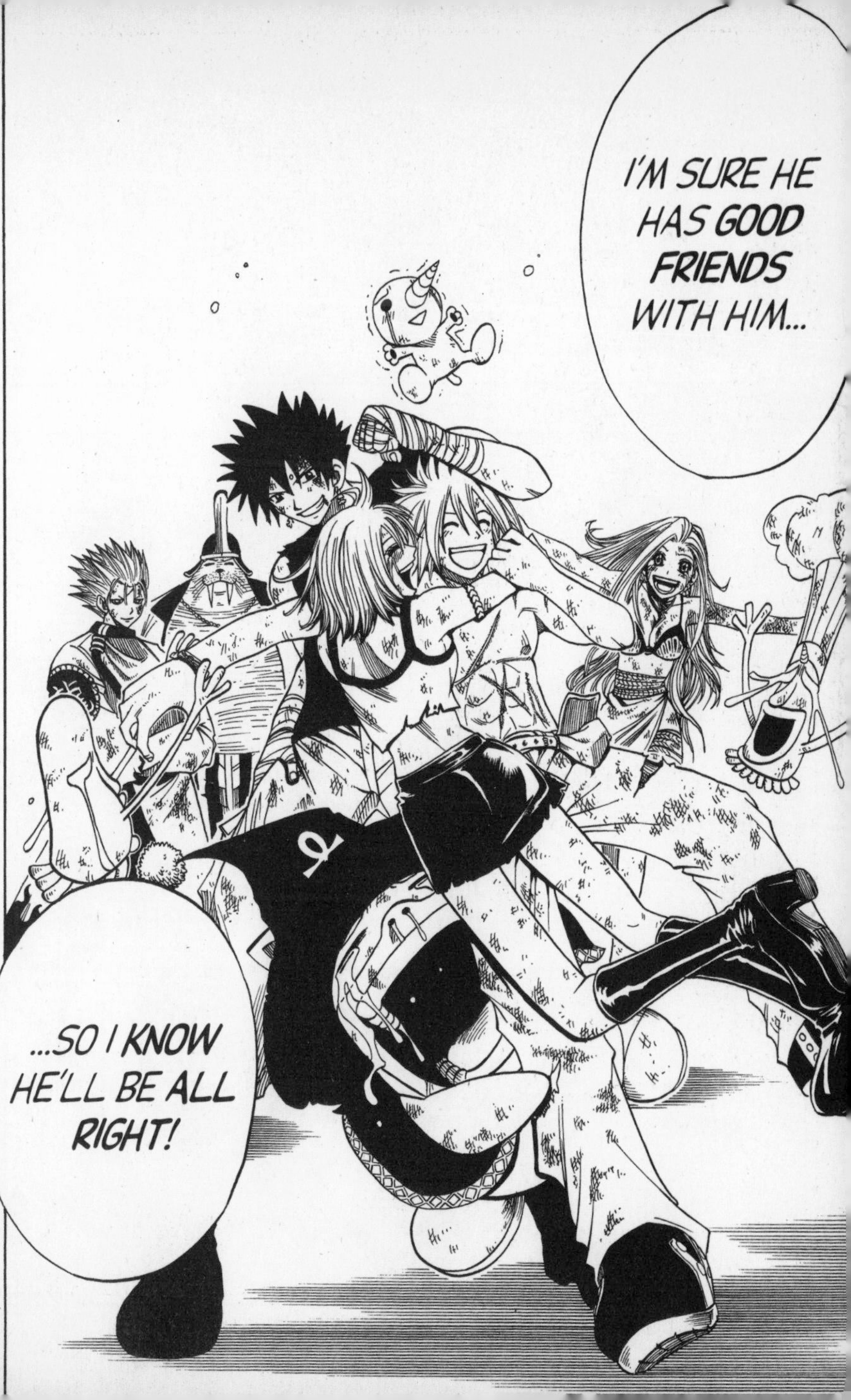
I'M SURE HE HAS GOOD FRIENDS WITH HIM...
...SO I KNOW HE'LL BE ALL RIGHT!

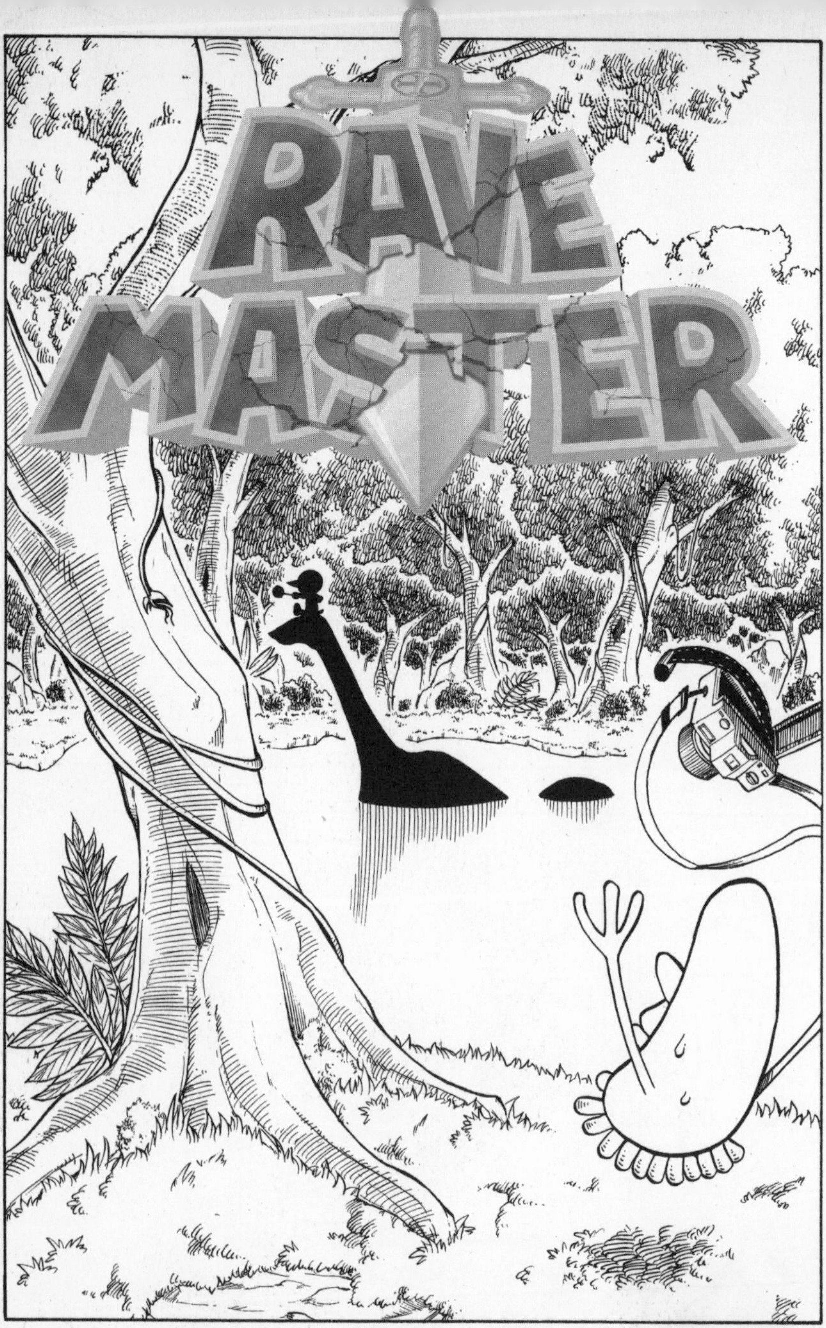
RAVE MASTER

RAVE:139 ✠ A KIND MIRACLE

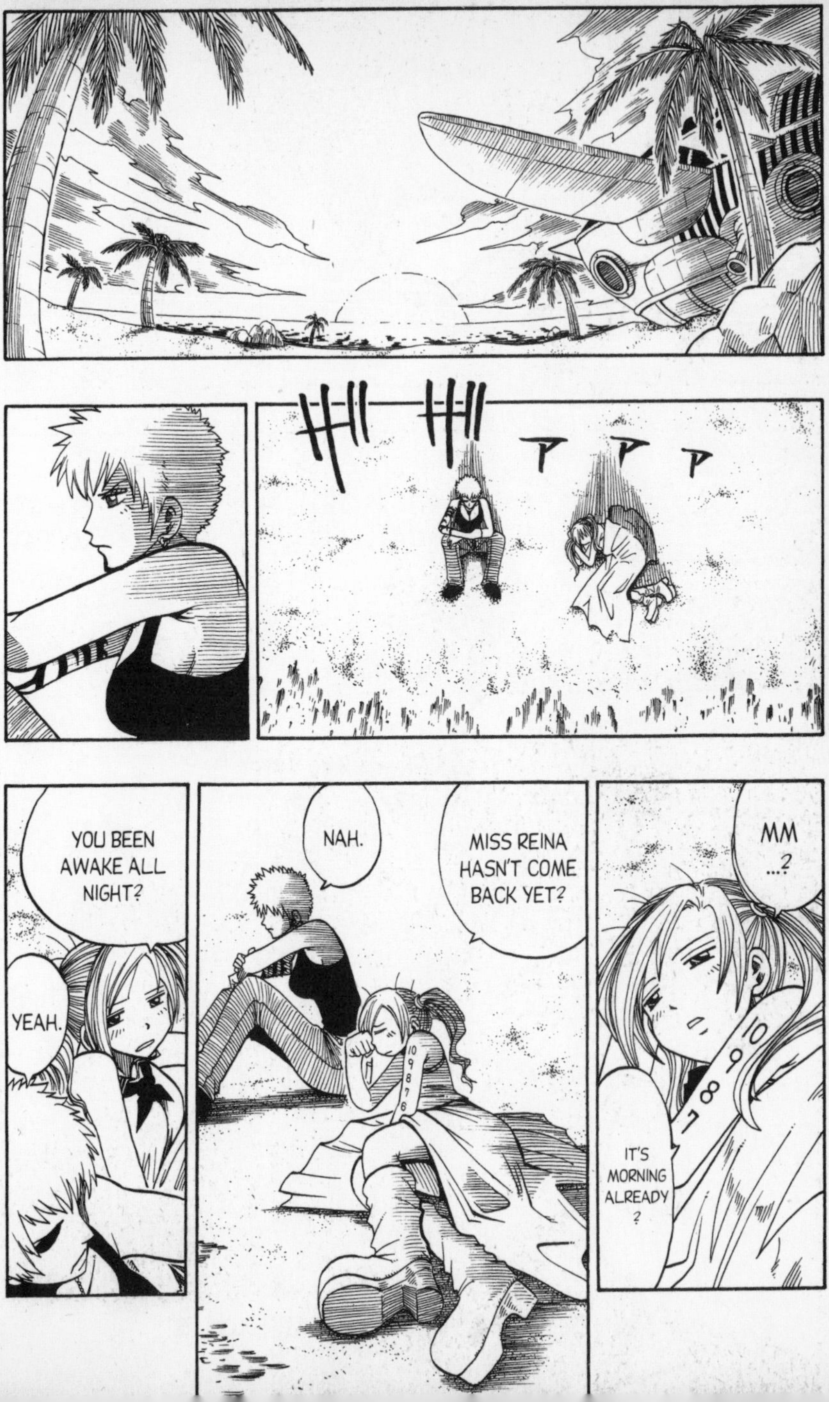
MM ...?
IT'S MORNING ALREADY ?
MISS REINA HASN'T COME BACK YET?
NAH.
YOU BEEN AWAKE ALL NIGHT?
YEAH.

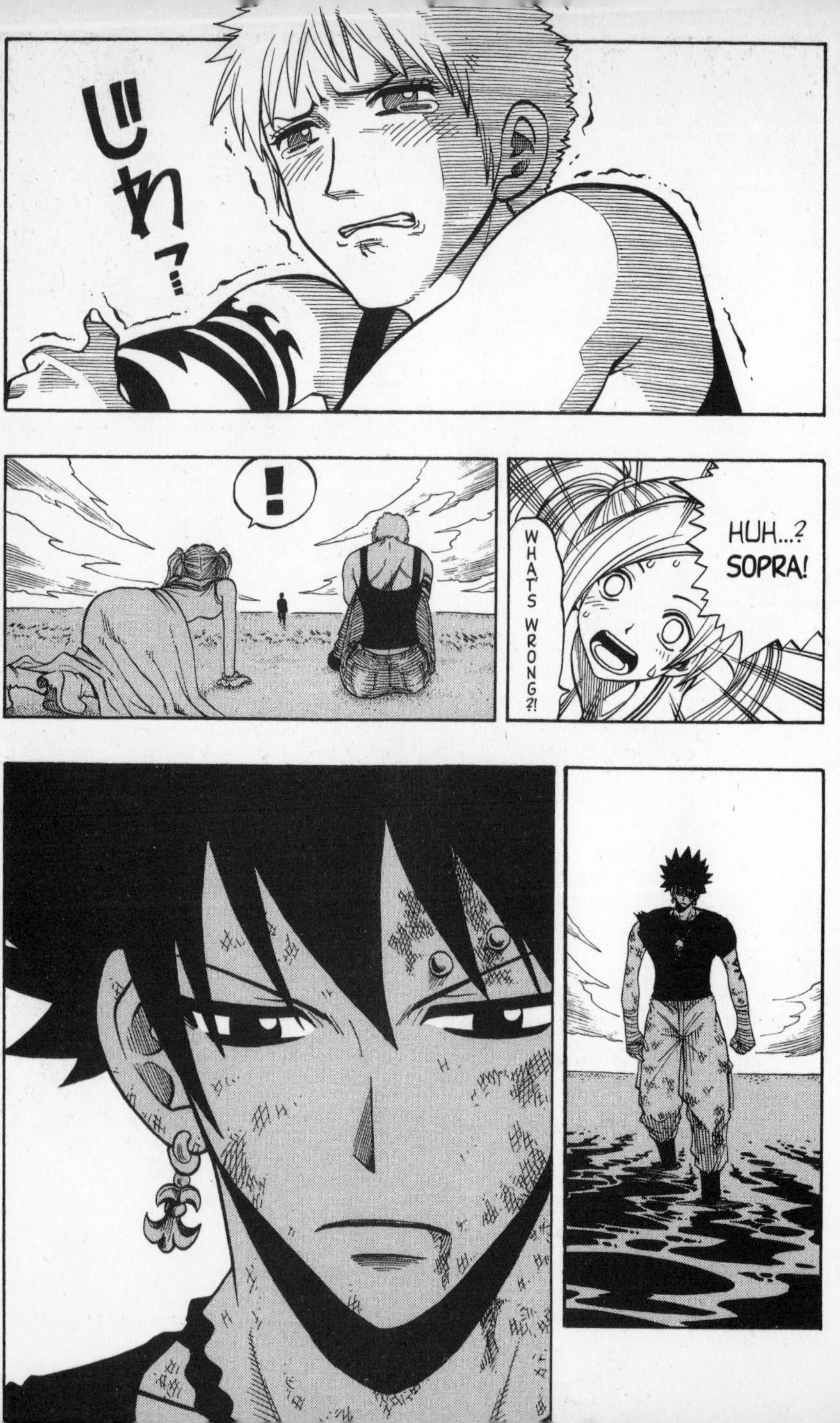
じわっ…
HUH...? SOPRA!
WHAT'S WRONG?!
!

I'M SORRY.

EH?

MISS REINA'S NOT...?

H-HEY...! SOPRA! SAY SOMETHING, HERE!

NOT... NOT THAT...

... RIGHT?

W-WAIT...! I DON'T...

WHAT ARE YOU SORRY FOR?!

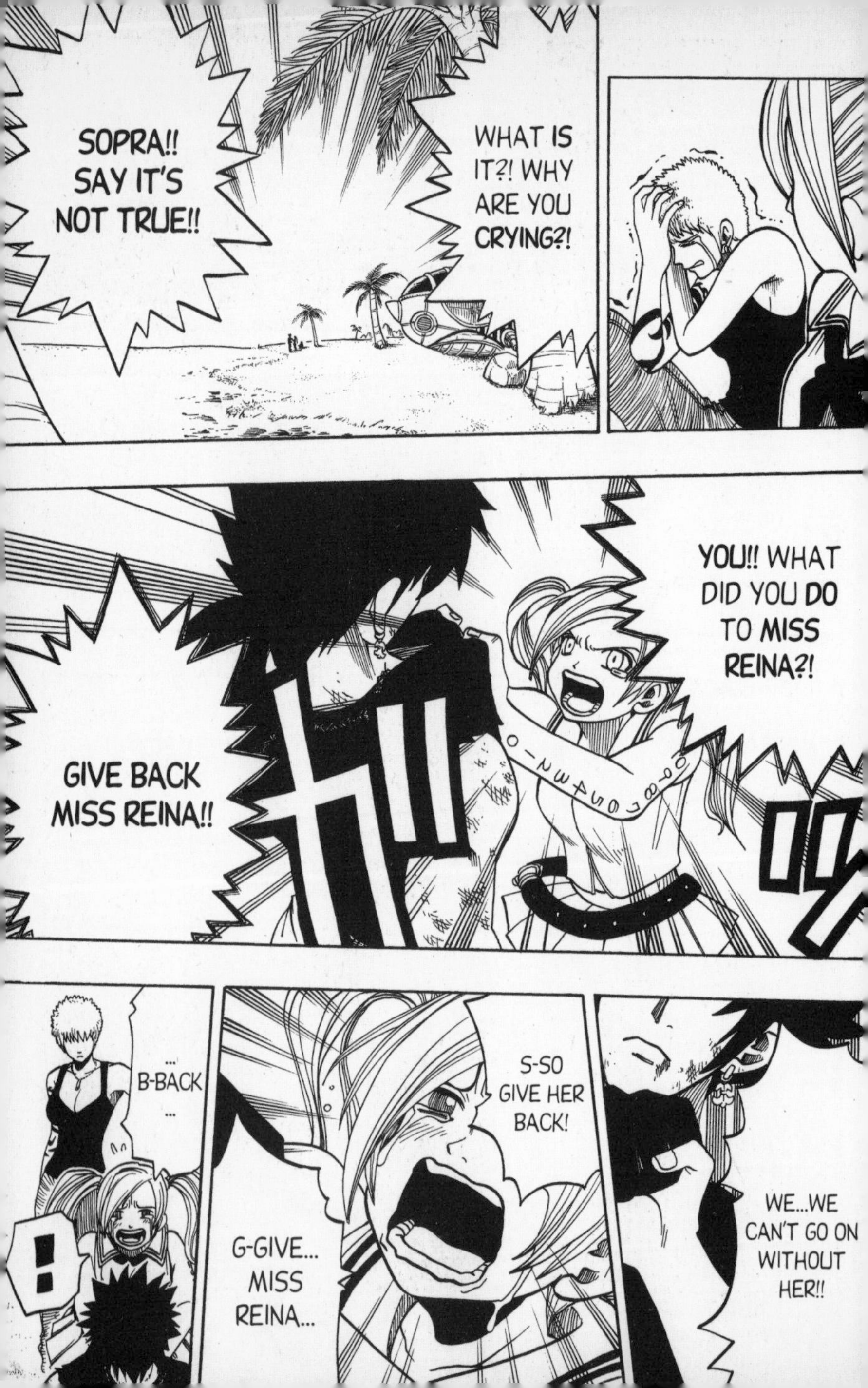
WHAT IS IT?! WHY ARE YOU CRYING?!
SOPRA!! SAY IT'S NOT TRUE!!
YOU!! WHAT DID YOU DO TO MISS REINA?!
GIVE BACK MISS REINA!!
WE...WE CAN'T GO ON WITHOUT HER!!
S-SO GIVE HER BACK!
G-GIVE... MISS REINA...
... B-BACK ...
!

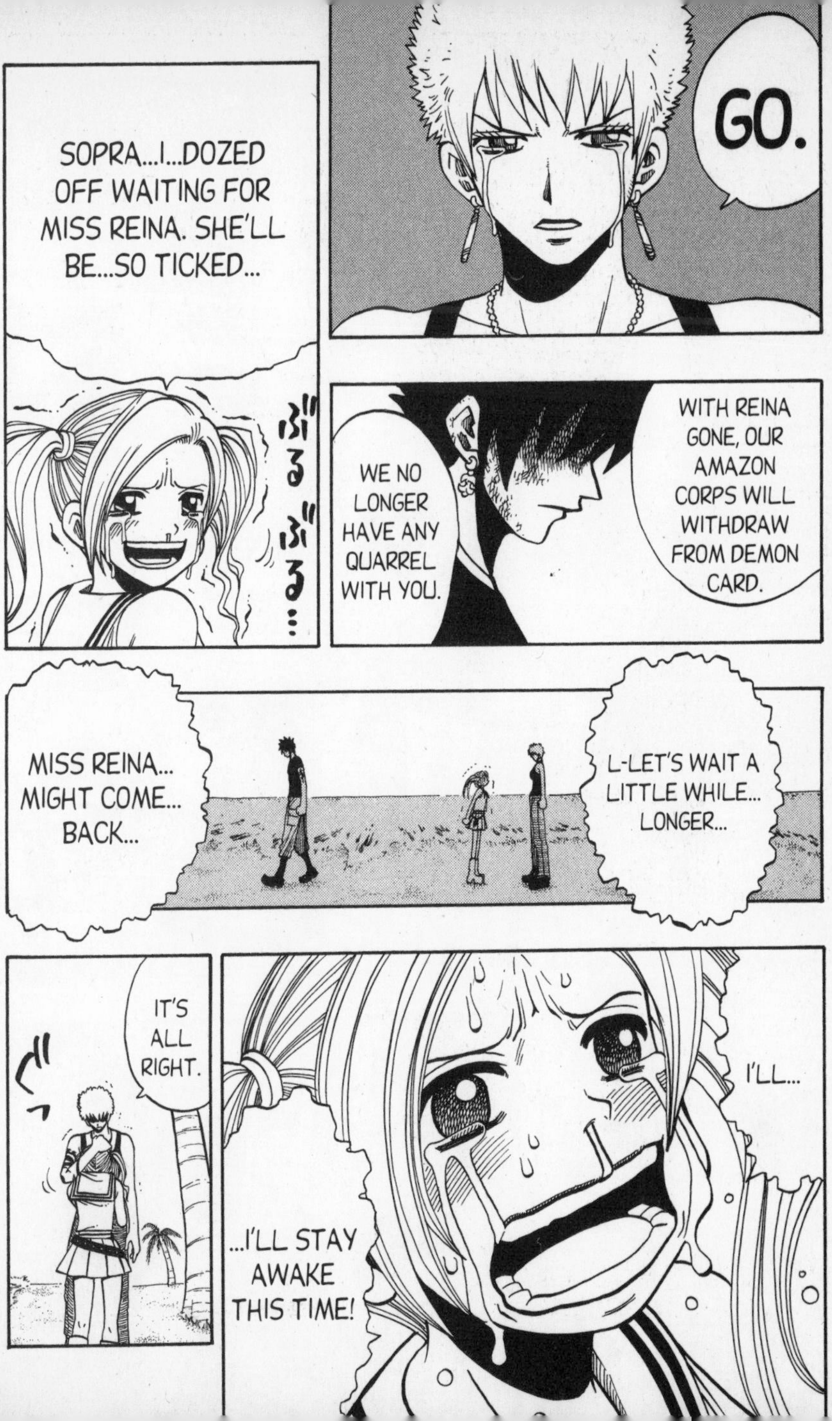
GO.
WITH REINA GONE, OUR AMAZON CORPS WILL WITHDRAW FROM DEMON CARD.
WE NO LONGER HAVE ANY QUARREL WITH YOU.
SOPRA...I...DOZED OFF WAITING FOR MISS REINA. SHE'LL BE...SO TICKED...
ぶるぶる…
L-LET'S WAIT A LITTLE WHILE... LONGER...
MISS REINA... MIGHT COME... BACK...
I'LL...
...I'LL STAY AWAKE THIS TIME!
IT'S ALL RIGHT.

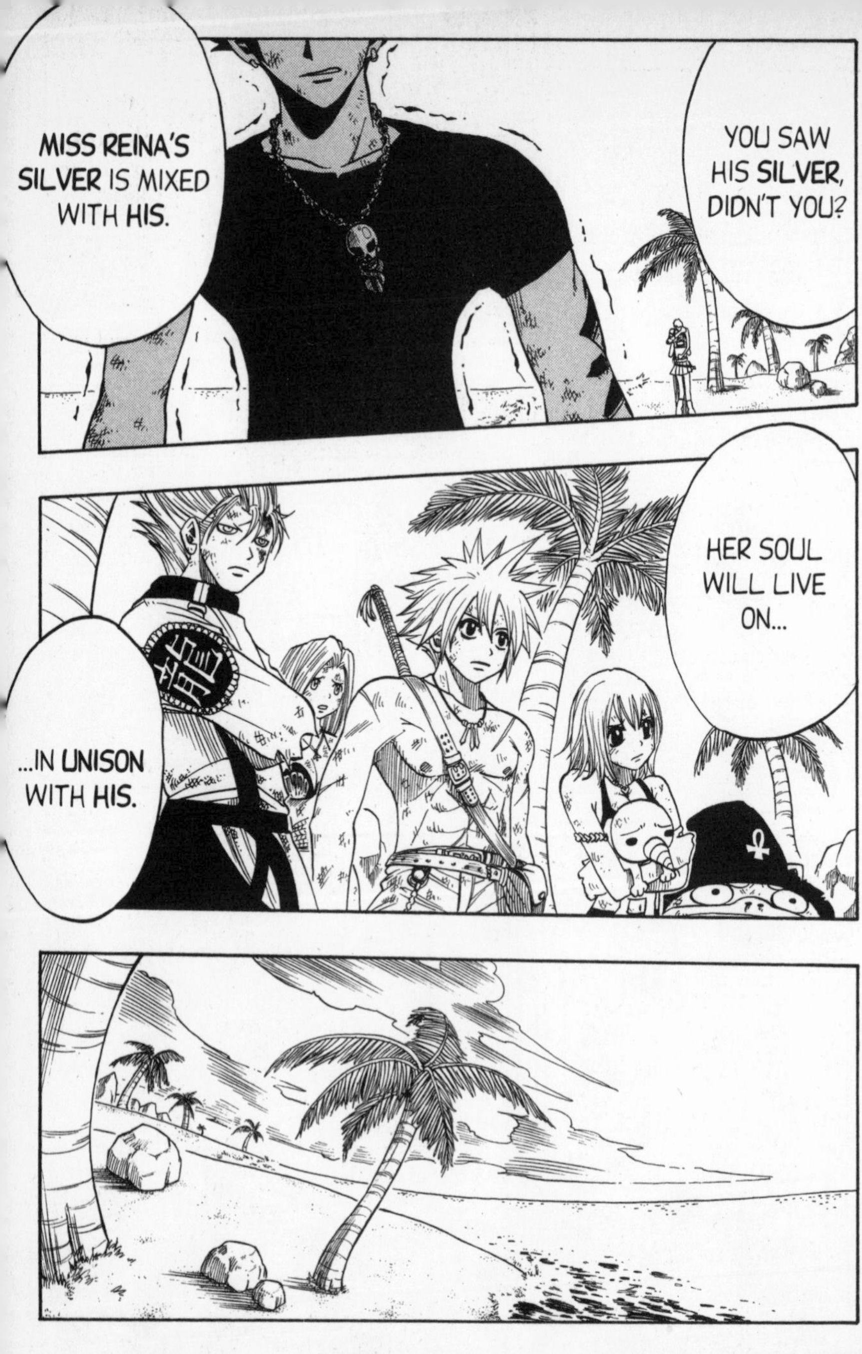
YOU SAW HIS SILVER, DIDN'T YOU?
MISS REINA'S SILVER IS MIXED WITH HIS.
HER SOUL WILL LIVE ON...
...IN UNISON WITH HIS.

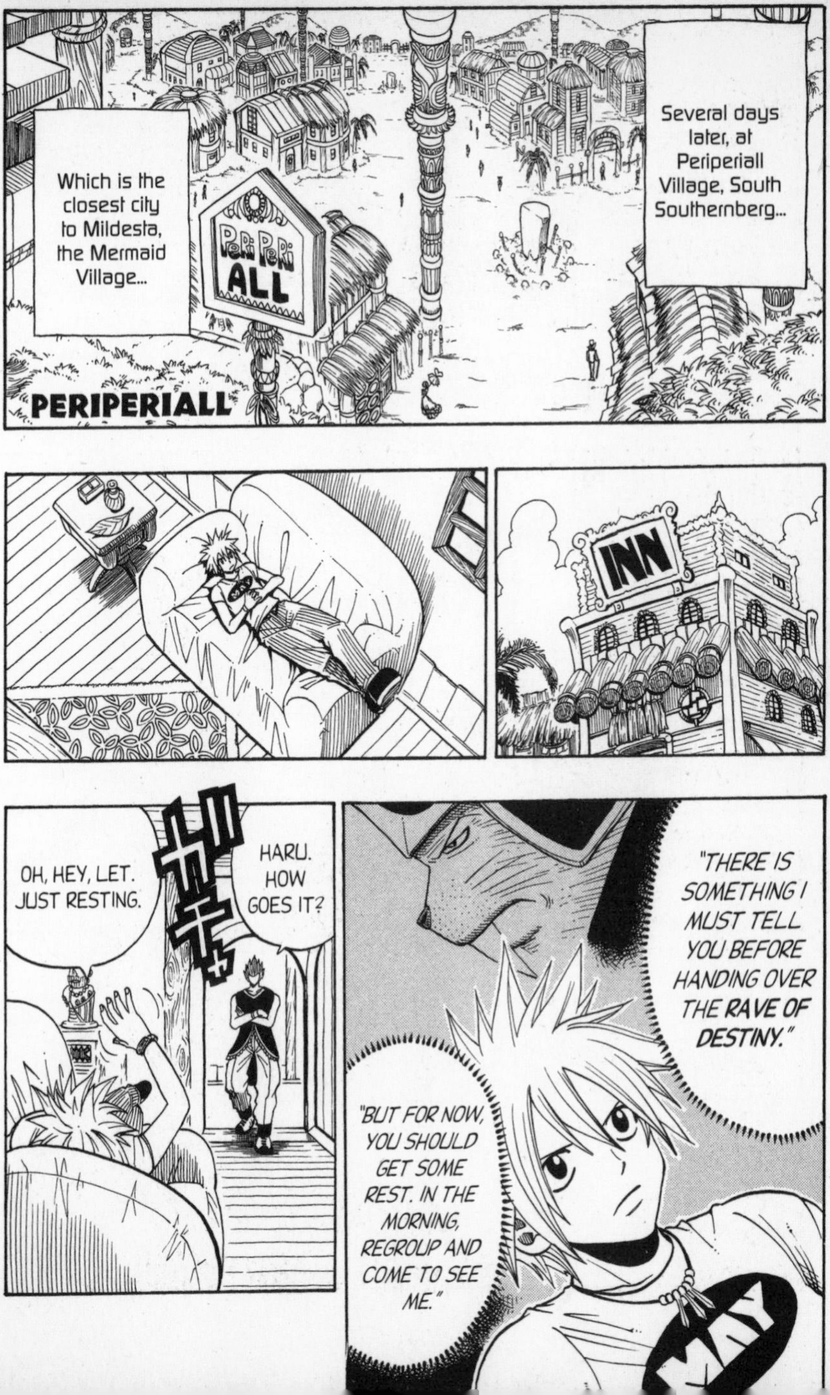
Several days later, at Periperiall Village, South Southernberg...
Which is the closest city to Mildesta, the Mermaid Village...
PeRi PeRi ALL
PERIPERIALL
INN
"THERE IS SOMETHING I MUST TELL YOU BEFORE HANDING OVER THE RAVE OF DESTINY."
"BUT FOR NOW, YOU SHOULD GET SOME REST. IN THE MORNING, REGROUP AND COME TO SEE ME."
HARU. HOW GOES IT?
OH, HEY, LET. JUST RESTING.

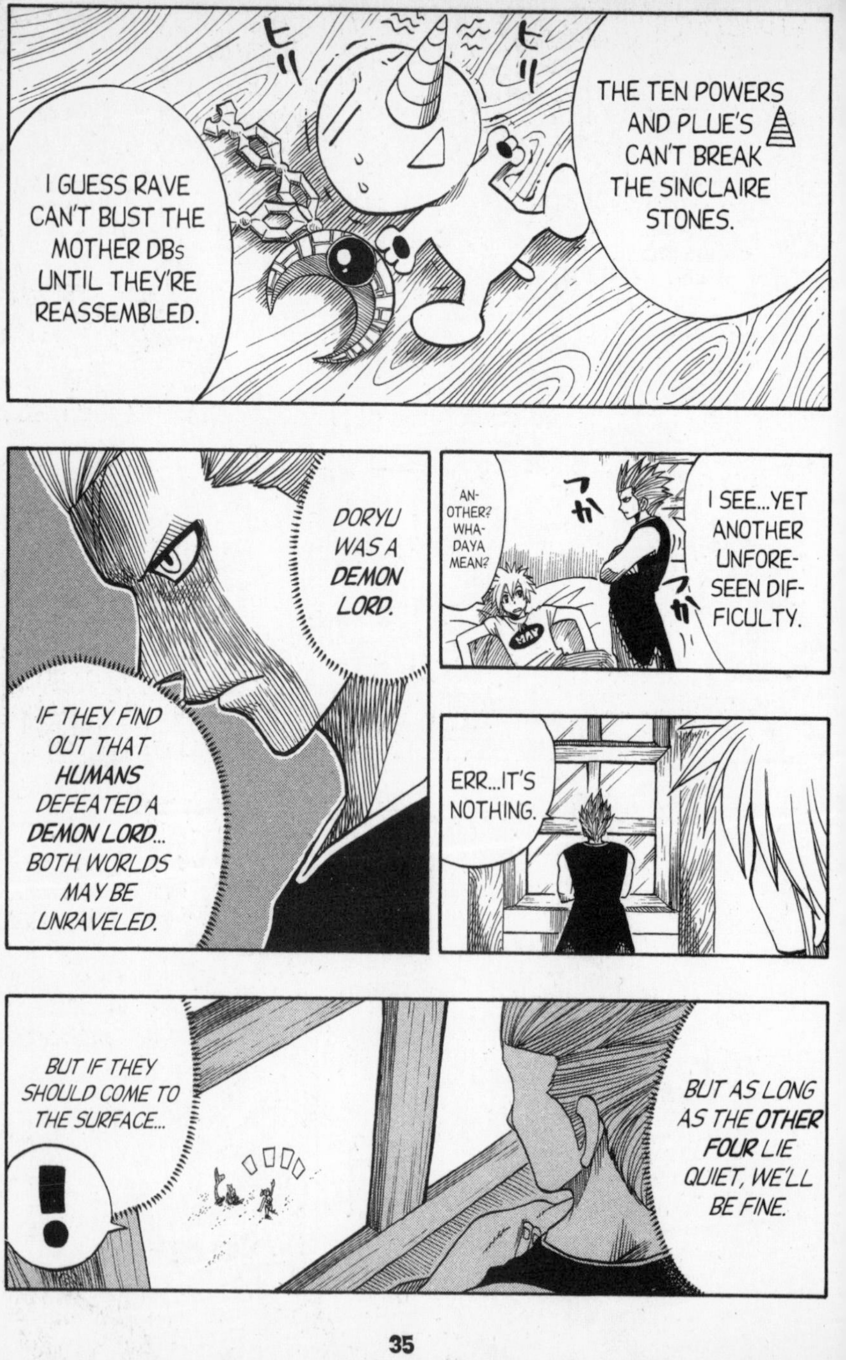
THE TEN POWERS AND PLUE'S CAN'T BREAK THE SINCLAIRE STONES.
I GUESS RAVE CAN'T BUST THE MOTHER DBs UNTIL THEY'RE REASSEMBLED.
I SEE...YET ANOTHER UNFORESEEN DIFFICULTY.
ANOTHER? WHADAYA MEAN?
ERR...IT'S NOTHING.
DORYU WAS A **DEMON LORD.**
IF THEY FIND OUT THAT **HUMANS** DEFEATED A **DEMON LORD**... BOTH WORLDS MAY BE UNRAVELED.
BUT AS LONG AS THE **OTHER FOUR** LIE QUIET, WE'LL BE FINE.
BUT IF THEY SHOULD COME TO THE SURFACE...
!

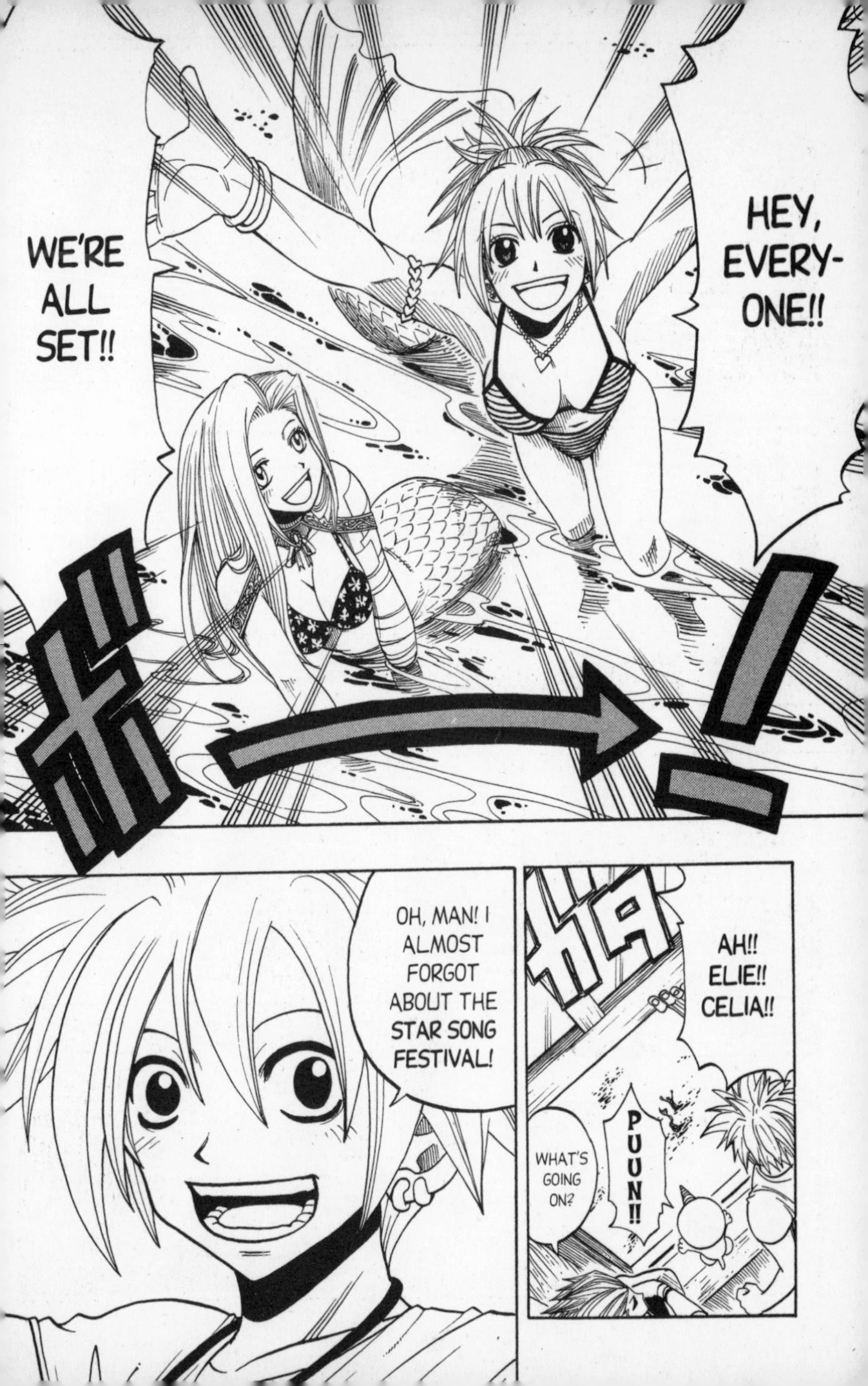
HEY, EVERYONE!!
WE'RE ALL SET!!
AH!! ELIE!! CELIA!!
PUUN!!
WHAT'S GOING ON?
OH, MAN! I ALMOST FORGOT ABOUT THE STAR SONG FESTIVAL!

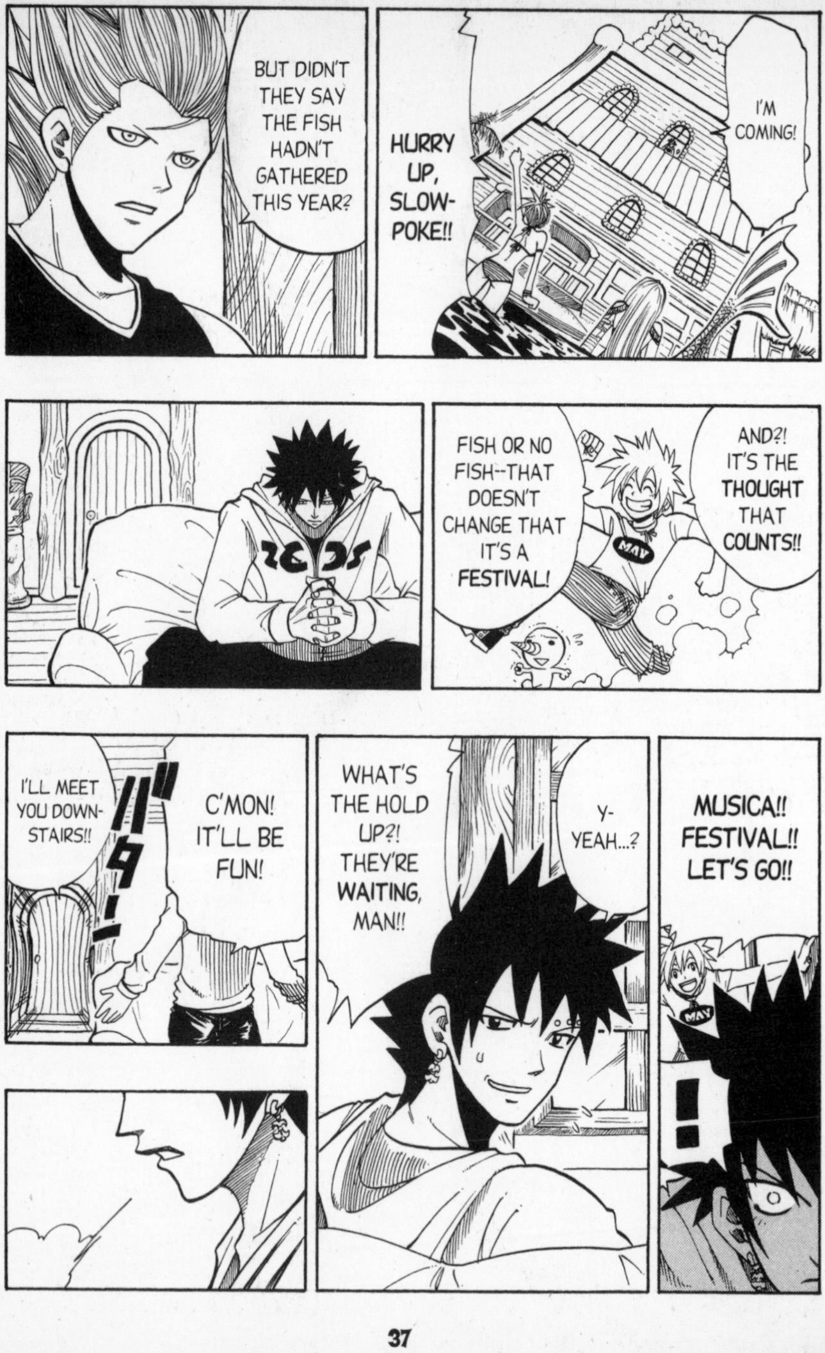
I'M COMING!
HURRY UP, SLOW-POKE!!
BUT DIDN'T THEY SAY THE FISH HADN'T GATHERED THIS YEAR?
AND?! IT'S THE THOUGHT THAT COUNTS!!
FISH OR NO FISH--THAT DOESN'T CHANGE THAT IT'S A FESTIVAL!
MUSICA!! FESTIVAL!! LET'S GO!!
Y-YEAH...?
WHAT'S THE HOLD UP?! THEY'RE WAITING, MAN!!
C'MON! IT'LL BE FUN!
I'LL MEET YOU DOWN-STAIRS!!

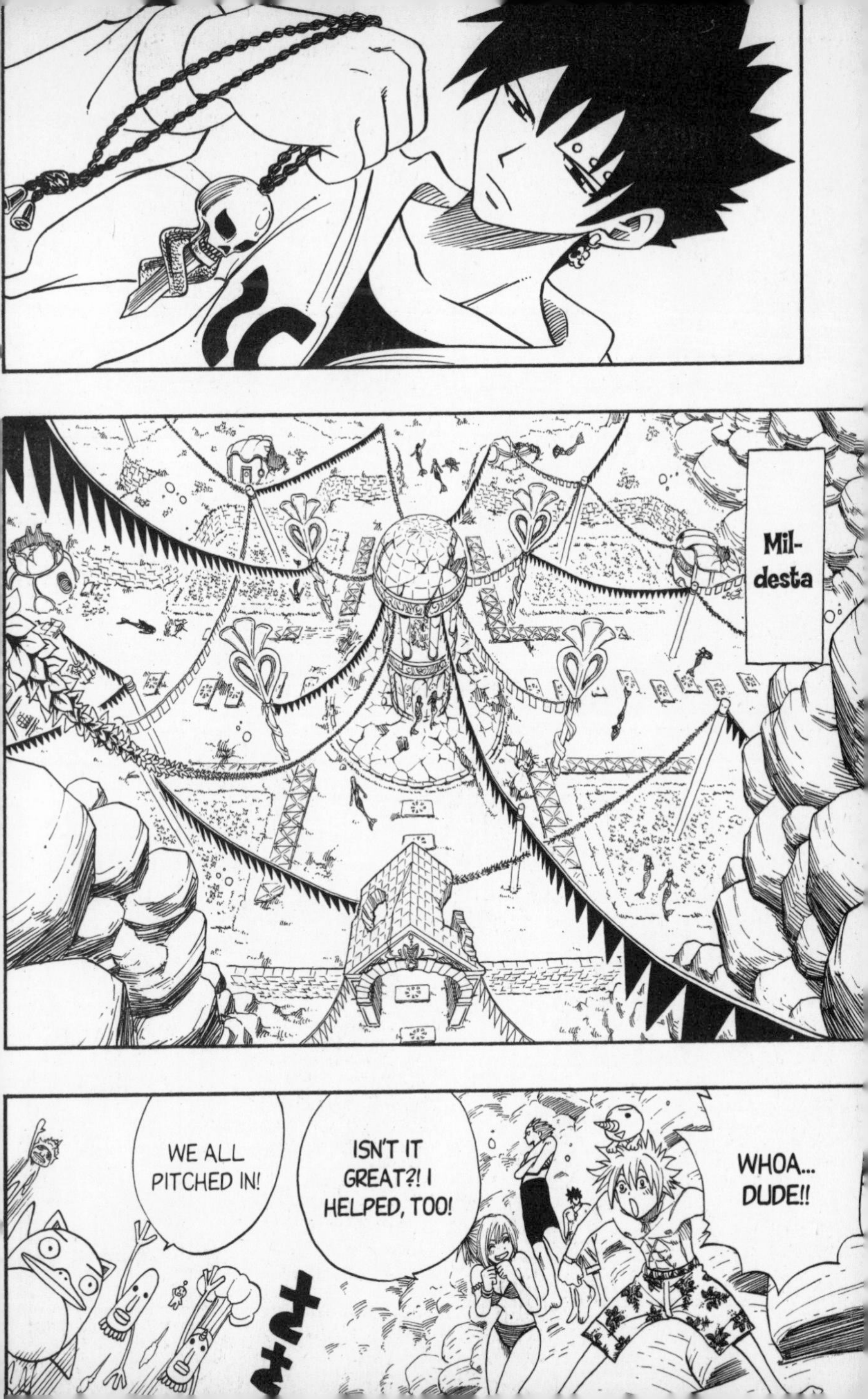
Mil-desta
WHOA... DUDE!!
ISN'T IT GREAT?! I HELPED, TOO!
WE ALL PITCHED IN!

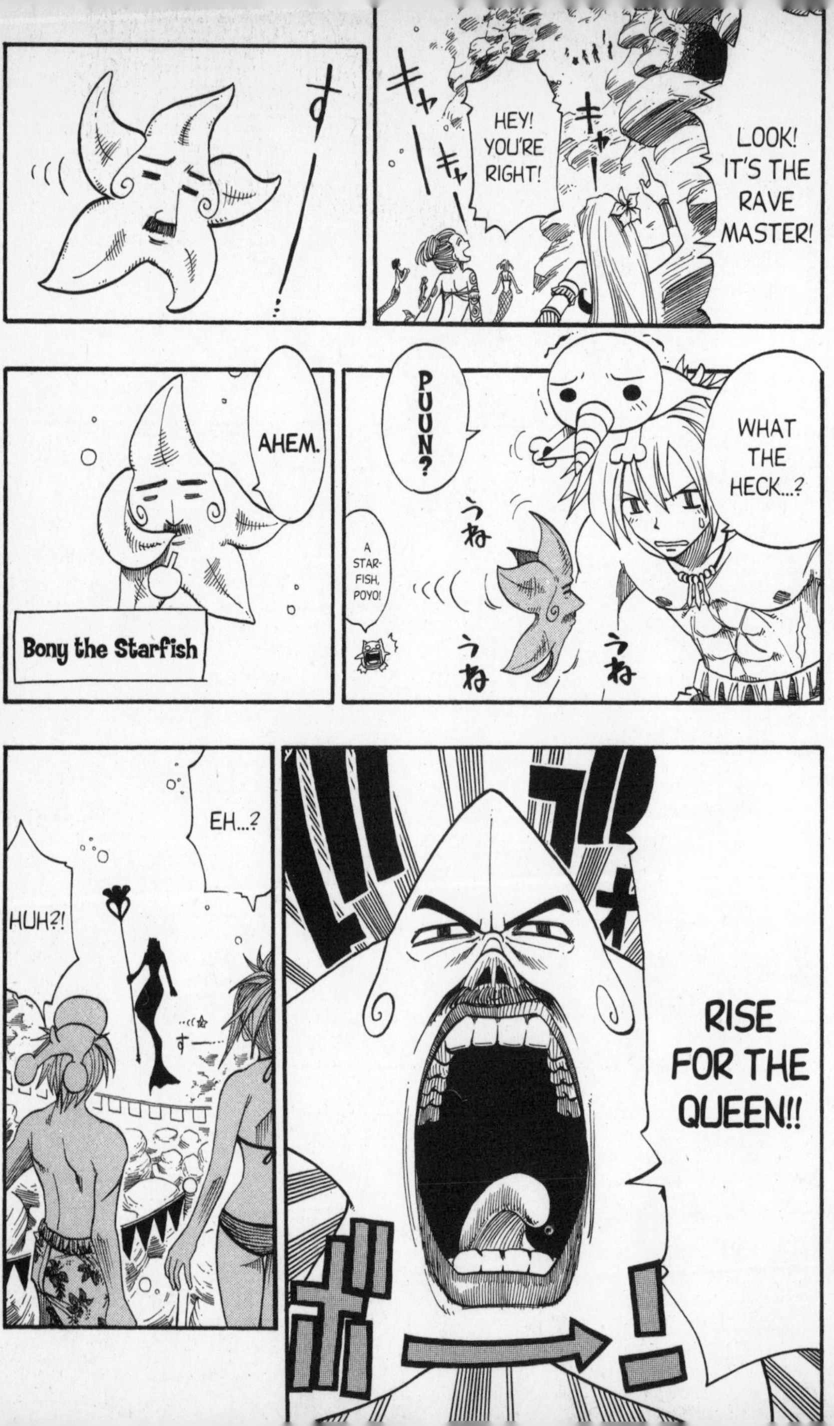
LOOK! IT'S THE RAVE MASTER!
キャー
HEY! YOU'RE RIGHT!
キャーキャー
すー!
WHAT THE HECK...?
PUUN?
A STARFISH, POYO!
うね
うね
うね
AHEM.
Bony the Starfish
RISE FOR THE QUEEN!!
EH...?
HUH?!
すー…☆

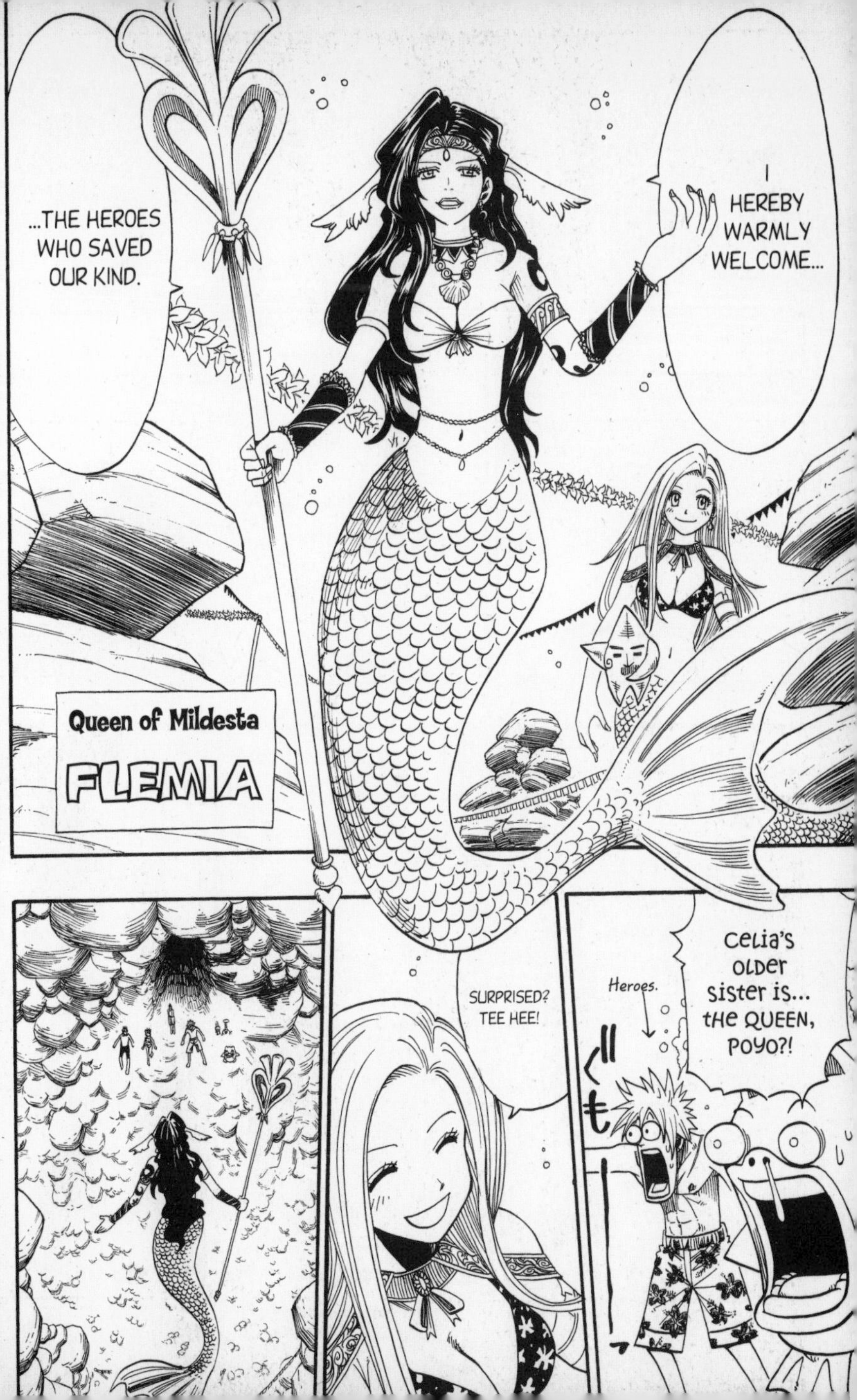
I HEREBY WARMLY WELCOME...
...THE HEROES WHO SAVED OUR KIND.
Queen of Mildesta
FLEMIA
Celia's older sister is... the QUEEN, POYO?!
Heroes.
SURPRISED? TEE HEE!

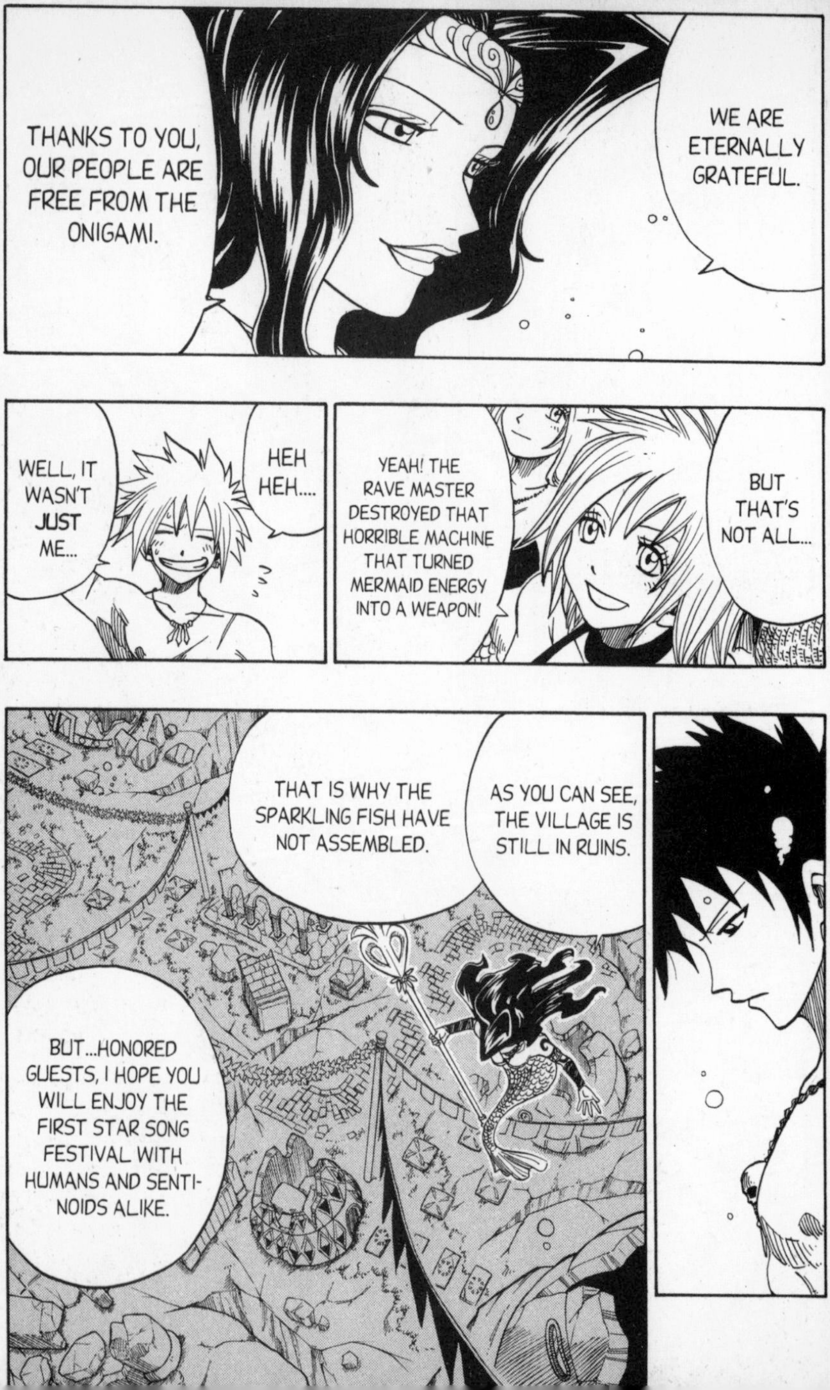
WE ARE ETERNALLY GRATEFUL.
THANKS TO YOU, OUR PEOPLE ARE FREE FROM THE ONIGAMI.
BUT THAT'S NOT ALL...
YEAH! THE RAVE MASTER DESTROYED THAT HORRIBLE MACHINE THAT TURNED MERMAID ENERGY INTO A WEAPON!
HEH HEH....
WELL, IT WASN'T **JUST** ME...
AS YOU CAN SEE, THE VILLAGE IS STILL IN RUINS.
THAT IS WHY THE SPARKLING FISH HAVE NOT ASSEMBLED.
BUT...HONORED GUESTS, I HOPE YOU WILL ENJOY THE FIRST STAR SONG FESTIVAL WITH HUMANS AND SENTI-NOIDS ALIKE.

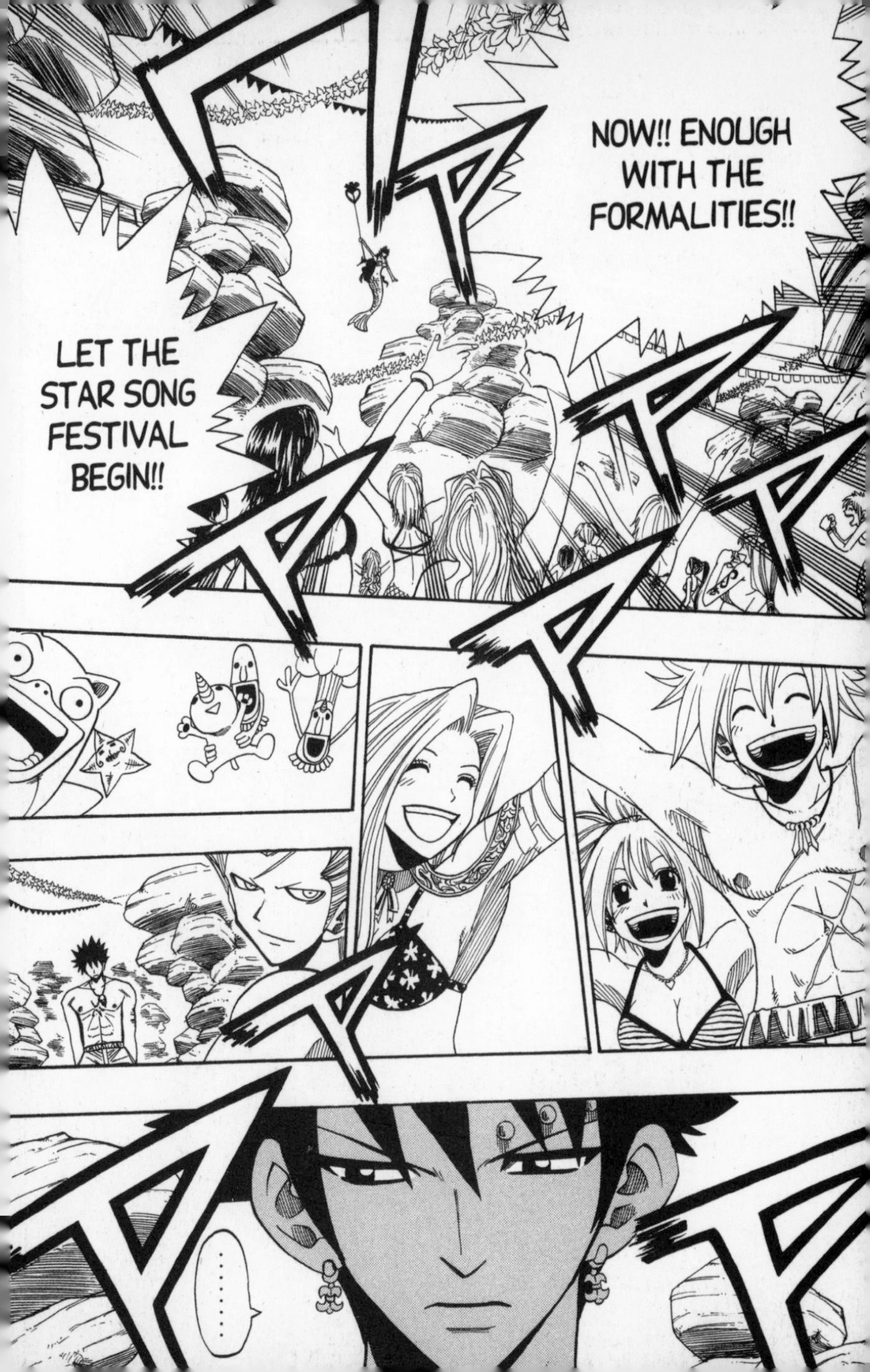

NOW!! ENOUGH WITH THE FORMALITIES!!
LET THE STAR SONG FESTIVAL BEGIN!!
....

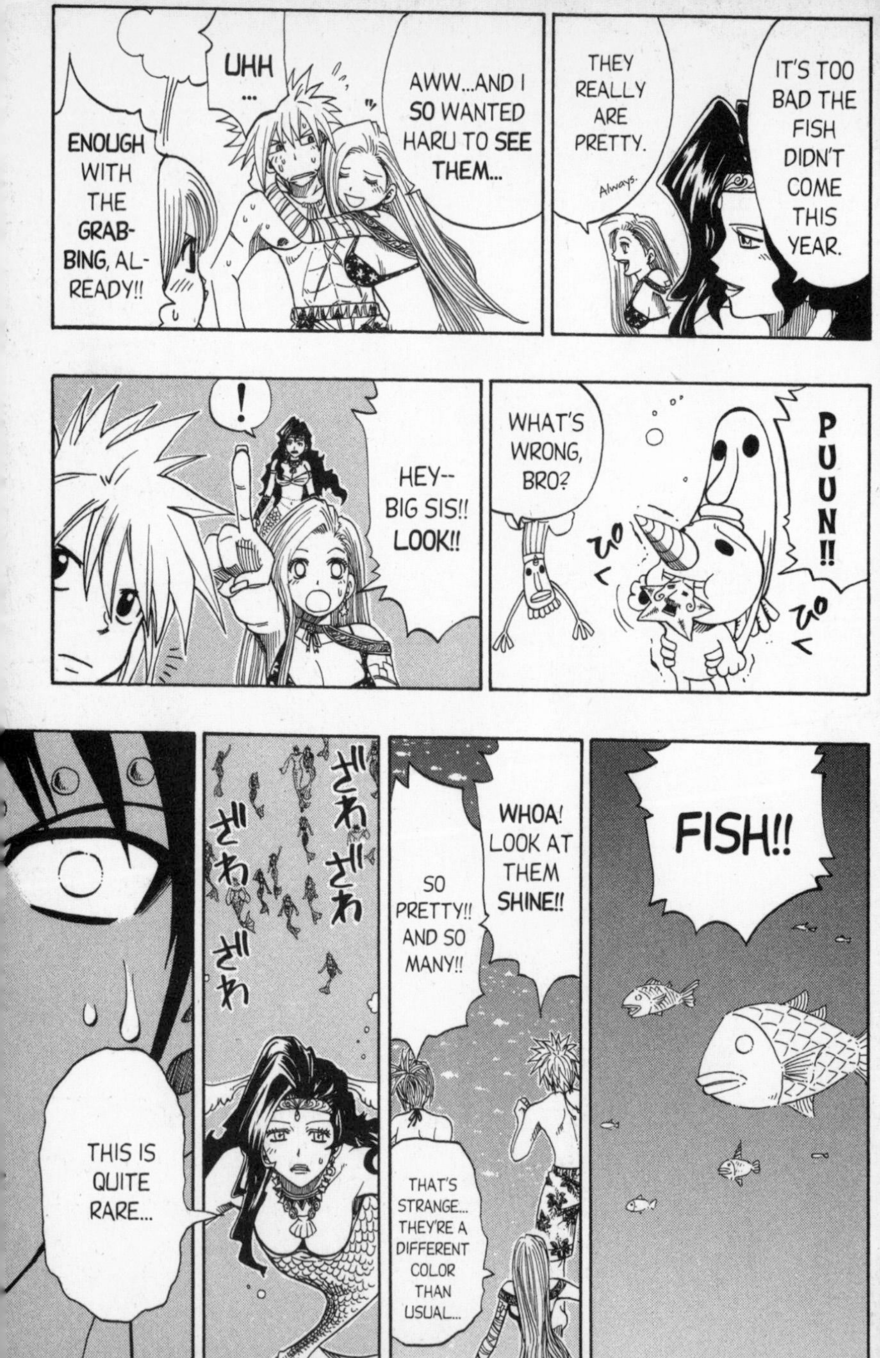
IT'S TOO BAD THE FISH DIDN'T COME THIS YEAR.
THEY REALLY ARE PRETTY.
Always.
AWW...AND I SO WANTED HARU TO SEE THEM...
UHH ...
ENOUGH WITH THE GRAB-BING, AL-READY!!
PUUN!!
ぴく
ぴく
WHAT'S WRONG, BRO?
!
HEY-- BIG SIS!! LOOK!!
FISH!!
WHOA! LOOK AT THEM SHINE!!
SO PRETTY!! AND SO MANY!!
THAT'S STRANGE... THEY'RE A DIFFERENT COLOR THAN USUAL...
ざわ ざわ
ざわ ざわ
ざわ
THIS IS QUITE RARE...

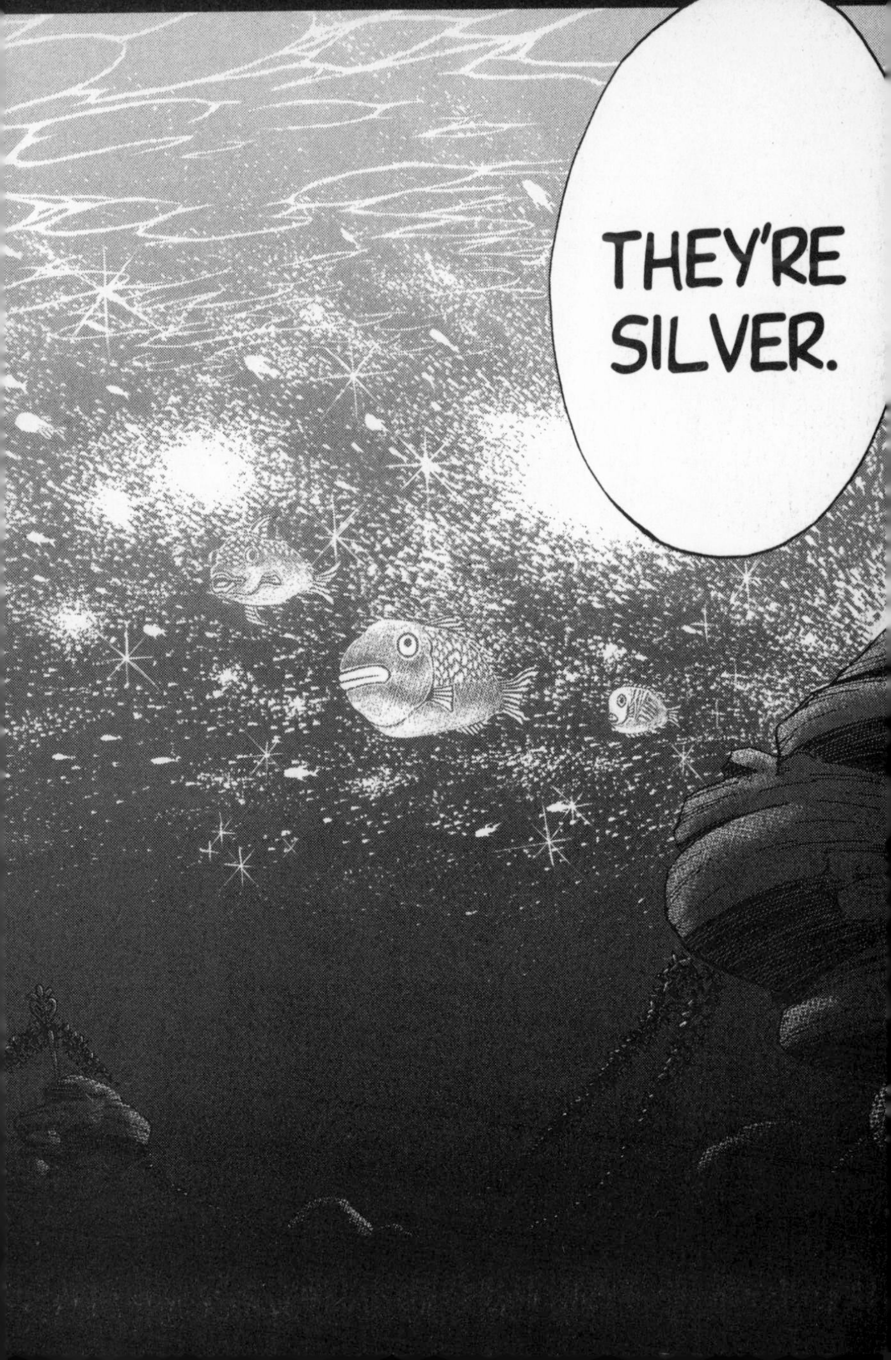
THEY'RE SILVER.

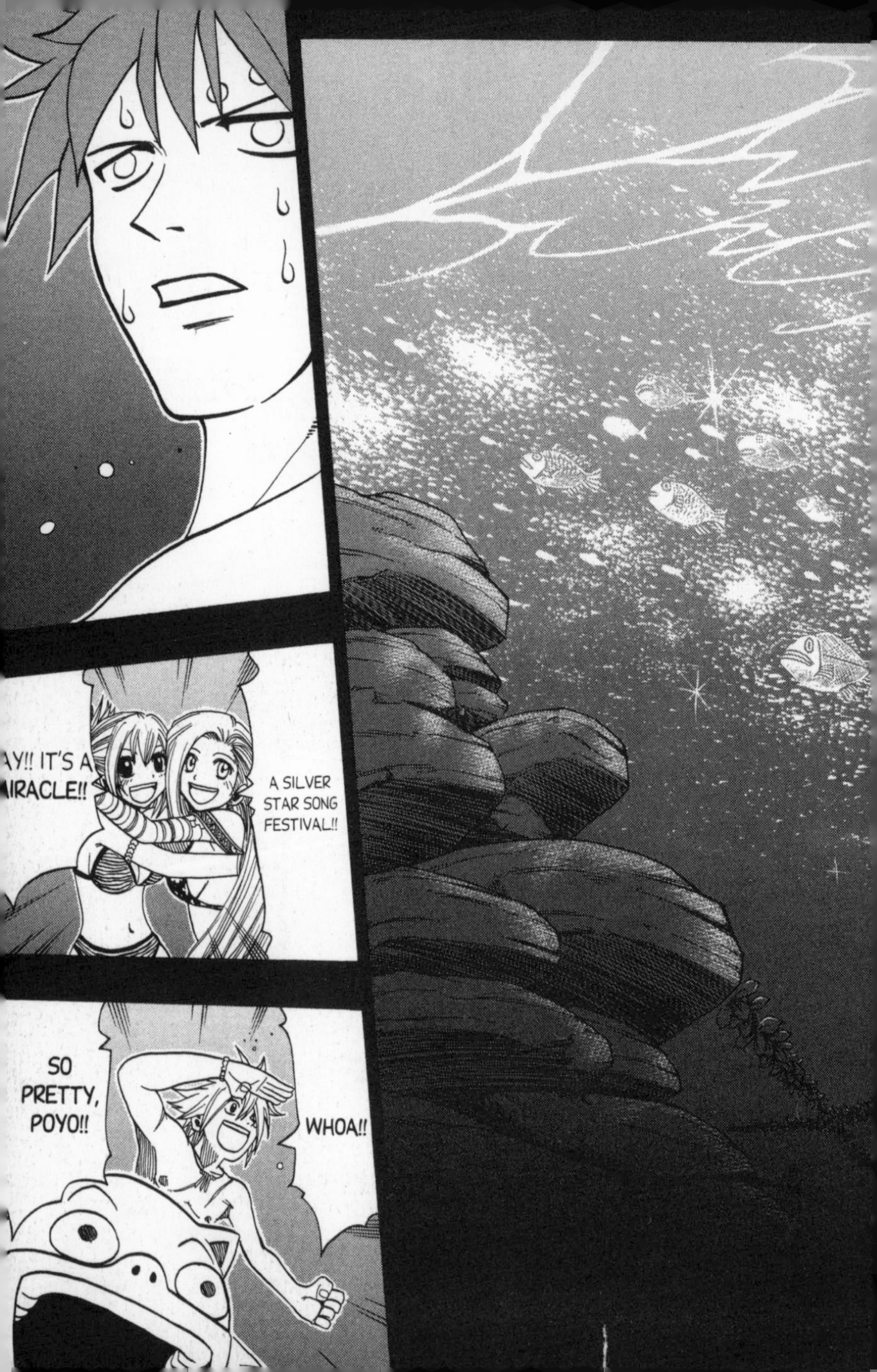
A SILVER STAR SONG FESTIVAL!!
AY!! IT'S A IRACLE!!
WHOA!!
SO PRETTY, POYO!!

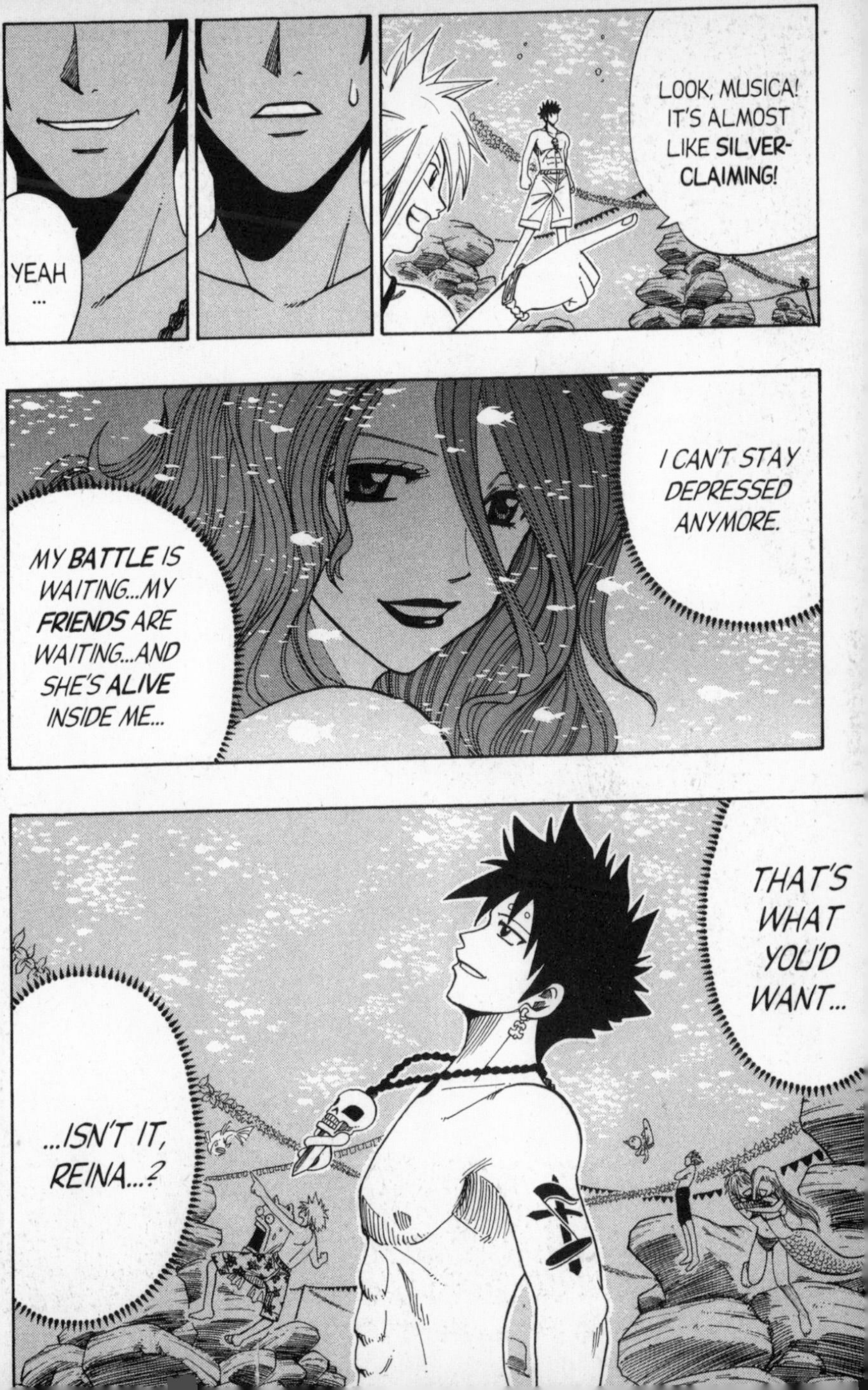
LOOK, MUSICA! IT'S ALMOST LIKE SILVER-CLAIMING!
YEAH ...
I CAN'T STAY DEPRESSED ANYMORE.
MY BATTLE IS WAITING...MY FRIENDS ARE WAITING...AND SHE'S ALIVE INSIDE ME...
THAT'S WHAT YOU'D WANT...
...ISN'T IT, REINA...?

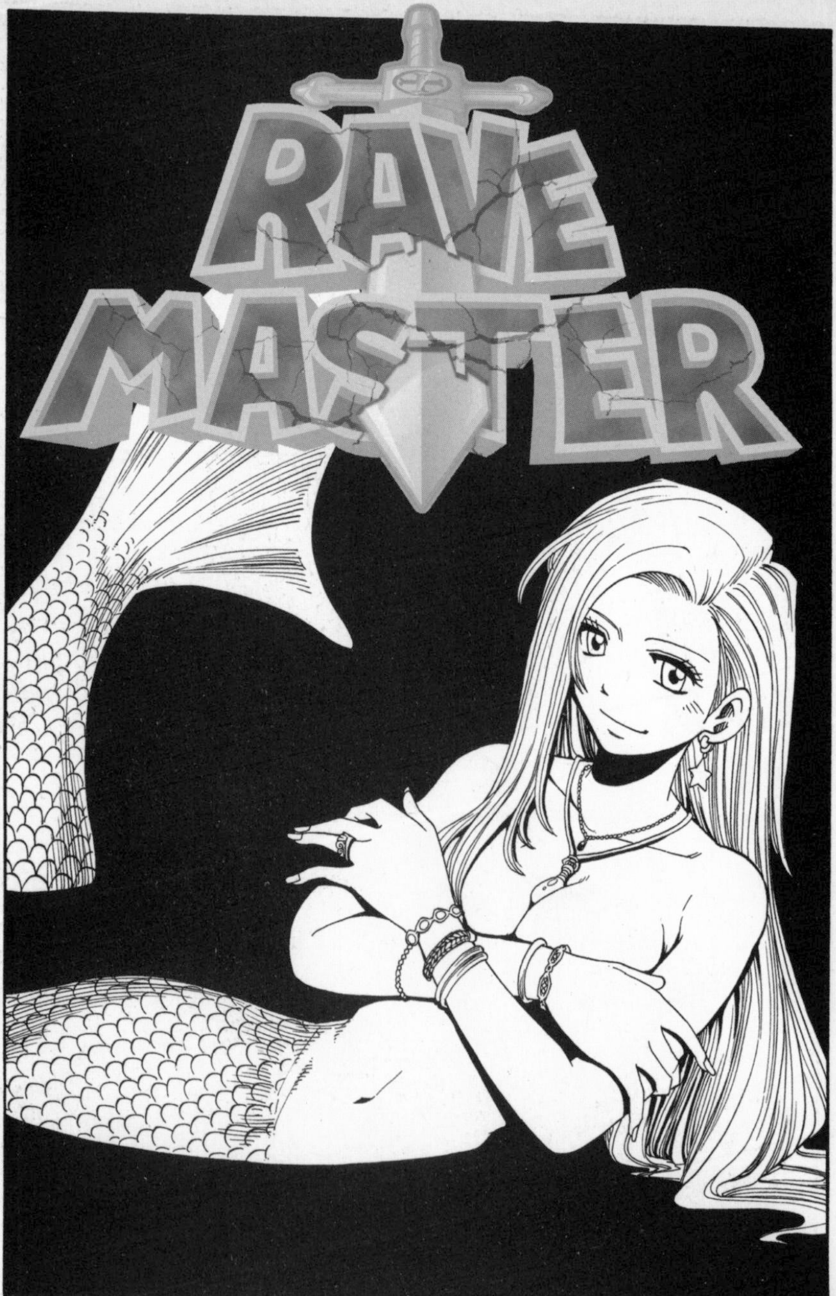
RAVE MASTER

RAVE:140 ✠ SMILING TOWARDS TOMORROW

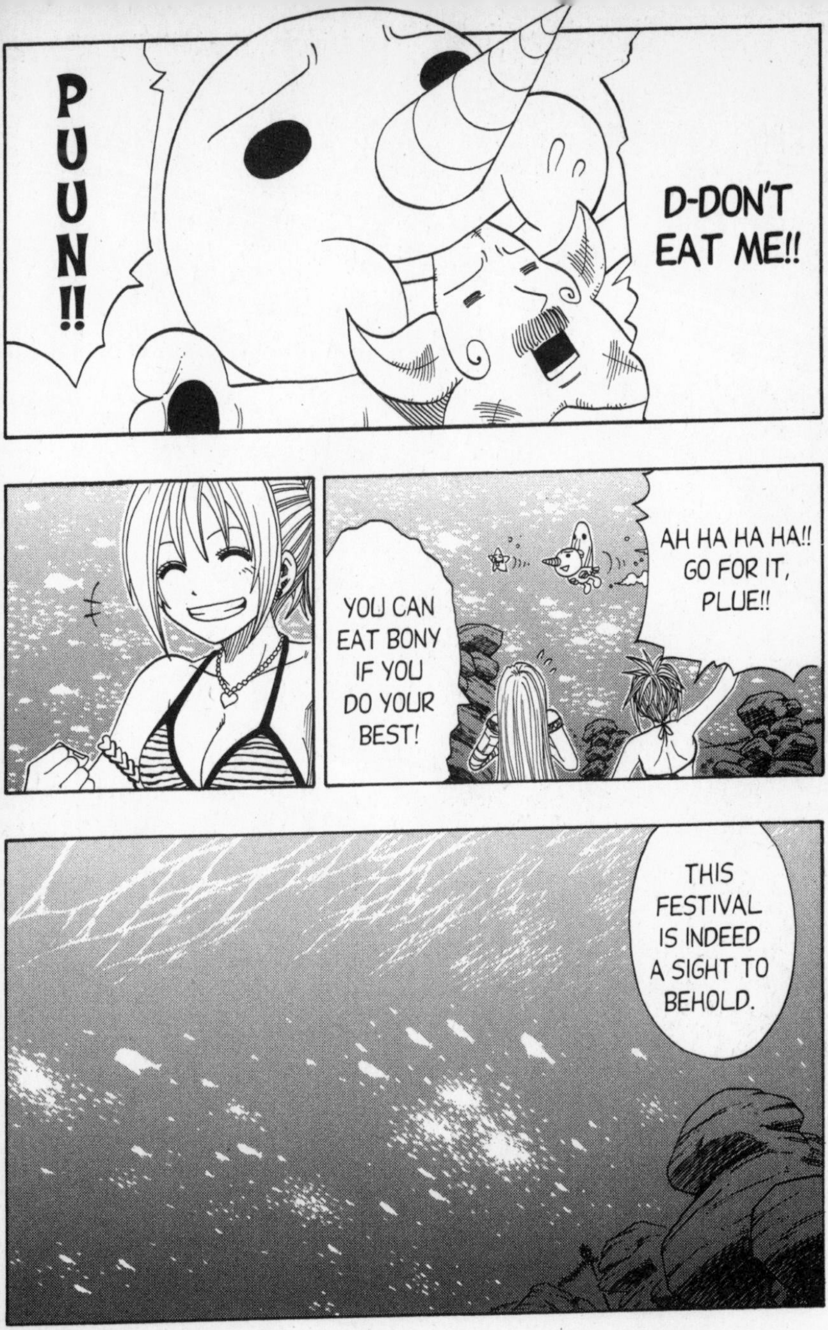
D-DON'T EAT ME!!
PUUN!!
AH HA HA HA!! GO FOR IT, PLUE!!
YOU CAN EAT BONY IF YOU DO YOUR BEST!
THIS FESTIVAL IS INDEED A SIGHT TO BEHOLD.

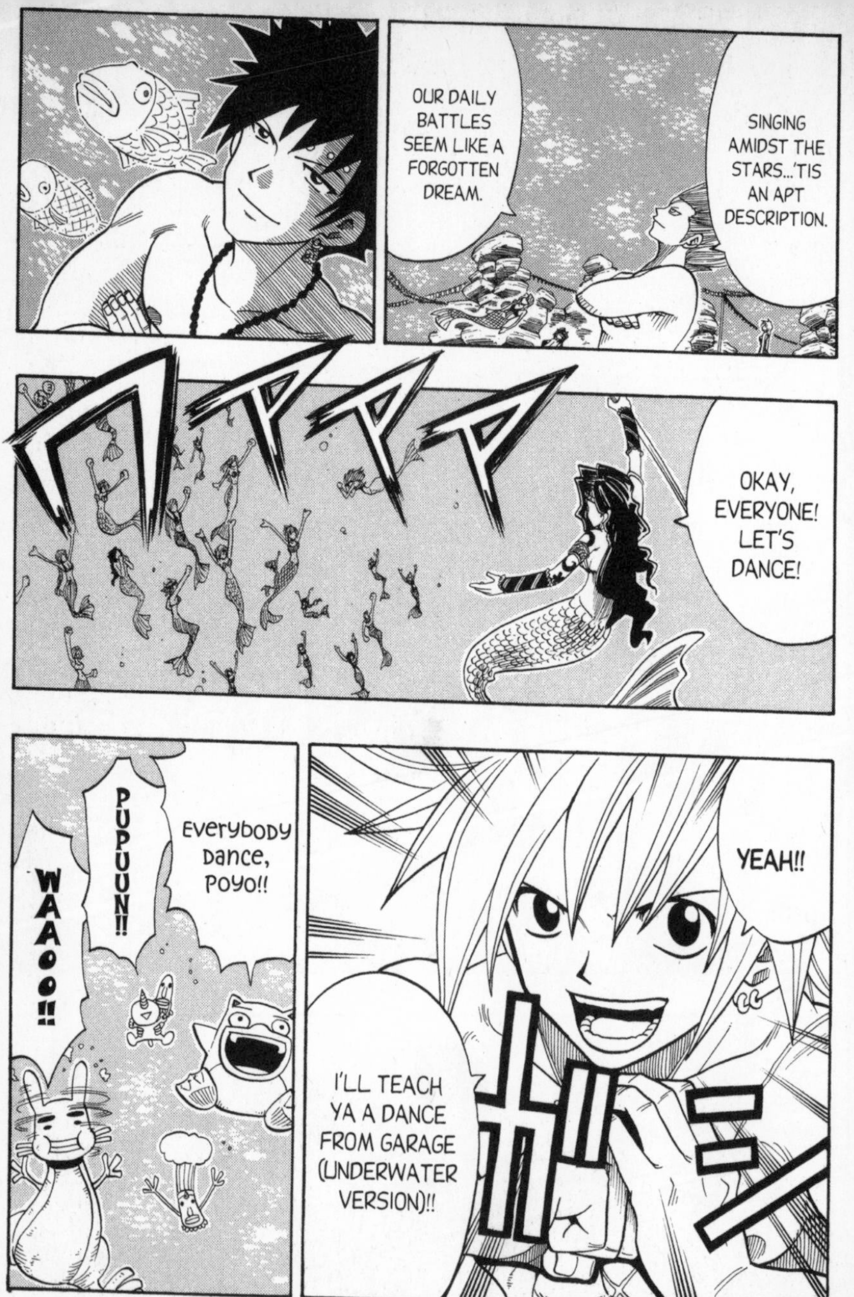
SINGING AMIDST THE STARS...'TIS AN APT DESCRIPTION.
OUR DAILY BATTLES SEEM LIKE A FORGOTTEN DREAM.
OKAY, EVERYONE! LET'S DANCE!
YEAH!!
I'LL TEACH YA A DANCE FROM GARAGE (UNDERWATER VERSION)!!
PUPUUN!!
Everybody Dance, Poyo!!
WAAOO!!

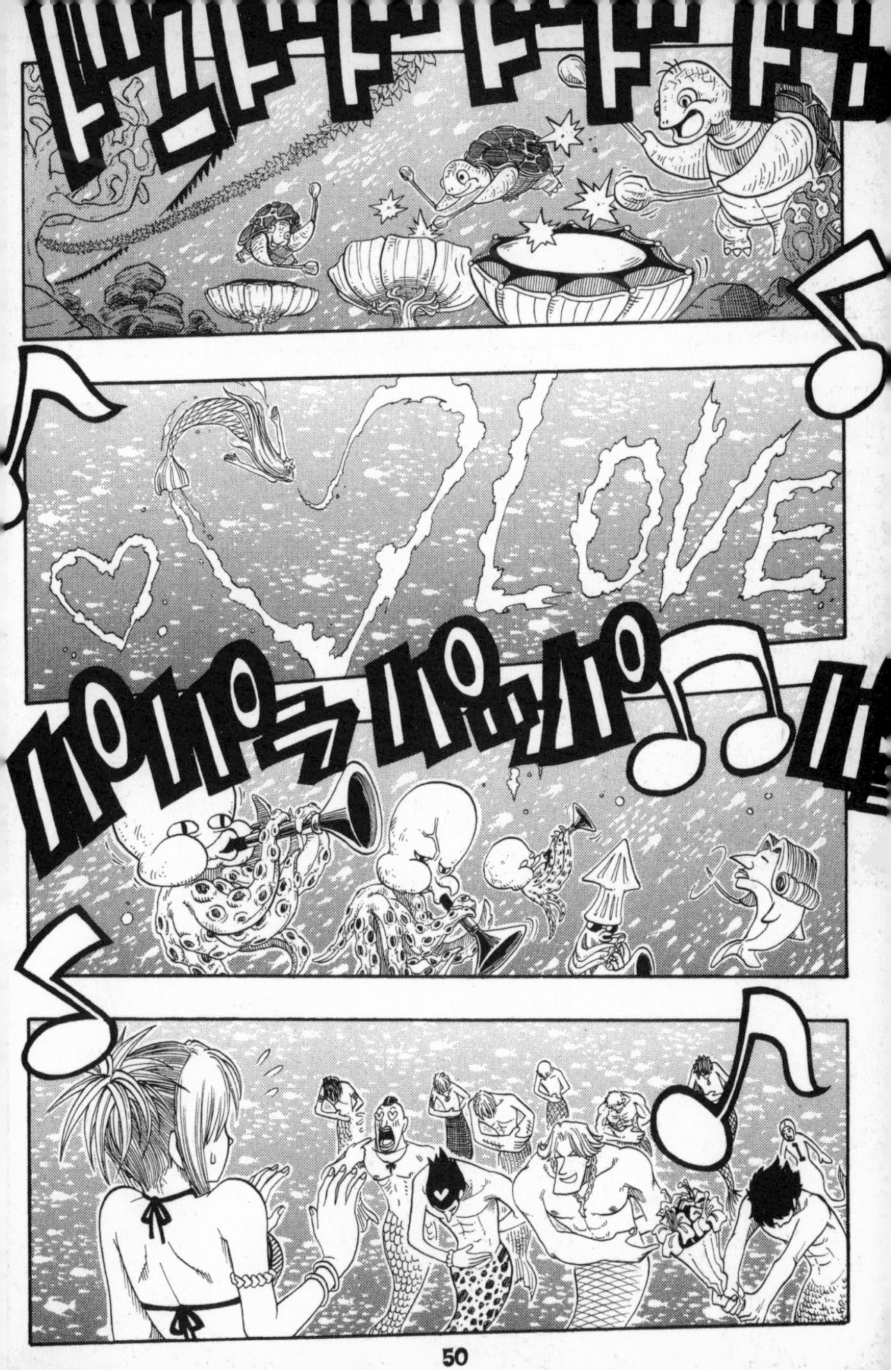
LOVE
パパパラパッパ

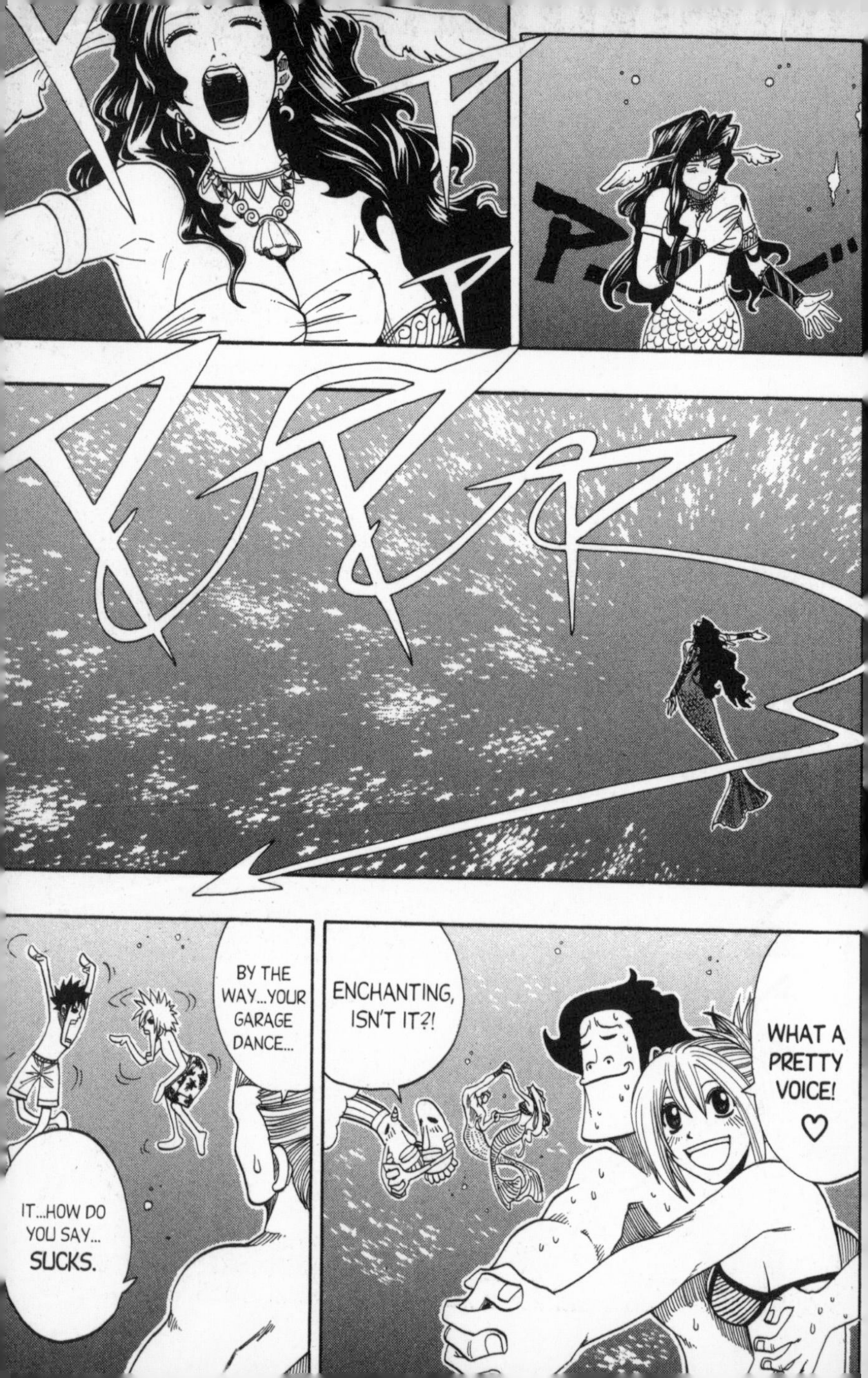
P...
WHAT A PRETTY VOICE! ♡
ENCHANTING, ISN'T IT?!
BY THE WAY...YOUR GARAGE DANCE...
IT...HOW DO YOU SAY... **SUCKS.**

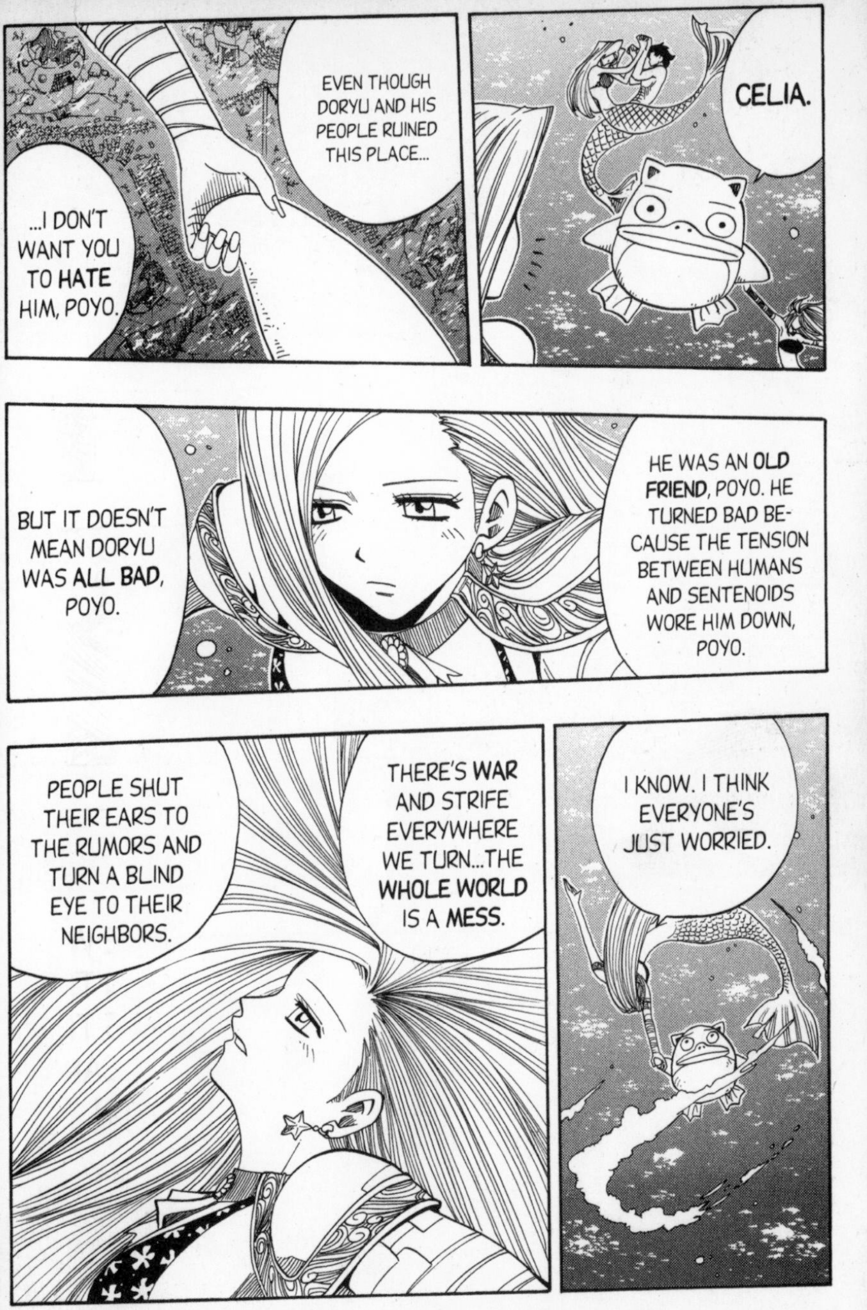

CELIA.
EVEN THOUGH DORYU AND HIS PEOPLE RUINED THIS PLACE...
...I DON'T WANT YOU TO **HATE** HIM, POYO.
HE WAS AN **OLD FRIEND**, POYO. HE TURNED BAD BE-CAUSE THE TENSION BETWEEN HUMANS AND SENTENOIDS WORE HIM DOWN, POYO.
BUT IT DOESN'T MEAN DORYU WAS **ALL BAD**, POYO.
I KNOW. I THINK EVERYONE'S JUST WORRIED.
THERE'S **WAR** AND STRIFE EVERYWHERE WE TURN...THE **WHOLE WORLD** IS A **MESS**.
PEOPLE SHUT THEIR EARS TO THE RUMORS AND TURN A BLIND EYE TO THEIR NEIGHBORS.

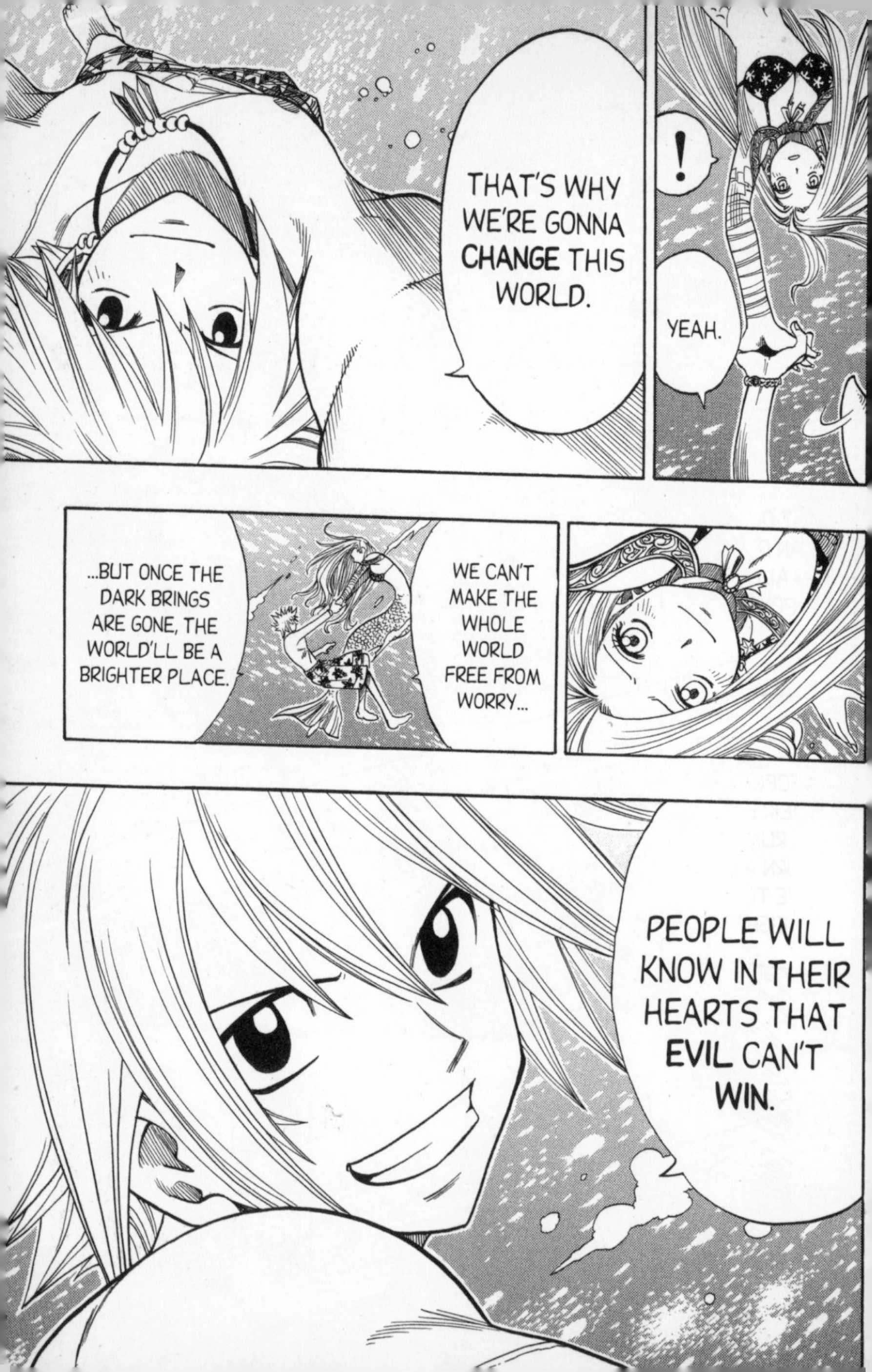
!
YEAH.
THAT'S WHY WE'RE GONNA CHANGE THIS WORLD.
WE CAN'T MAKE THE WHOLE WORLD FREE FROM WORRY...
...BUT ONCE THE DARK BRINGS ARE GONE, THE WORLD'LL BE A BRIGHTER PLACE.
PEOPLE WILL KNOW IN THEIR HEARTS THAT EVIL CAN'T WIN.

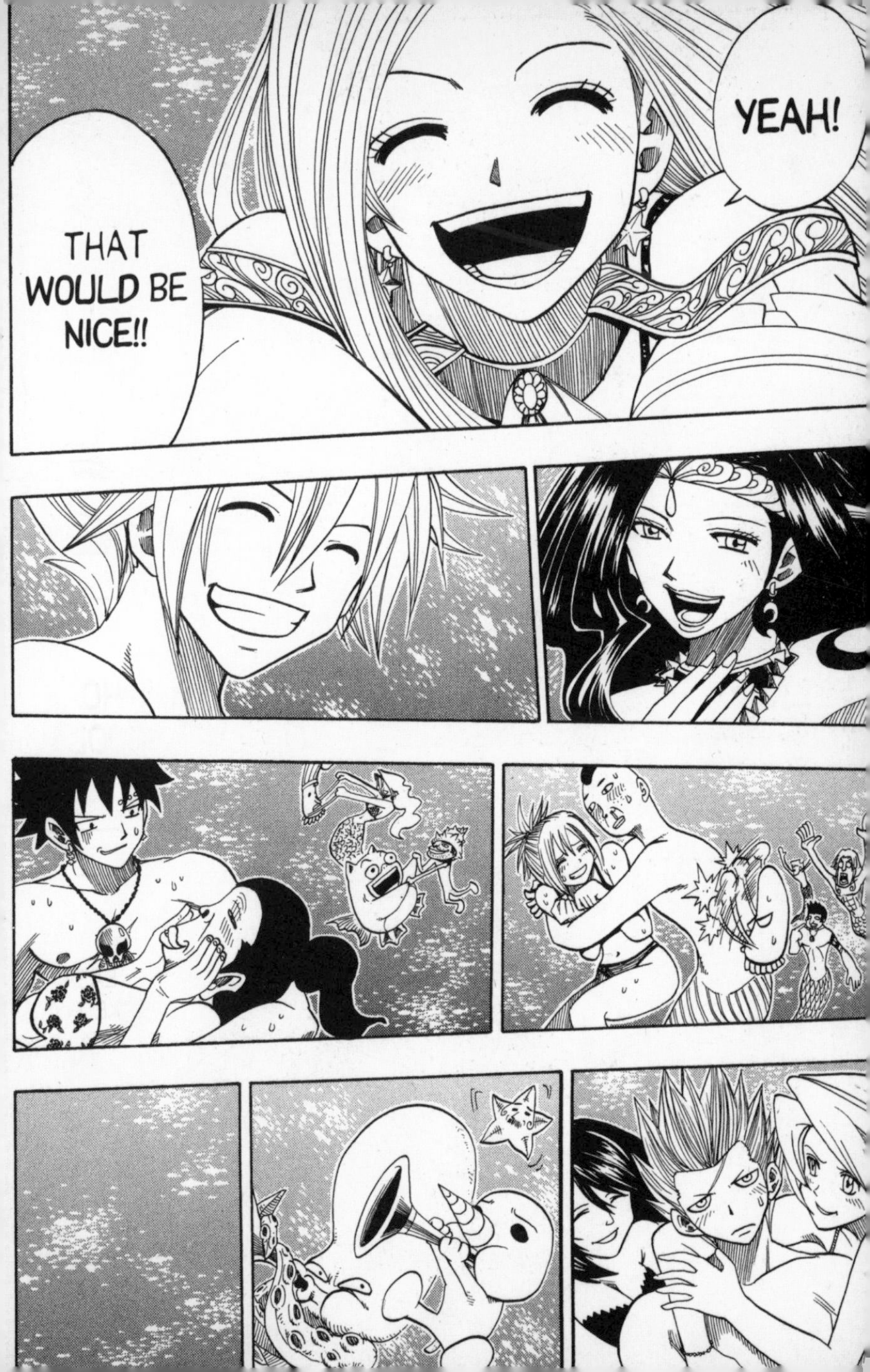
YEAH!
THAT WOULD BE NICE!!

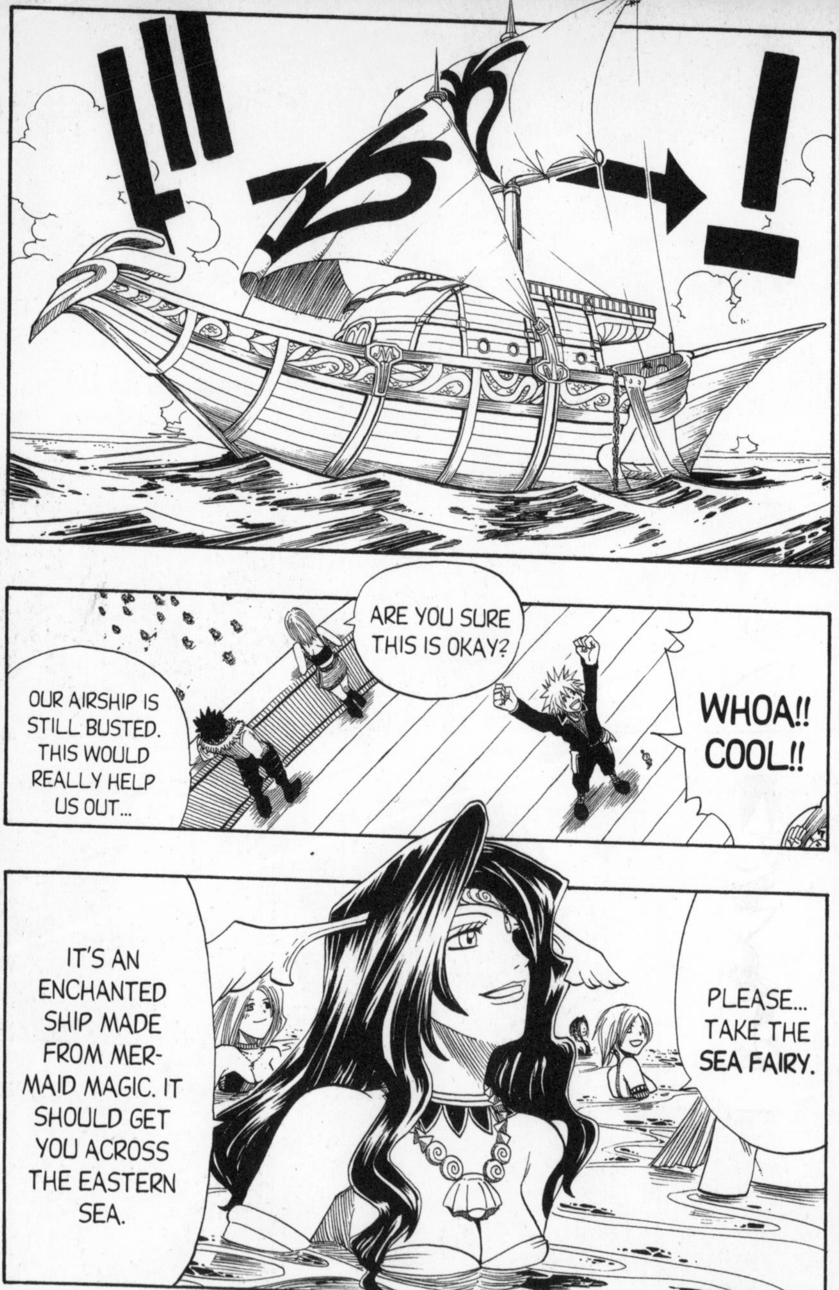
WHOA!! COOL!!
ARE YOU SURE THIS IS OKAY?
OUR AIRSHIP IS STILL BUSTED. THIS WOULD REALLY HELP US OUT...
PLEASE... TAKE THE SEA FAIRY.
IT'S AN ENCHANTED SHIP MADE FROM MER-MAID MAGIC. IT SHOULD GET YOU ACROSS THE EASTERN SEA.

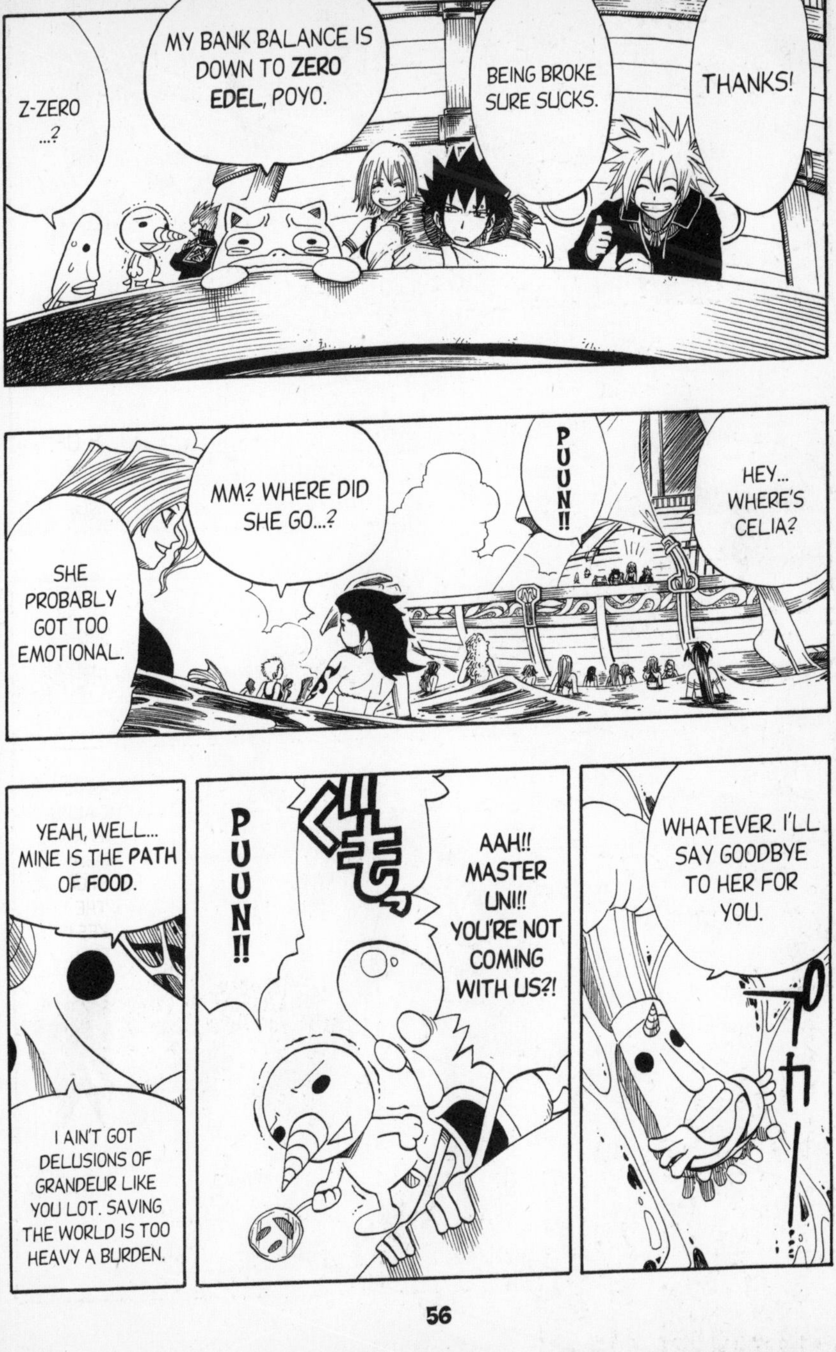
THANKS!
BEING BROKE SURE SUCKS.
MY BANK BALANCE IS DOWN TO ZERO EDEL, POYO.
Z-ZERO ...?
HEY... WHERE'S CELIA?
PUUN!!
MM? WHERE DID SHE GO...?
SHE PROBABLY GOT TOO EMOTIONAL.
WHATEVER. I'LL SAY GOODBYE TO HER FOR YOU.
AAH!! MASTER UNI!! YOU'RE NOT COMING WITH US?!
PUUN!!
YEAH, WELL... MINE IS THE PATH OF FOOD.
I AIN'T GOT DELUSIONS OF GRANDEUR LIKE YOU LOT. SAVING THE WORLD IS TOO HEAVY A BURDEN.

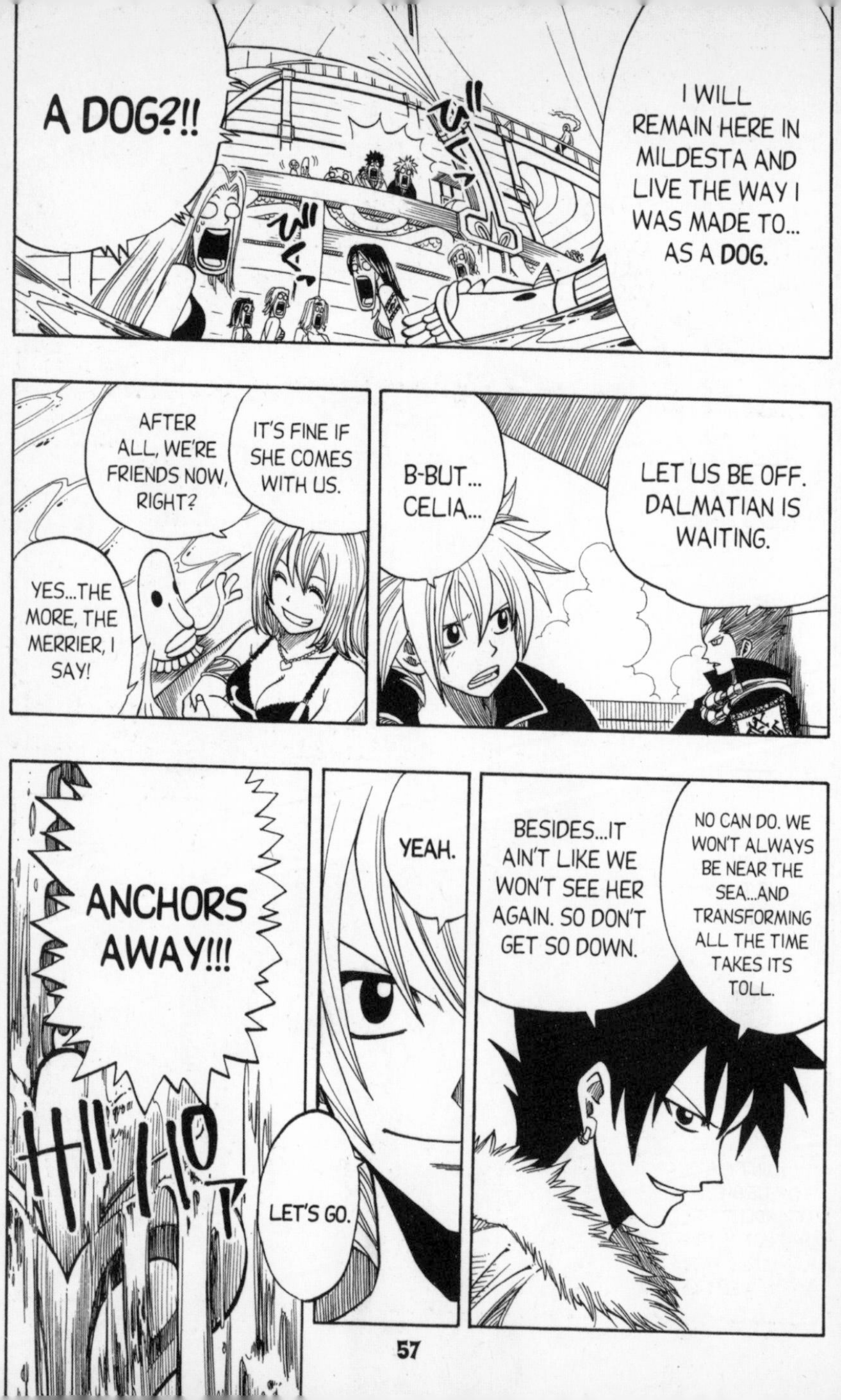
I WILL REMAIN HERE IN MILDESTA AND LIVE THE WAY I WAS MADE TO... AS A DOG.
A DOG?!!
LET US BE OFF. DALMATIAN IS WAITING.
B-BUT... CELIA...
IT'S FINE IF SHE COMES WITH US.
AFTER ALL, WE'RE FRIENDS NOW, RIGHT?
YES...THE MORE, THE MERRIER, I SAY!
NO CAN DO. WE WON'T ALWAYS BE NEAR THE SEA...AND TRANSFORMING ALL THE TIME TAKES ITS TOLL.
BESIDES...IT AIN'T LIKE WE WON'T SEE HER AGAIN. SO DON'T GET SO DOWN.
YEAH.
LET'S GO.
ANCHORS AWAY!!!

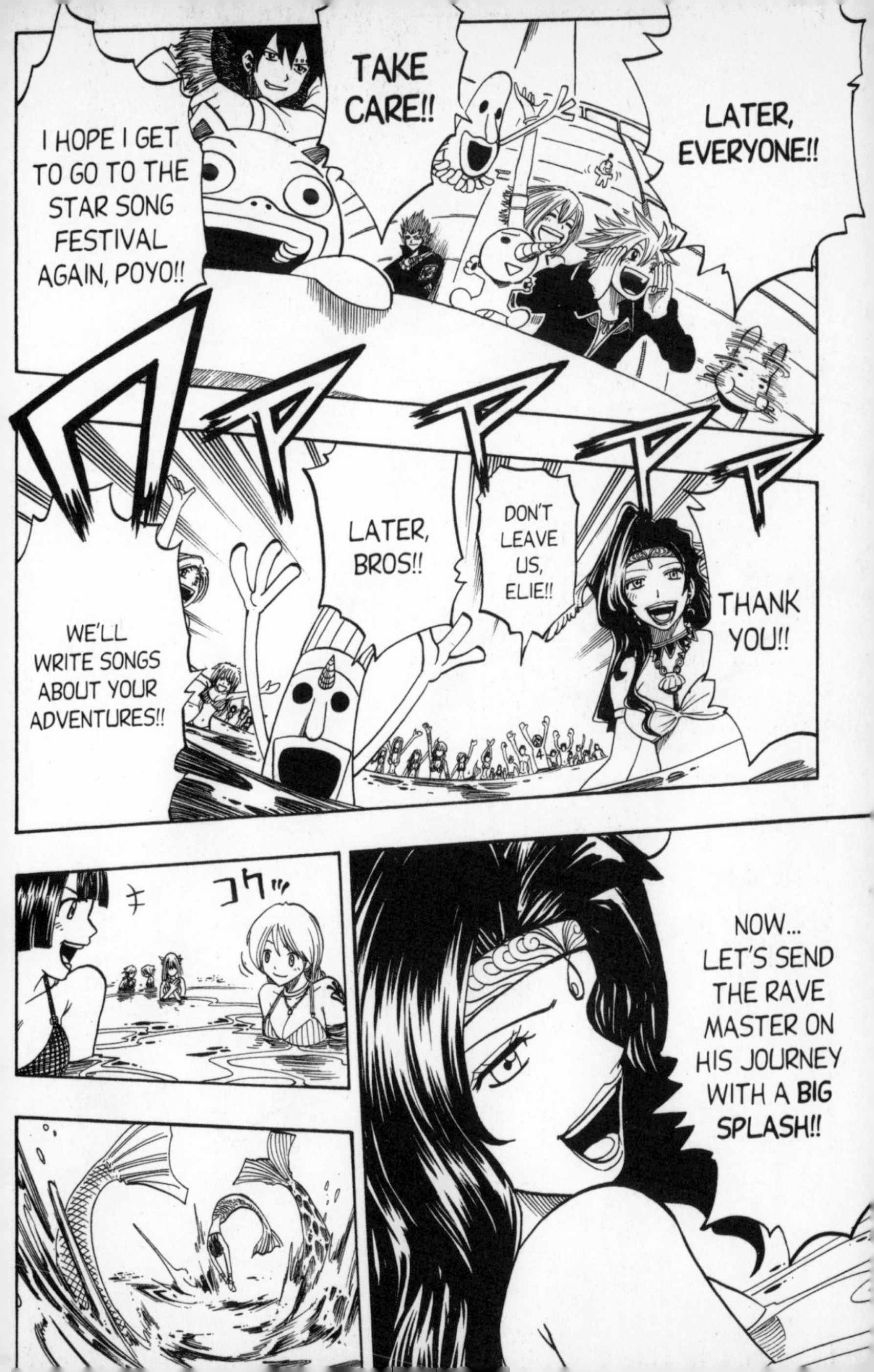
LATER, EVERYONE!!
TAKE CARE!!
I HOPE I GET TO GO TO THE STAR SONG FESTIVAL AGAIN, POYO!!
THANK YOU!!
DON'T LEAVE US, ELIE!!
LATER, BROS!!
WE'LL WRITE SONGS ABOUT YOUR ADVENTURES!!
NOW... LET'S SEND THE RAVE MASTER ON HIS JOURNEY WITH A **BIG SPLASH**!!
コクッ

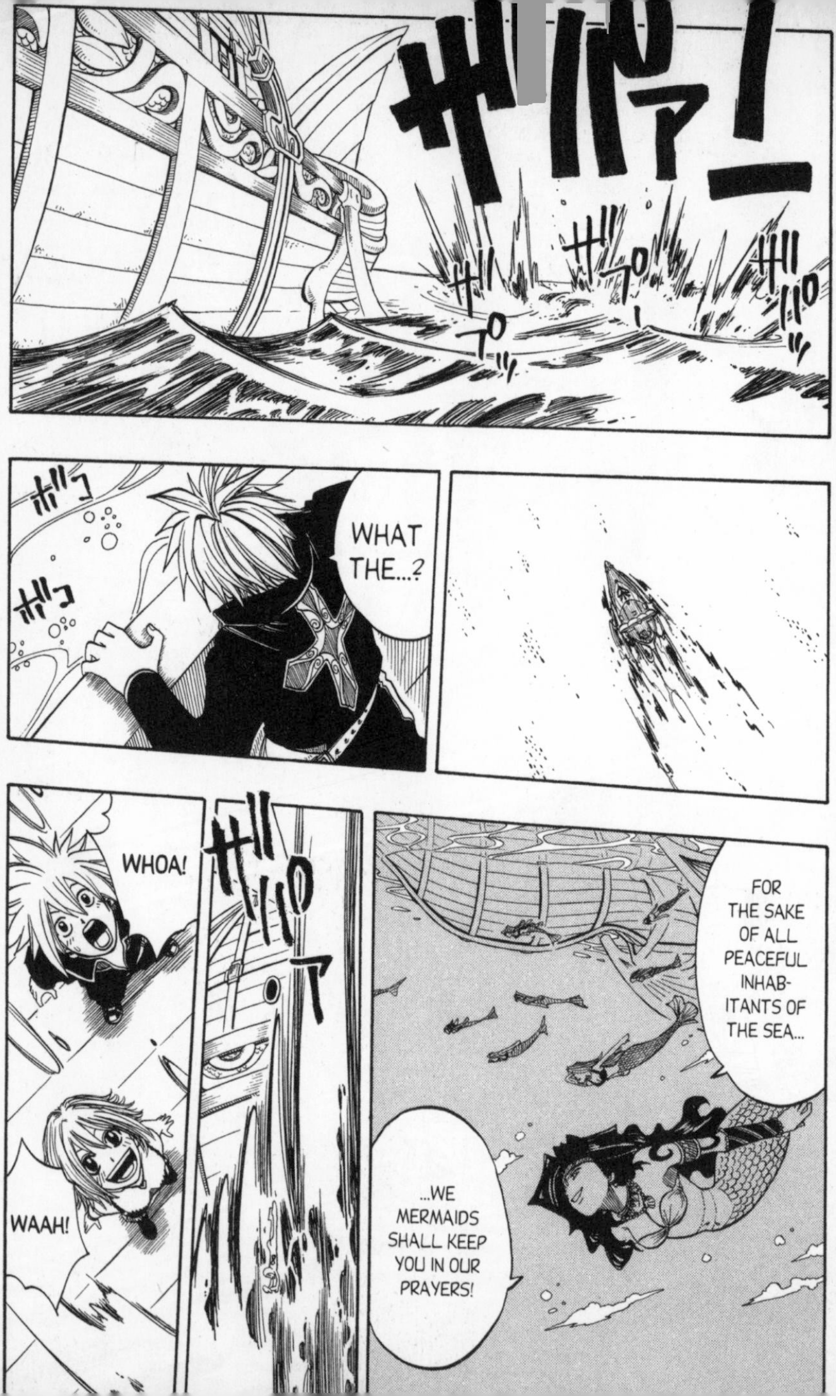
WHAT THE...?
FOR THE SAKE OF ALL PEACEFUL INHABITANTS OF THE SEA...
...WE MERMAIDS SHALL KEEP YOU IN OUR PRAYERS!
WHOA!
WAAH!

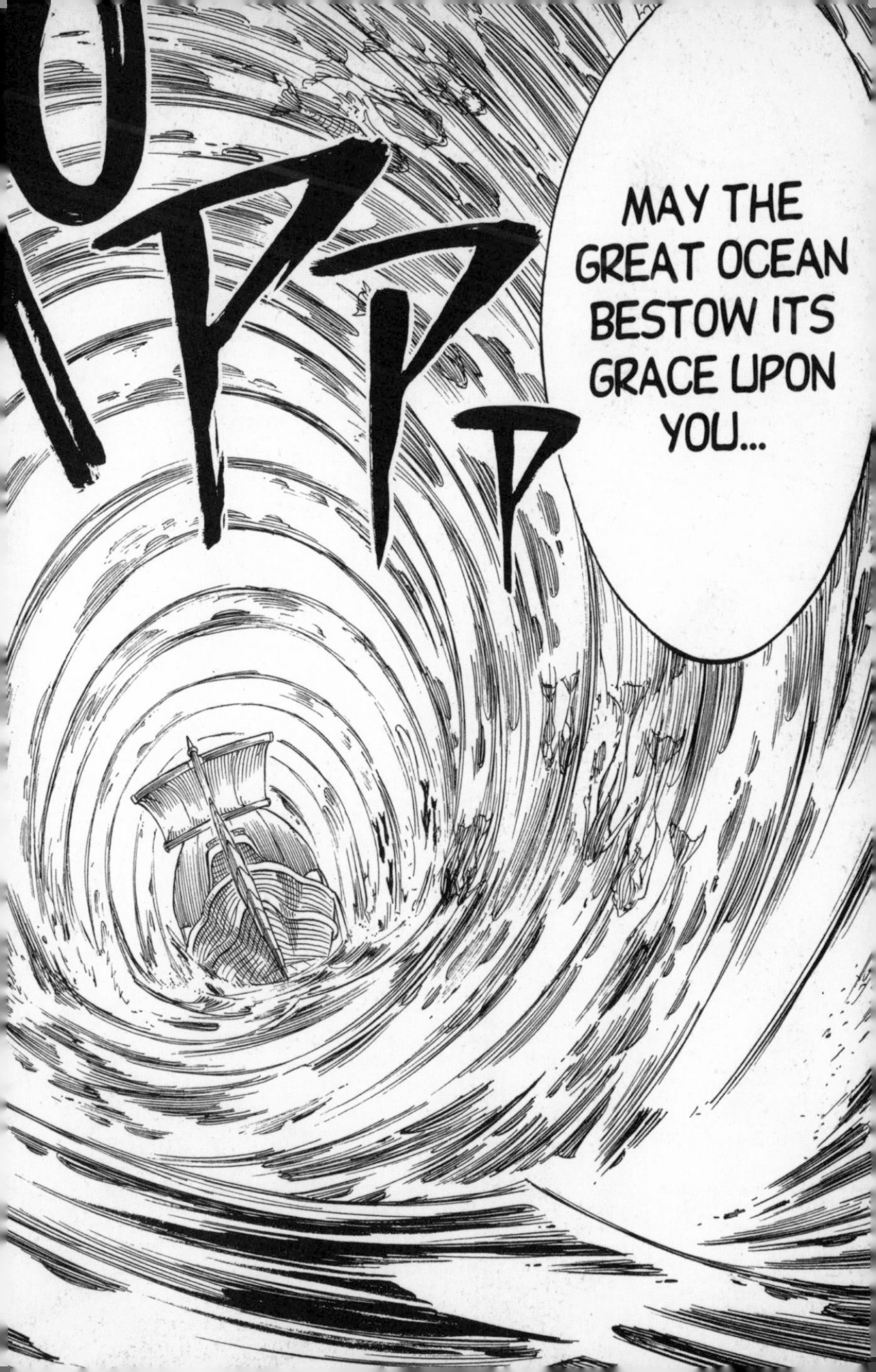
MAY THE GREAT OCEAN BESTOW ITS GRACE UPON YOU...

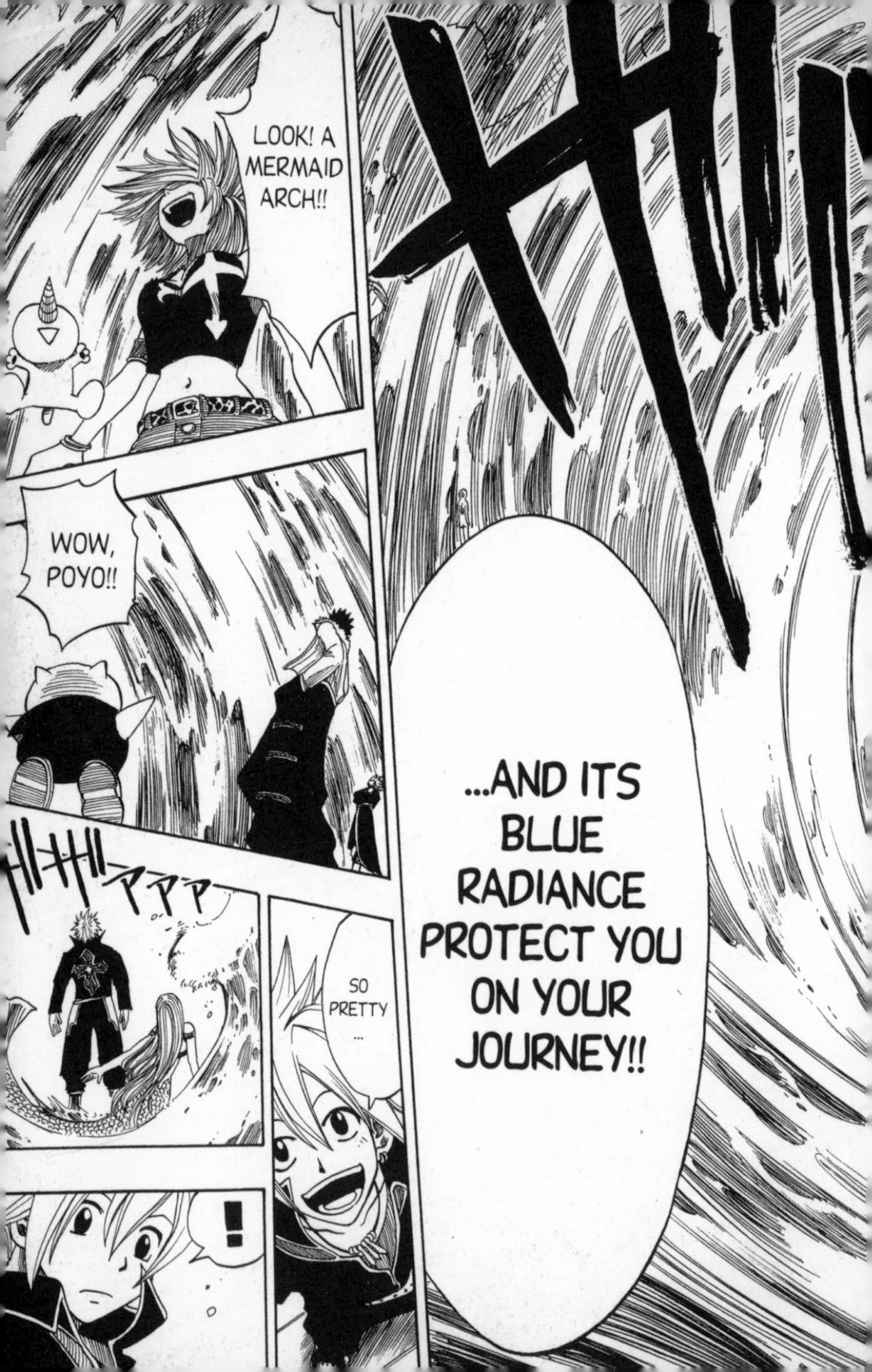
...AND ITS BLUE RADIANCE PROTECT YOU ON YOUR JOURNEY!!
LOOK! A MERMAID ARCH!!
WOW, POYO!!
SO PRETTY ...
!

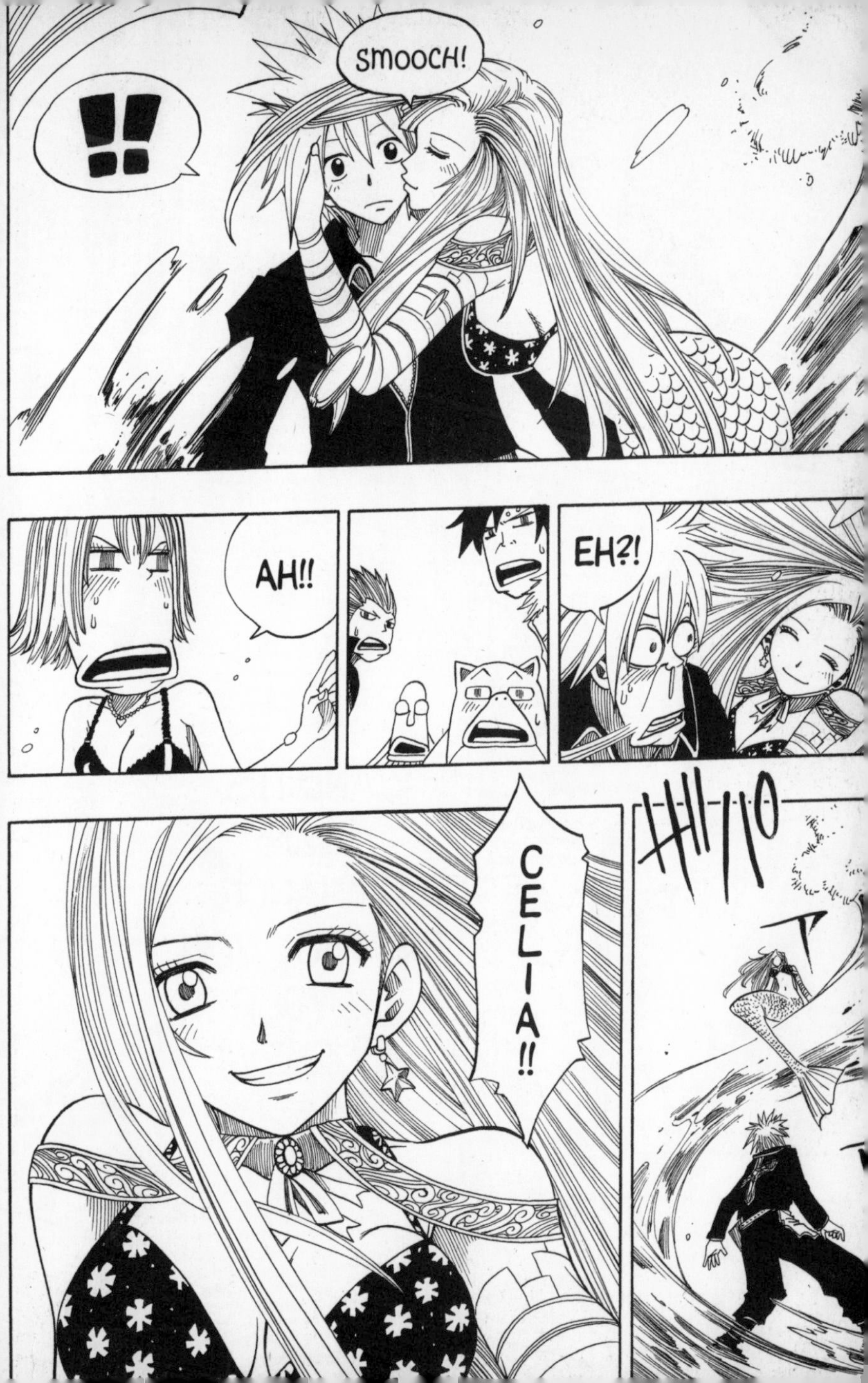
SMOOCH!
!!
EH?!
AH!!
CELIA!!

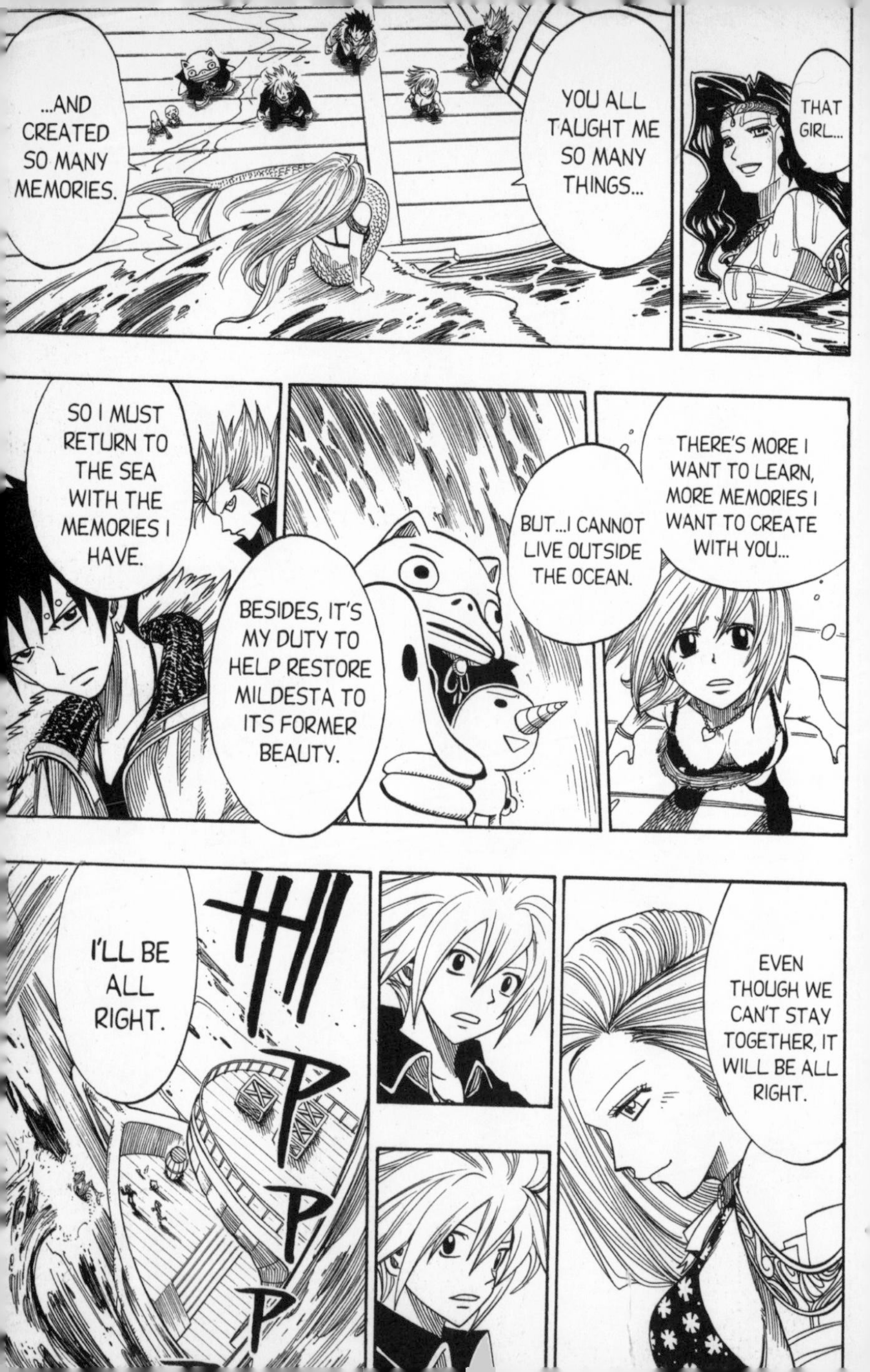
THAT GIRL...
YOU ALL TAUGHT ME SO MANY THINGS...
...AND CREATED SO MANY MEMORIES.
THERE'S MORE I WANT TO LEARN, MORE MEMORIES I WANT TO CREATE WITH YOU...
BUT...I CANNOT LIVE OUTSIDE THE OCEAN.
BESIDES, IT'S MY DUTY TO HELP RESTORE MILDESTA TO ITS FORMER BEAUTY.
SO I MUST RETURN TO THE SEA WITH THE MEMORIES I HAVE.
EVEN THOUGH WE CAN'T STAY TOGETHER, IT WILL BE ALL RIGHT.
I'LL BE ALL RIGHT.

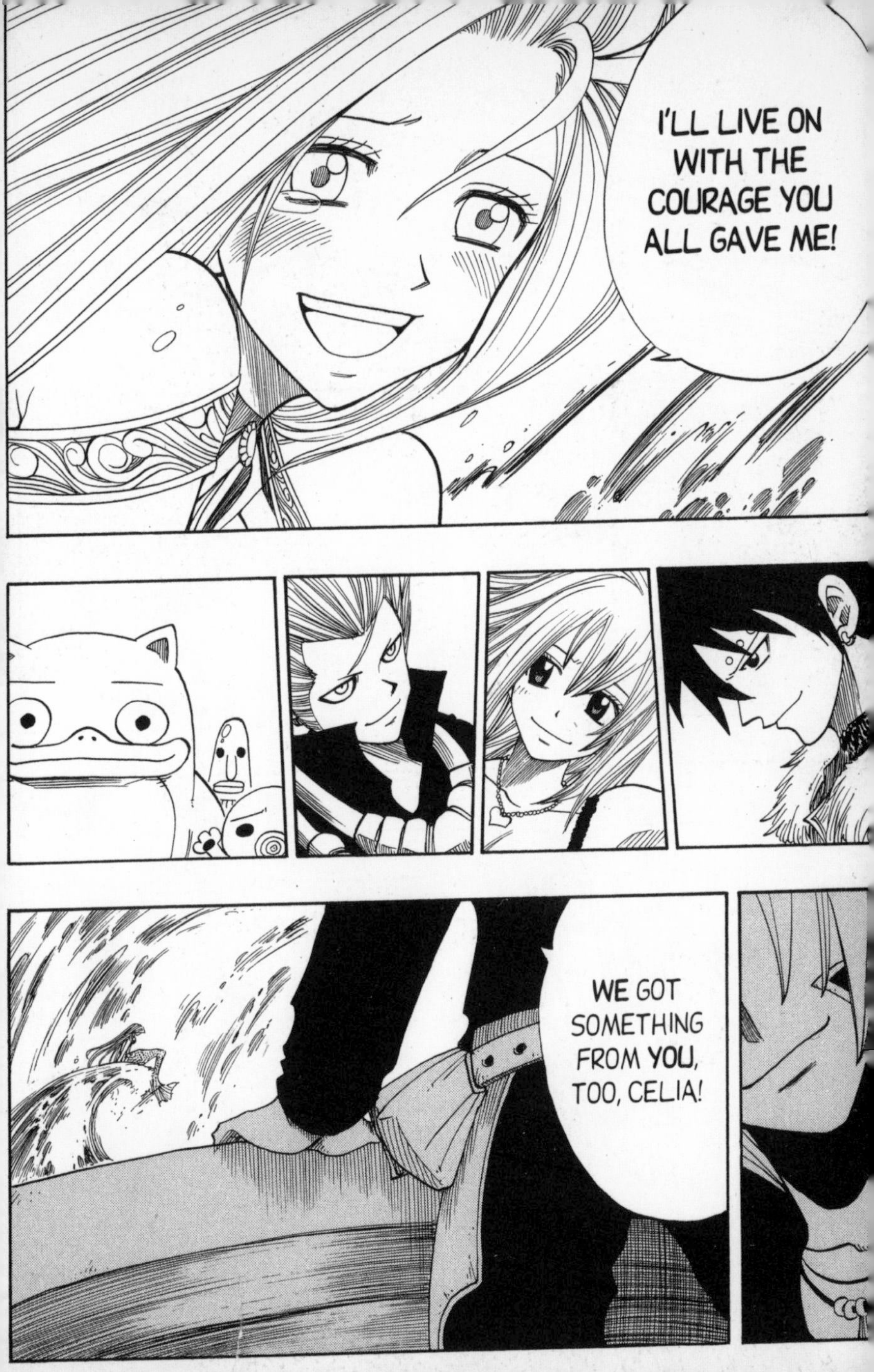
I'LL LIVE ON WITH THE COURAGE YOU ALL GAVE ME!
WE GOT SOMETHING FROM YOU, TOO, CELIA!

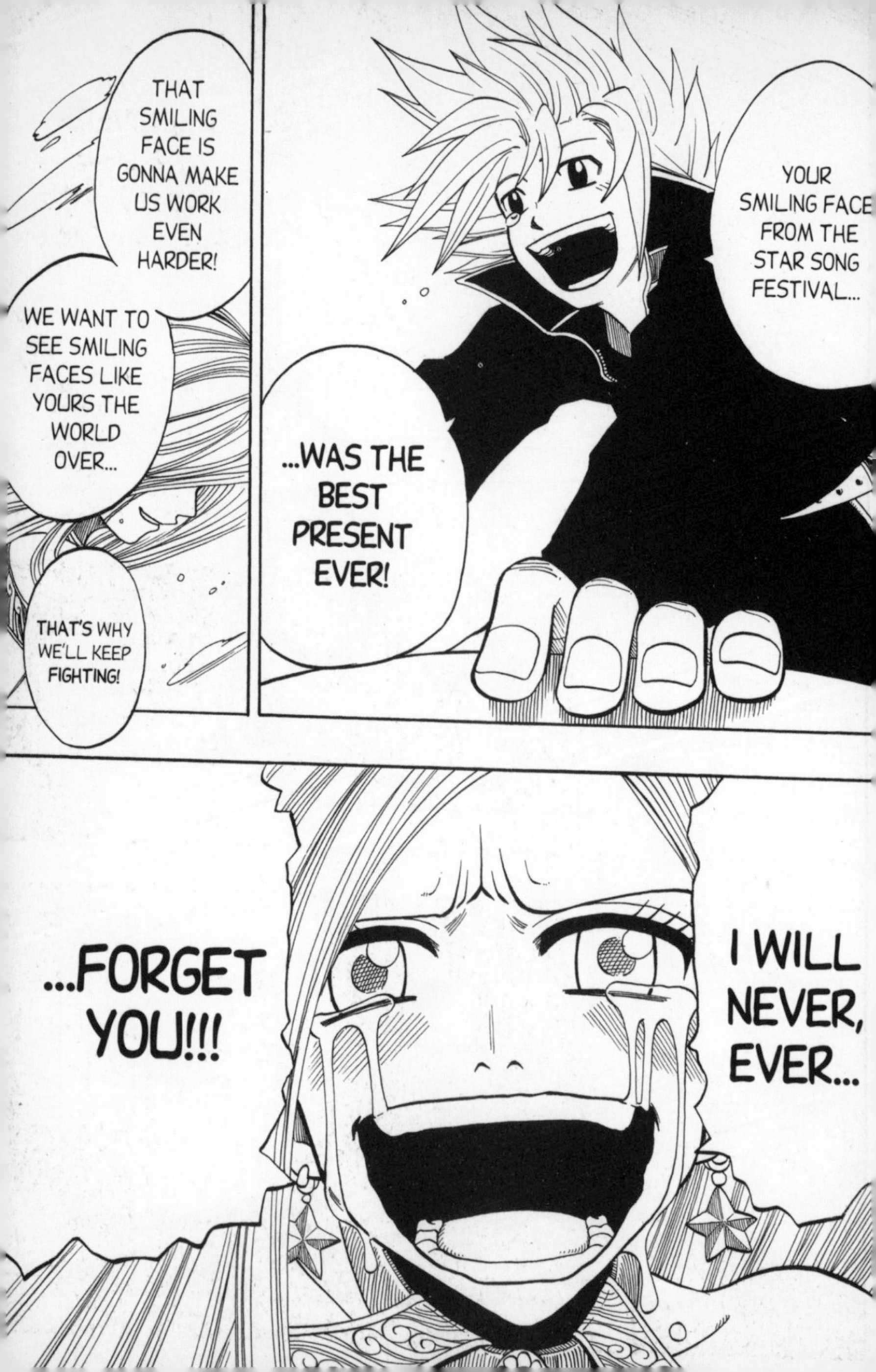
YOUR SMILING FACE FROM THE STAR SONG FESTIVAL...
...WAS THE BEST PRESENT EVER!
THAT SMILING FACE IS GONNA MAKE US WORK EVEN HARDER!
WE WANT TO SEE SMILING FACES LIKE YOURS THE WORLD OVER...
THAT'S WHY WE'LL KEEP FIGHTING!
I WILL NEVER, EVER...
...FORGET YOU!!!

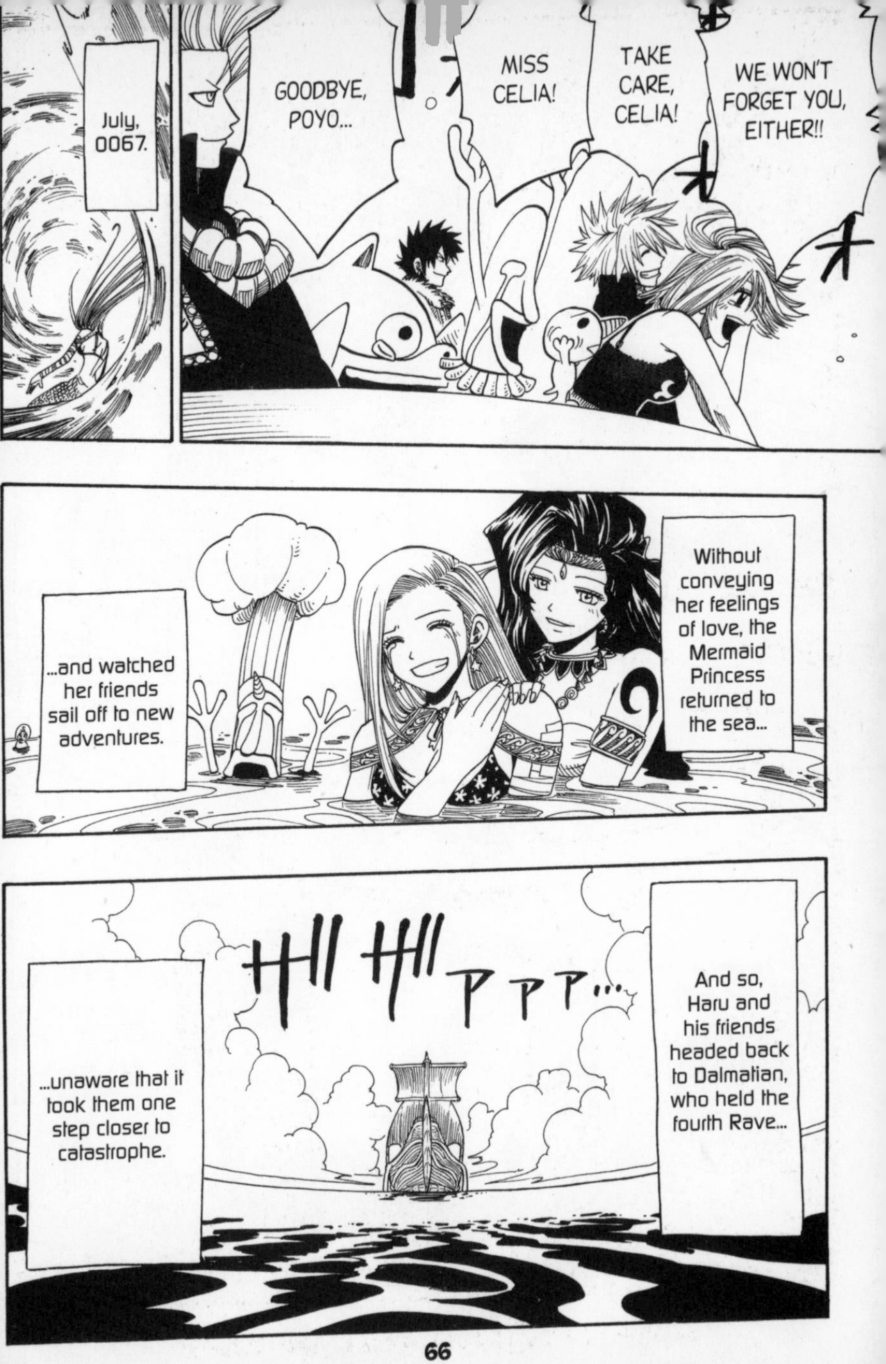
WE WON'T FORGET YOU, EITHER!!
TAKE CARE, CELIA!
MISS CELIA!
GOODBYE, POYO...
July, 0067.
Without conveying her feelings of love, the Mermaid Princess returned to the sea...
...and watched her friends sail off to new adventures.
And so, Haru and his friends headed back to Dalmatian, who held the fourth Rave...
...unaware that it took them one step closer to catastrophe.

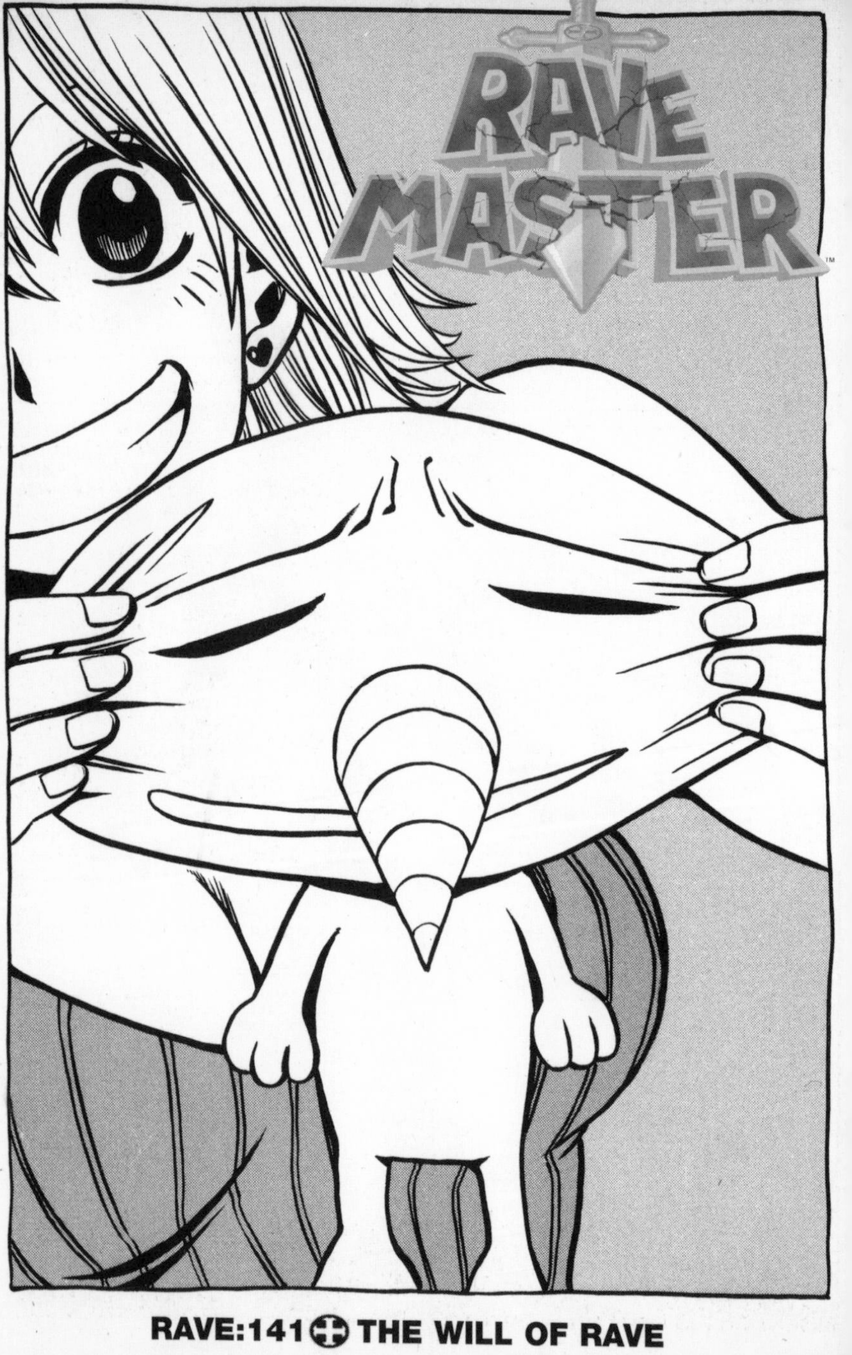
RAVE MASTER™

RAVE:141 ✚ THE WILL OF RAVE

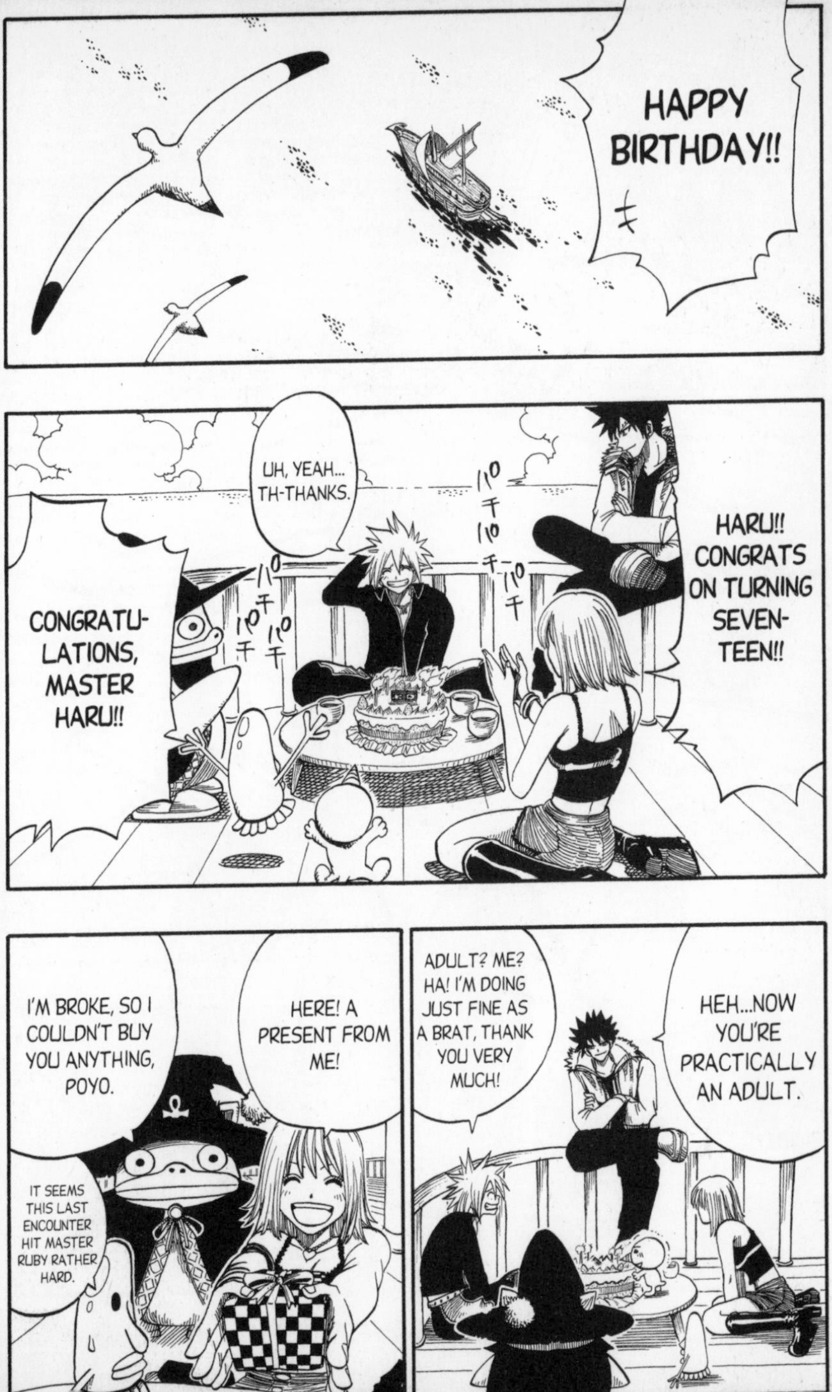
HAPPY BIRTHDAY!!
キ
HARU!! CONGRATS ON TURNING SEVENTEEN!!
パチパチ
UH, YEAH... TH-THANKS.
パチパチ
CONGRATU-LATIONS, MASTER HARU!!
HEH...NOW YOU'RE PRACTICALLY AN ADULT.
ADULT? ME? HA! I'M DOING JUST FINE AS A BRAT, THANK YOU VERY MUCH!
HERE! A PRESENT FROM ME!
I'M BROKE, SO I COULDN'T BUY YOU ANYTHING, POYO.
IT SEEMS THIS LAST ENCOUNTER HIT MASTER RUBY RATHER HARD.

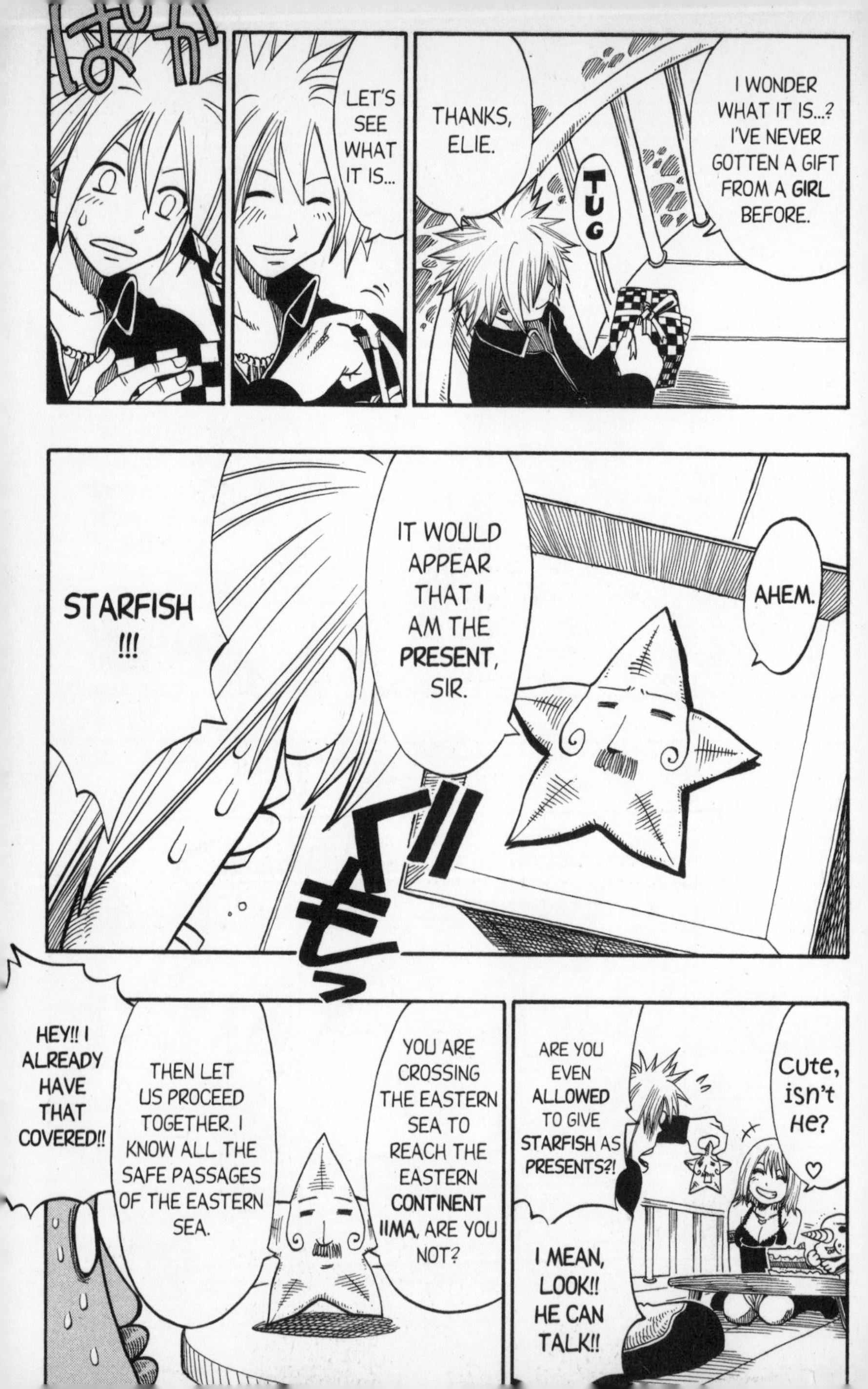
I WONDER WHAT IT IS...? I'VE NEVER GOTTEN A GIFT FROM A GIRL BEFORE.
THANKS, ELIE.
TUG
LET'S SEE WHAT IT IS...
ぱか
AHEM.
IT WOULD APPEAR THAT I AM THE PRESENT, SIR.
STARFISH !!!
Cute, isn't He? ♡
ARE YOU EVEN ALLOWED TO GIVE STARFISH AS PRESENTS?!
I MEAN, LOOK!! HE CAN TALK!!
YOU ARE CROSSING THE EASTERN SEA TO REACH THE EASTERN CONTINENT IIMA, ARE YOU NOT?
THEN LET US PROCEED TOGETHER. I KNOW ALL THE SAFE PASSAGES OF THE EASTERN SEA.
HEY!! I ALREADY HAVE THAT COVERED!!

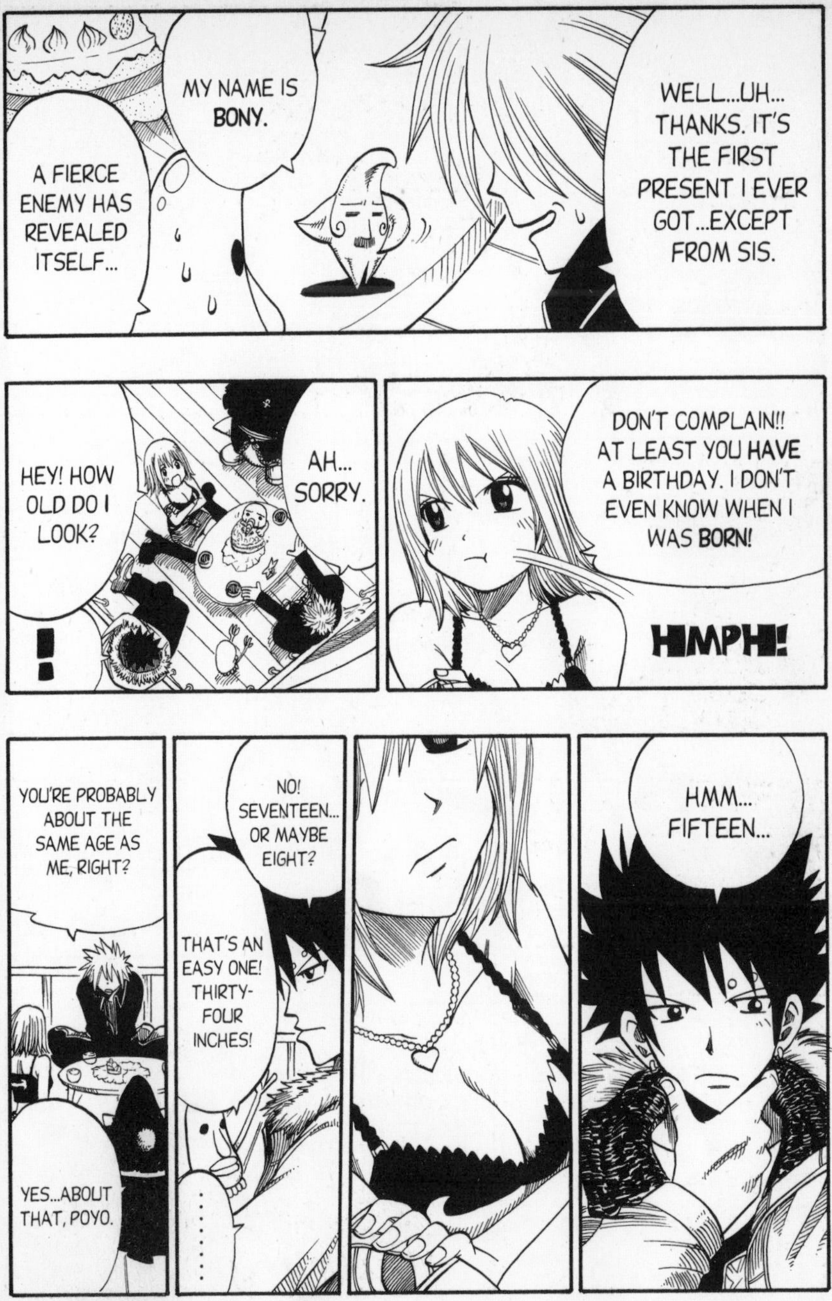
WELL...UH... THANKS. IT'S THE FIRST PRESENT I EVER GOT...EXCEPT FROM SIS.
MY NAME IS BONY.
A FIERCE ENEMY HAS REVEALED ITSELF...
DON'T COMPLAIN!! AT LEAST YOU HAVE A BIRTHDAY. I DON'T EVEN KNOW WHEN I WAS BORN!
HMPH!
AH... SORRY.
HEY! HOW OLD DO I LOOK?
!
HMM... FIFTEEN...
NO! SEVENTEEN... OR MAYBE EIGHT?
THAT'S AN EASY ONE! THIRTY-FOUR INCHES!
......
YOU'RE PROBABLY ABOUT THE SAME AGE AS ME, RIGHT?
YES...ABOUT THAT, POYO.

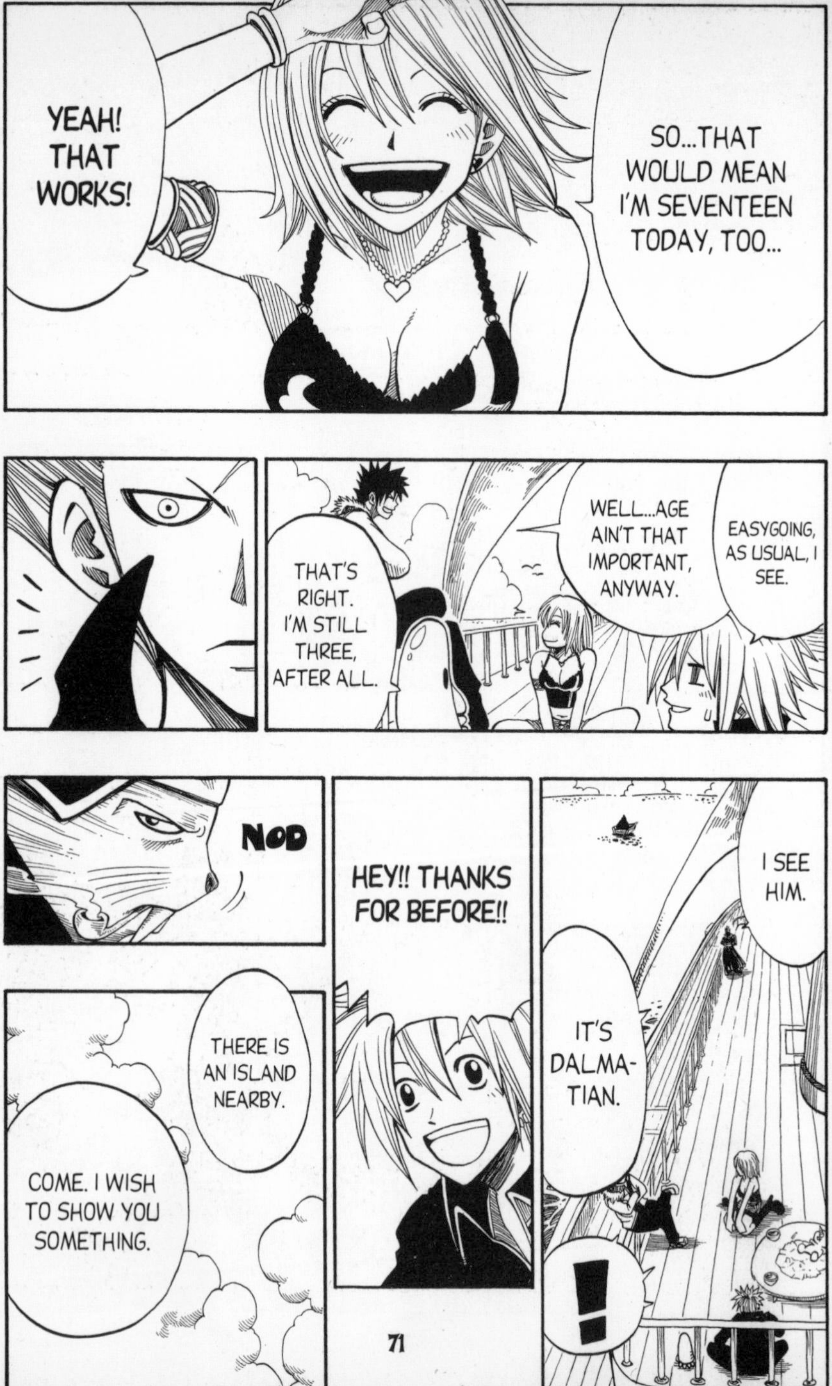
SO...THAT WOULD MEAN I'M SEVENTEEN TODAY, TOO...
YEAH! THAT WORKS!
EASYGOING, AS USUAL, I SEE.
WELL...AGE AIN'T THAT IMPORTANT, ANYWAY.
THAT'S RIGHT. I'M STILL THREE, AFTER ALL.
I SEE HIM.
IT'S DALMA-TIAN.
!
HEY!! THANKS FOR BEFORE!!
NOD
THERE IS AN ISLAND NEARBY.
COME. I WISH TO SHOW YOU SOMETHING.

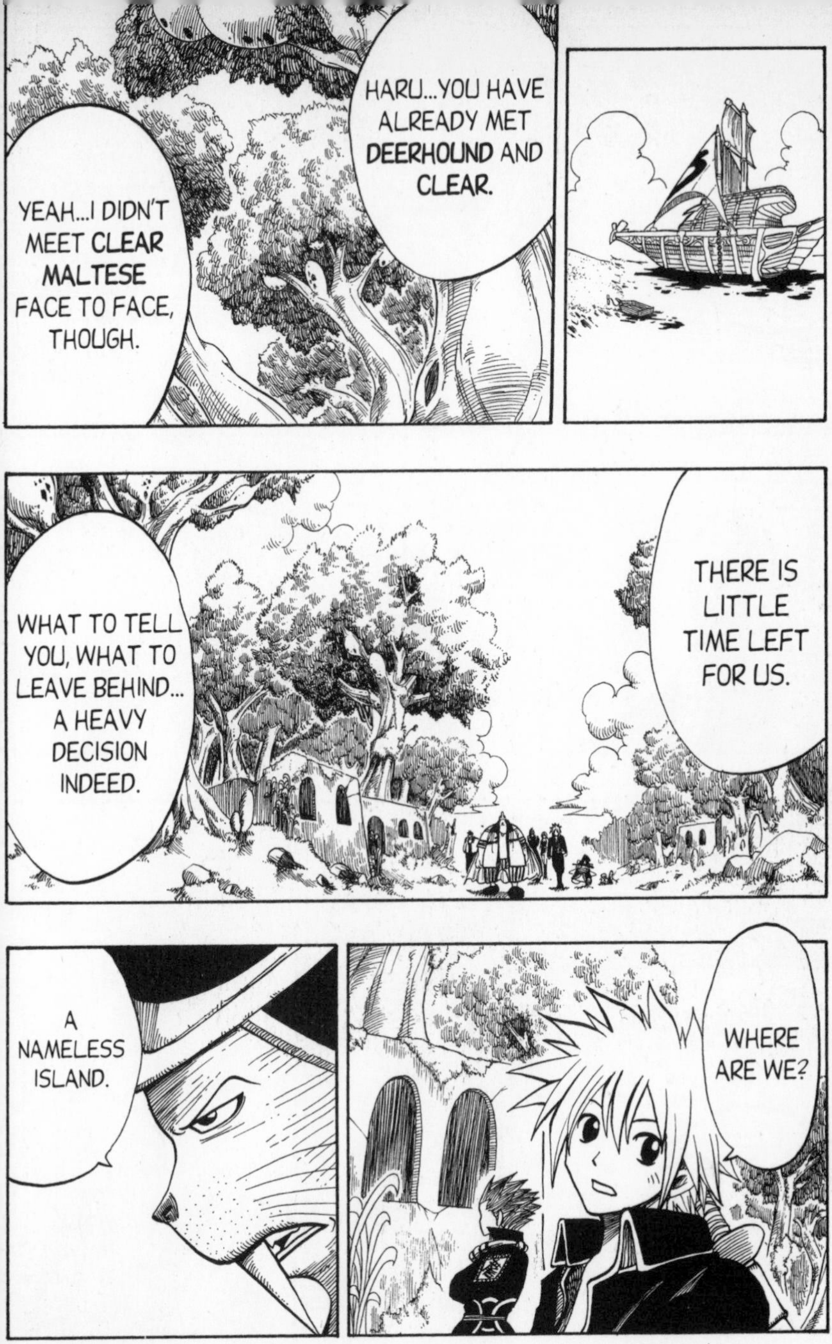
HARU...YOU HAVE ALREADY MET DEERHOUND AND CLEAR.
YEAH...I DIDN'T MEET CLEAR MALTESE FACE TO FACE, THOUGH.
THERE IS LITTLE TIME LEFT FOR US.
WHAT TO TELL YOU, WHAT TO LEAVE BEHIND... A HEAVY DECISION INDEED.
WHERE ARE WE?
A NAMELESS ISLAND.

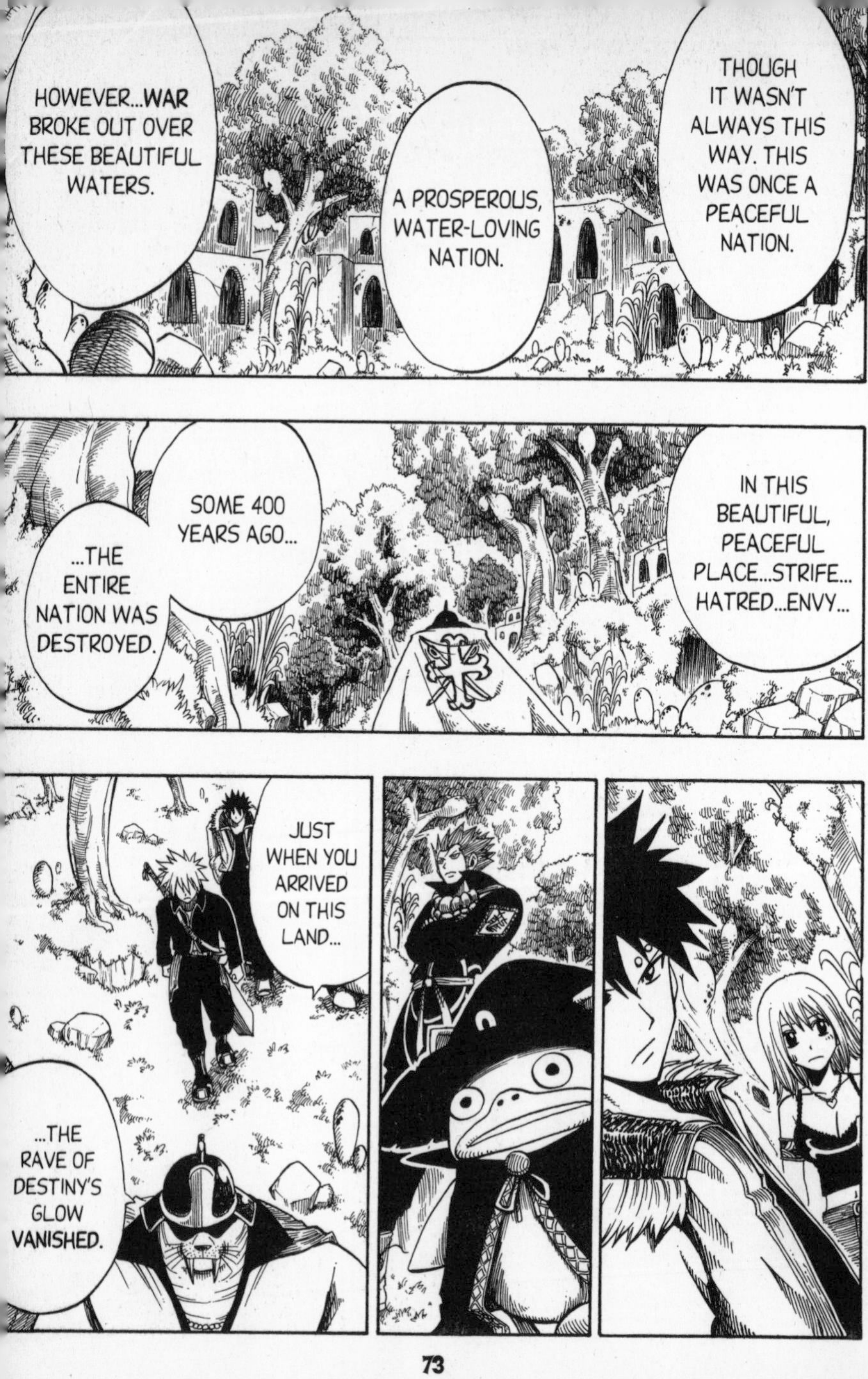
THOUGH IT WASN'T ALWAYS THIS WAY. THIS WAS ONCE A PEACEFUL NATION.
A PROSPEROUS, WATER-LOVING NATION.
HOWEVER...WAR BROKE OUT OVER THESE BEAUTIFUL WATERS.
IN THIS BEAUTIFUL, PEACEFUL PLACE...STRIFE... HATRED...ENVY...
SOME 400 YEARS AGO...
...THE ENTIRE NATION WAS DESTROYED.
JUST WHEN YOU ARRIVED ON THIS LAND...
...THE RAVE OF DESTINY'S GLOW VANISHED.

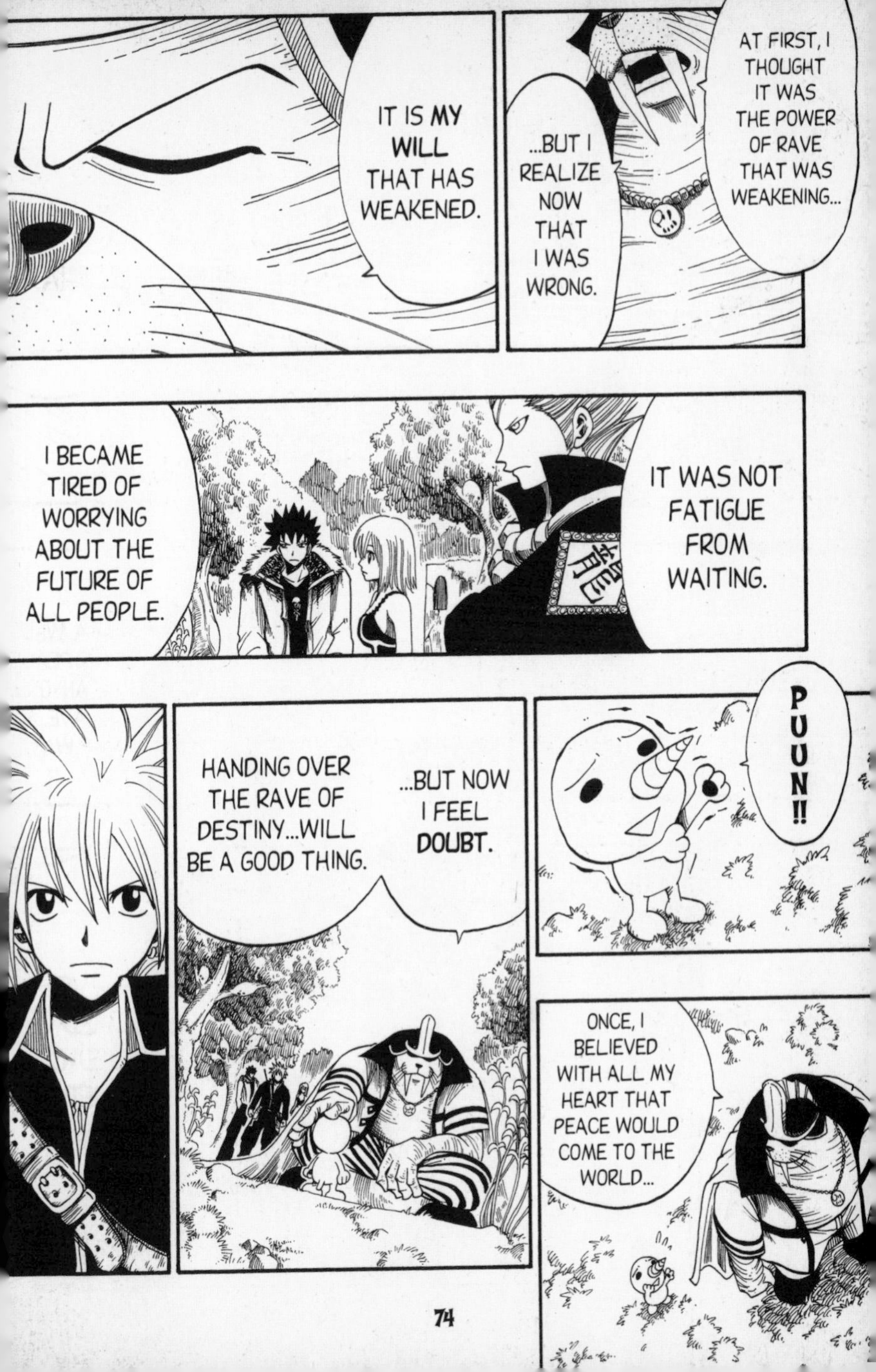
AT FIRST, I THOUGHT IT WAS THE POWER OF RAVE THAT WAS WEAKENING...
...BUT I REALIZE NOW THAT I WAS WRONG.
IT IS MY WILL THAT HAS WEAKENED.
IT WAS NOT FATIGUE FROM WAITING.
I BECAME TIRED OF WORRYING ABOUT THE FUTURE OF ALL PEOPLE.
PUUN!!
ONCE, I BELIEVED WITH ALL MY HEART THAT PEACE WOULD COME TO THE WORLD...
HANDING OVER THE RAVE OF DESTINY...WILL BE A GOOD THING.
...BUT NOW I FEEL DOUBT.

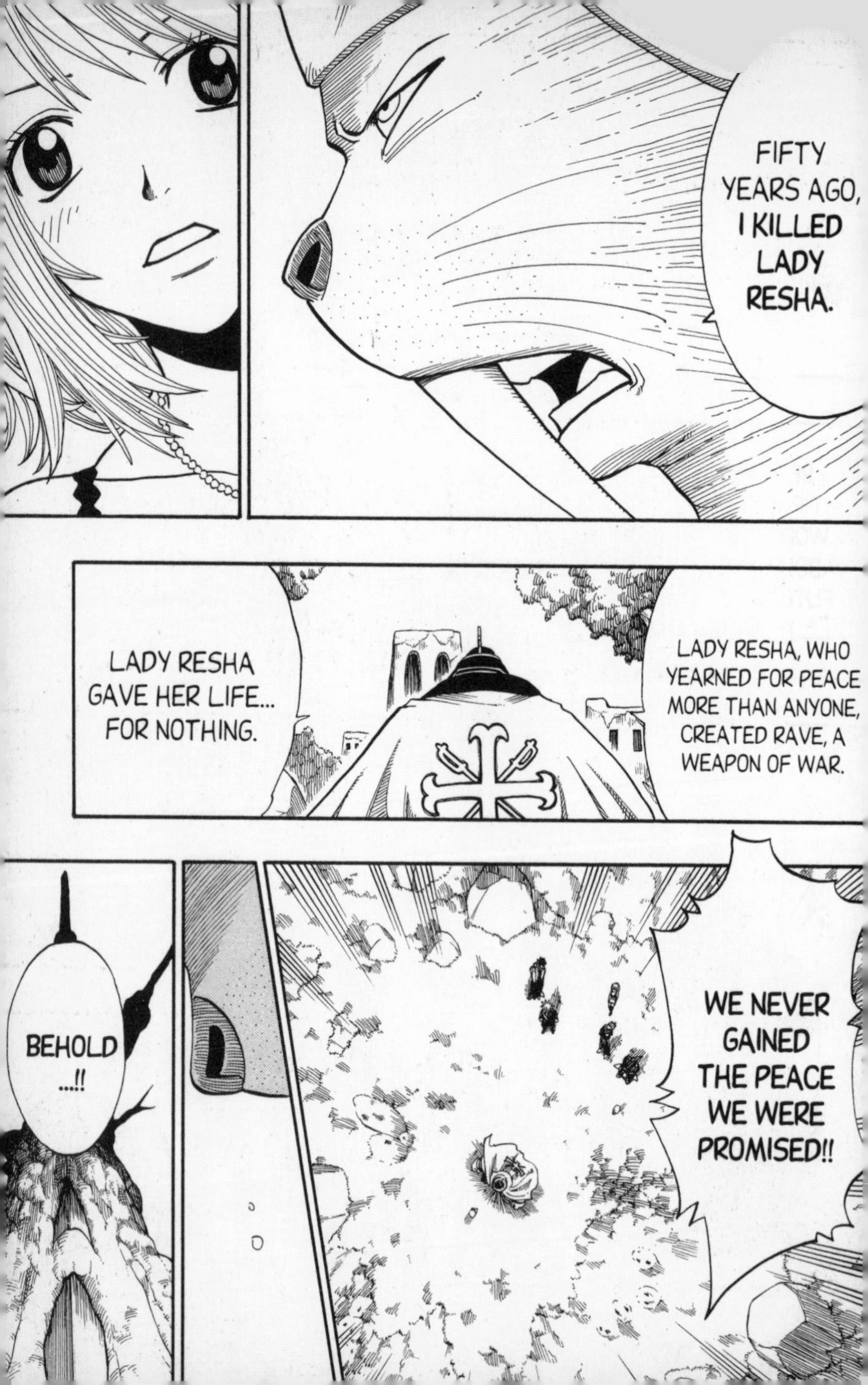
FIFTY YEARS AGO, I KILLED LADY RESHA.
LADY RESHA, WHO YEARNED FOR PEACE MORE THAN ANYONE, CREATED RAVE, A WEAPON OF WAR.
LADY RESHA GAVE HER LIFE... FOR NOTHING.
WE NEVER GAINED THE PEACE WE WERE PROMISED!!
BEHOLD ...!!

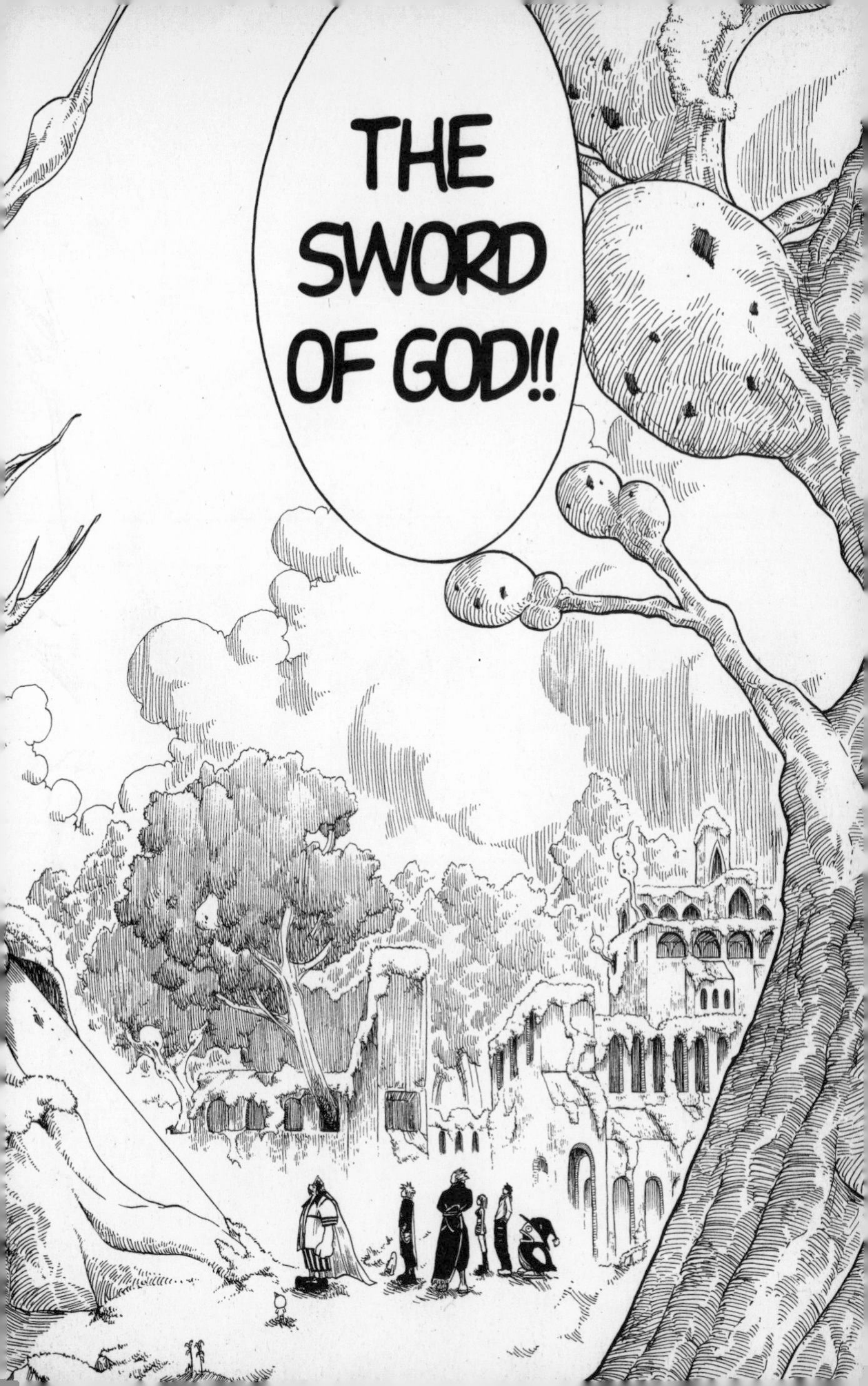
THE SWORD OF GOD!!

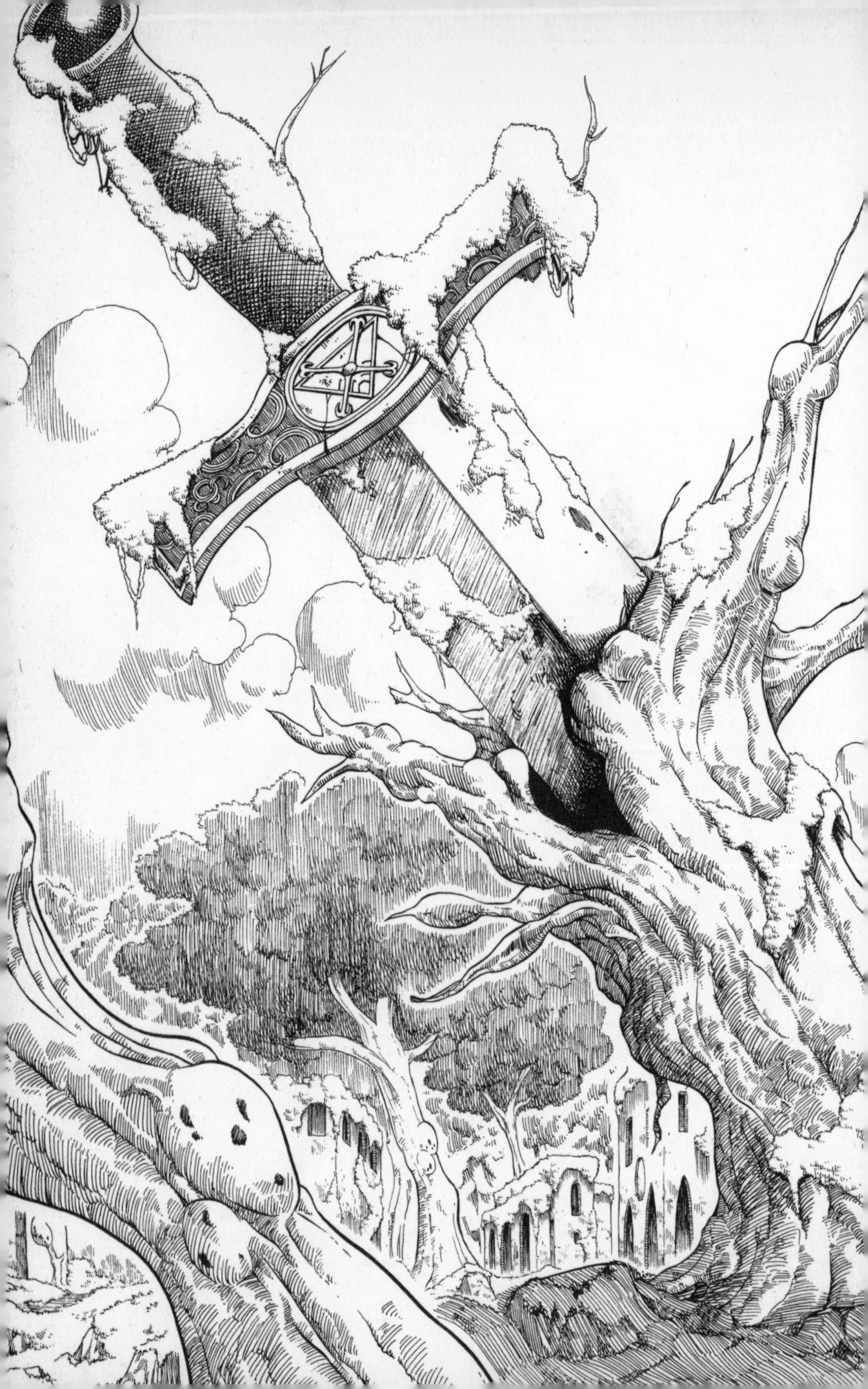

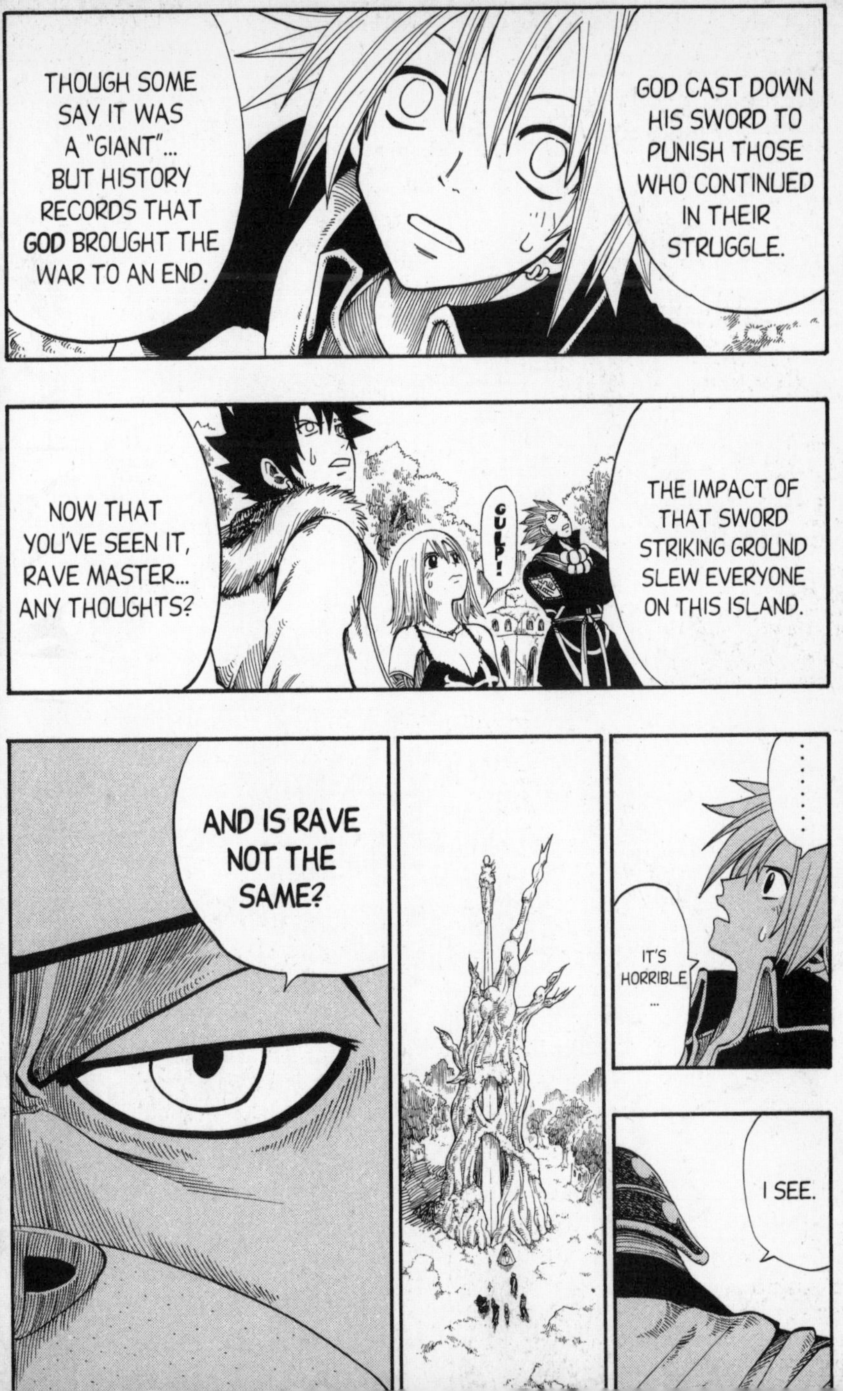
GOD CAST DOWN HIS SWORD TO PUNISH THOSE WHO CONTINUED IN THEIR STRUGGLE.
THOUGH SOME SAY IT WAS A "GIANT"... BUT HISTORY RECORDS THAT **GOD** BROUGHT THE WAR TO AN END.
THE IMPACT OF THAT SWORD STRIKING GROUND SLEW EVERYONE ON THIS ISLAND.
GULP!
NOW THAT YOU'VE SEEN IT, RAVE MASTER... ANY THOUGHTS?
......
IT'S HORRIBLE ...
I SEE.
AND IS RAVE NOT THE SAME?

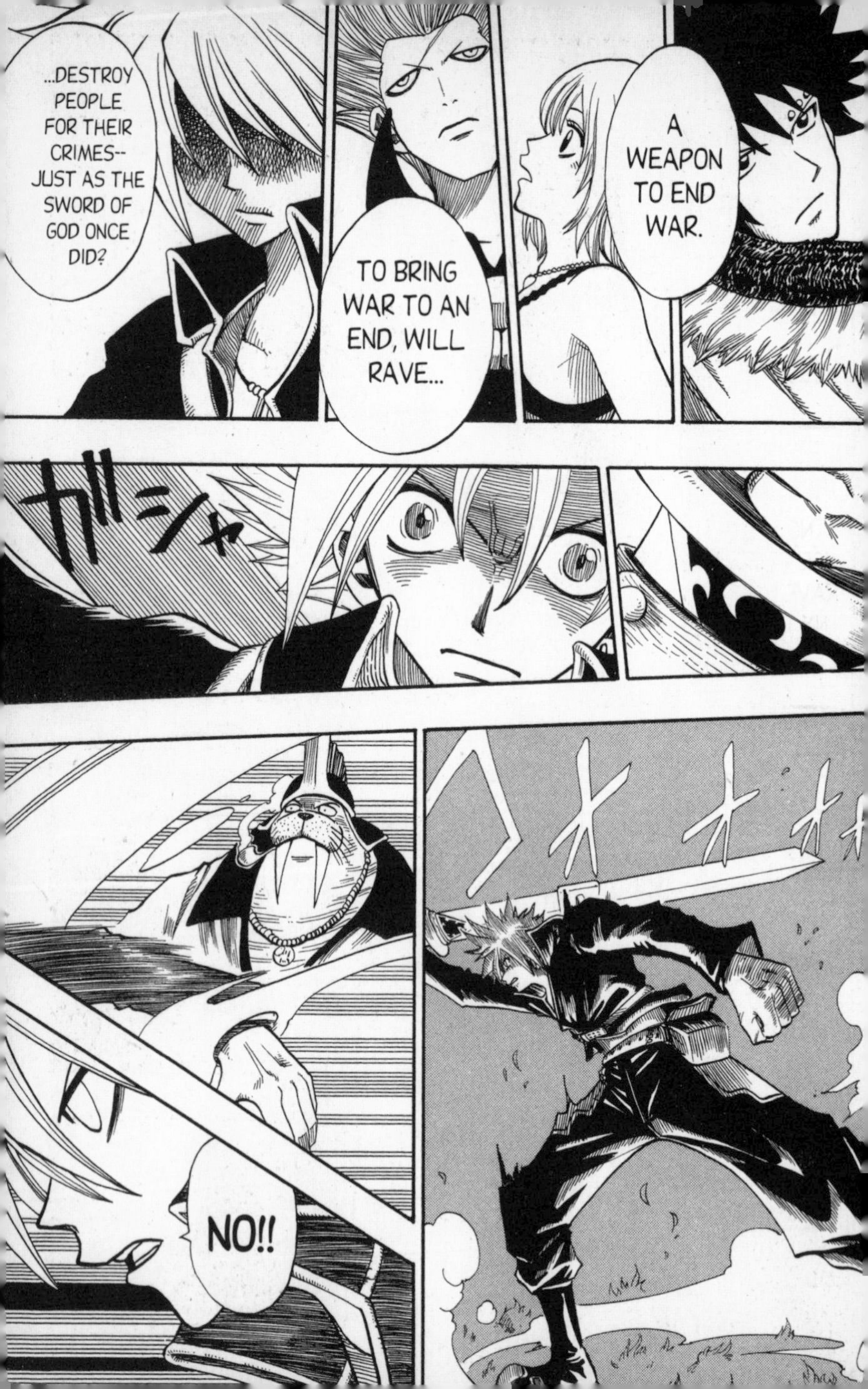
A WEAPON TO END WAR.
TO BRING WAR TO AN END, WILL RAVE...
...DESTROY PEOPLE FOR THEIR CRIMES-- JUST AS THE SWORD OF GOD ONCE DID?
ガシャ
NO!!

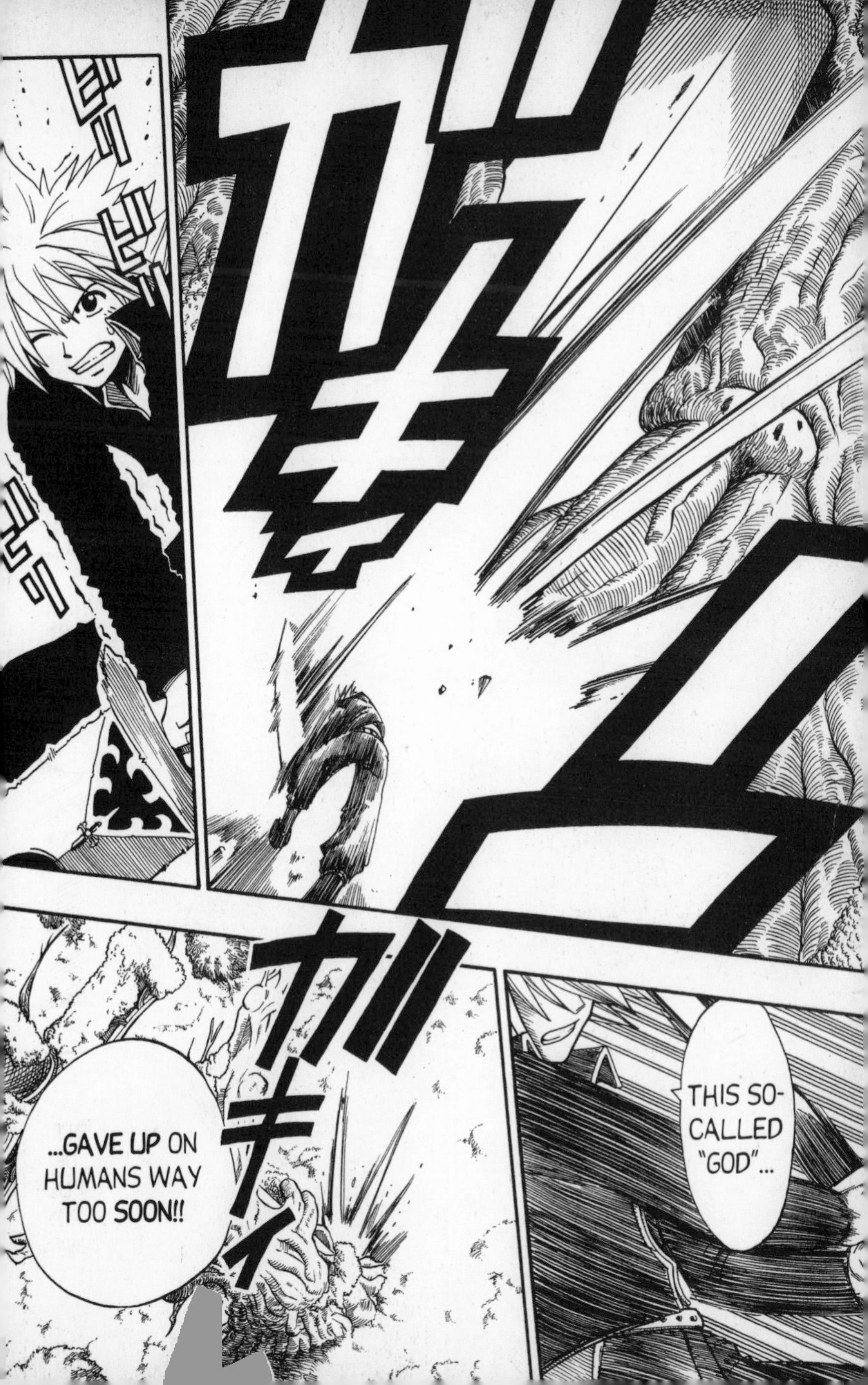
THIS SO-CALLED "GOD"...
...GAVE UP ON HUMANS WAY TOO SOON!!

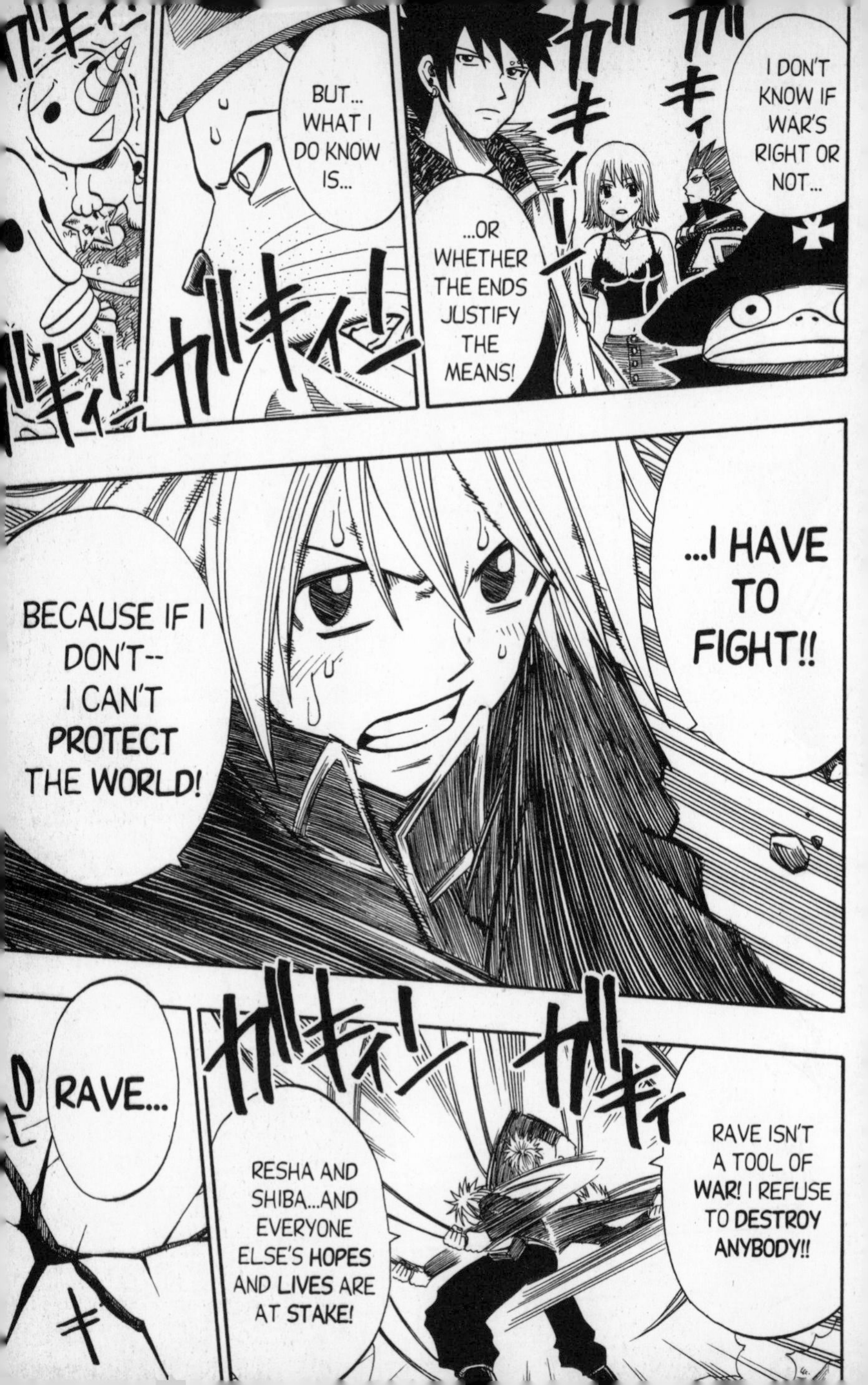
I DON'T KNOW IF WAR'S RIGHT OR NOT...
...OR WHETHER THE ENDS JUSTIFY THE MEANS!
BUT... WHAT I DO KNOW IS...
...I HAVE TO FIGHT!!
BECAUSE IF I DON'T-- I CAN'T PROTECT THE WORLD!
RAVE ISN'T A TOOL OF WAR! I REFUSE TO DESTROY ANYBODY!!
RESHA AND SHIBA...AND EVERYONE ELSE'S HOPES AND LIVES ARE AT STAKE!
ガキィン
ガキィ
RAVE...

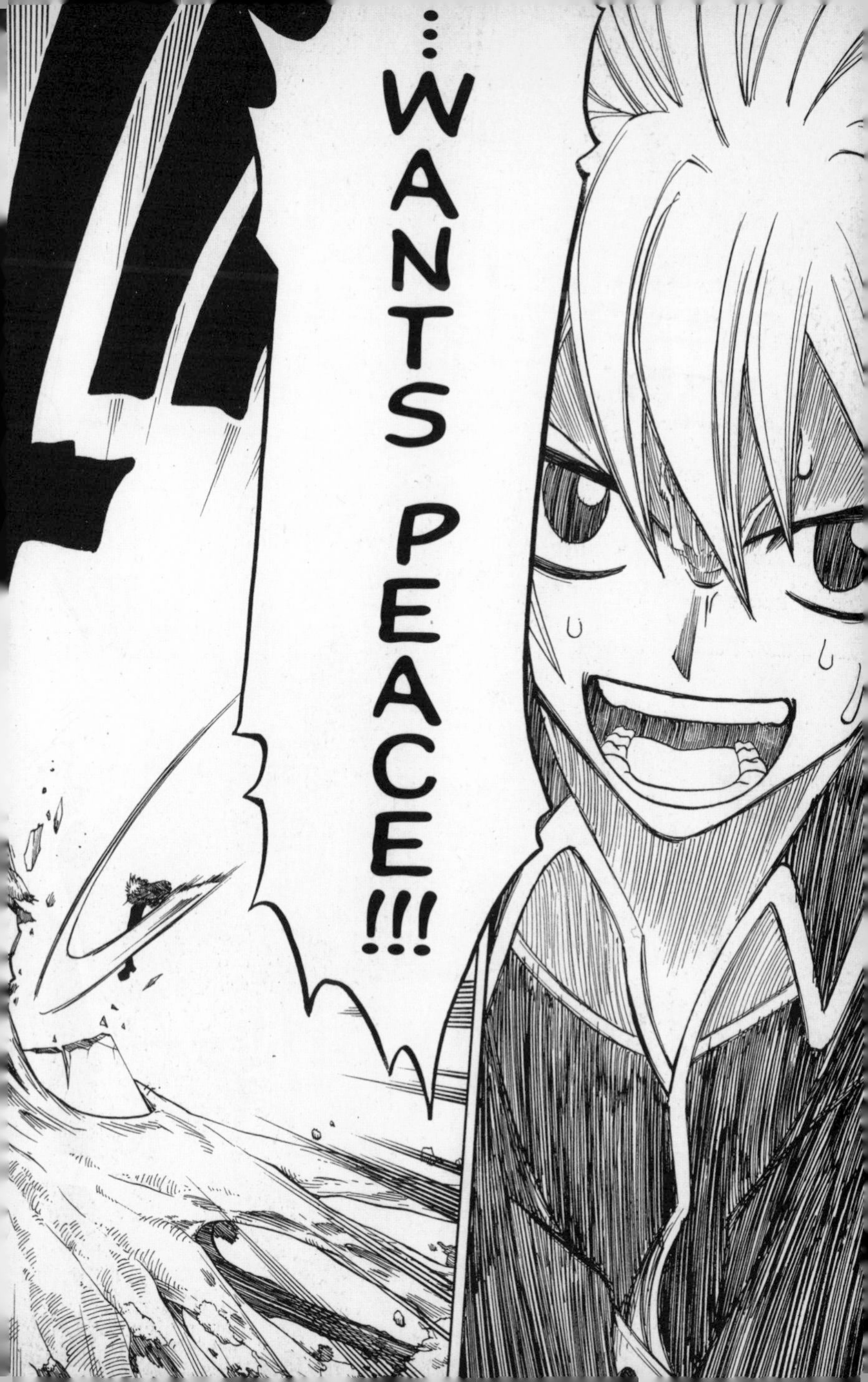
...WANTS PEACE!!!

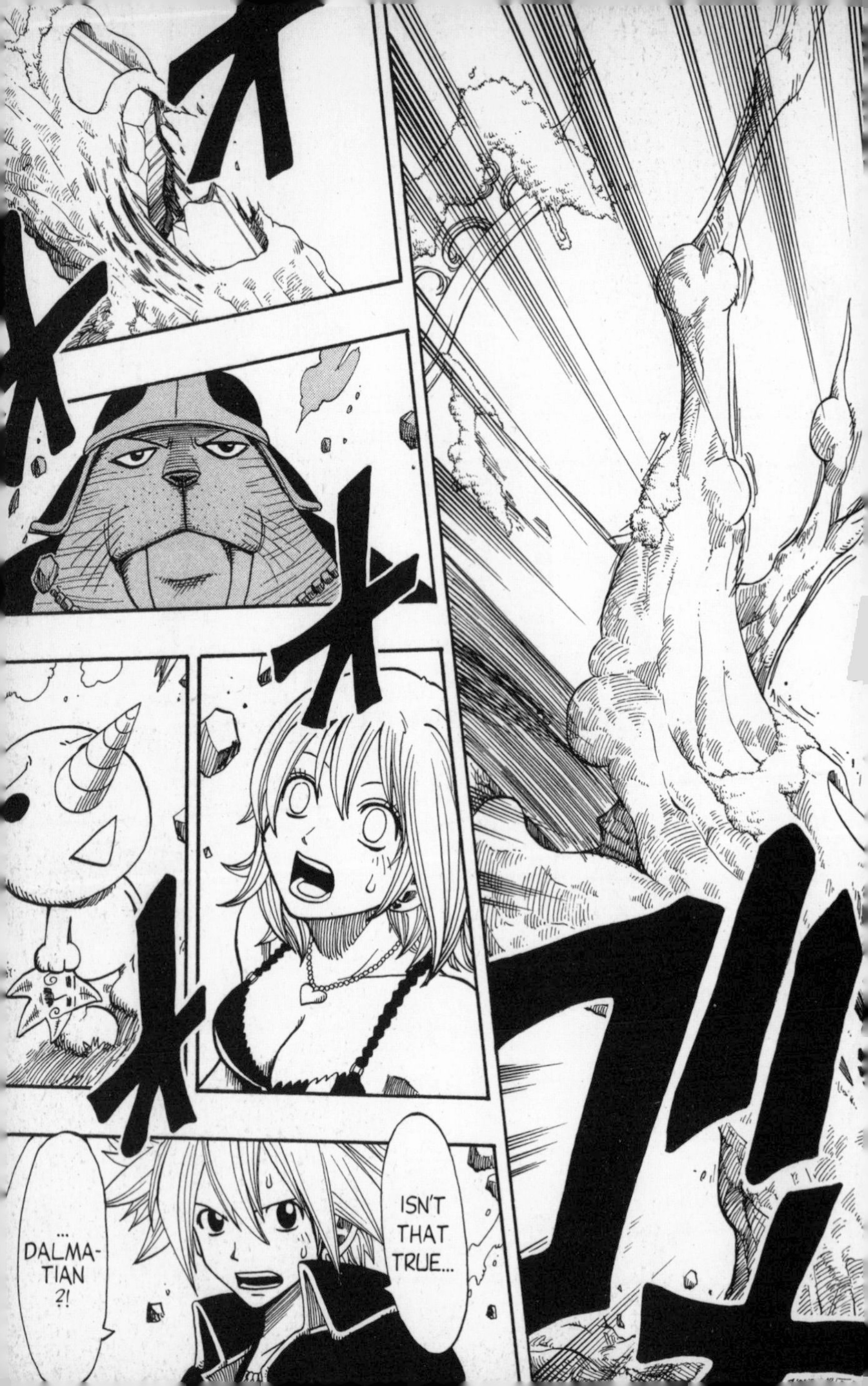
ISN'T THAT TRUE...
... DALMA-TIAN ?!

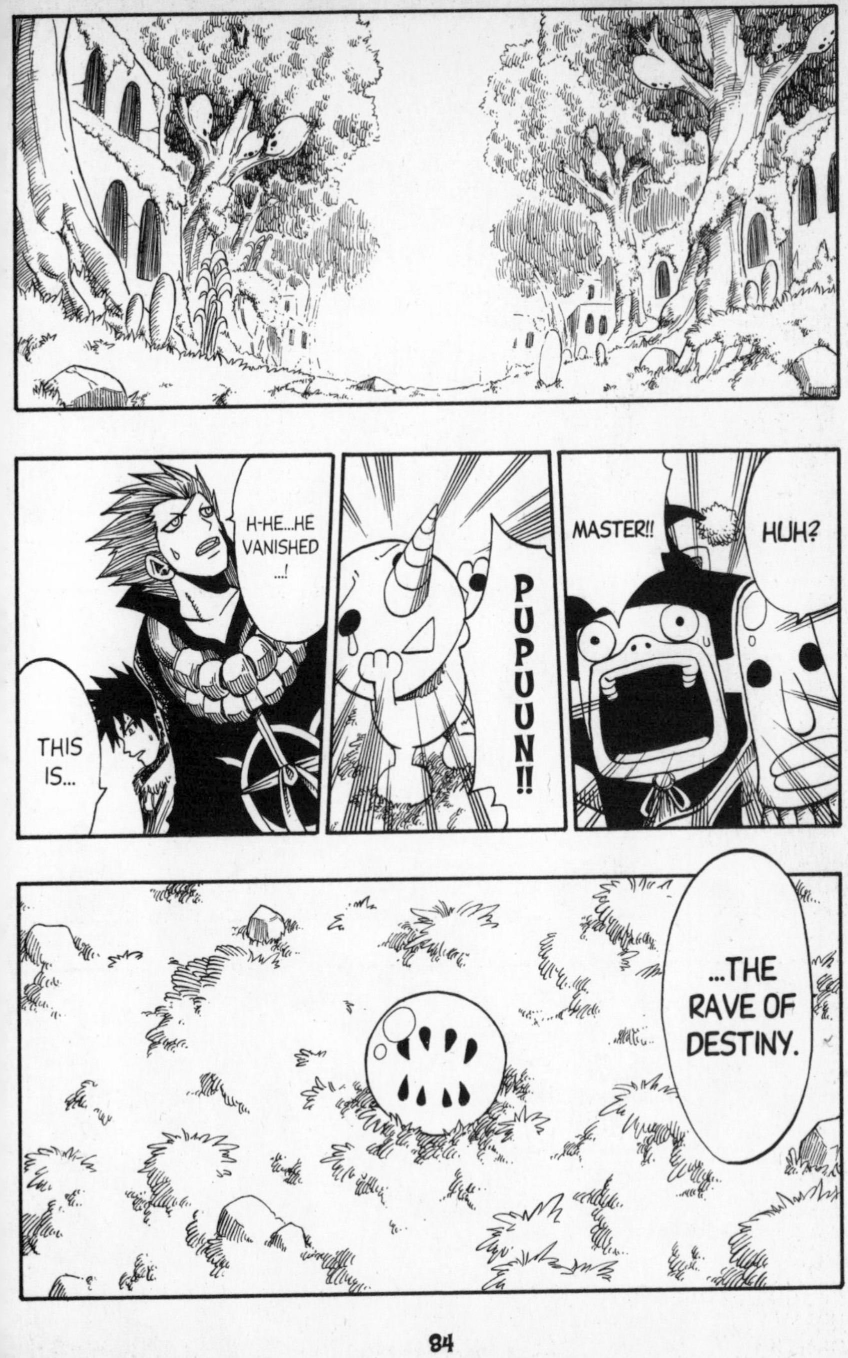
HUH?
MASTER!!
PUPUUN!!
H-HE...HE VANISHED ...!
THIS IS...
...THE RAVE OF DESTINY.

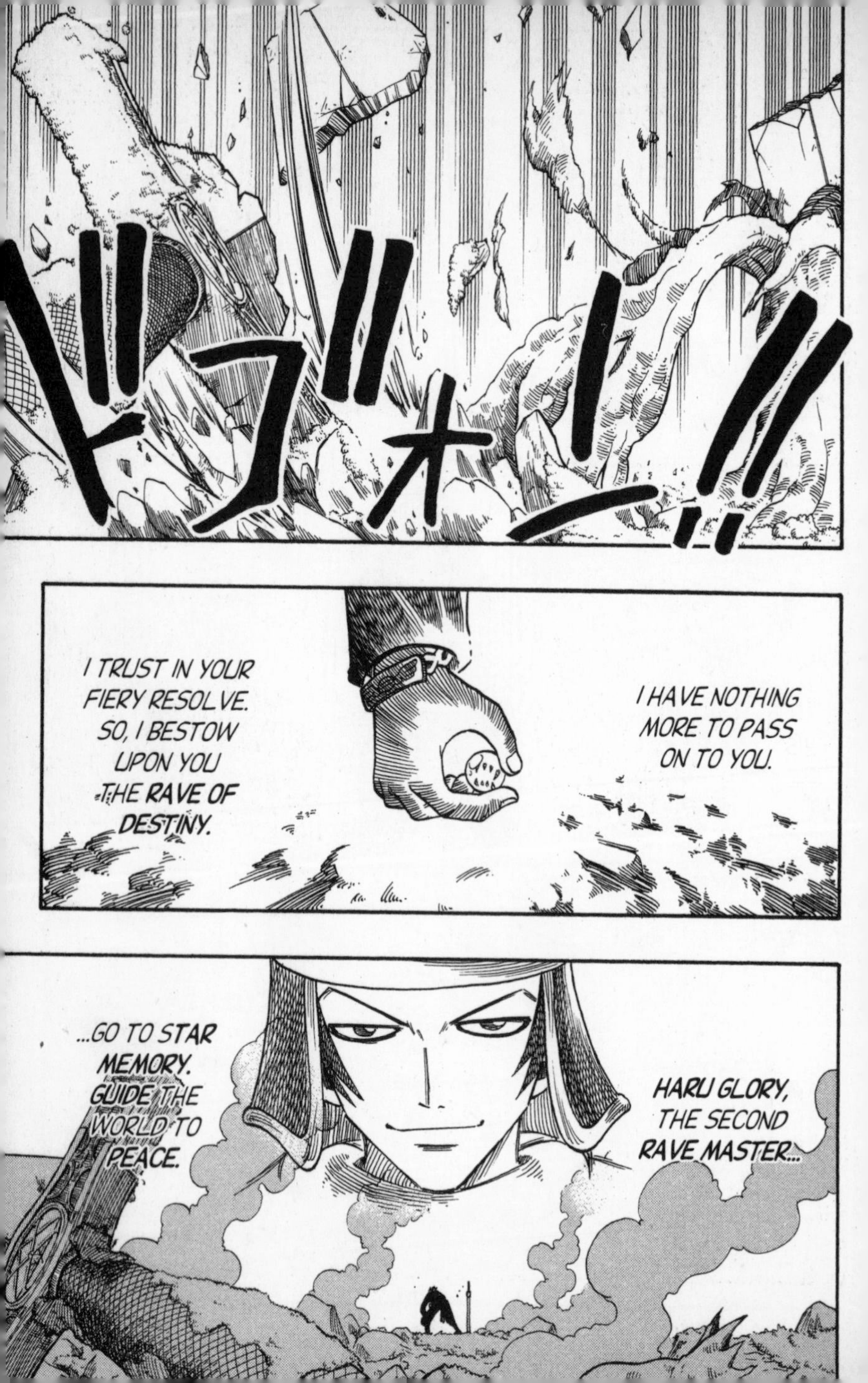
I HAVE NOTHING MORE TO PASS ON TO YOU.
I TRUST IN YOUR FIERY RESOLVE. SO, I BESTOW UPON YOU THE RAVE OF DESTINY.
HARU GLORY, THE SECOND RAVE MASTER...
...GO TO STAR MEMORY. GUIDE THE WORLD TO PEACE.

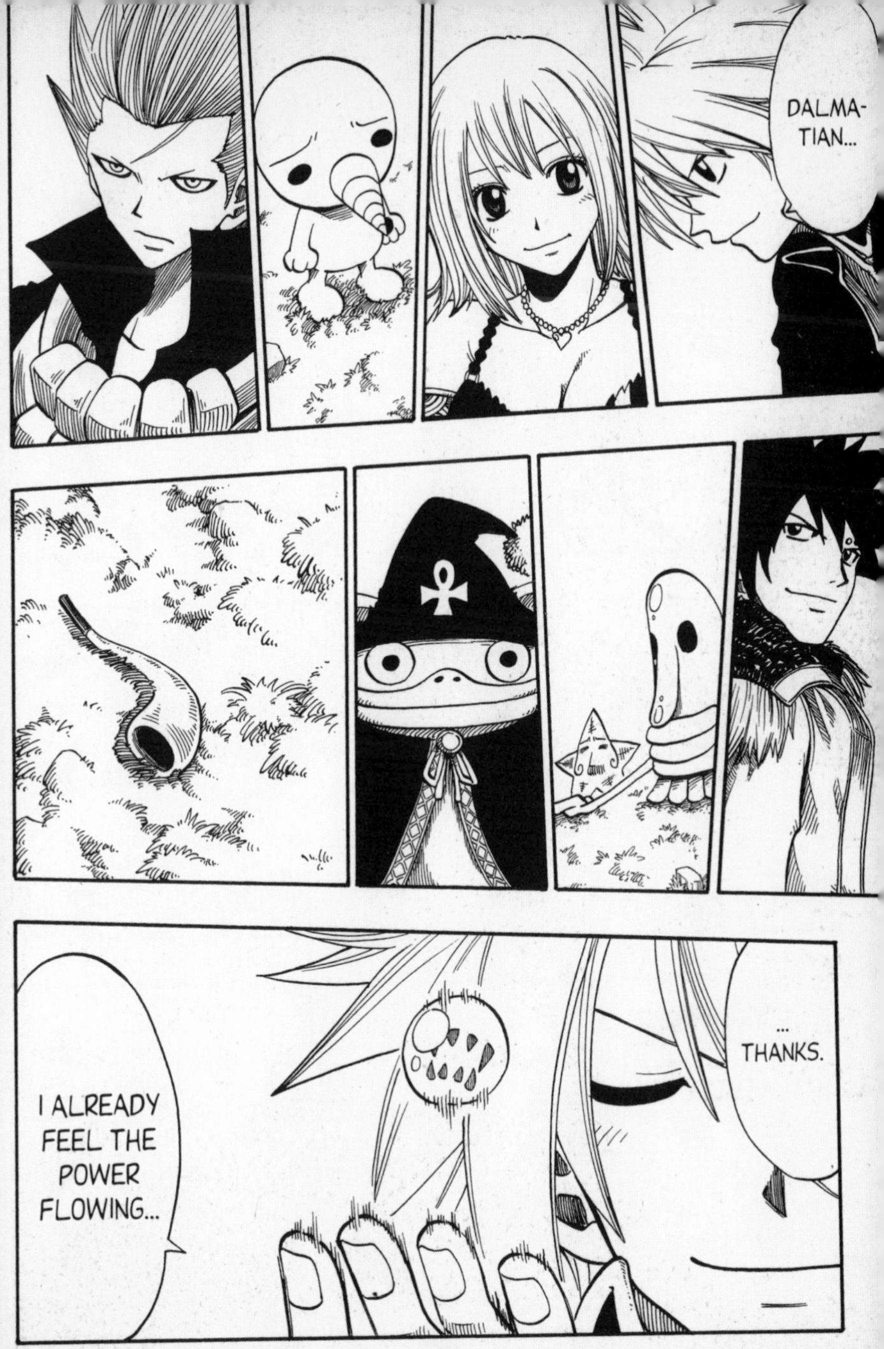
DALMA-
TIAN...
... THANKS.
I ALREADY FEEL THE POWER FLOWING...

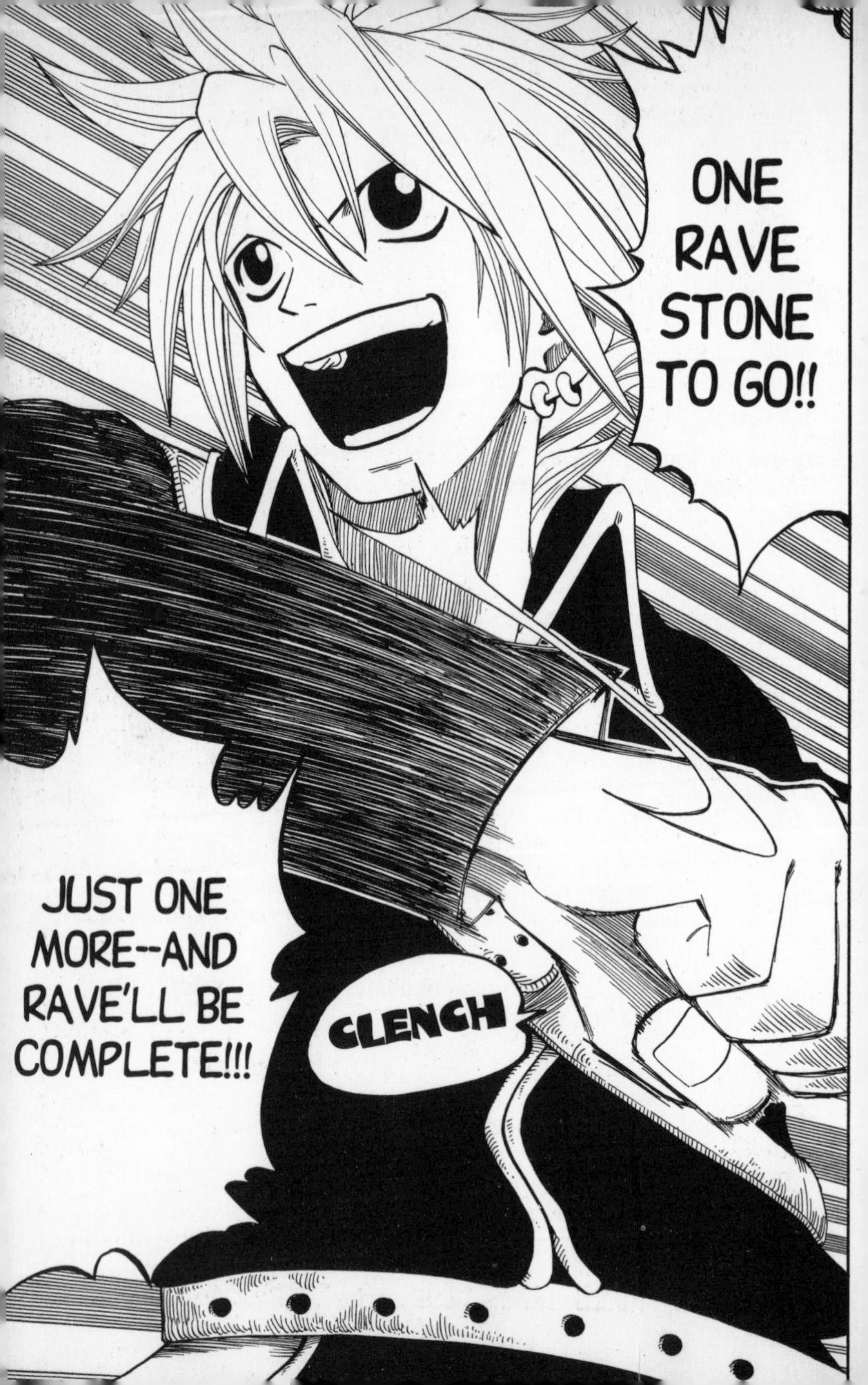
ONE RAVE STONE TO GO!!
JUST ONE MORE--AND RAVE'LL BE COMPLETE!!!
CLENCH

Q&A CORNER!!

Q. What's that mustache thing on the lower right corner of Vol. 9's cover? It looks like an obvious error. (OK - Saitama Prefecture)

A. Ya got me. I was using the laptop I bought to paint with digital colors, but...I messed up. Btw—I did this cover digitally, too...only without messing up.

Q. What does that kanji character on Haja's outfit say? Is it a word? (Hineto - Tokyo City)

A. It means "infinity." I used it as a word here, but it's a math concept. It means 10 to the 52nd power—meaning, going from 1 to 10, 100, 1000, 10,000, etc. up to 52 times. Beyond that, we'd just use an infinity symbol, right? Got it? (Or so a math teacher once told me.)

Q. How the heck do you get 100 points in "Plue's Adventure Diary" in Vol. 16? Please tell me! (Human - Yamaguchi Prefecture)

A. Okay! Big hint! It involves warping to somewhere! Pay attention to what the *sign* is telling you!!

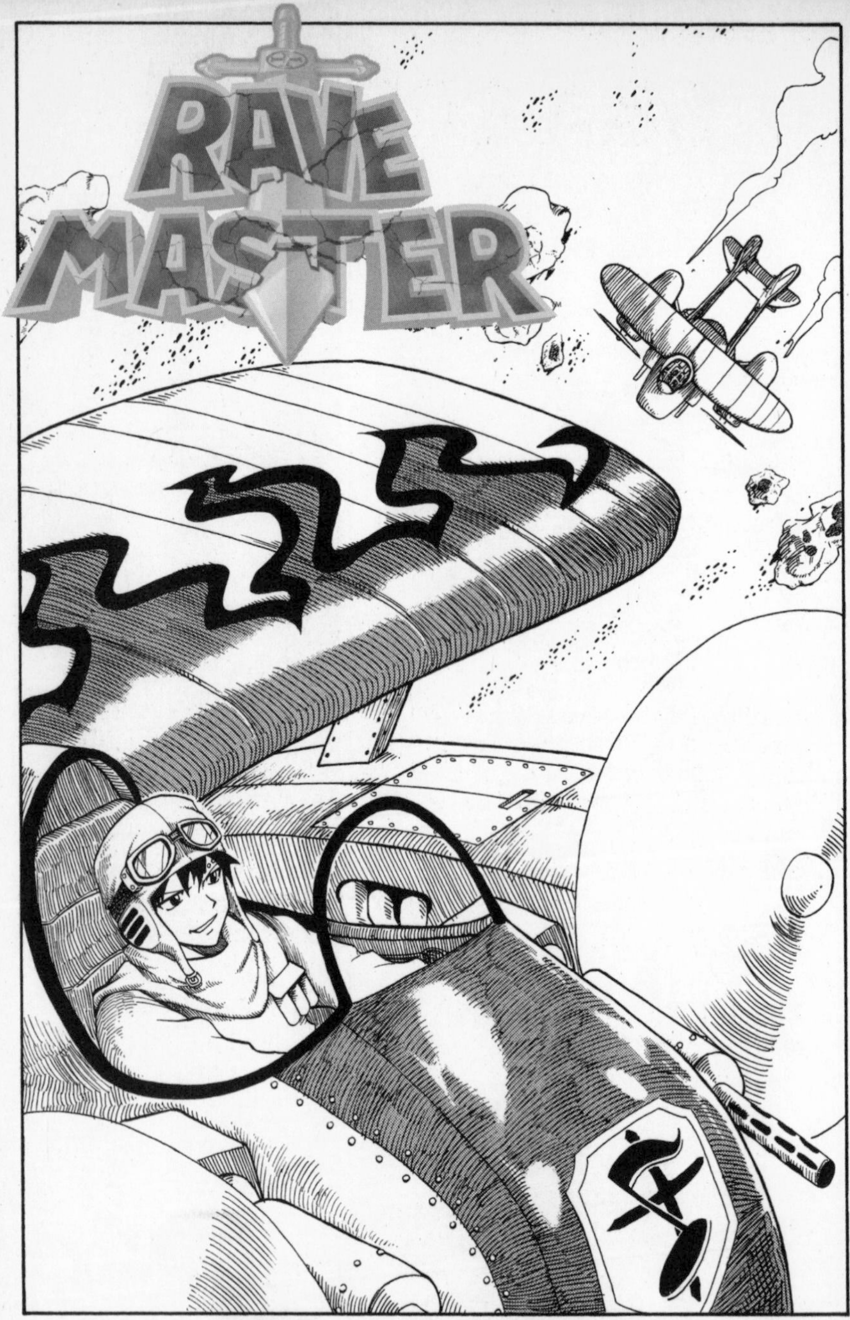
RAVE MASTER

RAVE:142 PROJECT DR

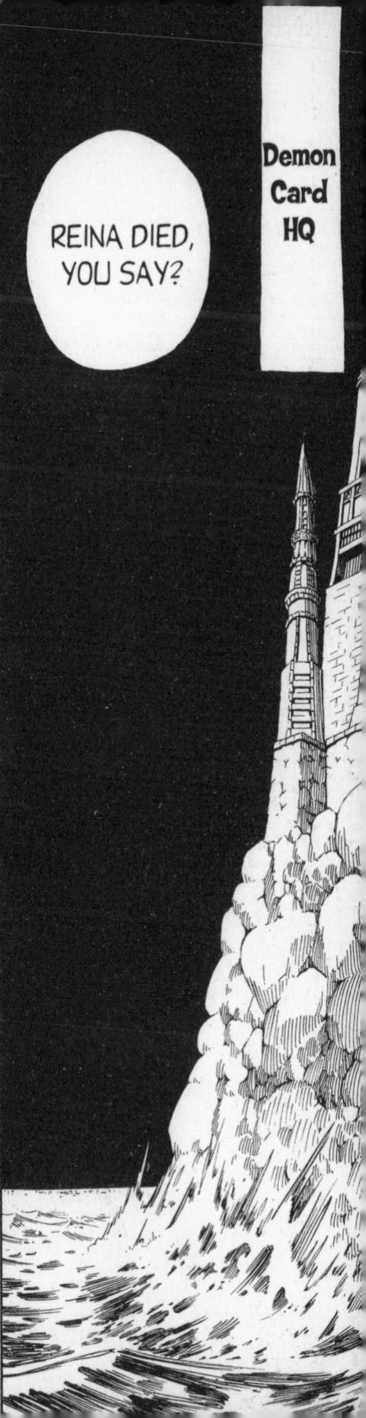
Demon Card HQ
REINA DIED, YOU SAY?

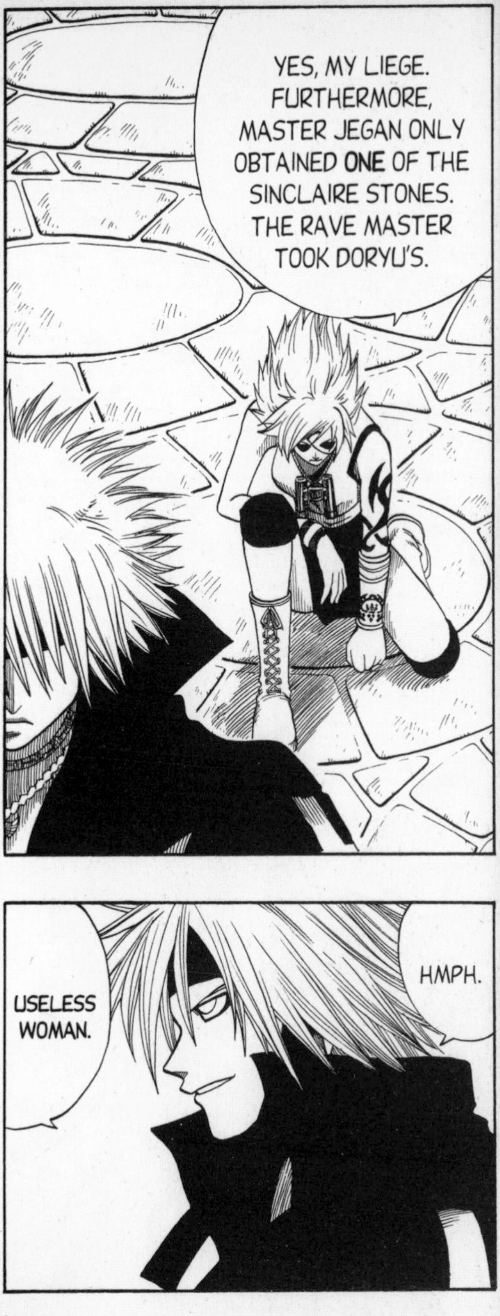
YES, MY LIEGE. FURTHERMORE, MASTER JEGAN ONLY OBTAINED **ONE** OF THE SINCLAIRE STONES. THE RAVE MASTER TOOK DORYU'S.
HMPH.
USELESS WOMAN.

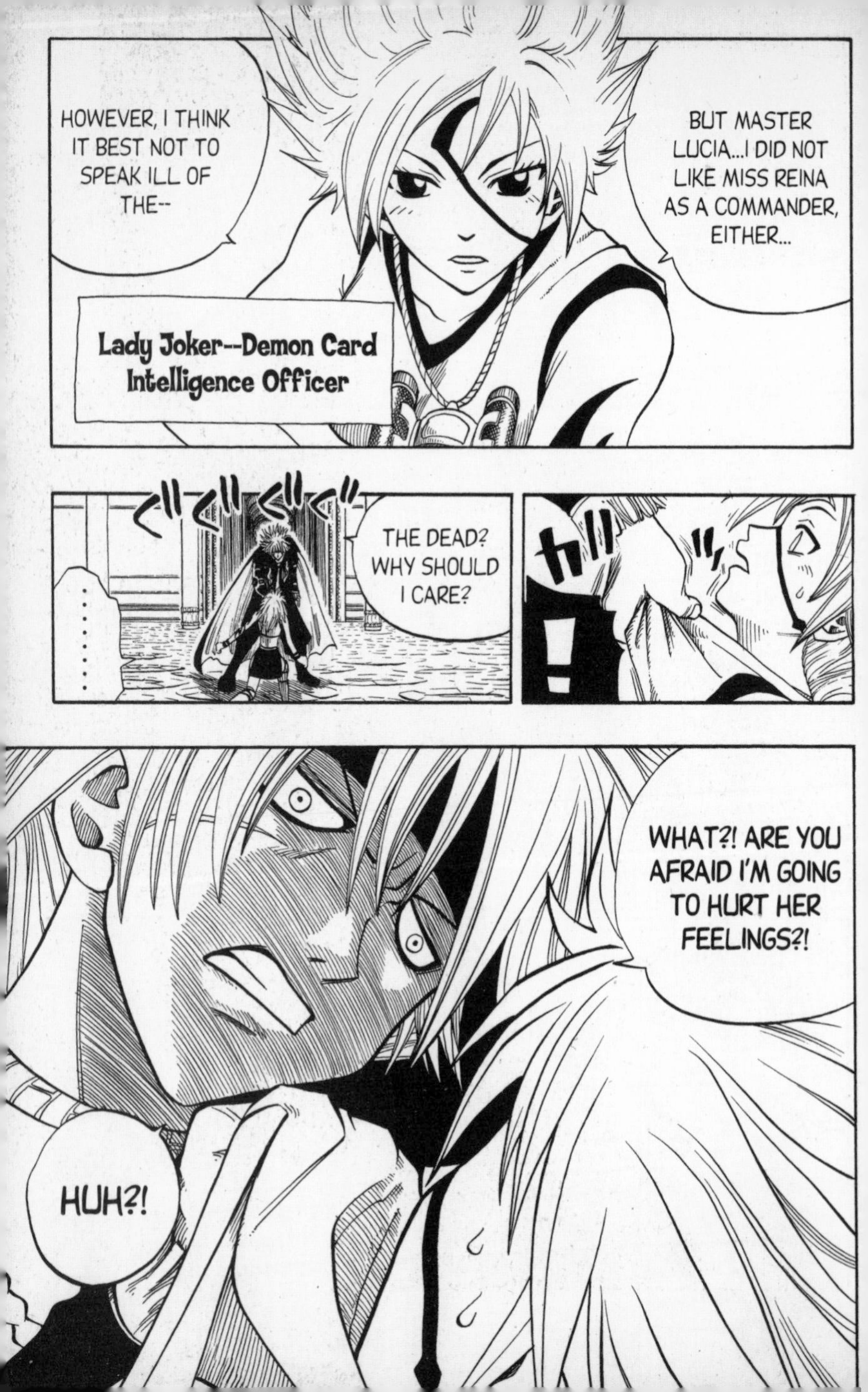
BUT MASTER LUCIA...I DID NOT LIKE MISS REINA AS A COMMANDER, EITHER...
HOWEVER, I THINK IT BEST NOT TO SPEAK ILL OF THE--
Lady Joker--Demon Card Intelligence Officer
!
THE DEAD? WHY SHOULD I CARE?
......
WHAT?! ARE YOU AFRAID I'M GOING TO HURT HER FEELINGS?!
HUH?!

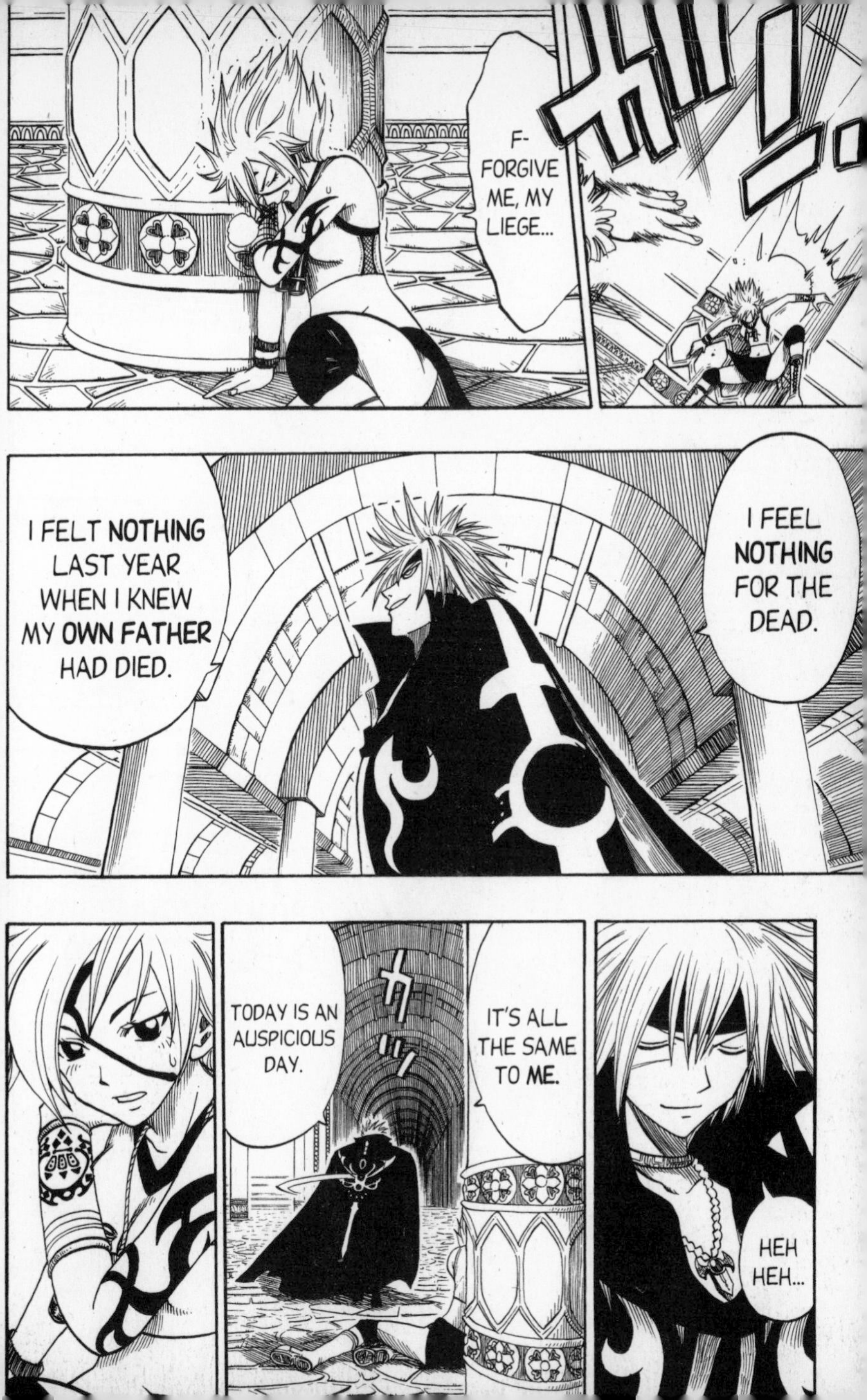
F- FORGIVE ME, MY LIEGE...
I FEEL NOTHING FOR THE DEAD.
I FELT NOTHING LAST YEAR WHEN I KNEW MY OWN FATHER HAD DIED.
HEH HEH...
IT'S ALL THE SAME TO ME.
TODAY IS AN AUSPICIOUS DAY.

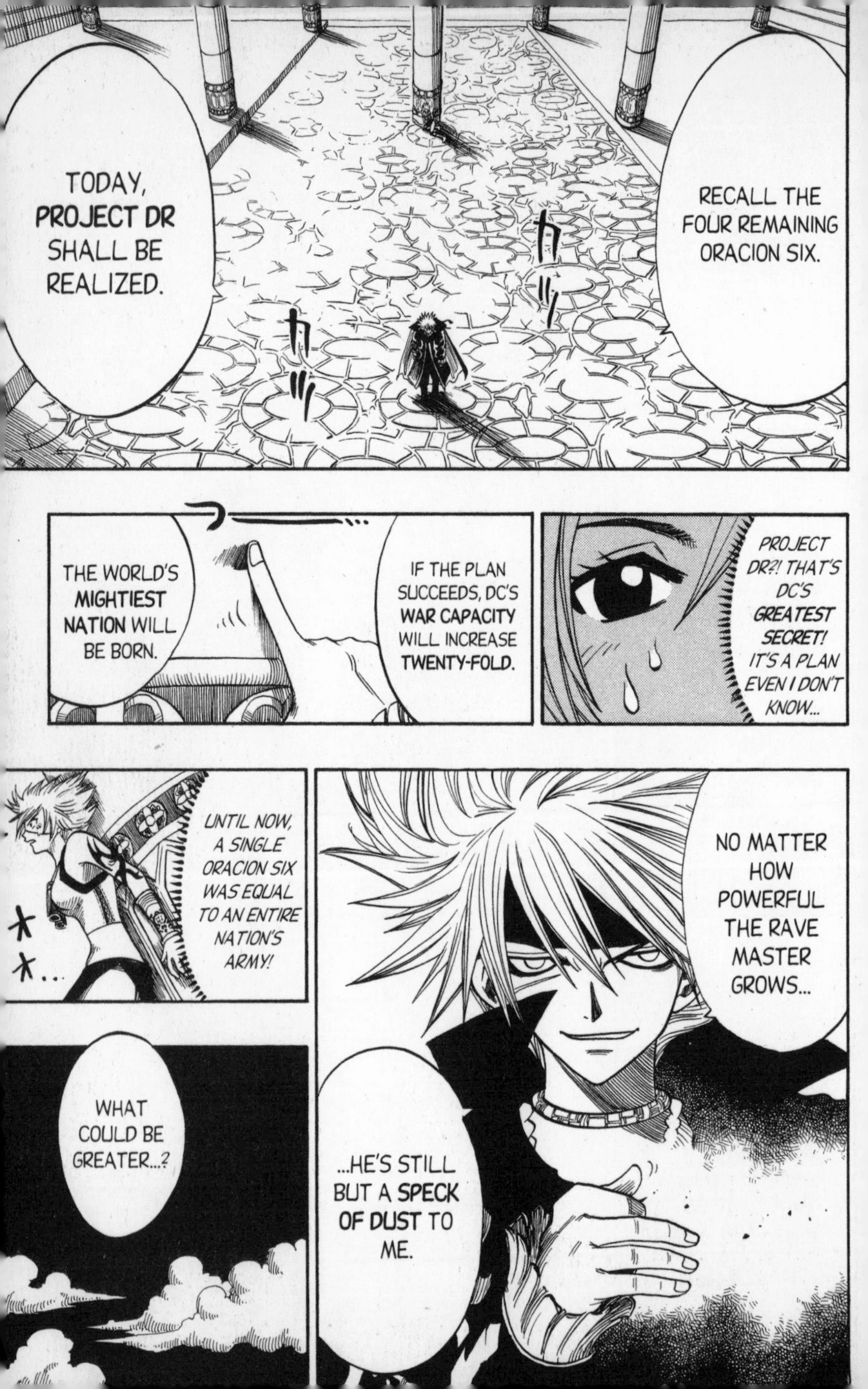
RECALL THE FOUR REMAINING ORACION SIX.
カッ
カッ
TODAY, PROJECT DR SHALL BE REALIZED.
PROJECT DR?! THAT'S DC'S GREATEST SECRET! IT'S A PLAN EVEN I DON'T KNOW...
IF THE PLAN SUCCEEDS, DC'S WAR CAPACITY WILL INCREASE TWENTY-FOLD.
THE WORLD'S MIGHTIEST NATION WILL BE BORN.
NO MATTER HOW POWERFUL THE RAVE MASTER GROWS...
...HE'S STILL BUT A SPECK OF DUST TO ME.
UNTIL NOW, A SINGLE ORACION SIX WAS EQUAL TO AN ENTIRE NATION'S ARMY!
WHAT COULD BE GREATER...?

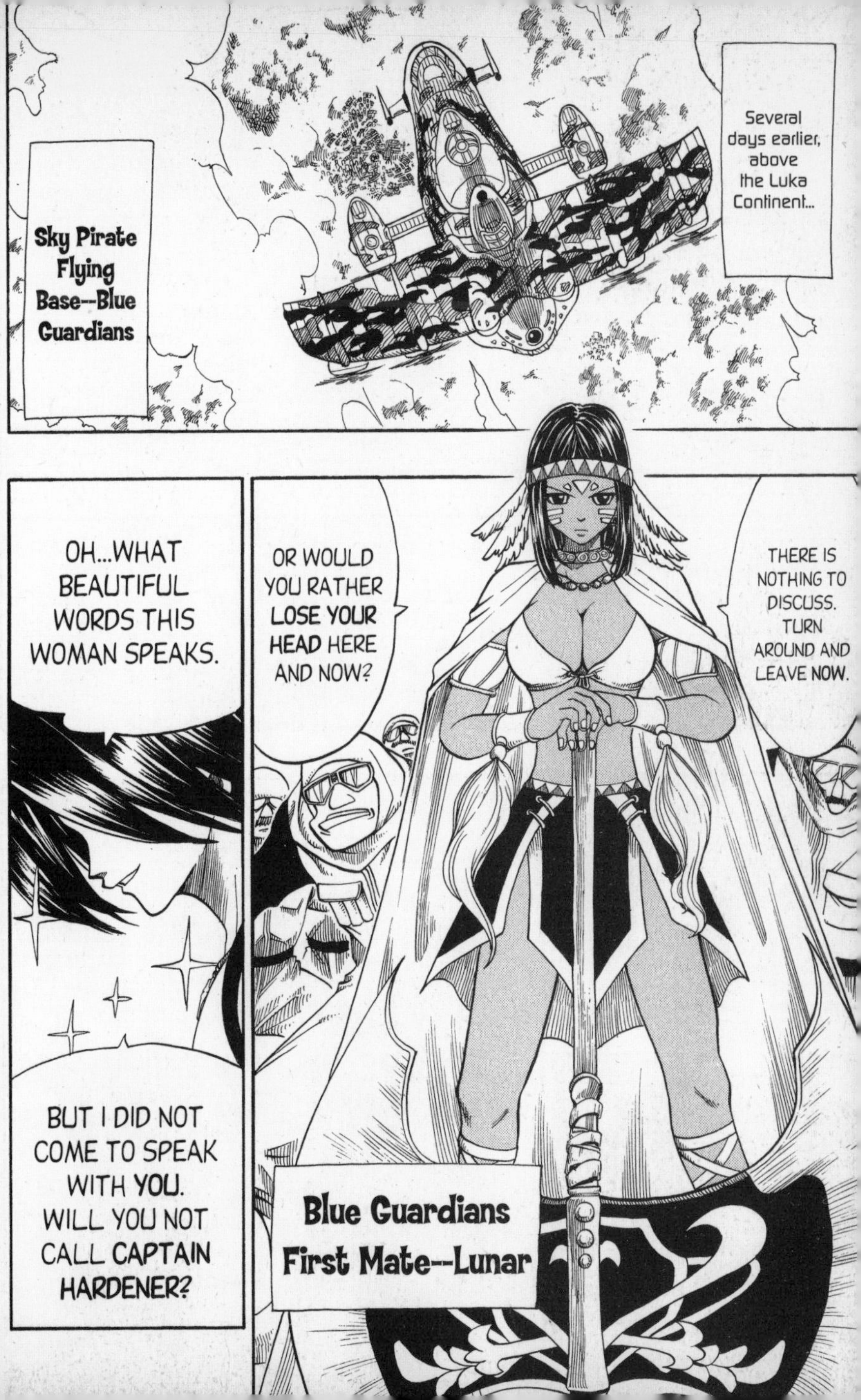
Several days earlier, above the Luka Continent...
Sky Pirate Flying Base--Blue Guardians
THERE IS NOTHING TO DISCUSS. TURN AROUND AND LEAVE NOW.
OR WOULD YOU RATHER LOSE YOUR HEAD HERE AND NOW?
Blue Guardians First Mate--Lunar
OH...WHAT BEAUTIFUL WORDS THIS WOMAN SPEAKS.
BUT I DID NOT COME TO SPEAK WITH YOU. WILL YOU NOT CALL CAPTAIN HARDENER?

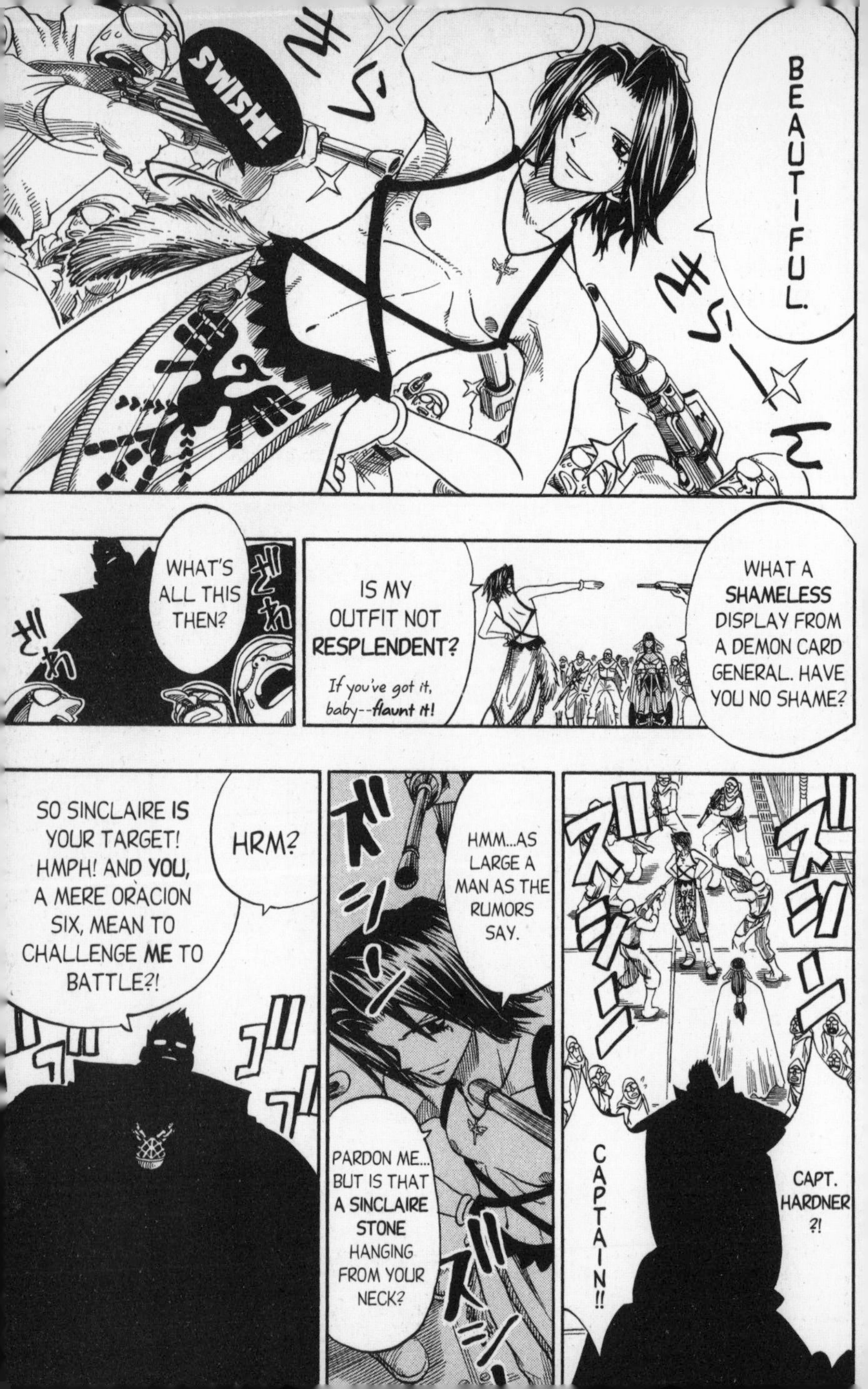
BEAUTIFUL.
SWISH!
WHAT A **SHAMELESS** DISPLAY FROM A DEMON CARD GENERAL. HAVE YOU NO SHAME?
IS MY OUTFIT NOT **RESPLENDENT?**
*If you've got it, baby--**flaunt it!***
WHAT'S ALL THIS THEN?
CAPT. HARDNER?!
CAPTAIN!!
HMM...AS LARGE A MAN AS THE RUMORS SAY.
PARDON ME... BUT IS THAT **A SINCLAIRE STONE** HANGING FROM YOUR NECK?
HRM?
SO SINCLAIRE **IS** YOUR TARGET! HMPH! AND **YOU**, A MERE ORACION SIX, MEAN TO CHALLENGE **ME** TO BATTLE?!

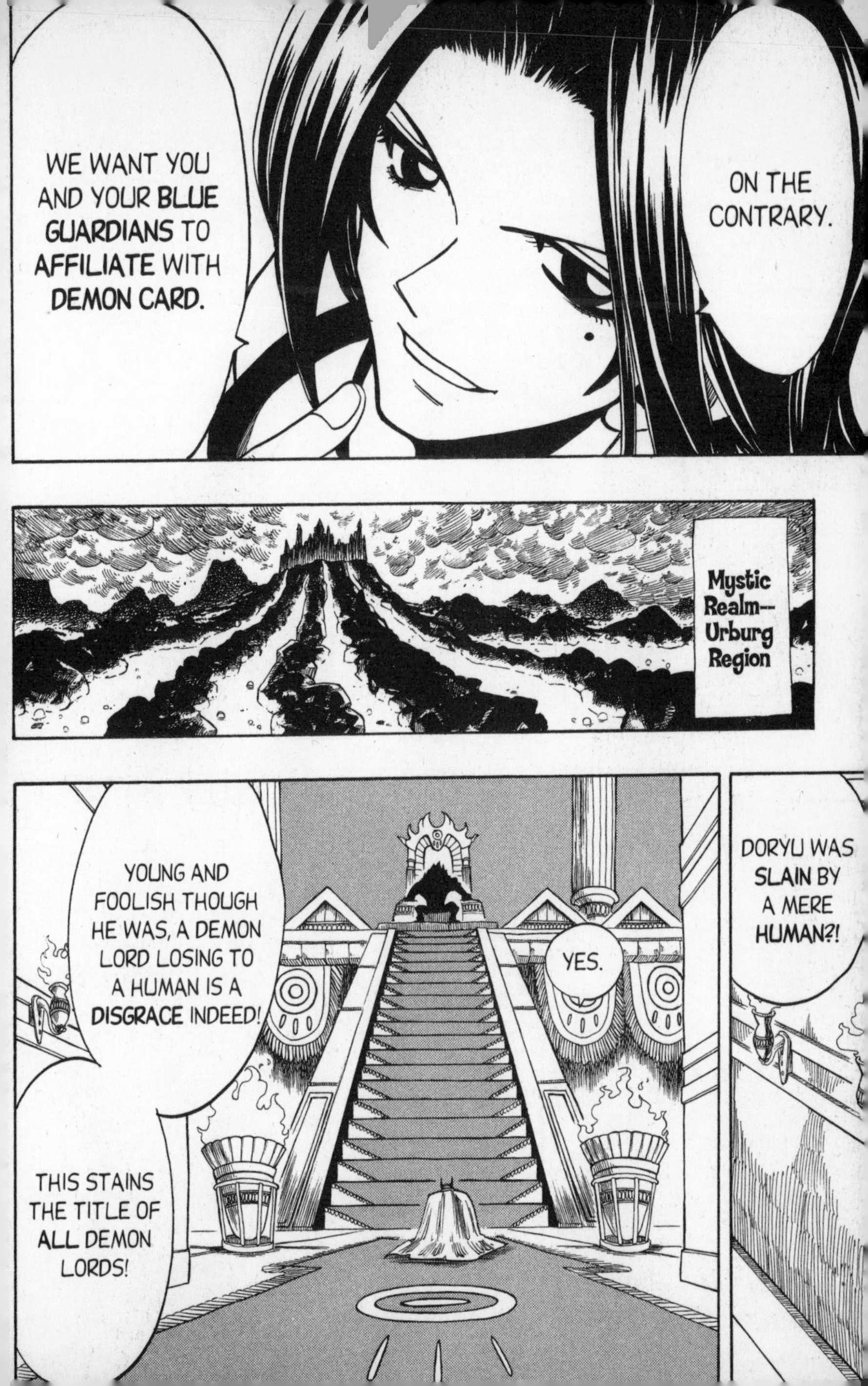
ON THE CONTRARY.
WE WANT YOU AND YOUR BLUE GUARDIANS TO AFFILIATE WITH DEMON CARD.
Mystic Realm-- Urburg Region
DORYU WAS SLAIN BY A MERE HUMAN?!
YES.
YOUNG AND FOOLISH THOUGH HE WAS, A DEMON LORD LOSING TO A HUMAN IS A DISGRACE INDEED!
THIS STAINS THE TITLE OF ALL DEMON LORDS!

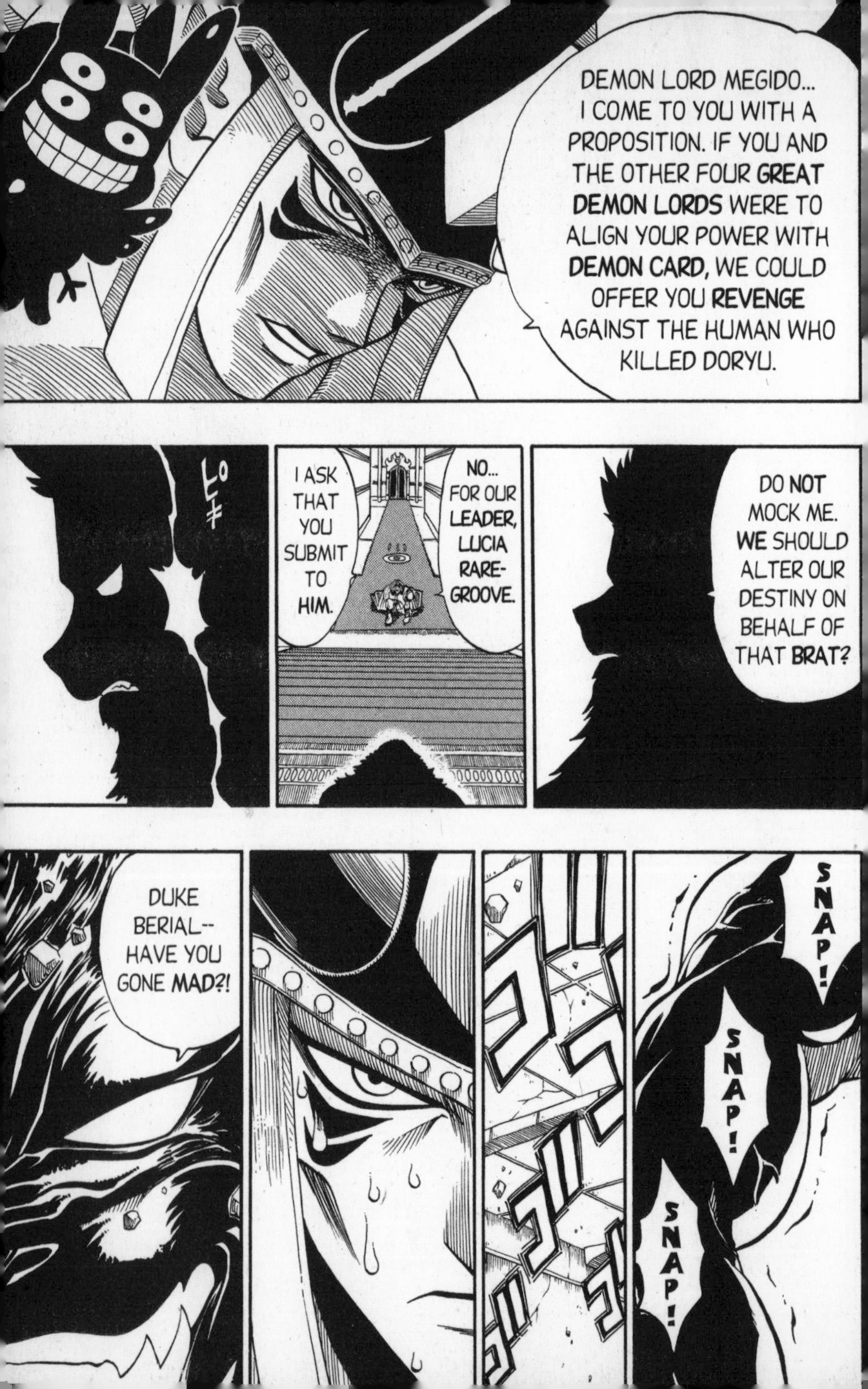
DEMON LORD MEGIDO... I COME TO YOU WITH A PROPOSITION. IF YOU AND THE OTHER FOUR GREAT DEMON LORDS WERE TO ALIGN YOUR POWER WITH DEMON CARD, WE COULD OFFER YOU REVENGE AGAINST THE HUMAN WHO KILLED DORYU.
DO NOT MOCK ME. WE SHOULD ALTER OUR DESTINY ON BEHALF OF THAT BRAT?
NO... FOR OUR LEADER, LUCIA RARE-GROOVE.
I ASK THAT YOU SUBMIT TO HIM.
ピキ
SNAP!
SNAP!
SNAP!
DUKE BERIAL-- HAVE YOU GONE MAD?!

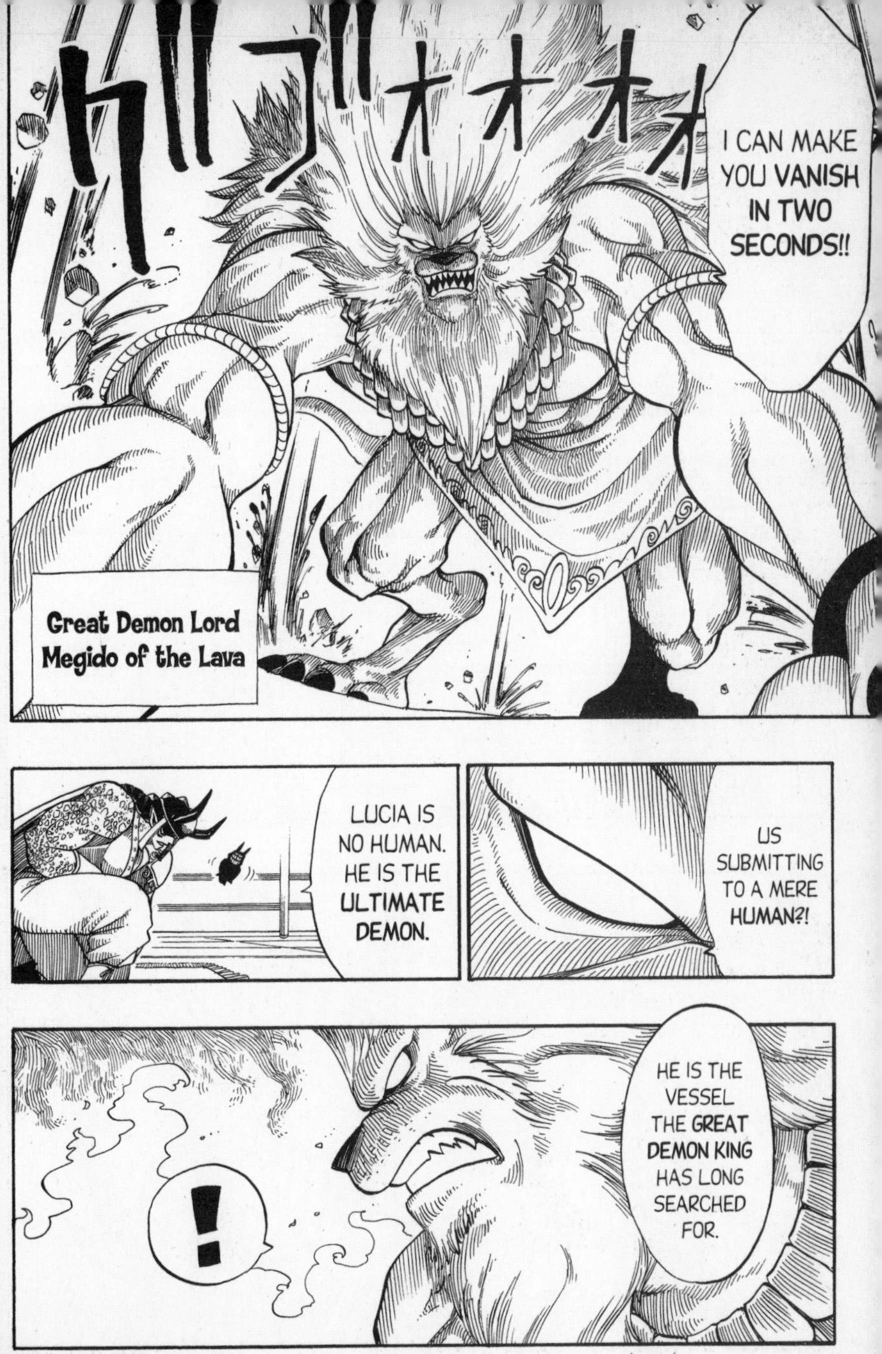
I CAN MAKE YOU VANISH IN TWO SECONDS!!
グゴオオオオ
Great Demon Lord Megido of the Lava
US SUBMITTING TO A MERE HUMAN?!
LUCIA IS NO HUMAN. HE IS THE ULTIMATE DEMON.
HE IS THE VESSEL THE GREAT DEMON KING HAS LONG SEARCHED FOR.
!

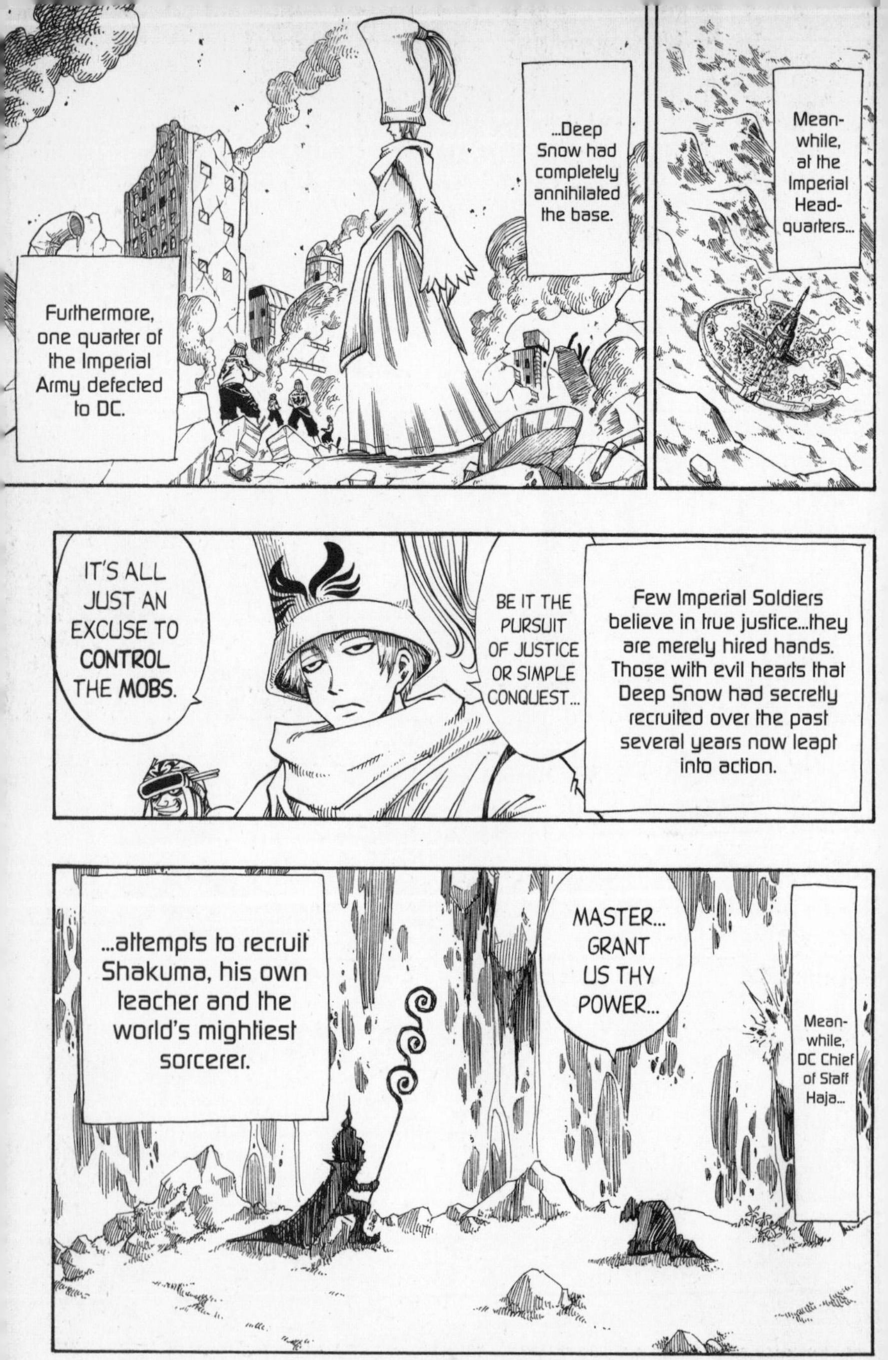

Meanwhile, at the Imperial Headquarters...
...Deep Snow had completely annihilated the base.
Furthermore, one quarter of the Imperial Army defected to DC.
Few Imperial Soldiers believe in true justice...they are merely hired hands. Those with evil hearts that Deep Snow had secretly recruited over the past several years now leapt into action.
BE IT THE PURSUIT OF JUSTICE OR SIMPLE CONQUEST...
IT'S ALL JUST AN EXCUSE TO CONTROL THE MOBS.
Meanwhile, DC Chief of Staff Haja...
MASTER... GRANT US THY POWER...
...attempts to recruit Shakuma, his own teacher and the world's mightiest sorcerer.

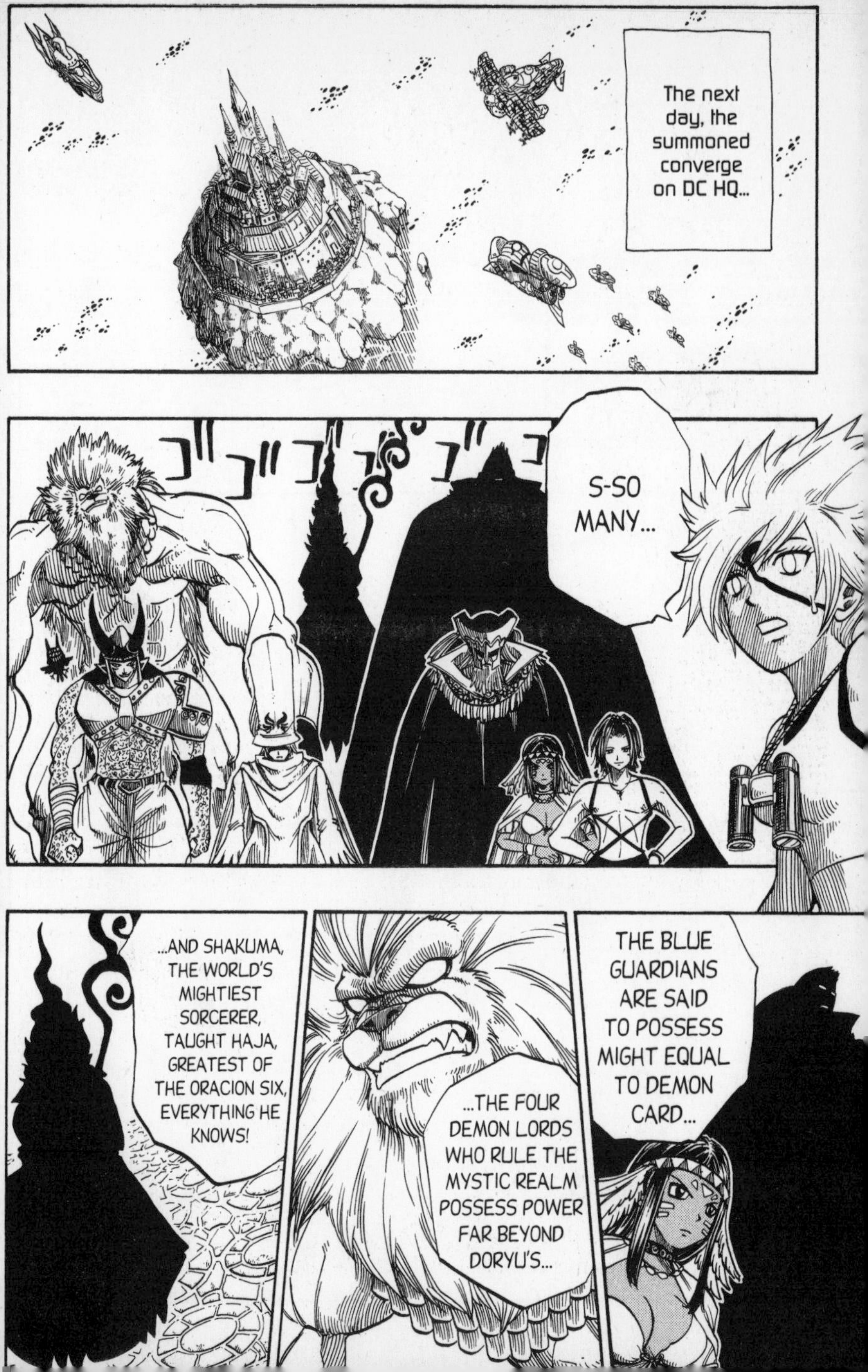

The next day, the summoned converge on DC HQ...
S-SO MANY...
THE BLUE GUARDIANS ARE SAID TO POSSESS MIGHT EQUAL TO DEMON CARD...
...THE FOUR DEMON LORDS WHO RULE THE MYSTIC REALM POSSESS POWER FAR BEYOND DORYU'S...
...AND SHAKUMA, THE WORLD'S MIGHTIEST SORCERER, TAUGHT HAJA, GREATEST OF THE ORACION SIX, EVERYTHING HE KNOWS!

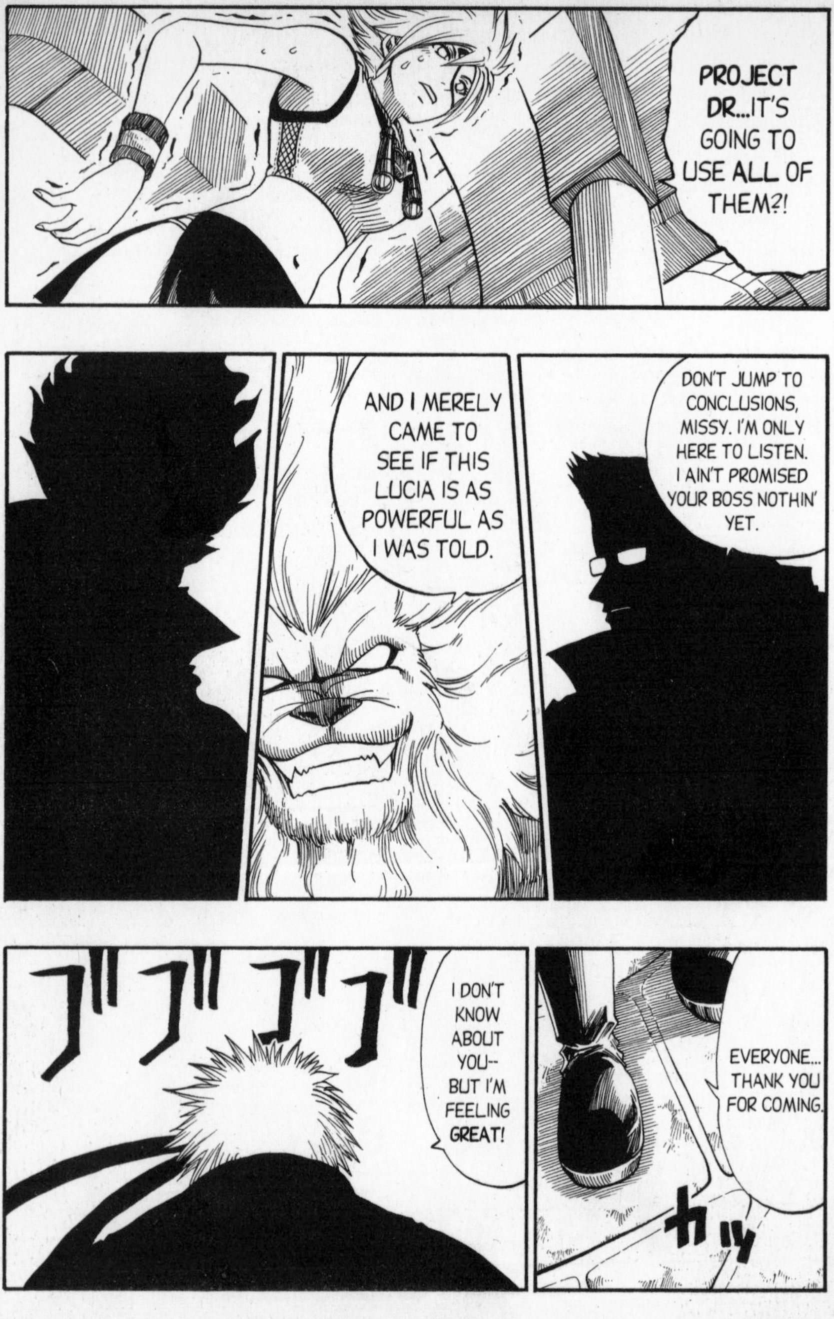
PROJECT DR...IT'S GOING TO USE ALL OF THEM?!
DON'T JUMP TO CONCLUSIONS, MISSY. I'M ONLY HERE TO LISTEN. I AIN'T PROMISED YOUR BOSS NOTHIN' YET.
AND I MERELY CAME TO SEE IF THIS LUCIA IS AS POWERFUL AS I WAS TOLD.
EVERYONE... THANK YOU FOR COMING.
カッ
ゴゴゴゴ
I DON'T KNOW ABOUT YOU-- BUT I'M FEELING GREAT!

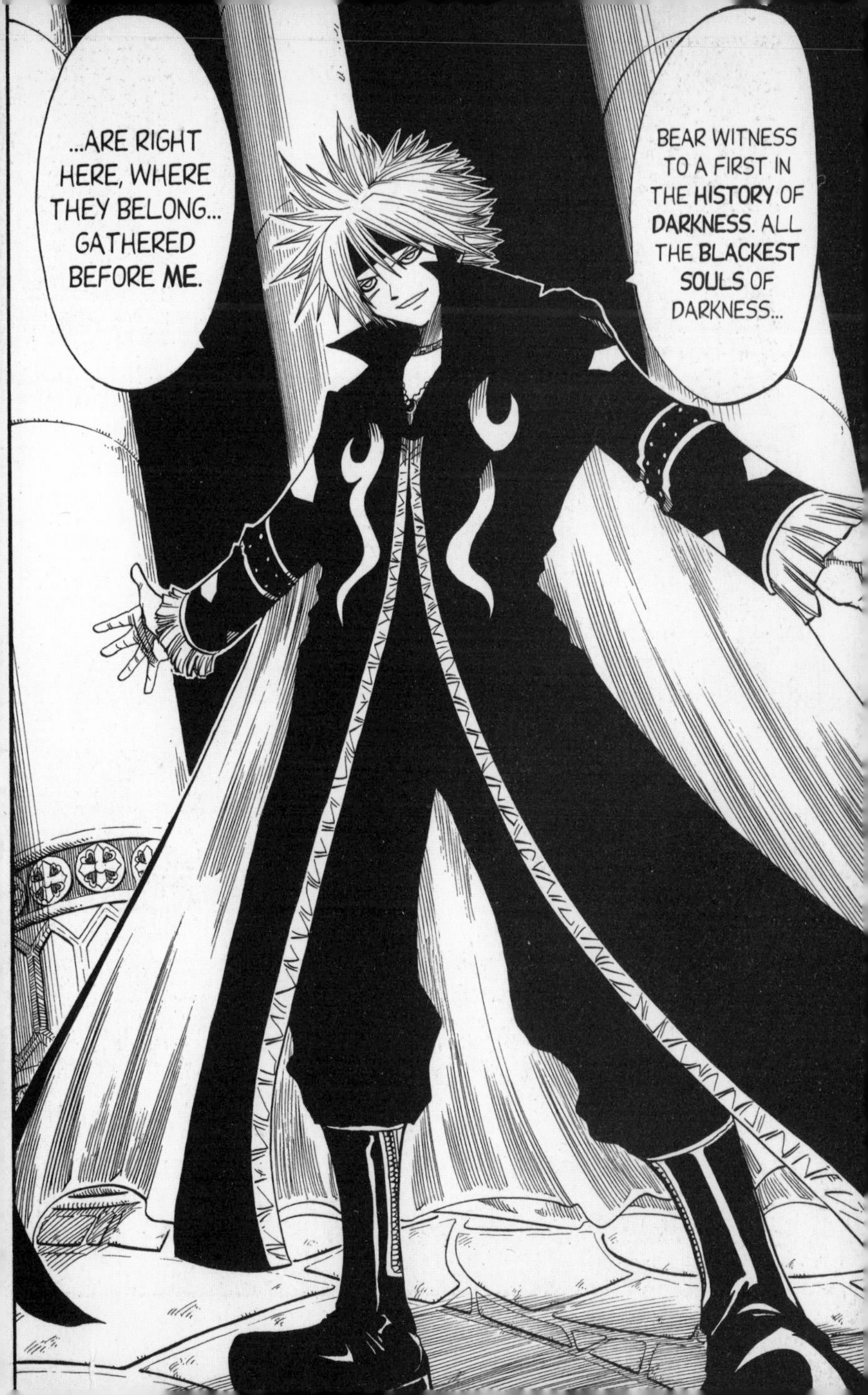
BEAR WITNESS TO A FIRST IN THE HISTORY OF DARKNESS. ALL THE BLACKEST SOULS OF DARKNESS...
...ARE RIGHT HERE, WHERE THEY BELONG... GATHERED BEFORE ME.

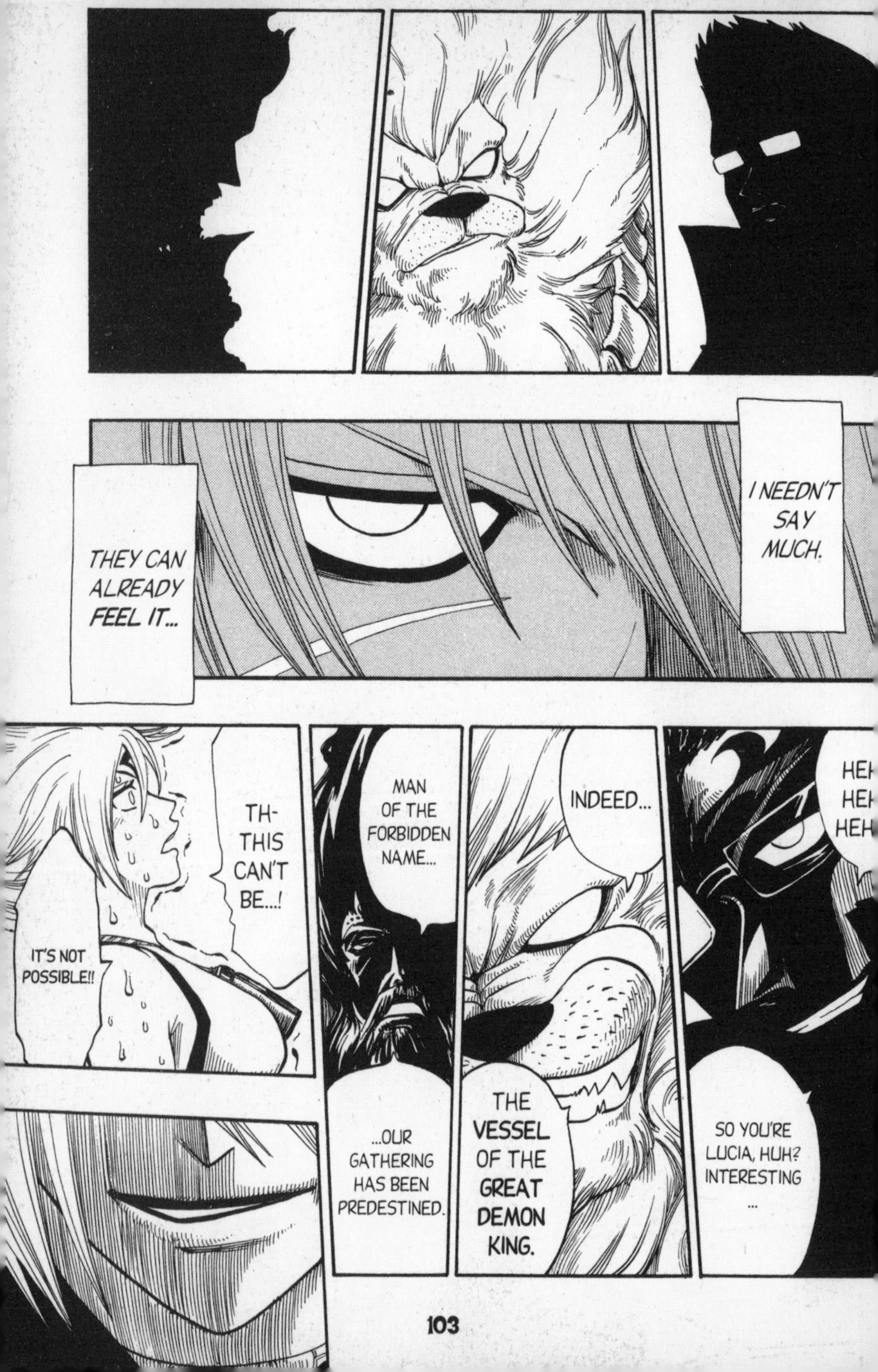
I NEEDN'T SAY MUCH.
THEY CAN ALREADY FEEL IT...
HEH HEH HEH
INDEED...
MAN OF THE FORBIDDEN NAME...
TH- THIS CAN'T BE...!
IT'S NOT POSSIBLE!!
SO YOU'RE LUCIA, HUH? INTERESTING ...
THE VESSEL OF THE GREAT DEMON KING.
...OUR GATHERING HAS BEEN PREDESTINED.

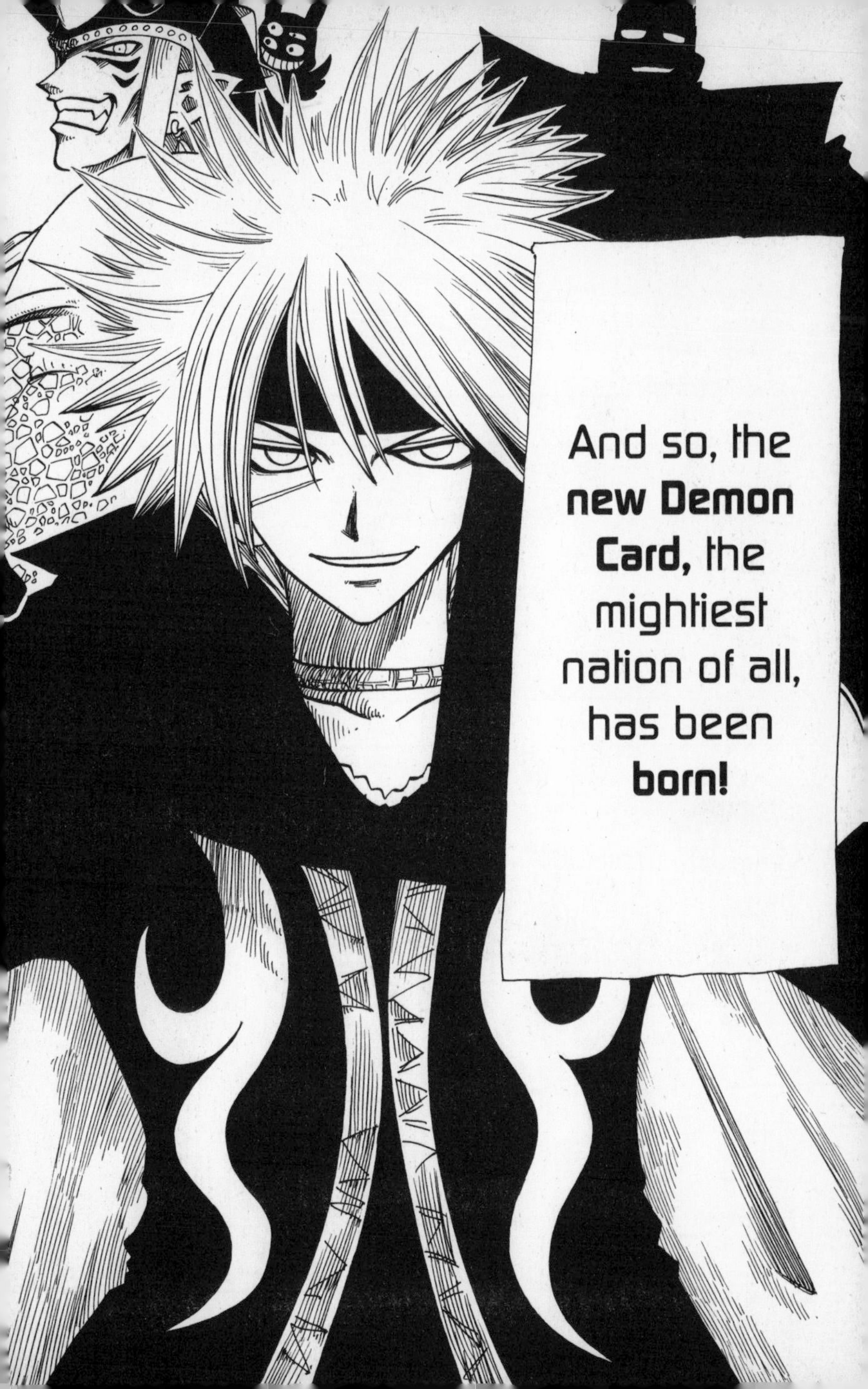
And so, the new Demon Card, the mightiest nation of all, has been born!

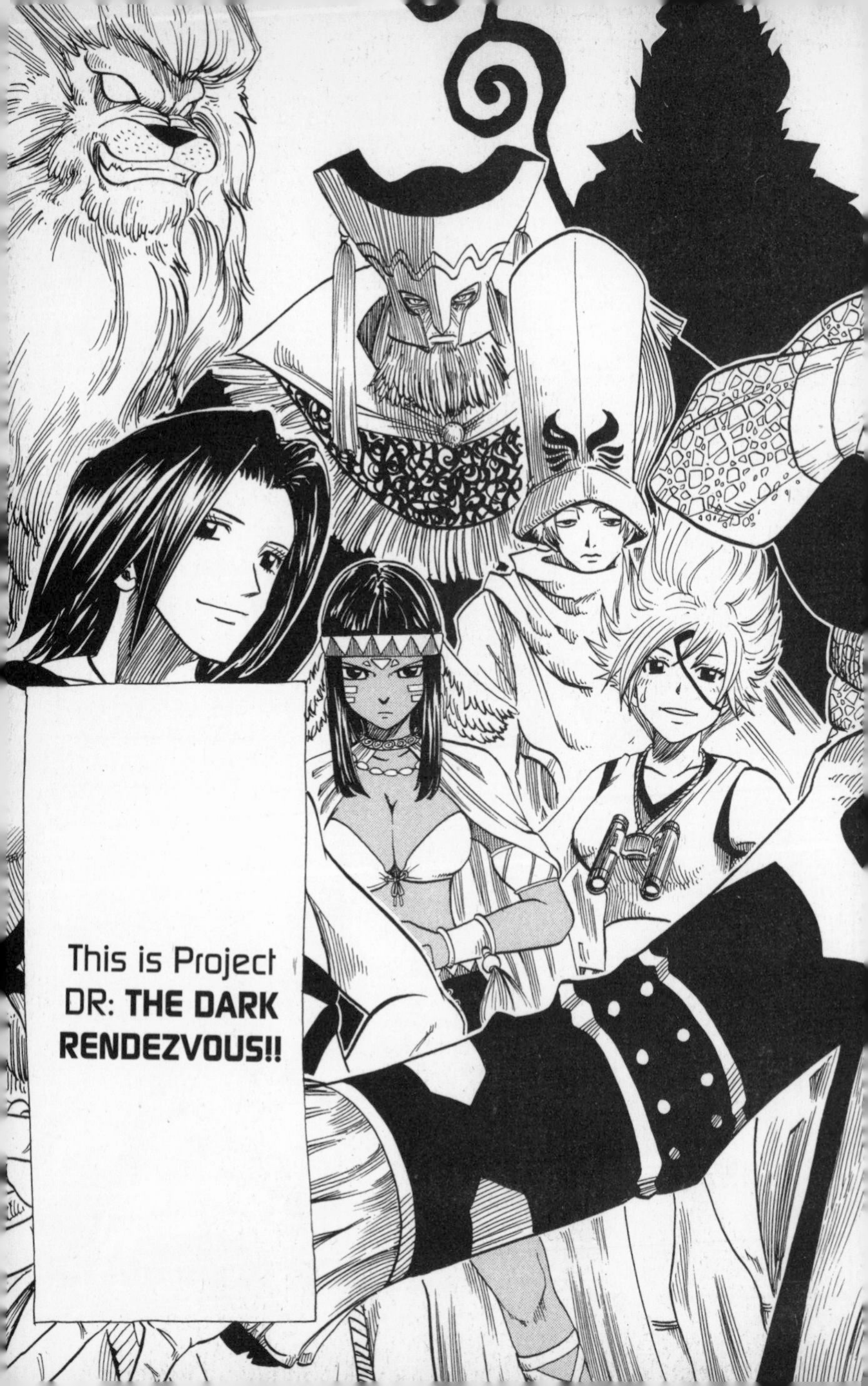
This is Project DR: THE DARK RENDEZVOUS!!

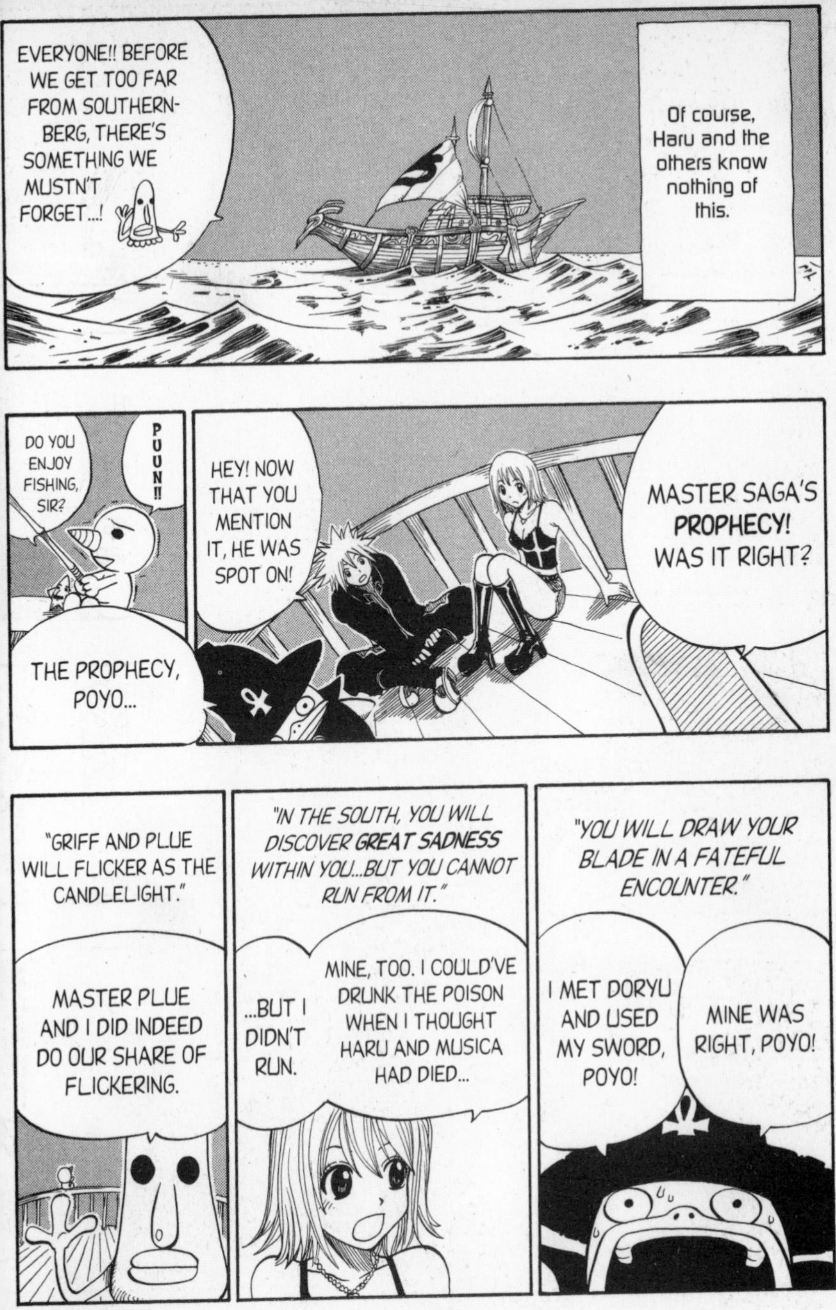
Of course, Haru and the others know nothing of this.
EVERYONE!! BEFORE WE GET TOO FAR FROM SOUTHERNBERG, THERE'S SOMETHING WE MUSTN'T FORGET...!
MASTER SAGA'S **PROPHECY!** WAS IT RIGHT?
HEY! NOW THAT YOU MENTION IT, HE WAS SPOT ON!
PUUN!!
DO YOU ENJOY FISHING, SIR?
THE PROPHECY, POYO...
"YOU WILL DRAW YOUR BLADE IN A FATEFUL ENCOUNTER."
MINE WAS RIGHT, POYO!
I MET DORYU AND USED MY SWORD, POYO!
*"IN THE SOUTH, YOU WILL DISCOVER **GREAT SADNESS** WITHIN YOU...BUT YOU CANNOT RUN FROM IT."*
MINE, TOO. I COULD'VE DRUNK THE POISON WHEN I THOUGHT HARU AND MUSICA HAD DIED...
...BUT I DIDN'T RUN.
"GRIFF AND PLUE WILL FLICKER AS THE CANDLELIGHT."
MASTER PLUE AND I DID INDEED DO OUR SHARE OF FLICKERING.

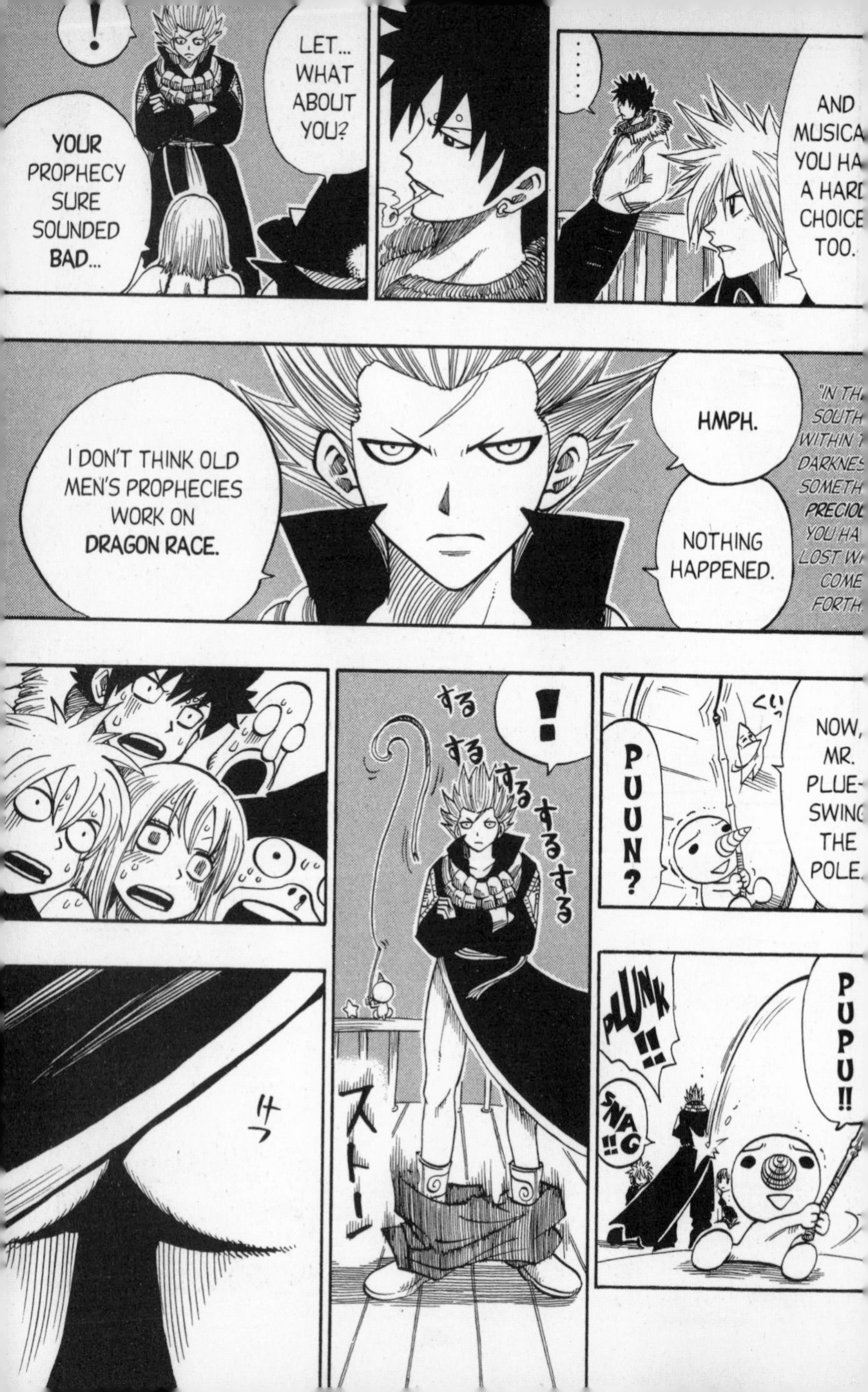
AND MUSICA YOU HA A HARD CHOICE TOO.
.....
LET... WHAT ABOUT YOU?
YOUR PROPHECY SURE SOUNDED BAD...
!
"IN TH SOUTH WITHIN T DARKNES SOMETH PRECIOU YOU HA LOST W COME FORTH.
HMPH.
NOTHING HAPPENED.
I DON'T THINK OLD MEN'S PROPHECIES WORK ON DRAGON RACE.
くいっ
NOW, MR. PLUE- SWING THE POLE.
PUUN?
PUPU!!
PLUNK!!
SNAG!!
!
するするするするする
ストーン

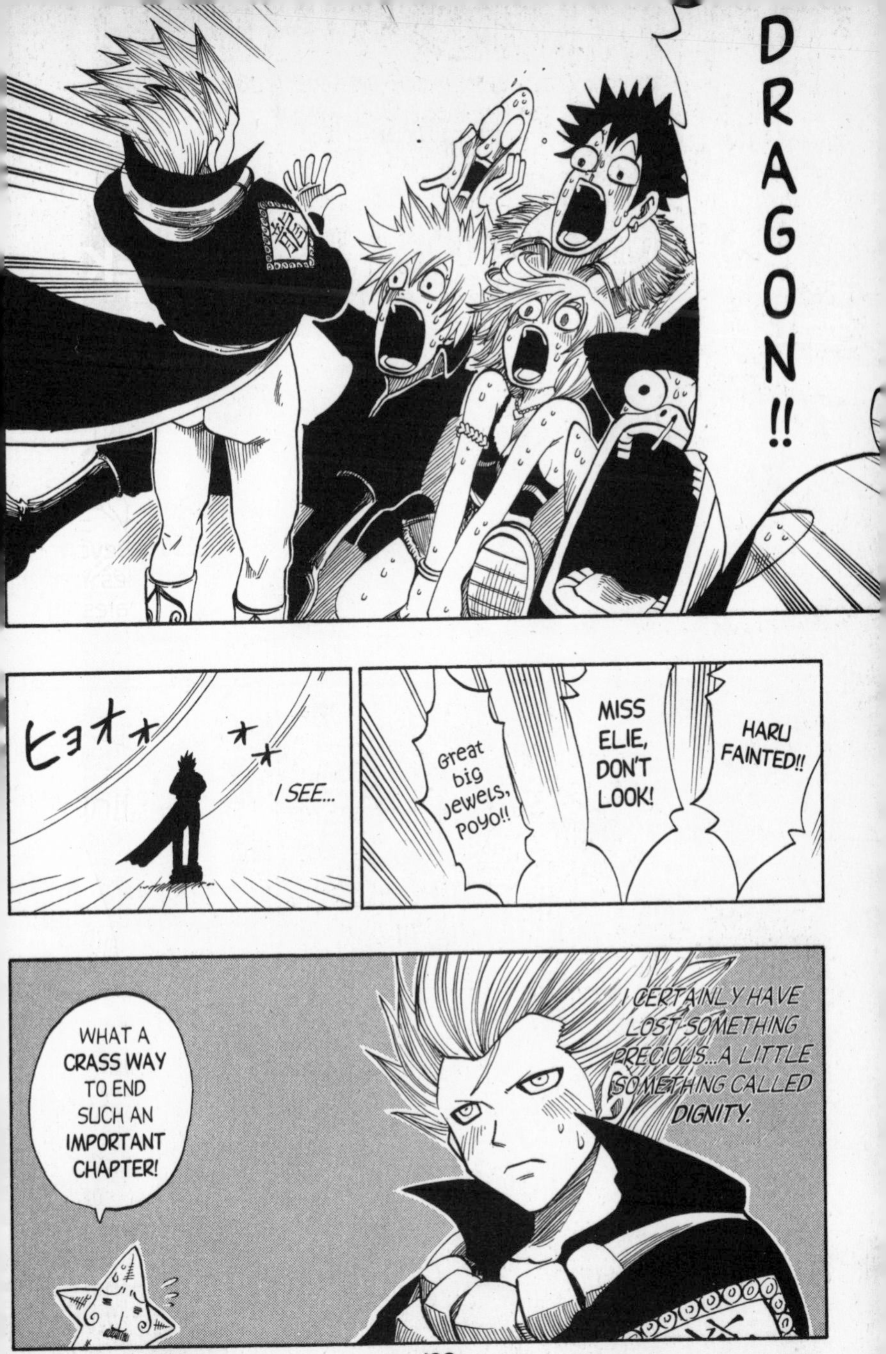
DRAGON!!
HARU FAINTED!!
MISS ELIE, DON'T LOOK!
Great big jewels, poyo!!
ヒョオォ
I SEE...
I CERTAINLY HAVE LOST SOMETHING PRECIOUS...A LITTLE SOMETHING CALLED DIGNITY.
WHAT A CRASS WAY TO END SUCH AN IMPORTANT CHAPTER!

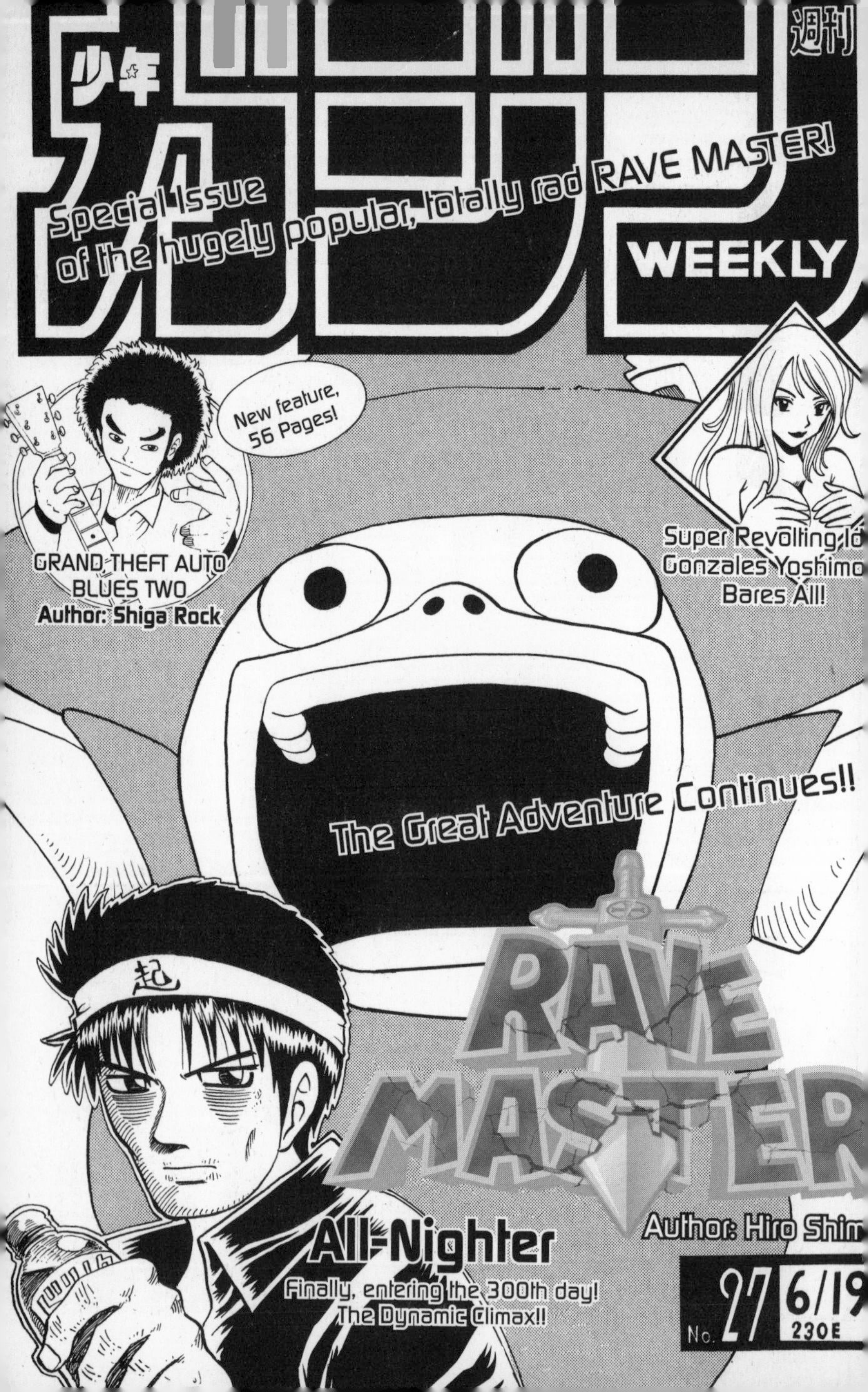
週刊
少年
WEEKLY
Special Issue of the hugely popular, totally rad RAVE MASTER!
New feature, 56 Pages!
Super Revolting Id
Gonzales Yoshimo
Bares All!
GRAND THEFT AUTO BLUES TWO
Author: Shiga Rock
The Great Adventure Continues!!
RAVE MASTER
Author: Hiro Shim
All-Nighter
Finally, entering the 300th day!
The Dynamic Climax!!
No. 27
6/19
230E

RAVE:143 ✠ ARE THESE GUYS STUPID OR WHAT?!

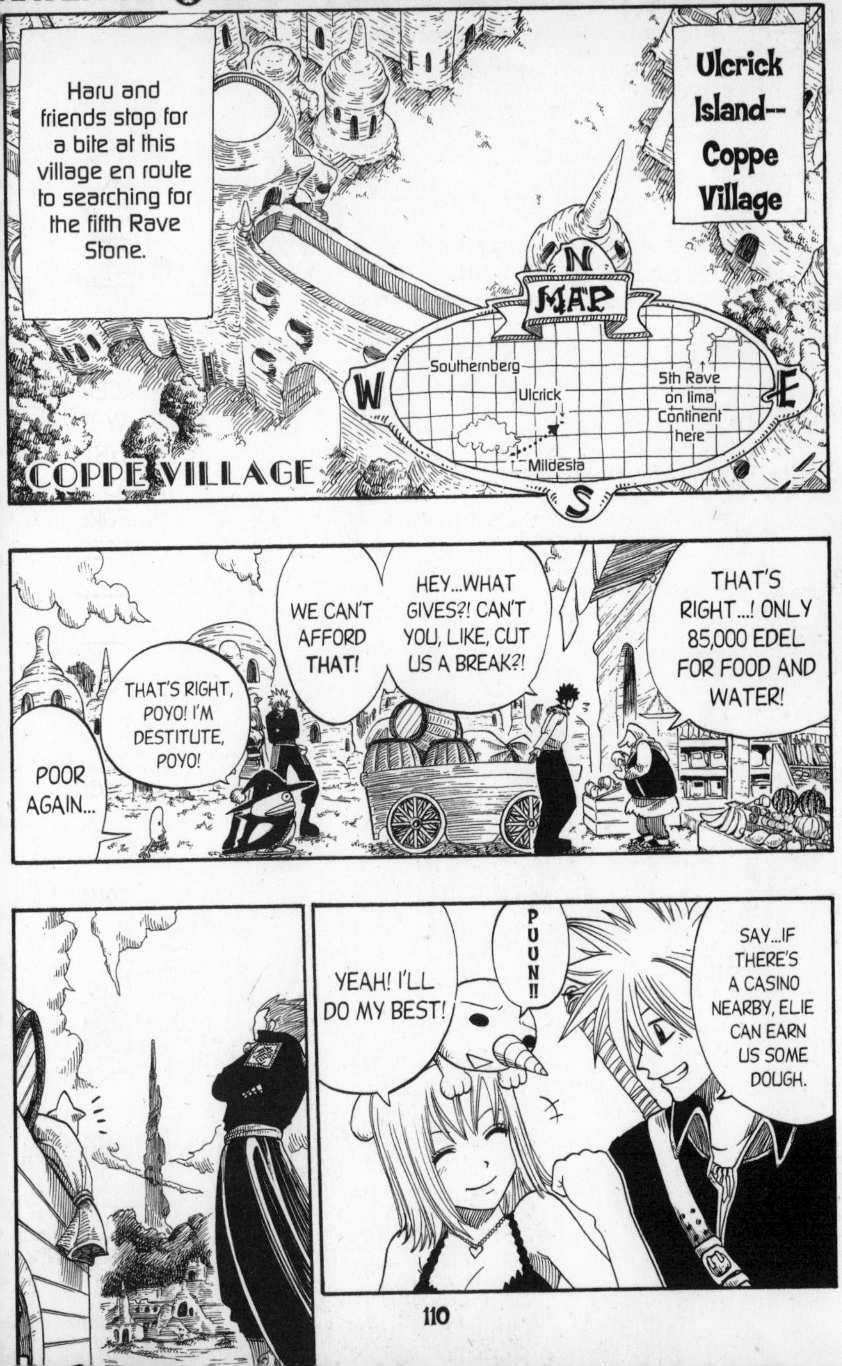

Ulcrick Island-- Coppe Village
Haru and friends stop for a bite at this village en route to searching for the fifth Rave Stone.
N
MAP
W
E
S
Southernberg
Ulcrick
5th Rave on Iima Continent here
Mildesta
COPPE VILLAGE
THAT'S RIGHT...! ONLY 85,000 EDEL FOR FOOD AND WATER!
HEY...WHAT GIVES?! CAN'T YOU, LIKE, CUT US A BREAK?!
WE CAN'T AFFORD THAT!
THAT'S RIGHT, POYO! I'M DESTITUTE, POYO!
POOR AGAIN...
SAY...IF THERE'S A CASINO NEARBY, ELIE CAN EARN US SOME DOUGH.
PUUN!!
YEAH! I'LL DO MY BEST!

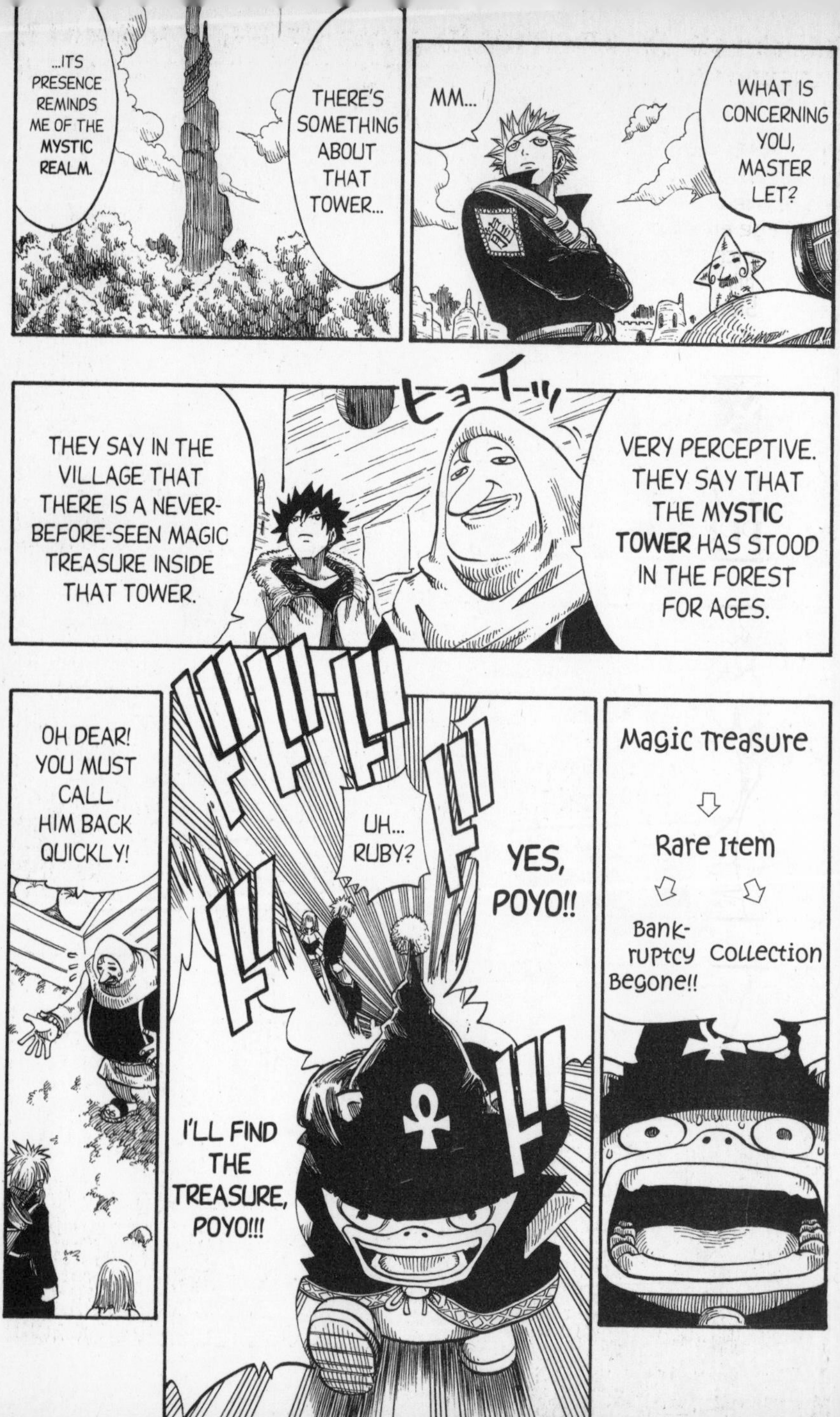

WHAT IS CONCERNING YOU, MASTER LET?
MM...
THERE'S SOMETHING ABOUT THAT TOWER...
...ITS PRESENCE REMINDS ME OF THE MYSTIC REALM.
ヒョーイーッ
VERY PERCEPTIVE. THEY SAY THAT THE MYSTIC TOWER HAS STOOD IN THE FOREST FOR AGES.
THEY SAY IN THE VILLAGE THAT THERE IS A NEVER-BEFORE-SEEN MAGIC TREASURE INSIDE THAT TOWER.
Magic Treasure
Rare Item
Bank-ruptcy Begone!!
Collection
YES, POYO!!
UH... RUBY?
I'LL FIND THE TREASURE, POYO!!!
OH DEAR! YOU MUST CALL HIM BACK QUICKLY!

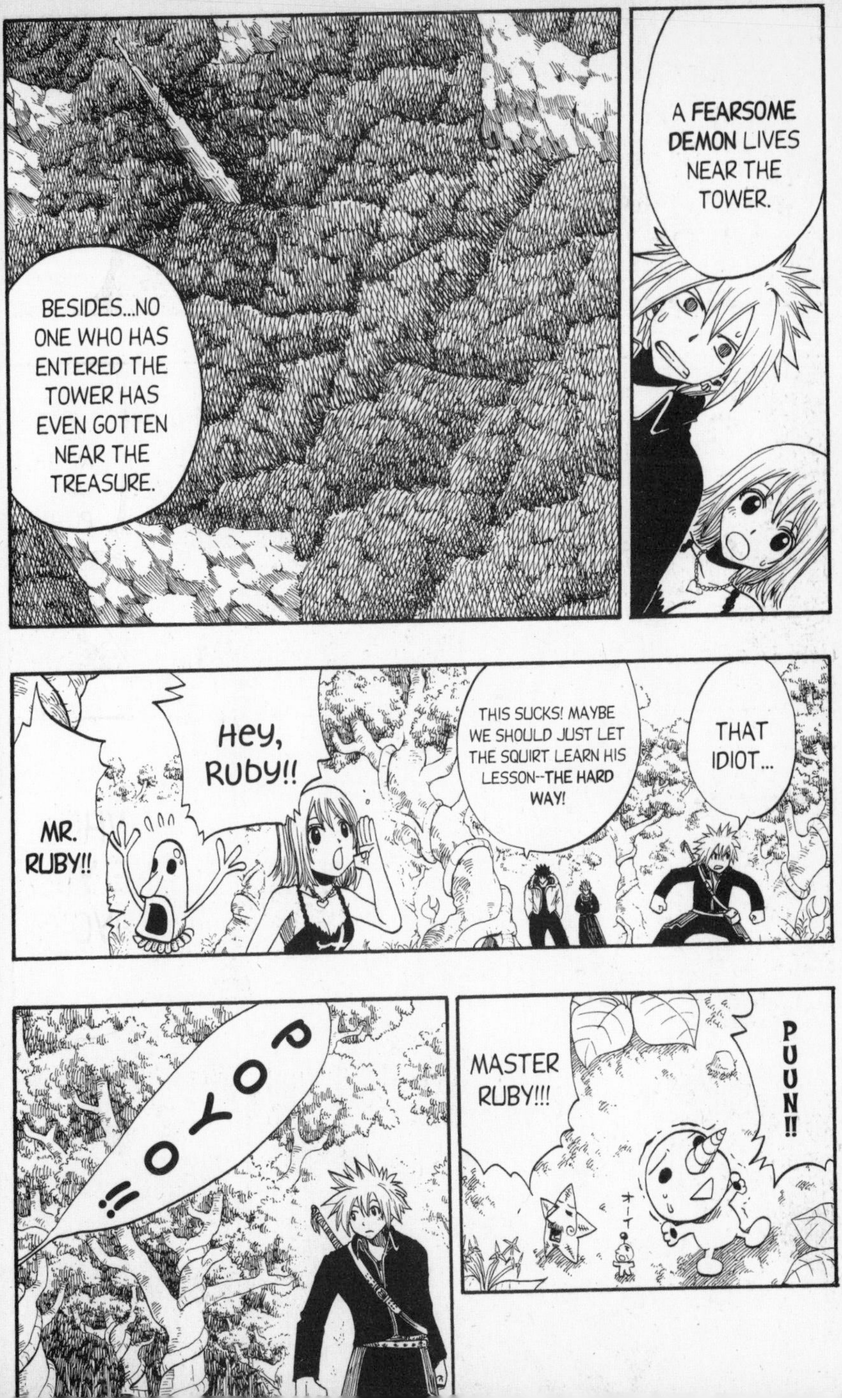
A FEARSOME DEMON LIVES NEAR THE TOWER.
BESIDES...NO ONE WHO HAS ENTERED THE TOWER HAS EVEN GOTTEN NEAR THE TREASURE.
THAT IDIOT...
THIS SUCKS! MAYBE WE SHOULD JUST LET THE SQUIRT LEARN HIS LESSON--THE HARD WAY!
Hey, Ruby!!
MR. RUBY!!
PUUN!!
MASTER RUBY!!!
オーイ
POYO!!

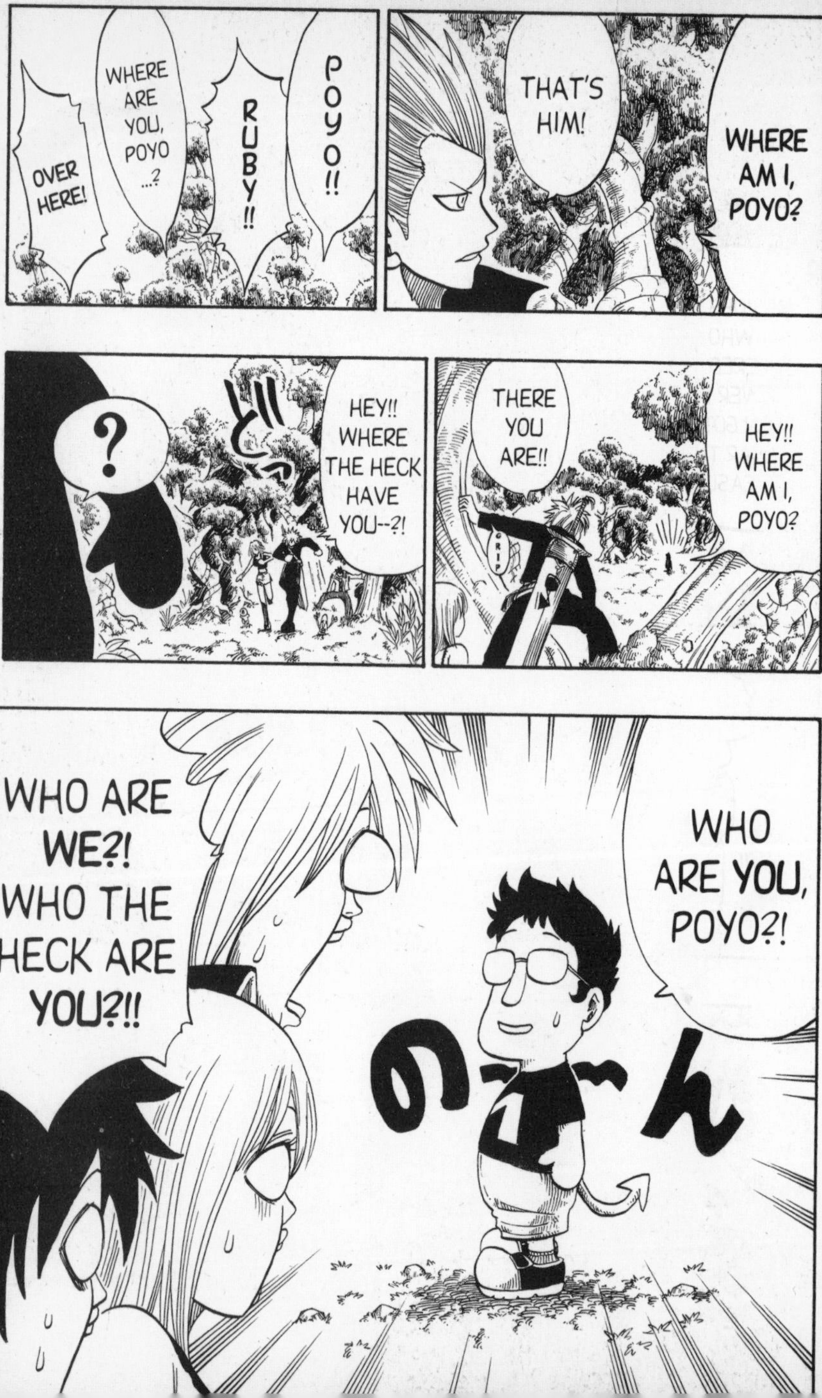
WHERE AM I, POYO?
THAT'S HIM!
POYO!!
RUBY!!
WHERE ARE YOU, POYO ...?
OVER HERE!
HEY!! WHERE AM I, POYO?
THERE YOU ARE!!
GRIP
HEY!! WHERE THE HECK HAVE YOU--?!
?
WHO ARE YOU, POYO?!
のーん
WHO ARE WE?! WHO THE HECK ARE YOU?!!

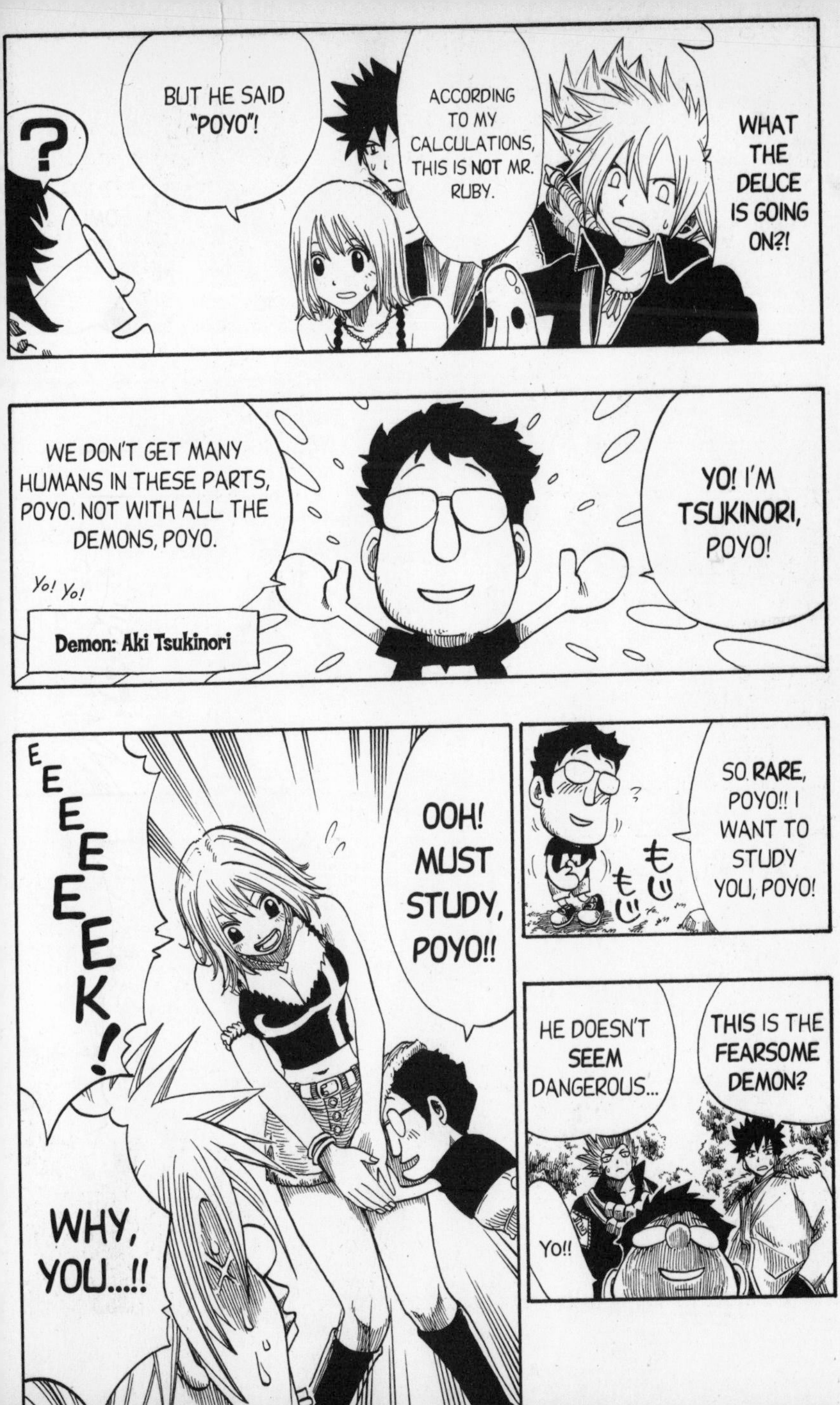
WHAT THE DEUCE IS GOING ON?!
ACCORDING TO MY CALCULATIONS, THIS IS NOT MR. RUBY.
BUT HE SAID "POYO"!
?
YO! I'M TSUKINORI, POYO!
WE DON'T GET MANY HUMANS IN THESE PARTS, POYO. NOT WITH ALL THE DEMONS, POYO.
Yo! Yo!
Demon: Aki Tsukinori
SO RARE, POYO!! I WANT TO STUDY YOU, POYO!
もじもじ
THIS IS THE FEARSOME DEMON?
HE DOESN'T SEEM DANGEROUS...
Yo!!
OOH! MUST STUDY, POYO!!
EEEEEEEK!
WHY, YOU...!!

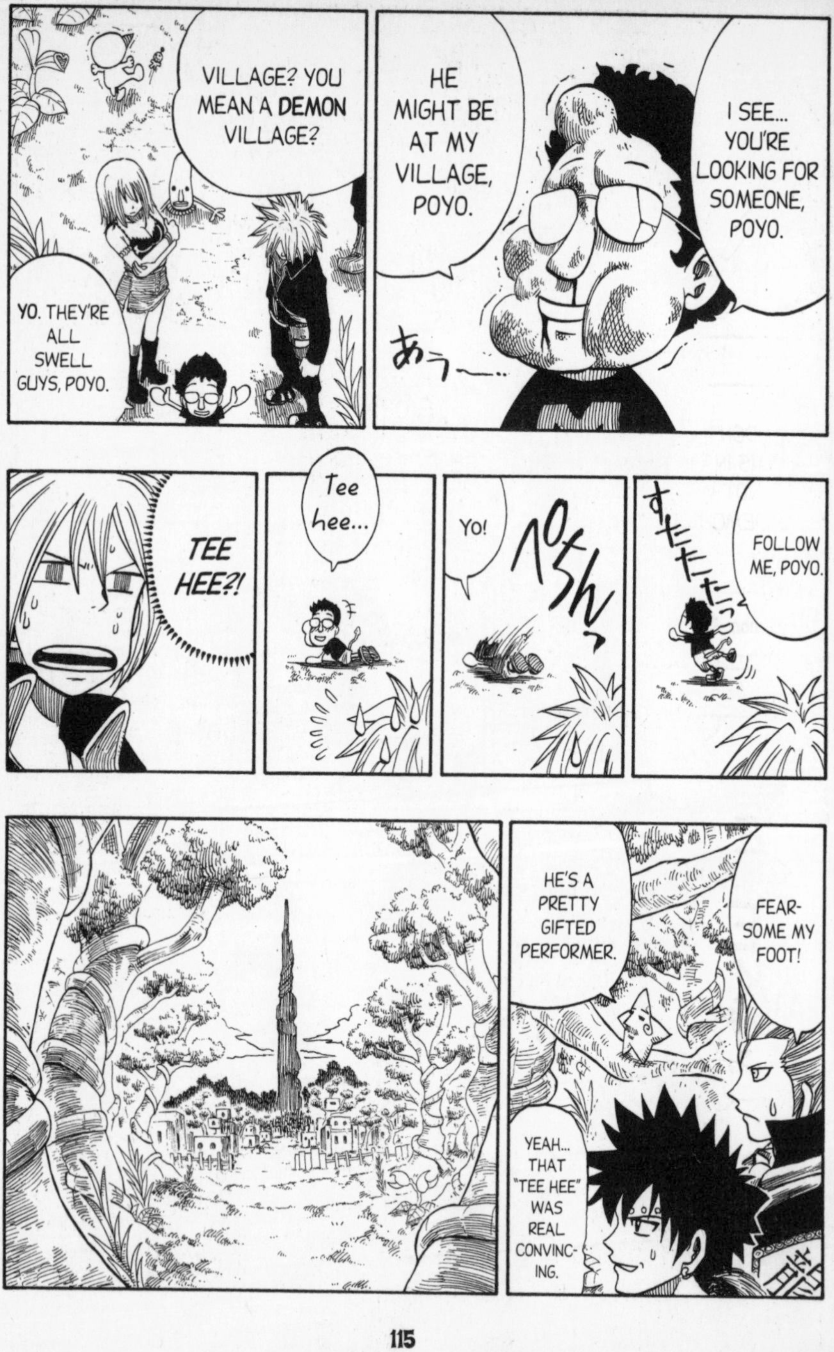
I SEE... YOU'RE LOOKING FOR SOMEONE, POYO.
HE MIGHT BE AT MY VILLAGE, POYO.
あう〜…
VILLAGE? YOU MEAN A DEMON VILLAGE?
YO. THEY'RE ALL SWELL GUYS, POYO.
FOLLOW ME, POYO.
すたたたたっ
Yo!
ぺちん
Tee hee...
TEE HEE?!
FEAR-SOME MY FOOT!
HE'S A PRETTY GIFTED PERFORMER.
YEAH... THAT "TEE HEE" WAS REAL CONVINCING.

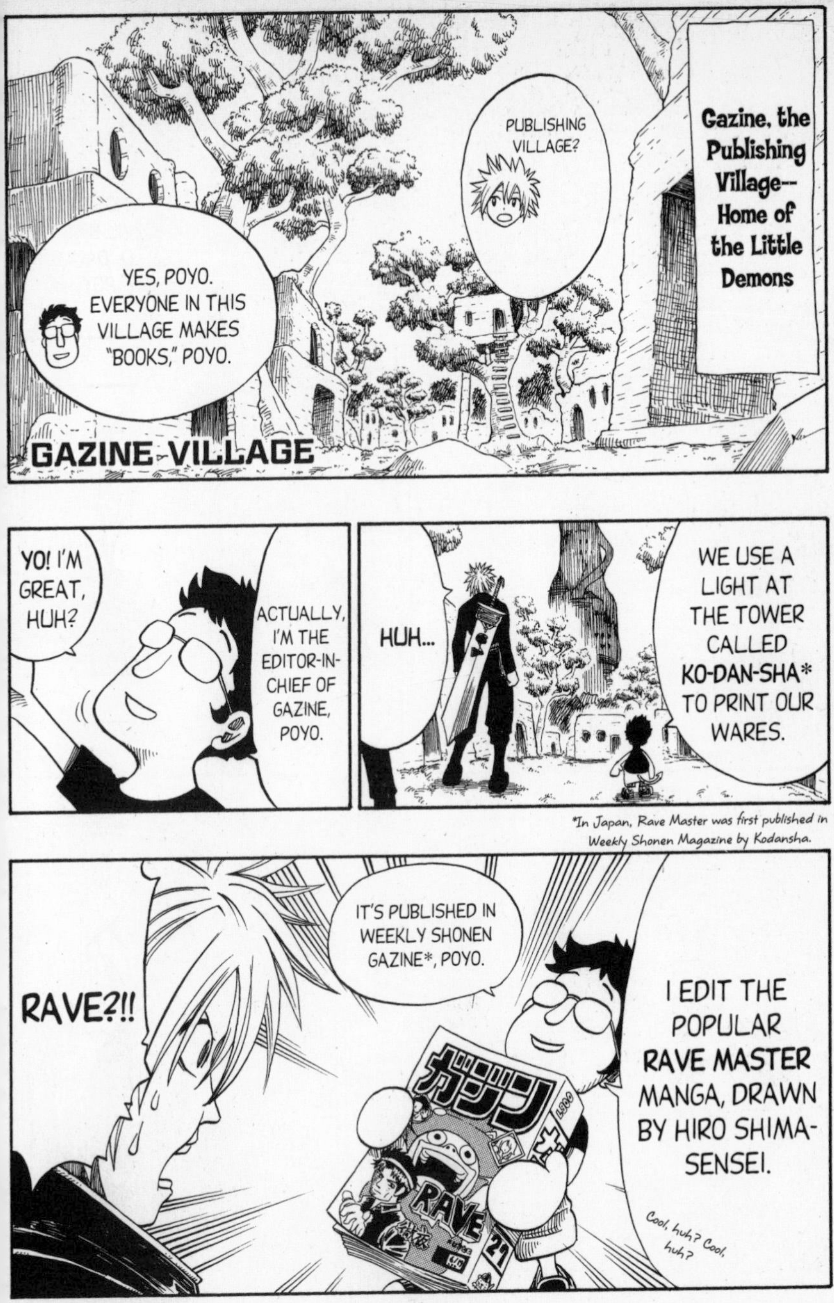
Gazine, the Publishing Village-- Home of the Little Demons
PUBLISHING VILLAGE?
YES, POYO. EVERYONE IN THIS VILLAGE MAKES "BOOKS," POYO.
GAZINE VILLAGE
WE USE A LIGHT AT THE TOWER CALLED KO-DAN-SHA* TO PRINT OUR WARES.
HUH...
ACTUALLY, I'M THE EDITOR-IN-CHIEF OF GAZINE, POYO.
YO! I'M GREAT, HUH?
I EDIT THE POPULAR RAVE MASTER MANGA, DRAWN BY HIRO SHIMA-SENSEI.
Cool, huh? Cool, huh?
IT'S PUBLISHED IN WEEKLY SHONEN GAZINE*, POYO.
RAVE?!!
RAVE

*In Japan, Rave Master was first published in Weekly Shonen Magazine by Kodansha.

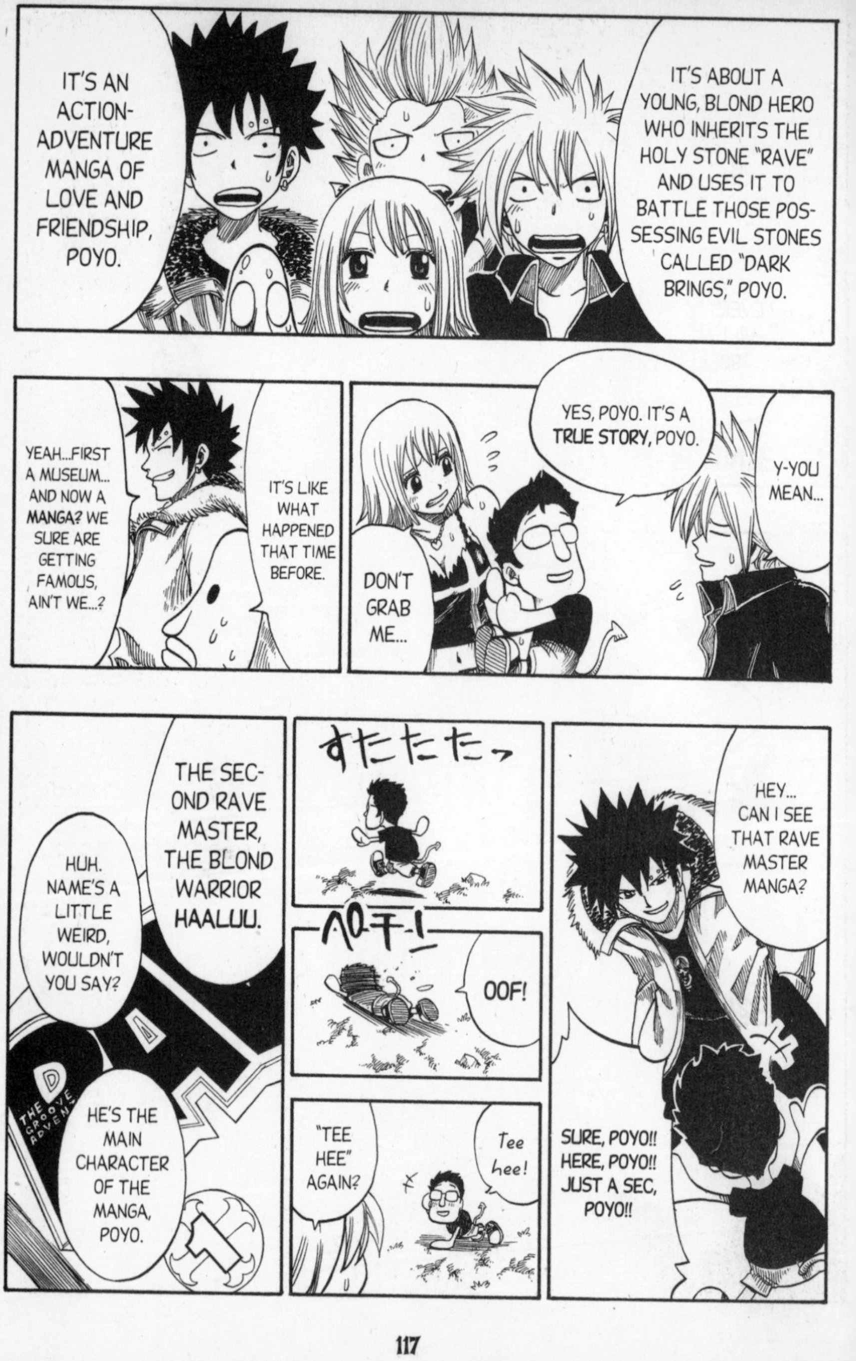
IT'S ABOUT A YOUNG, BLOND HERO WHO INHERITS THE HOLY STONE "RAVE" AND USES IT TO BATTLE THOSE POSSESSING EVIL STONES CALLED "DARK BRINGS," POYO.
IT'S AN ACTION-ADVENTURE MANGA OF LOVE AND FRIENDSHIP, POYO.
Y-YOU MEAN...
YES, POYO. IT'S A TRUE STORY, POYO.
DON'T GRAB ME...
IT'S LIKE WHAT HAPPENED THAT TIME BEFORE.
YEAH...FIRST A MUSEUM... AND NOW A MANGA? WE SURE ARE GETTING FAMOUS, AIN'T WE...?
HEY... CAN I SEE THAT RAVE MASTER MANGA?
SURE, POYO!! HERE, POYO!! JUST A SEC, POYO!!
すたたたっ
OOF!
Tee hee!
"TEE HEE" AGAIN?
THE SECOND RAVE MASTER, THE BLOND WARRIOR HAALUU.
HUH. NAME'S A LITTLE WEIRD, WOULDN'T YOU SAY?
HE'S THE MAIN CHARACTER OF THE MANGA, POYO.

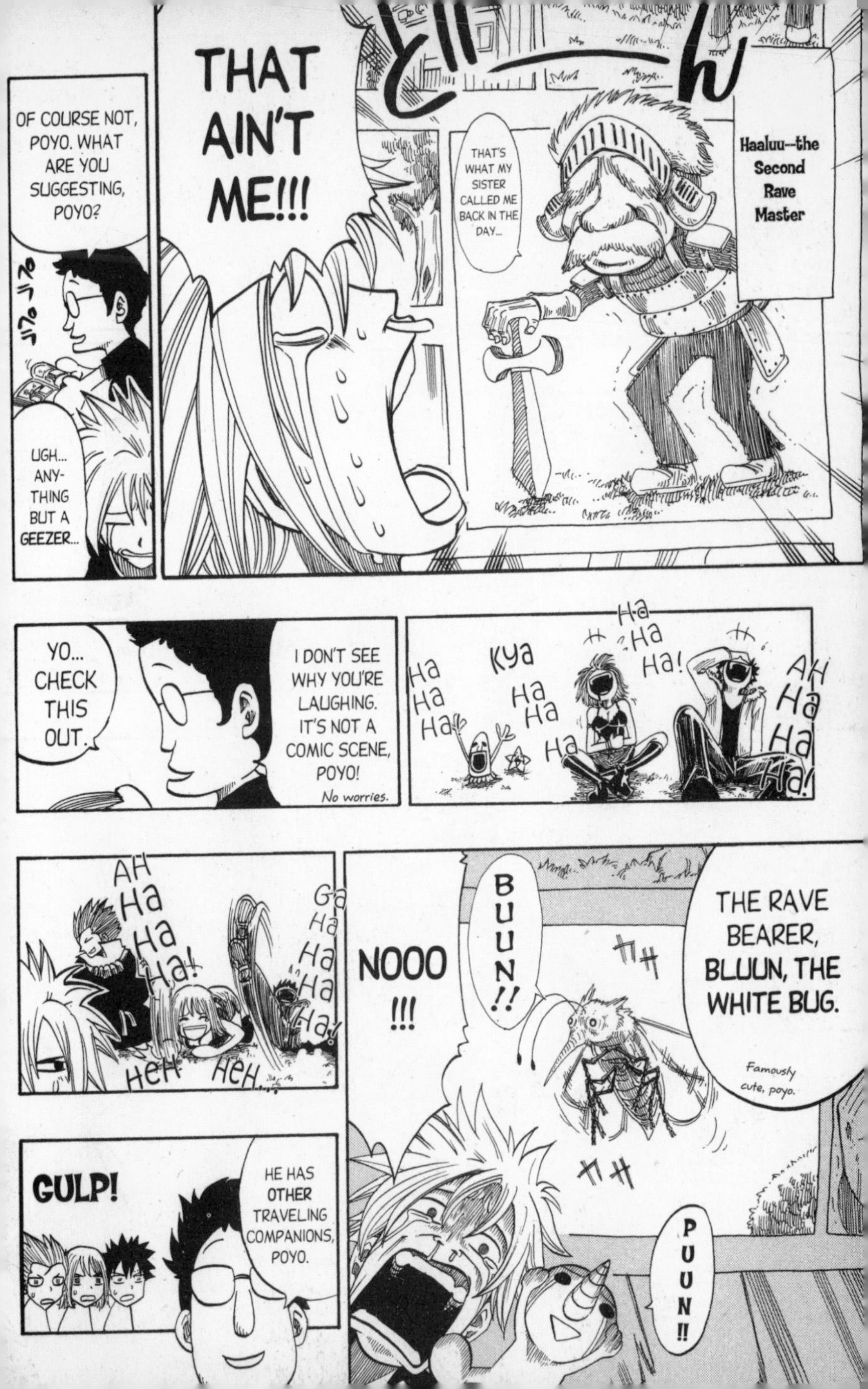
Haaluu--the Second Rave Master
THAT'S WHAT MY SISTER CALLED ME BACK IN THE DAY...
THAT AIN'T ME!!!
OF COURSE NOT, POYO. WHAT ARE YOU SUGGESTING, POYO?
UGH... ANY-THING BUT A GEEZER...
AH Ha Ha Ha!
Ha Ha Ha!
Kya Ha Ha Ha
Ha Ha Ha
I DON'T SEE WHY YOU'RE LAUGHING. IT'S NOT A COMIC SCENE, POYO!
No worries.
YO... CHECK THIS OUT.
THE RAVE BEARER, BLUUN, THE WHITE BUG.
Famously cute, poyo.
BUUN!!
NOOO!!!
PUUN!!
AH Ha Ha Ha!
Ga Ha Ha Ha Ha!
HeH HeH...
HE HAS OTHER TRAVELING COMPANIONS, POYO.
GULP!

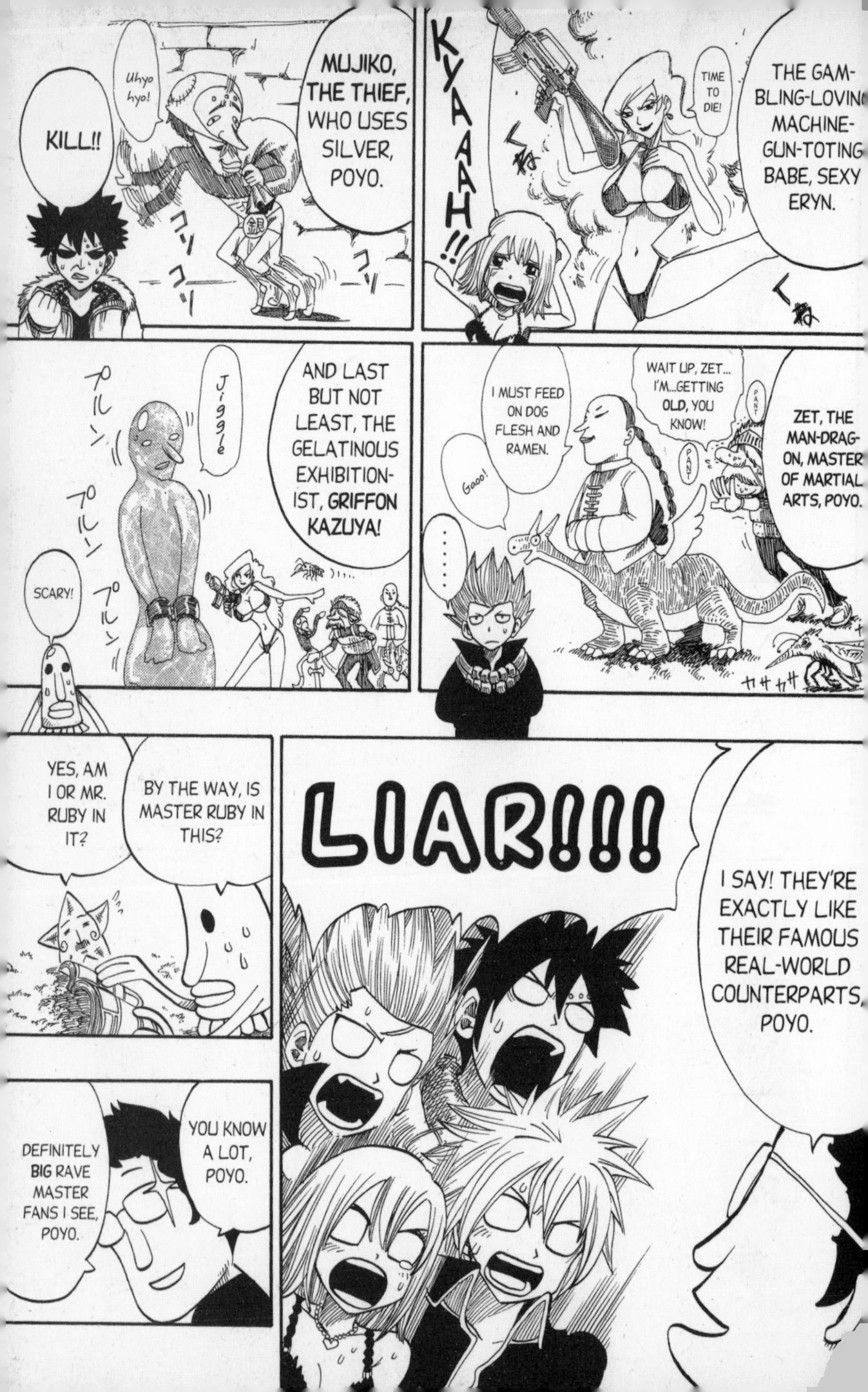
THE GAMBLING-LOVING MACHINE-GUN-TOTING BABE, SEXY ERYN.
TIME TO DIE!
KYAAAH!!
MUJIKO, THE THIEF, WHO USES SILVER, POYO.
Uhyo hyo!
KILL!!
ZET, THE MAN-DRAGON, MASTER OF MARTIAL ARTS, POYO.
WAIT UP, ZET... I'M...GETTING OLD, YOU KNOW!
PANT
PANT
I MUST FEED ON DOG FLESH AND RAMEN.
Gaoo!
......
AND LAST BUT NOT LEAST, THE GELATINOUS EXHIBITIONIST, GRIFFON KAZUYA!
Jiggle
SCARY!
I SAY! THEY'RE EXACTLY LIKE THEIR FAMOUS REAL-WORLD COUNTERPARTS, POYO.
LIAR!!!
BY THE WAY, IS MASTER RUBY IN THIS?
YES, AM I OR MR. RUBY IN IT?
YOU KNOW A LOT, POYO.
DEFINITELY BIG RAVE MASTER FANS I SEE, POYO.

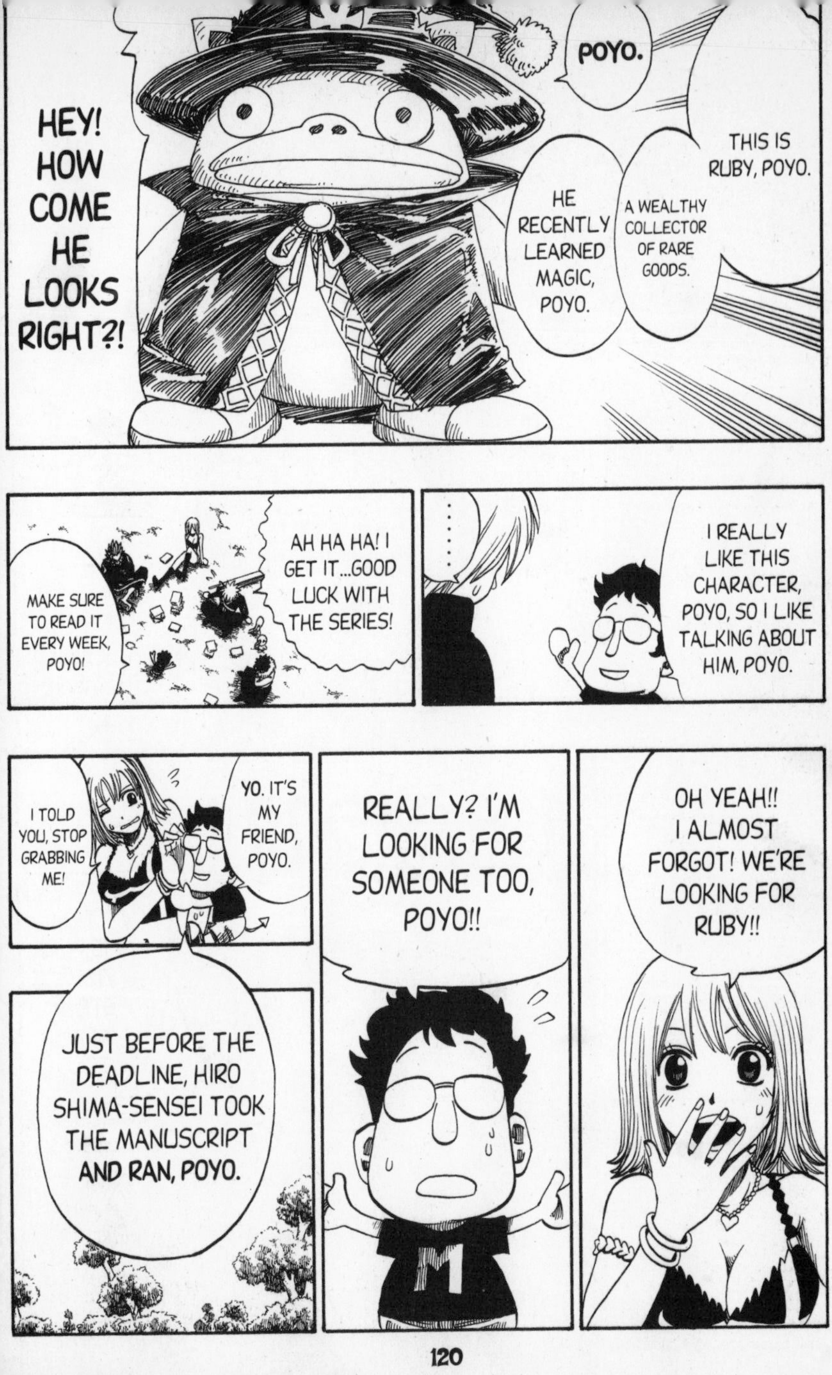
POYO.
THIS IS RUBY, POYO.
A WEALTHY COLLECTOR OF RARE GOODS.
HE RECENTLY LEARNED MAGIC, POYO.
HEY! HOW COME HE LOOKS RIGHT?!
I REALLY LIKE THIS CHARACTER, POYO, SO I LIKE TALKING ABOUT HIM, POYO.
......
AH HA HA! I GET IT...GOOD LUCK WITH THE SERIES!
MAKE SURE TO READ IT EVERY WEEK, POYO!
OH YEAH!! I ALMOST FORGOT! WE'RE LOOKING FOR RUBY!!
REALLY? I'M LOOKING FOR SOMEONE TOO, POYO!!
YO. IT'S MY FRIEND, POYO.
I TOLD YOU, STOP GRABBING ME!
JUST BEFORE THE DEADLINE, HIRO SHIMA-SENSEI TOOK THE MANUSCRIPT AND RAN, POYO.

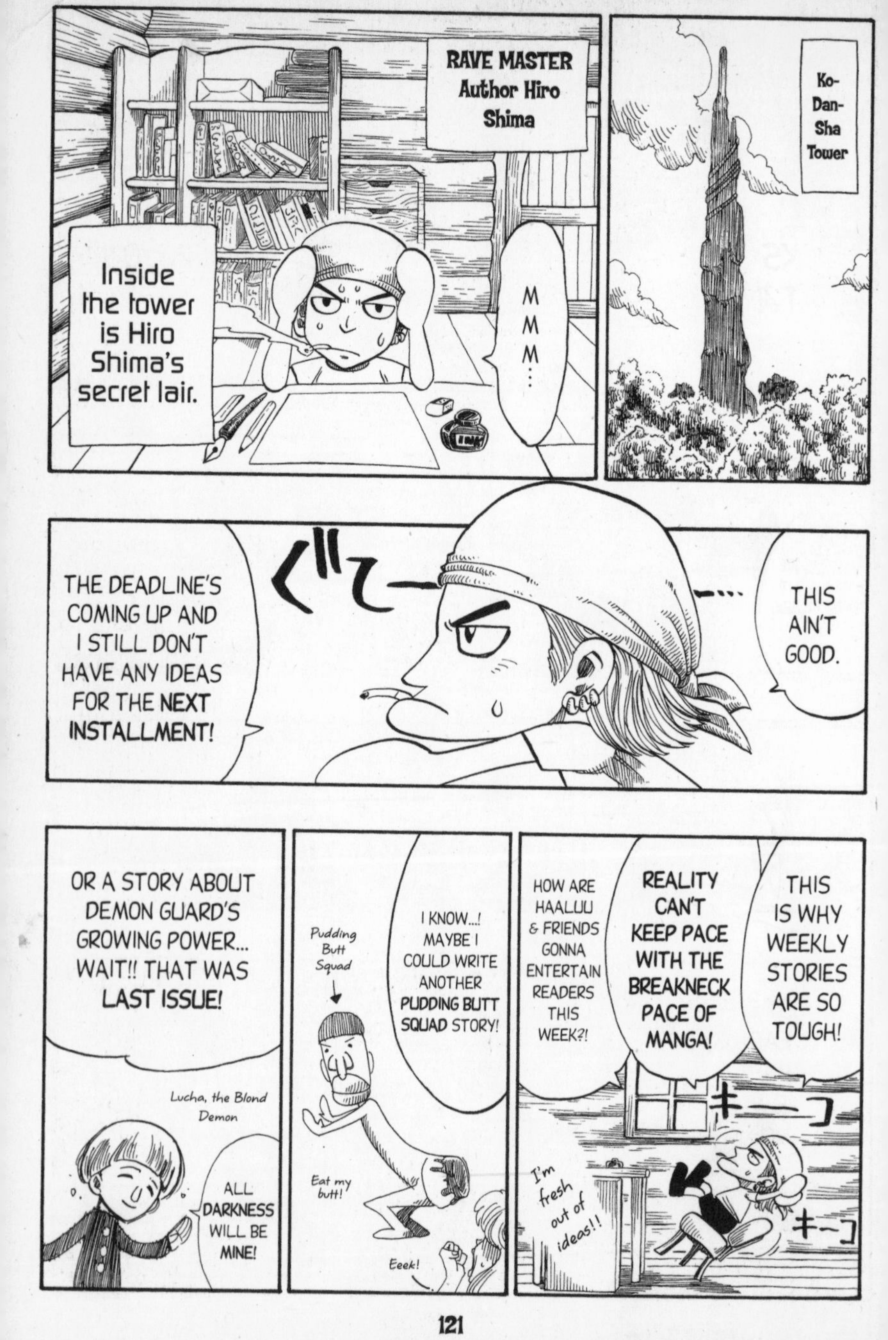

Ko-Dan-Sha Tower
RAVE MASTER Author Hiro Shima
MMM...
Inside the tower is Hiro Shima's secret lair.
THIS AIN'T GOOD.
ぐでー…
THE DEADLINE'S COMING UP AND I STILL DON'T HAVE ANY IDEAS FOR THE NEXT INSTALLMENT!
THIS IS WHY WEEKLY STORIES ARE SO TOUGH!
REALITY CAN'T KEEP PACE WITH THE BREAKNECK PACE OF MANGA!
HOW ARE HAALUU & FRIENDS GONNA ENTERTAIN READERS THIS WEEK?!
キーコ
I'm fresh out of ideas!!
キーコ
I KNOW...! MAYBE I COULD WRITE ANOTHER PUDDING BUTT SQUAD STORY!
Pudding Butt Squad
Eat my butt!
Eeek!
OR A STORY ABOUT DEMON GUARD'S GROWING POWER... WAIT!! THAT WAS LAST ISSUE!
Lucha, the Blond Demon
ALL DARKNESS WILL BE MINE!

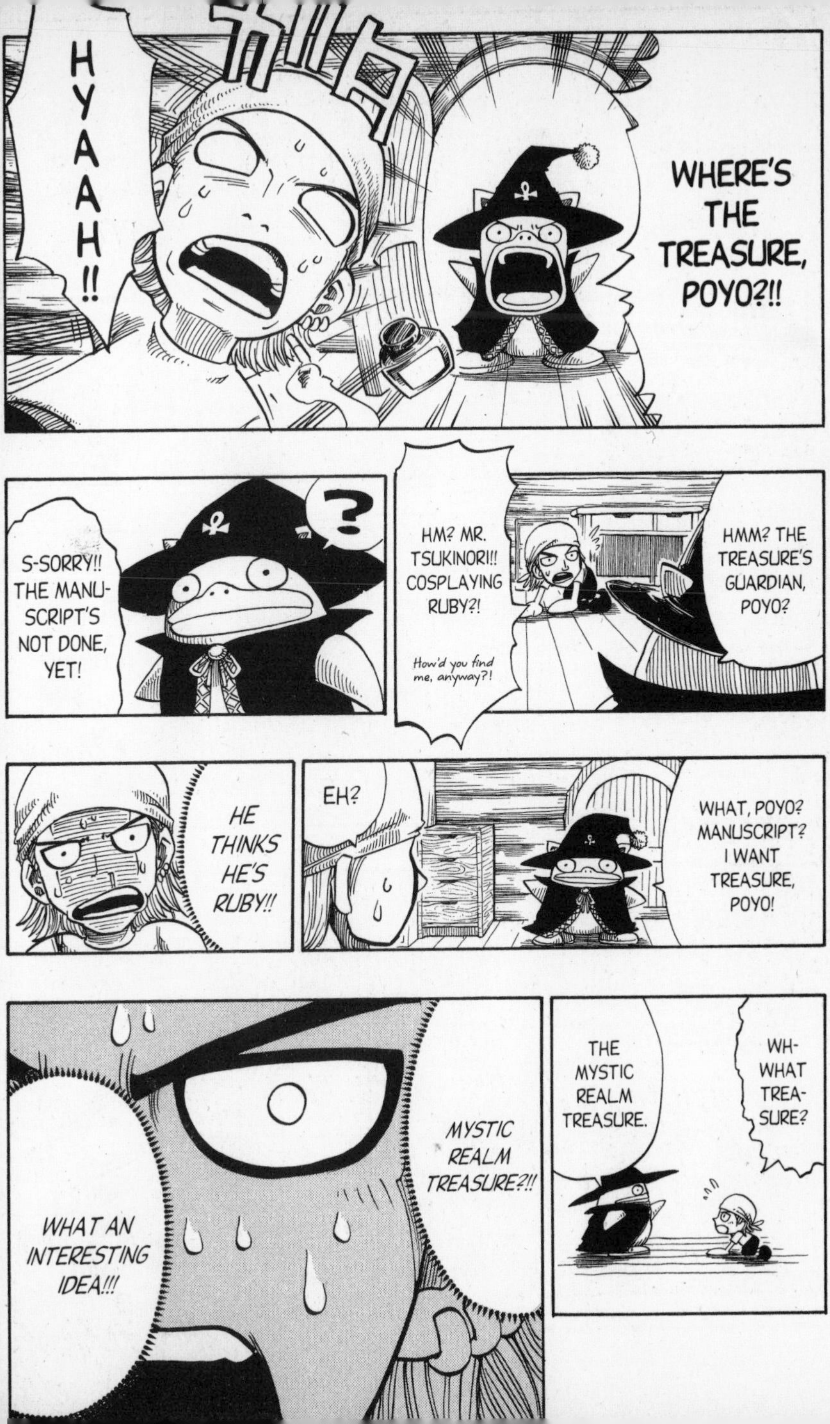
WHERE'S THE TREASURE, POYO?!!
HYAAH!!
HMM? THE TREASURE'S GUARDIAN, POYO?
HM? MR. TSUKINORI!! COSPLAYING RUBY?!
How'd you find me, anyway?!
?
S-SORRY!! THE MANU-SCRIPT'S NOT DONE, YET!
WHAT, POYO? MANUSCRIPT? I WANT TREASURE, POYO!
EH?
HE THINKS HE'S RUBY!!
WH-WHAT TREA-SURE?
THE MYSTIC REALM TREASURE.
MYSTIC REALM TREASURE?!!
WHAT AN INTERESTING IDEA!!!

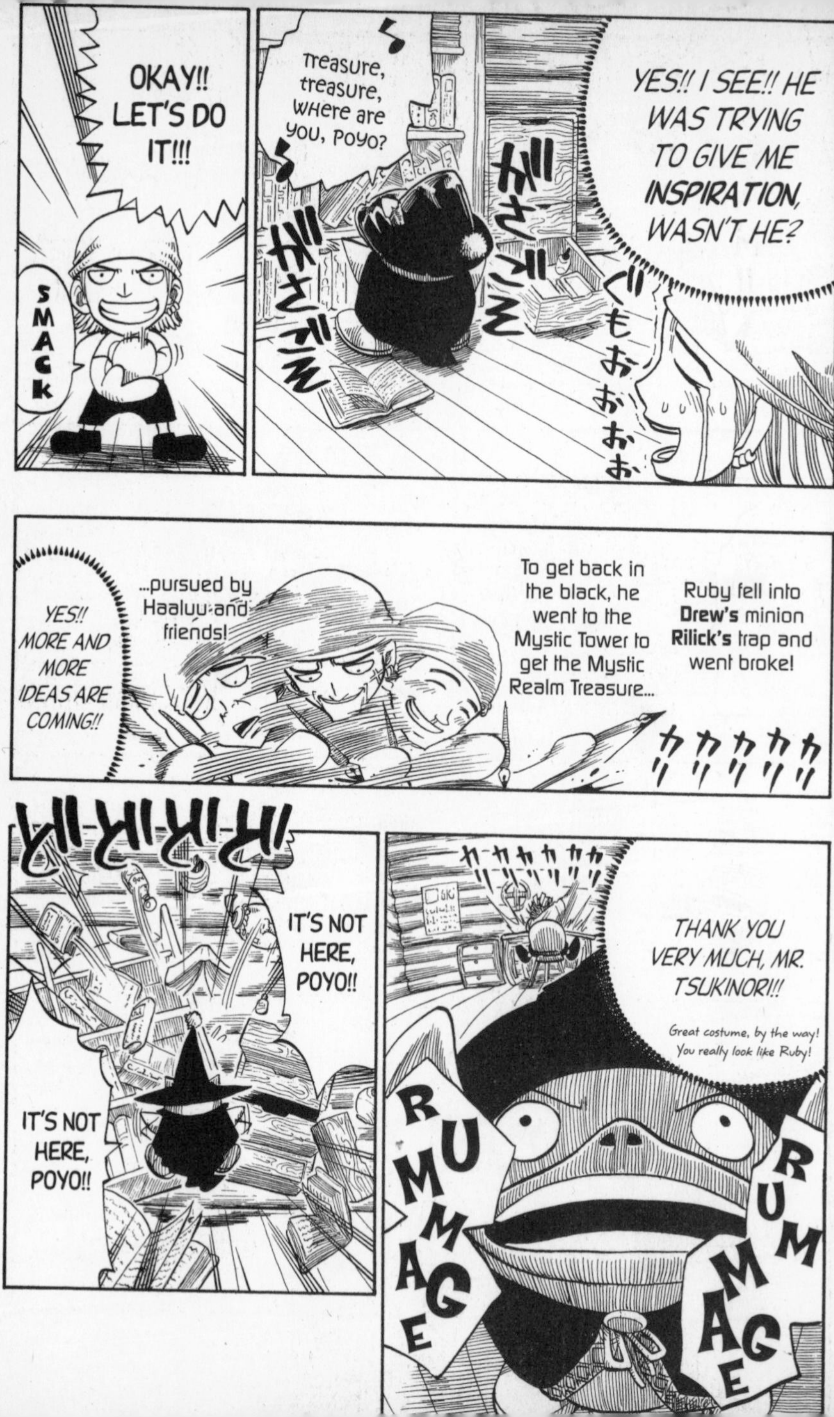
YES!! I SEE!! HE WAS TRYING TO GIVE ME INSPIRATION, WASN'T HE?
ぐもおおおおお
Treasure, treasure, where are you, poyo?
がさごそ
がさごそ
OKAY!! LET'S DO IT!!!
SMACK
Ruby fell into **Drew's** minion **Rilick's** trap and went broke!
To get back in the black, he went to the Mystic Tower to get the Mystic Realm Treasure...
...pursued by Haaluu and friends!
YES!! MORE AND MORE IDEAS ARE COMING!!
カリカリカリカリカリ
THANK YOU VERY MUCH, MR. TSUKINORI!!
Great costume, by the way! You really look like Ruby!
RUMMAGE
RUMMAGE
IT'S NOT HERE, POYO!!
IT'S NOT HERE, POYO!!

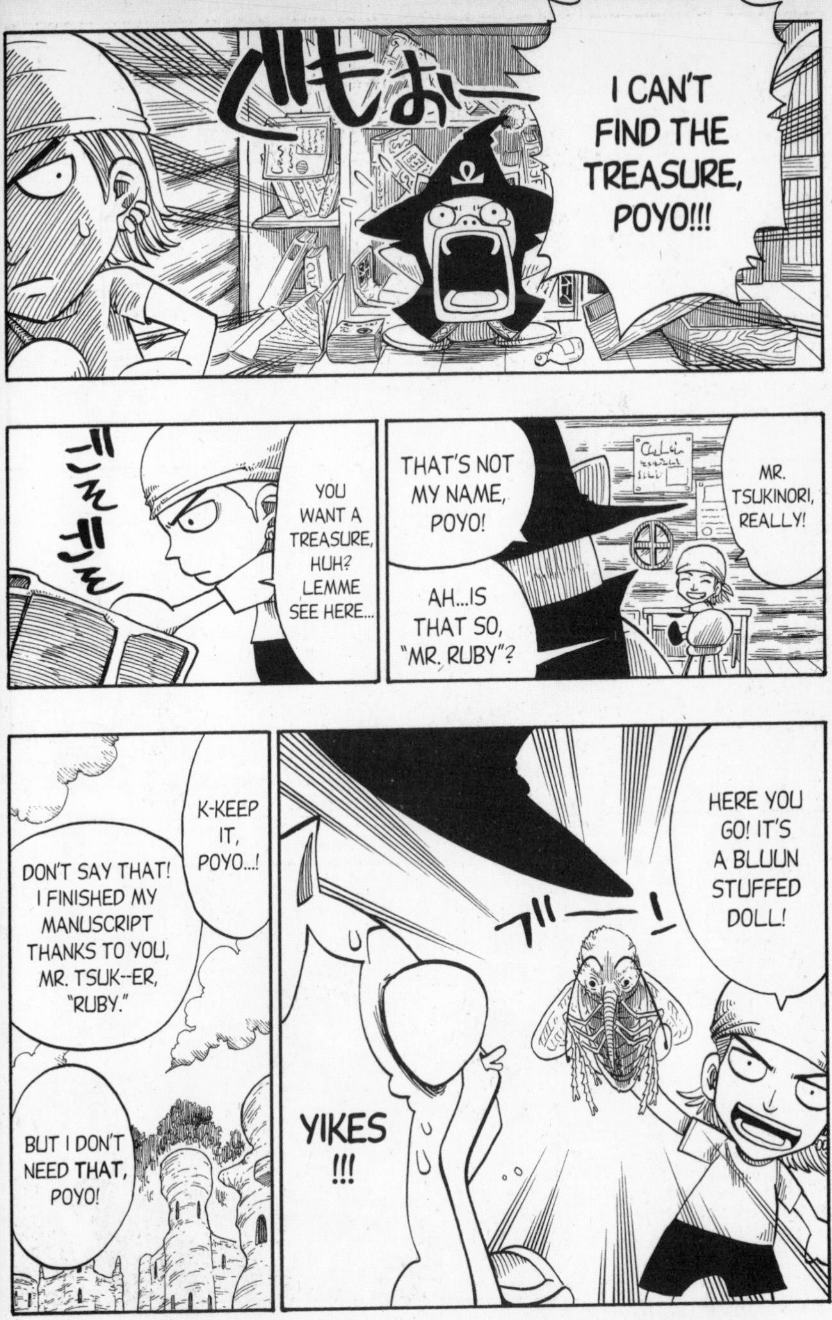
くもぉー
I CAN'T FIND THE TREASURE, POYO!!!
MR. TSUKINORI, REALLY!
THAT'S NOT MY NAME, POYO!
AH...IS THAT SO, "MR. RUBY"?
YOU WANT A TREASURE, HUH? LEMME SEE HERE...
ごそごそ
HERE YOU GO! IT'S A BLUUN STUFFED DOLL!
ブーーン
YIKES!!!
K-KEEP IT, POYO...!
DON'T SAY THAT! I FINISHED MY MANUSCRIPT THANKS TO YOU, MR. TSUK--ER, "RUBY."
BUT I DON'T NEED THAT, POYO!

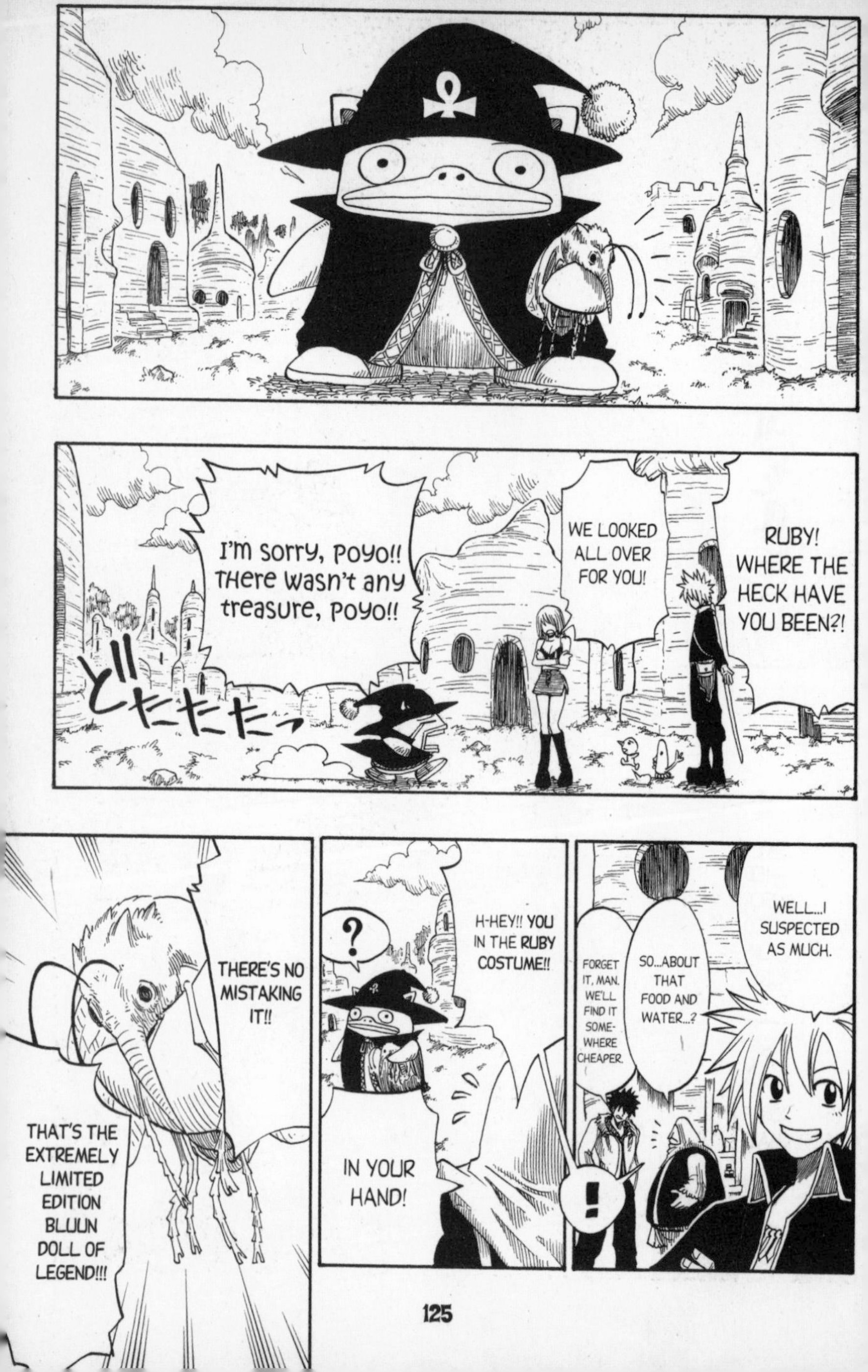
RUBY! WHERE THE HECK HAVE YOU BEEN?!
WE LOOKED ALL OVER FOR YOU!
I'm sorry, Poyo!! There wasn't any treasure, Poyo!!
どたたたっ
WELL...I SUSPECTED AS MUCH.
SO...ABOUT THAT FOOD AND WATER...?
FORGET IT, MAN. WE'LL FIND IT SOME-WHERE CHEAPER.
!
H-HEY!! YOU IN THE RUBY COSTUME!!
?
IN YOUR HAND!
THERE'S NO MISTAKING IT!!
THAT'S THE EXTREMELY LIMITED EDITION BLUUN DOLL OF LEGEND!!!

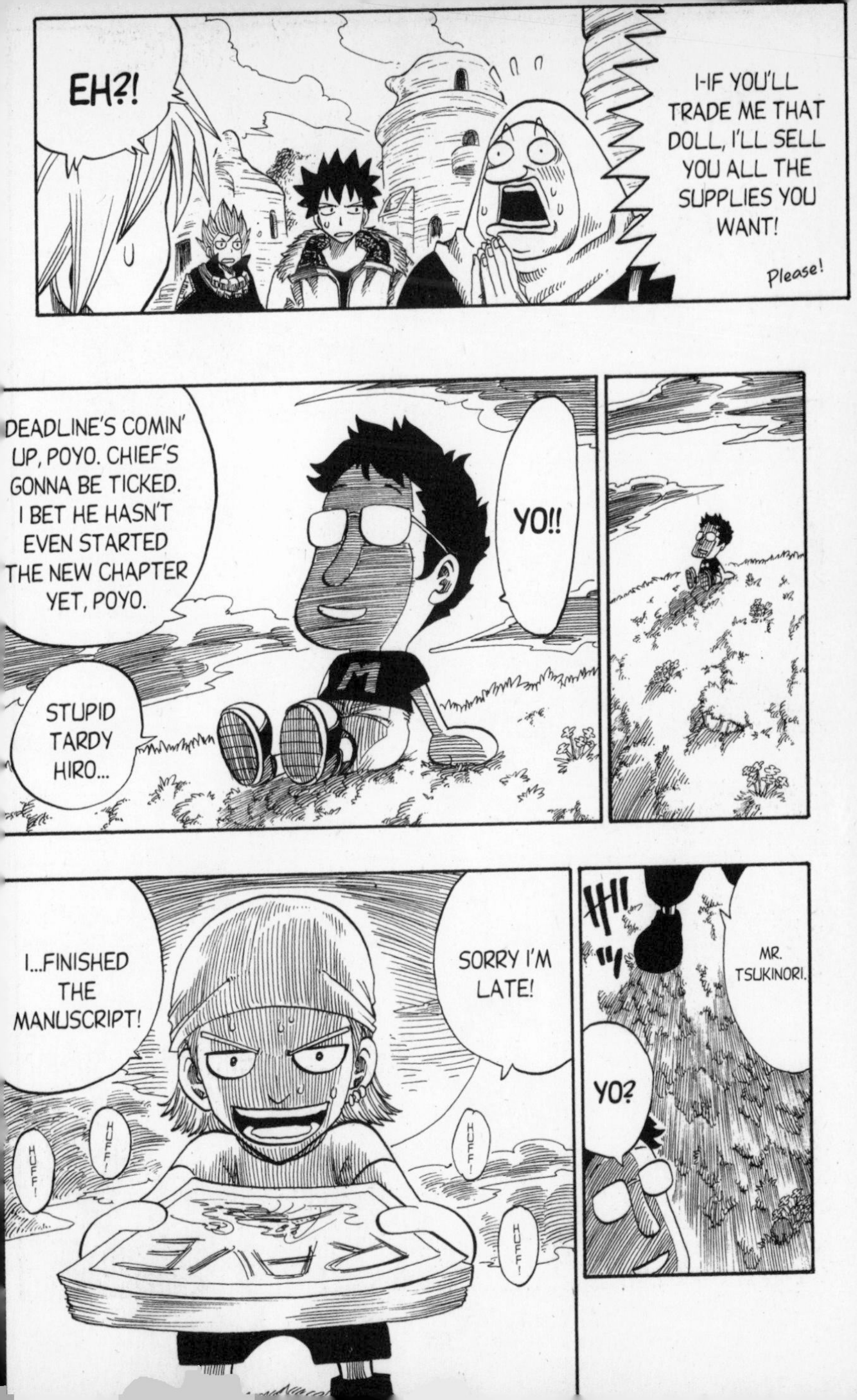
I-IF YOU'LL TRADE ME THAT DOLL, I'LL SELL YOU ALL THE SUPPLIES YOU WANT!
Please!
EH?!
YO!!
DEADLINE'S COMIN' UP, POYO. CHIEF'S GONNA BE TICKED. I BET HE HASN'T EVEN STARTED THE NEW CHAPTER YET, POYO.
STUPID TARDY HIRO...
MR. TSUKINORI.
YO?
SORRY I'M LATE!
I...FINISHED THE MANUSCRIPT!
HUF!
HUF!
HUF!
HUF!
RAVE

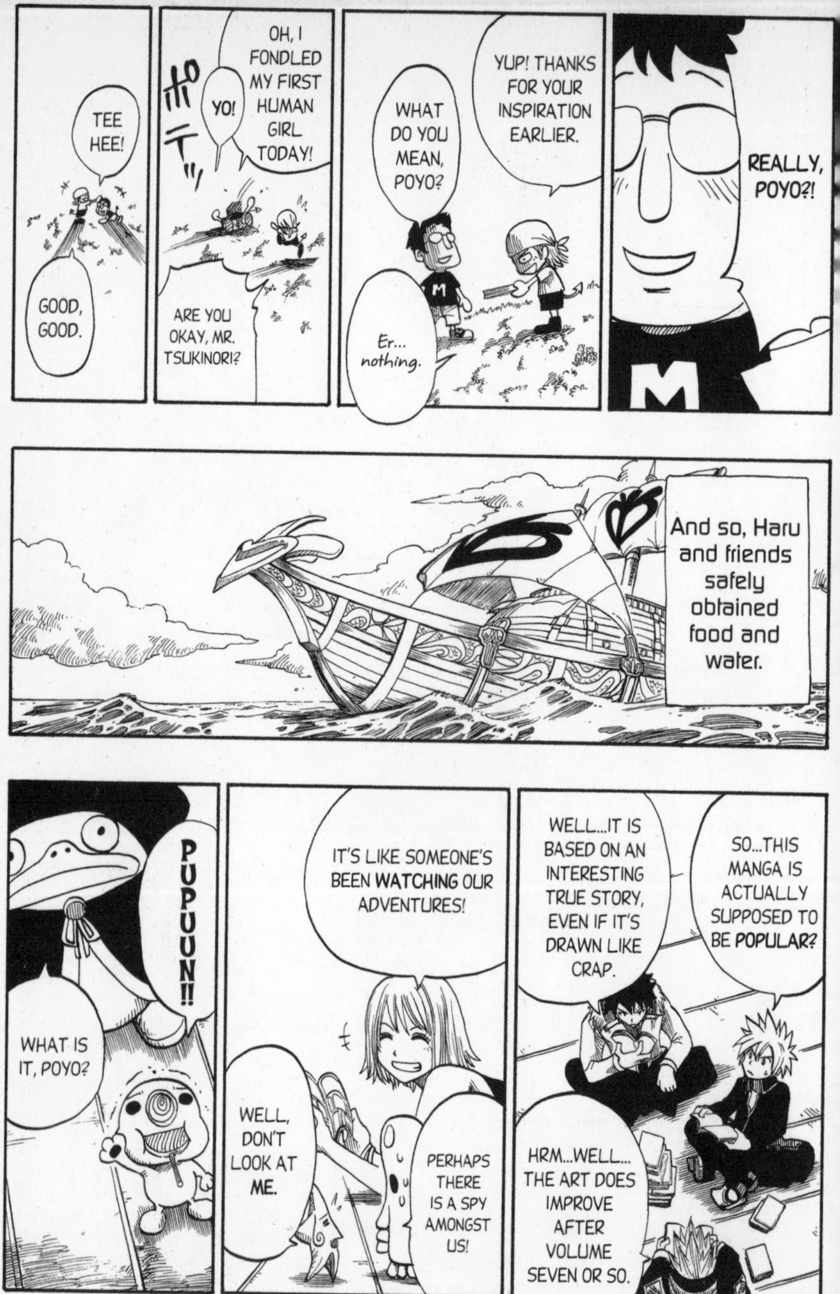
REALLY, POYO?!
YUP! THANKS FOR YOUR INSPIRATION EARLIER.
WHAT DO YOU MEAN, POYO?
Er... nothing.
OH, I FONDLED MY FIRST HUMAN GIRL TODAY!
YO!
ARE YOU OKAY, MR. TSUKINORI!?
TEE HEE!
GOOD, GOOD.
And so, Haru and friends safely obtained food and water.
SO...THIS MANGA IS ACTUALLY SUPPOSED TO BE POPULAR?
WELL...IT IS BASED ON AN INTERESTING TRUE STORY, EVEN IF IT'S DRAWN LIKE CRAP.
HRM...WELL... THE ART DOES IMPROVE AFTER VOLUME SEVEN OR SO.
IT'S LIKE SOMEONE'S BEEN WATCHING OUR ADVENTURES!
PERHAPS THERE IS A SPY AMONGST US!
WELL, DON'T LOOK AT ME.
PUPUUN!!
WHAT IS IT, POYO?

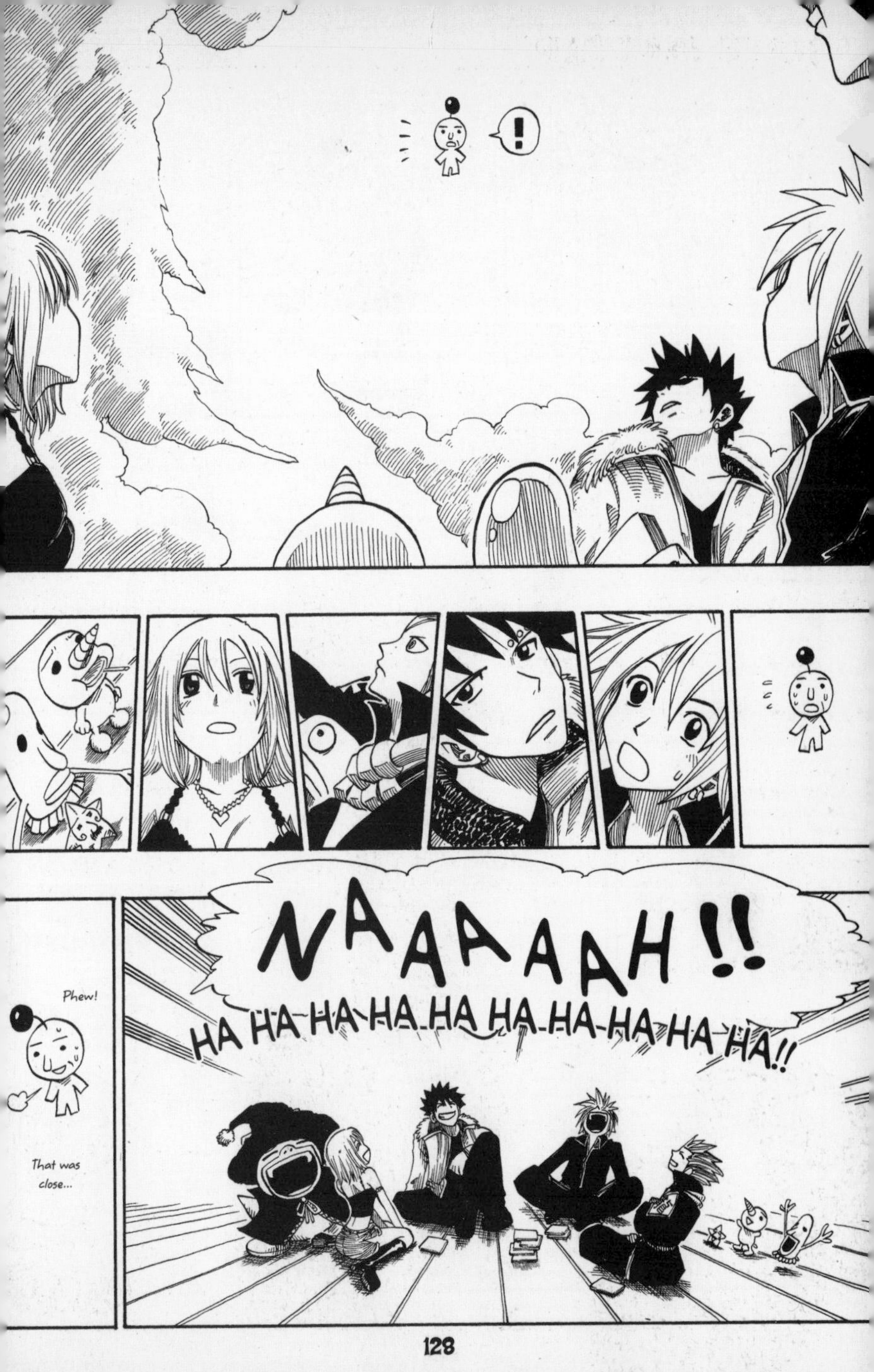
!
NAAAAAH!!
HA HA HA HA HA HA HA HA HA HA HA!!
Phew!
That was close...

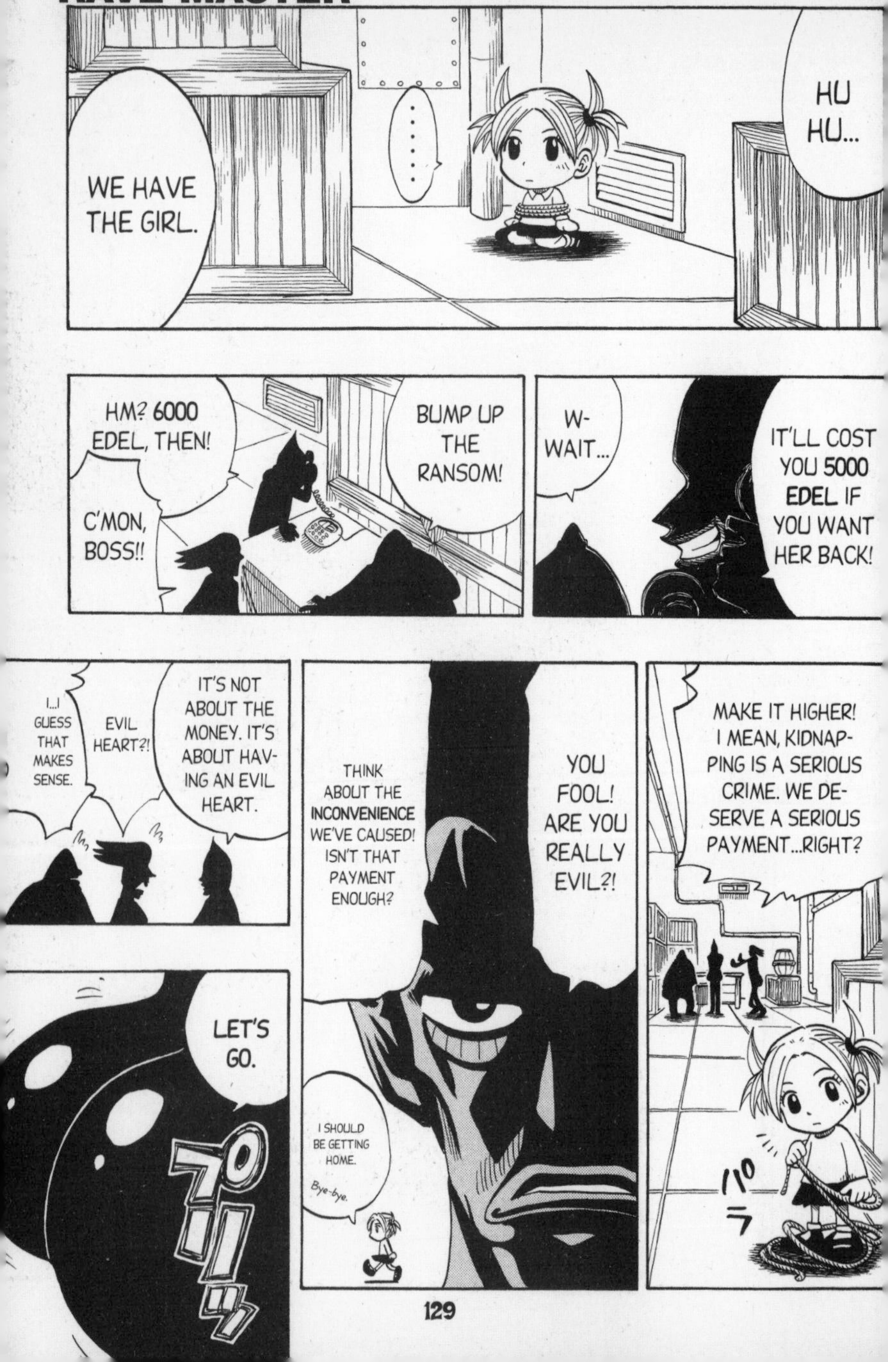
HU HU...
...
WE HAVE THE GIRL.
IT'LL COST YOU 5000 EDEL IF YOU WANT HER BACK!
W-WAIT...
BUMP UP THE RANSOM!
HM? 6000 EDEL, THEN!
C'MON, BOSS!!
MAKE IT HIGHER! I MEAN, KIDNAPPING IS A SERIOUS CRIME. WE DESERVE A SERIOUS PAYMENT...RIGHT?
YOU FOOL! ARE YOU REALLY EVIL?!
THINK ABOUT THE INCONVENIENCE WE'VE CAUSED! ISN'T THAT PAYMENT ENOUGH?
I SHOULD BE GETTING HOME.
Bye-bye.
IT'S NOT ABOUT THE MONEY. IT'S ABOUT HAVING AN EVIL HEART.
EVIL HEART?!
I...I GUESS THAT MAKES SENSE.
LET'S GO.

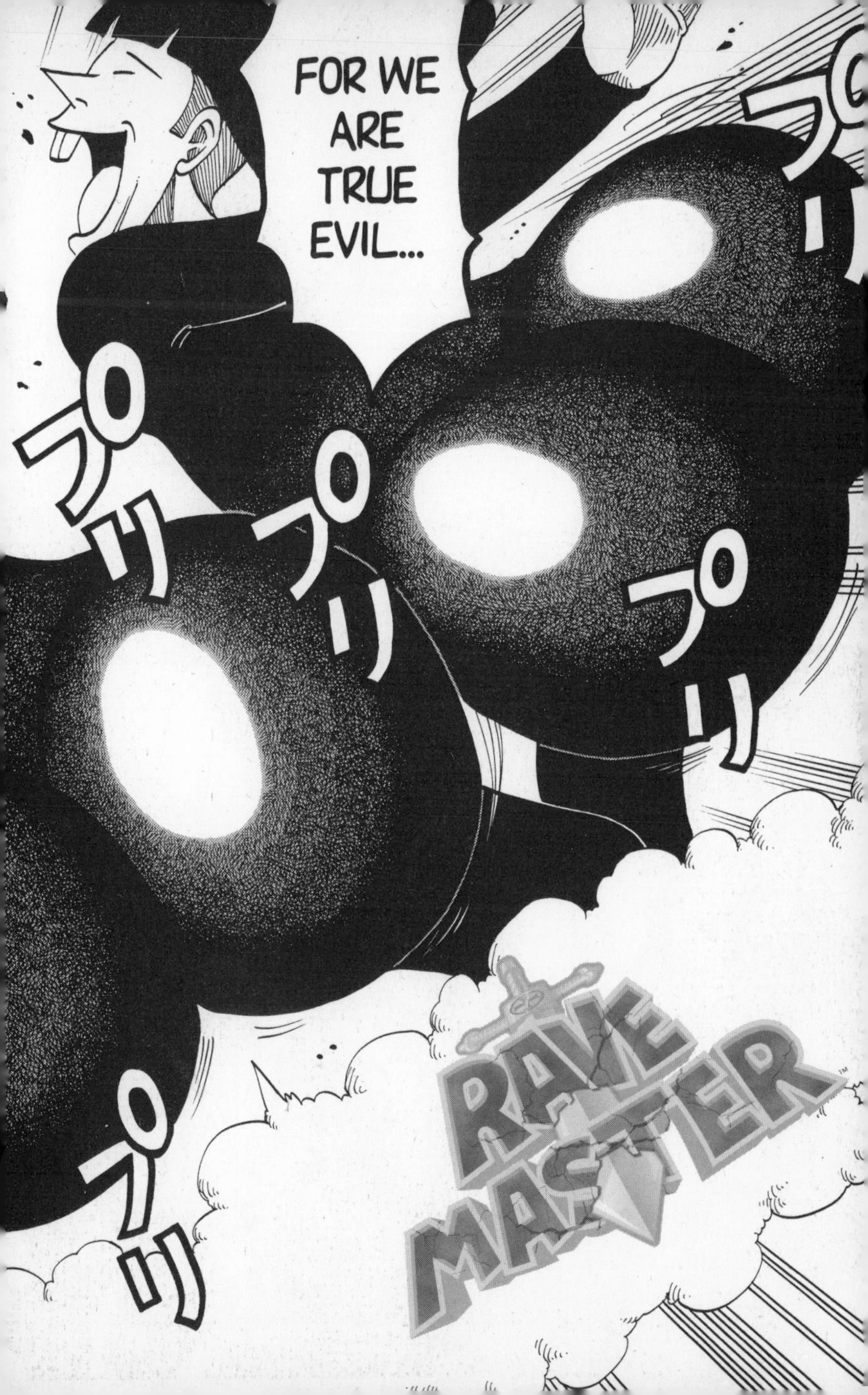
FOR WE ARE TRUE EVIL...
プリ
プリ
プリ
プリ
プリ
RAVE MASTER™

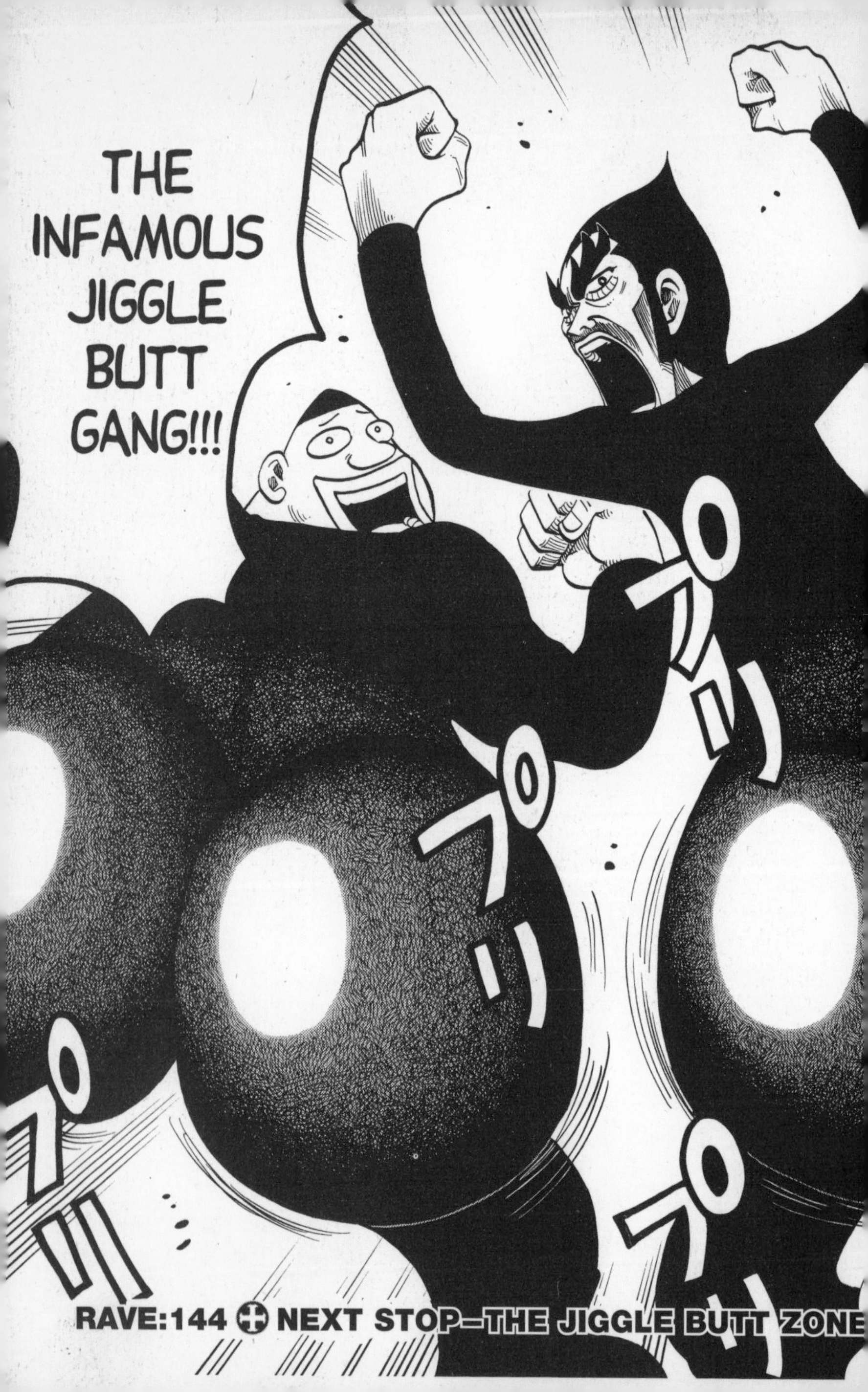
THE INFAMOUS JIGGLE BUTT GANG!!!

RAVE:144 ✚ NEXT STOP—THE JIGGLE BUTT ZONE

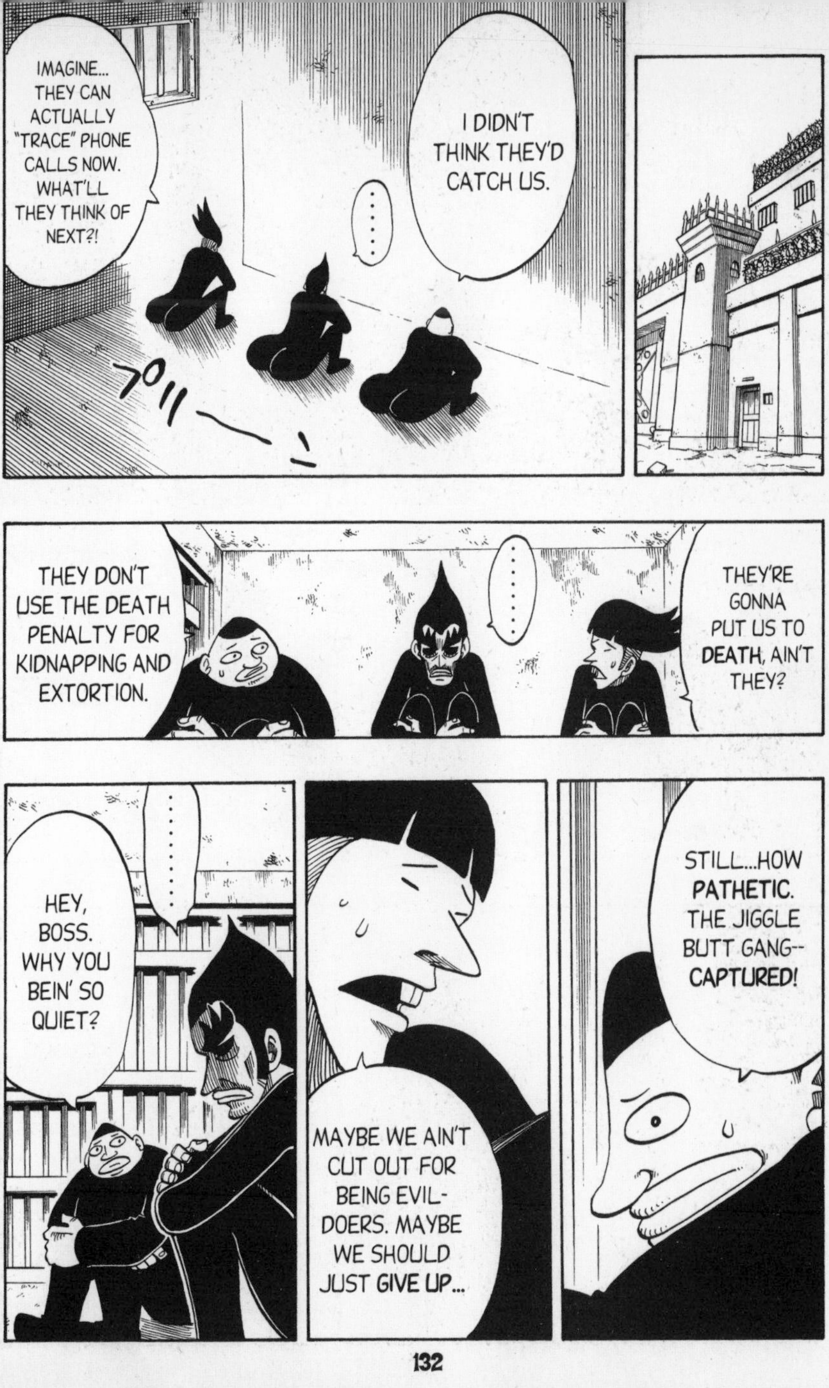
I DIDN'T THINK THEY'D CATCH US.
......
IMAGINE... THEY CAN ACTUALLY "TRACE" PHONE CALLS NOW. WHAT'LL THEY THINK OF NEXT?!
THEY'RE GONNA PUT US TO **DEATH**, AIN'T THEY?
......
THEY DON'T USE THE DEATH PENALTY FOR KIDNAPPING AND EXTORTION.
STILL...HOW **PATHETIC**. THE JIGGLE BUTT GANG--**CAPTURED!**
MAYBE WE AIN'T CUT OUT FOR BEING EVIL-DOERS. MAYBE WE SHOULD JUST **GIVE UP...**
......
HEY, BOSS. WHY YOU BEIN' SO QUIET?

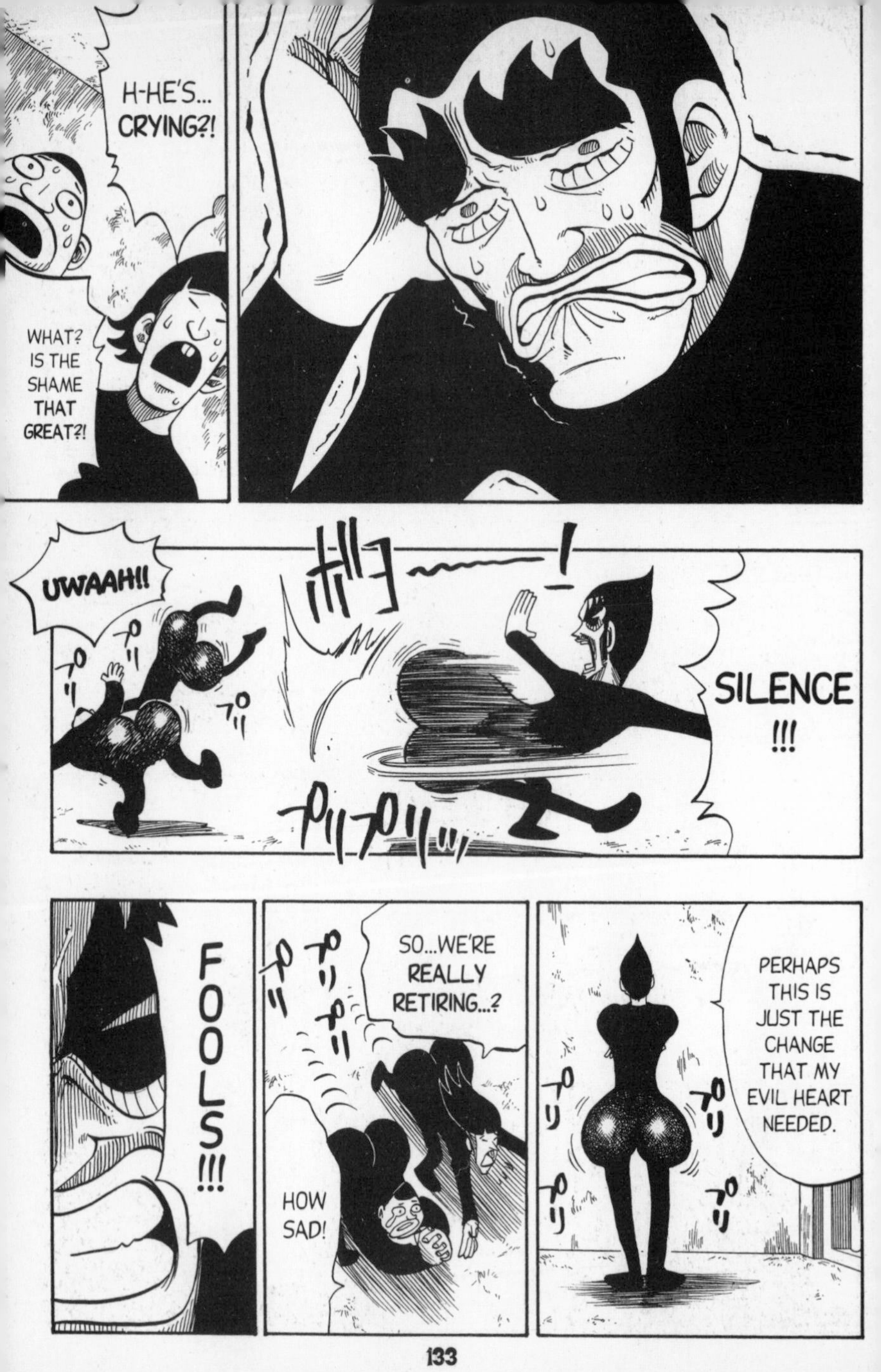
H-HE'S... CRYING?!
WHAT? IS THE SHAME THAT GREAT?!
SILENCE!!!
UWAAH!!
PERHAPS THIS IS JUST THE CHANGE THAT MY EVIL HEART NEEDED.
SO...WE'RE REALLY RETIRING...?
HOW SAD!
FOOLS!!!

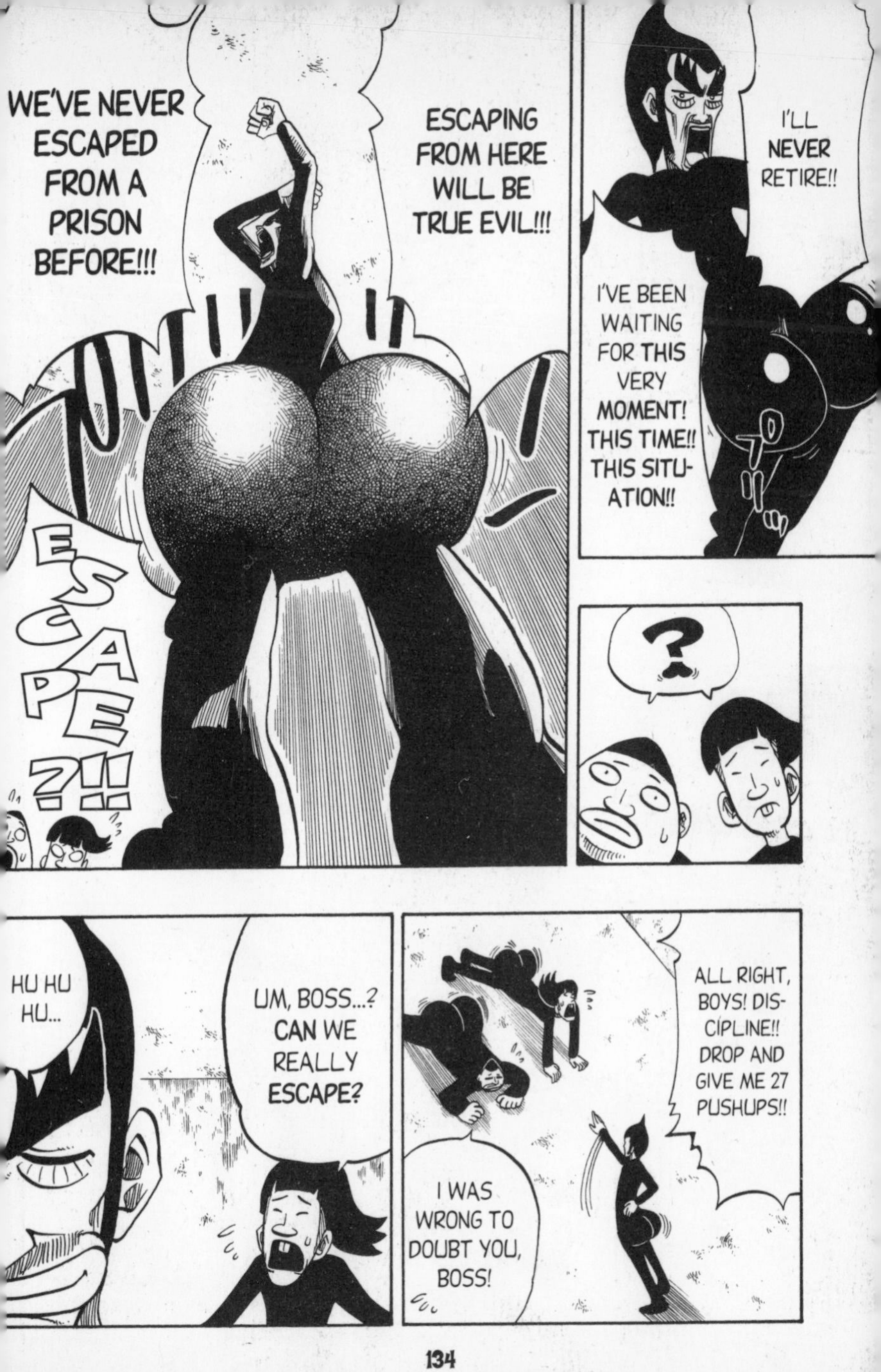
I'LL NEVER RETIRE!!
I'VE BEEN WAITING FOR THIS VERY MOMENT! THIS TIME!! THIS SITU-ATION!!
?
ESCAPING FROM HERE WILL BE TRUE EVIL!!!
WE'VE NEVER ESCAPED FROM A PRISON BEFORE!!!
ESCAPE?!!
ALL RIGHT, BOYS! DIS-CIPLINE!! DROP AND GIVE ME 27 PUSHUPS!!
I WAS WRONG TO DOUBT YOU, BOSS!
UM, BOSS...? CAN WE REALLY ESCAPE?
HU HU HU...

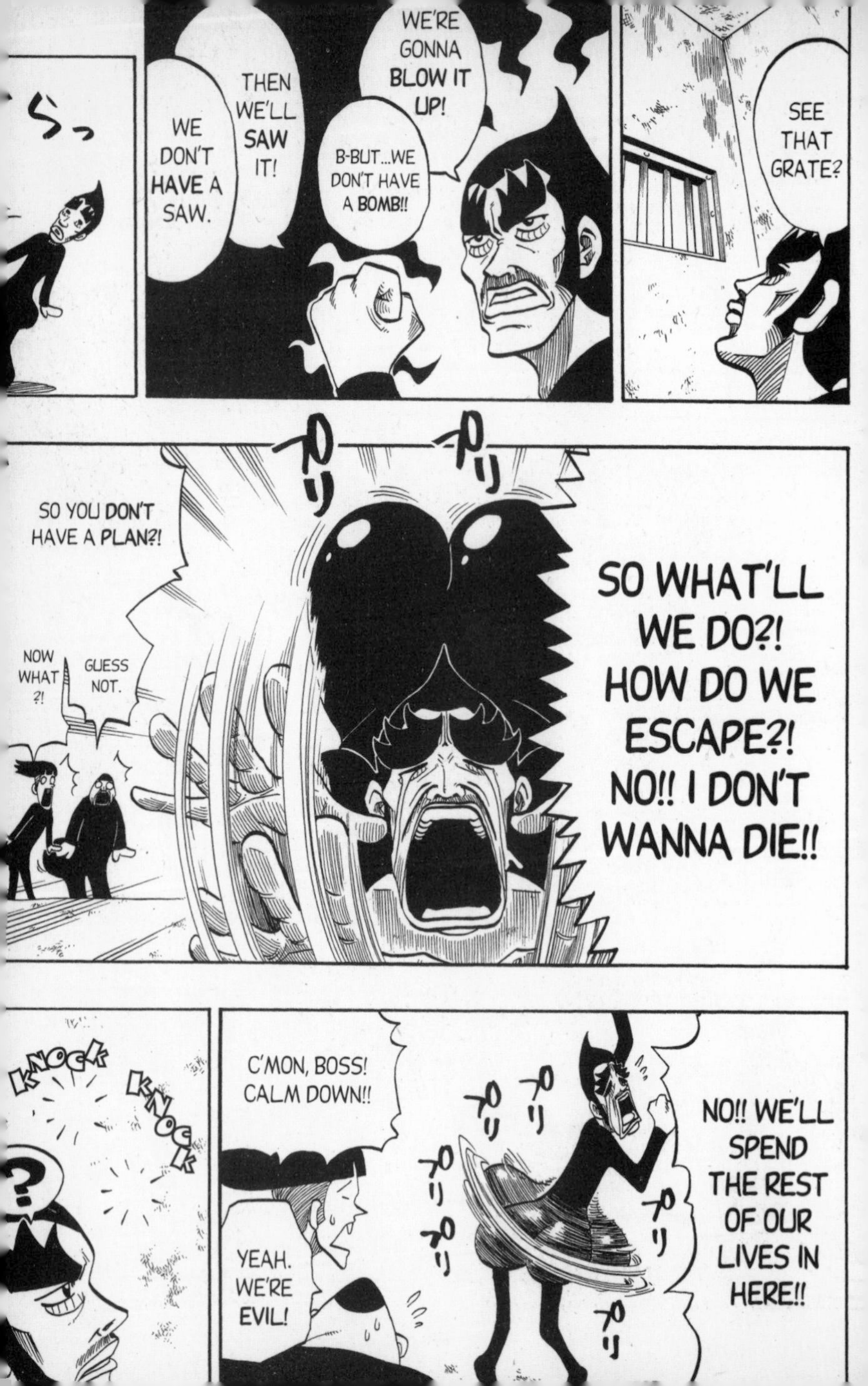
SEE THAT GRATE?
WE'RE GONNA BLOW IT UP!
B-BUT...WE DON'T HAVE A BOMB!!
THEN WE'LL SAW IT!
WE DON'T HAVE A SAW.
らっ
SO WHAT'LL WE DO?! HOW DO WE ESCAPE?! NO!! I DON'T WANNA DIE!!
プリ
プリ
SO YOU DON'T HAVE A PLAN?!
GUESS NOT.
NOW WHAT?!
NO!! WE'LL SPEND THE REST OF OUR LIVES IN HERE!!
プリ
プリ
プリ
プリ
プリ
プリ
C'MON, BOSS! CALM DOWN!!
YEAH. WE'RE EVIL!
KNOCK
KNOCK
?

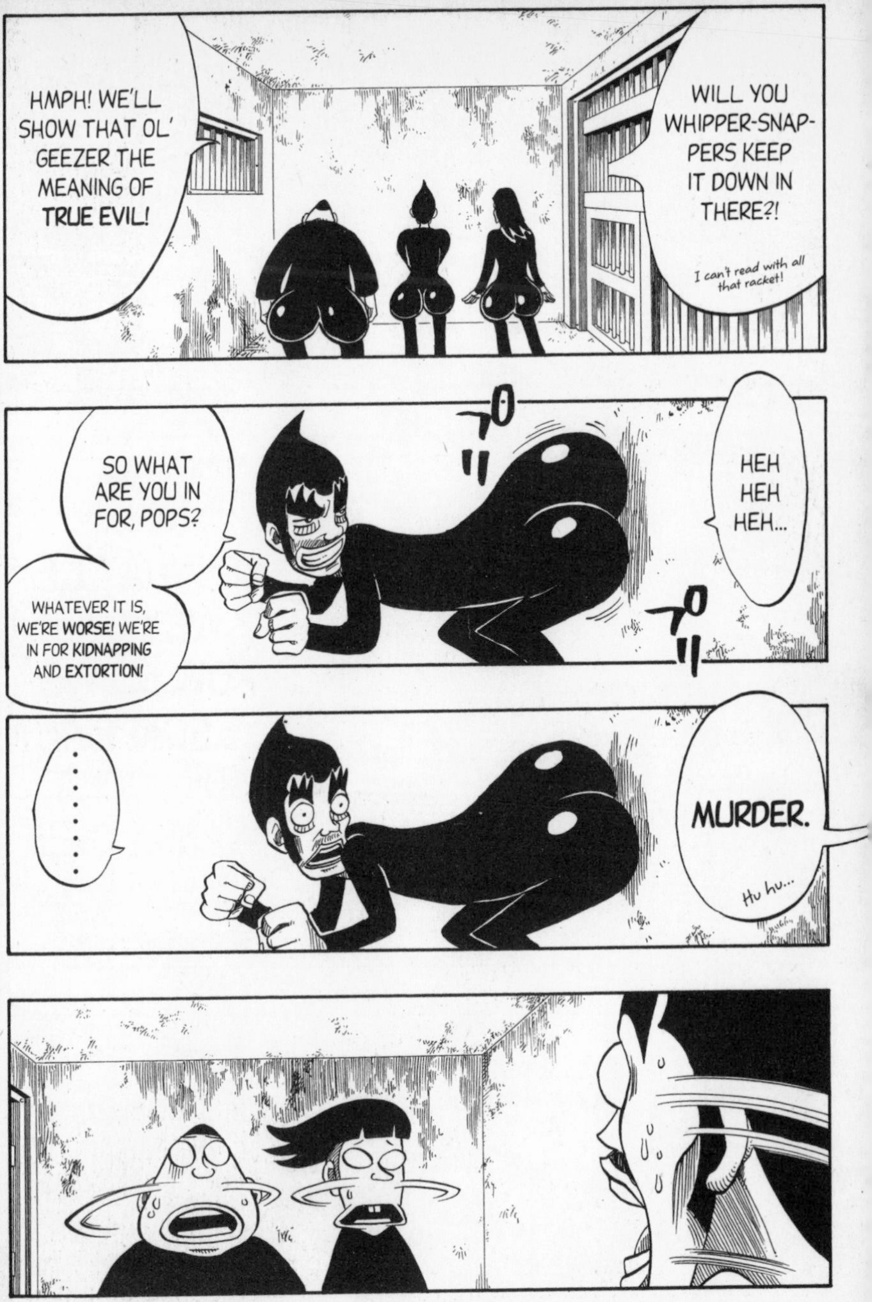
WILL YOU WHIPPER-SNAPPERS KEEP IT DOWN IN THERE?!
I can't read with all that racket!
HMPH! WE'LL SHOW THAT OL' GEEZER THE MEANING OF **TRUE EVIL!**
HEH HEH HEH...
SO WHAT ARE YOU IN FOR, POPS?
WHATEVER IT IS, WE'RE **WORSE!** WE'RE IN FOR **KIDNAPPING** AND **EXTORTION!**
MURDER.
Hu hu...
....

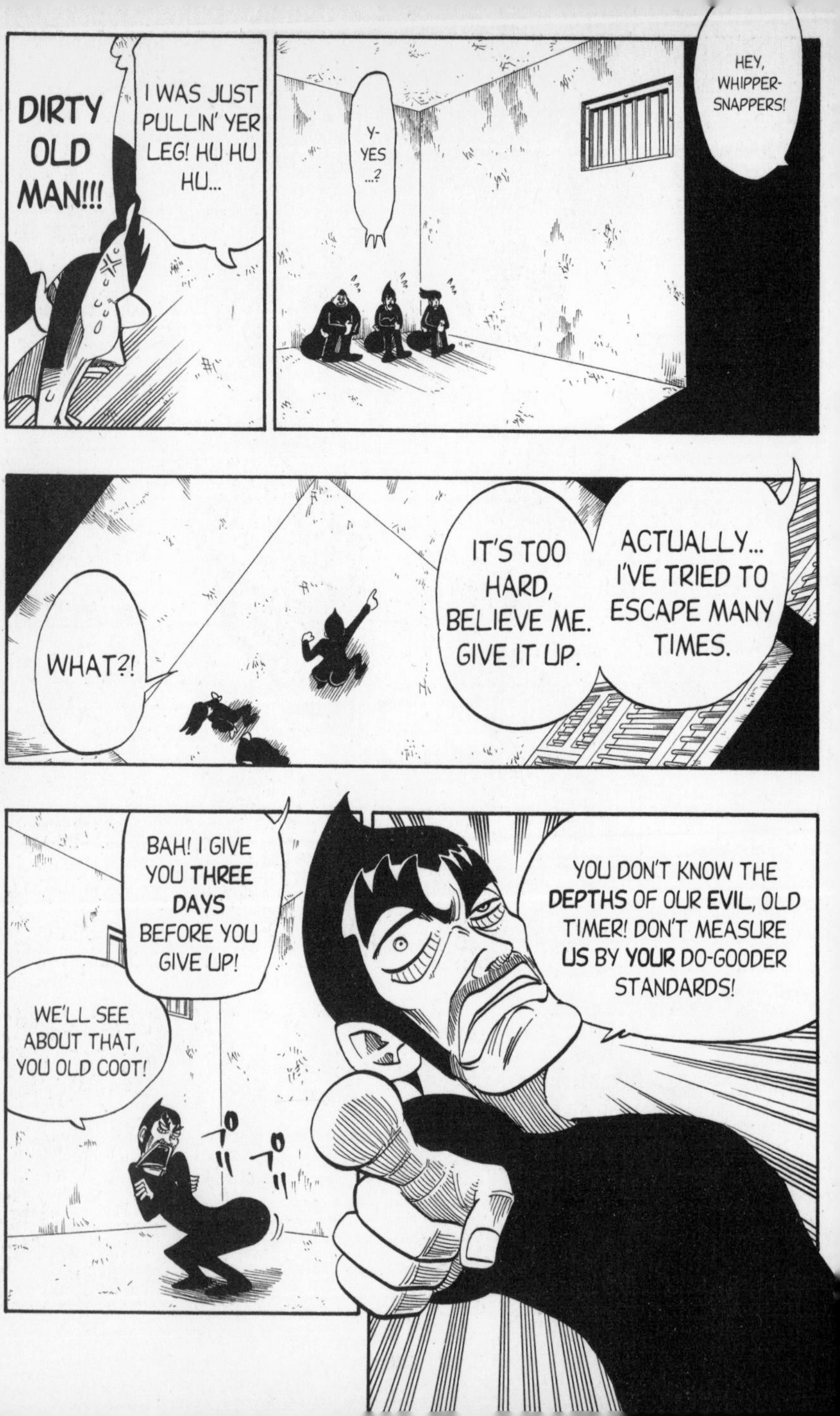
HEY, WHIPPER-SNAPPERS!
Y-YES ...?
I WAS JUST PULLIN' YER LEG! HU HU HU...
DIRTY OLD MAN!!!
ACTUALLY... I'VE TRIED TO ESCAPE MANY TIMES.
IT'S TOO HARD, BELIEVE ME. GIVE IT UP.
WHAT?!
YOU DON'T KNOW THE DEPTHS OF OUR EVIL, OLD TIMER! DON'T MEASURE US BY YOUR DO-GOODER STANDARDS!
BAH! I GIVE YOU THREE DAYS BEFORE YOU GIVE UP!
WE'LL SEE ABOUT THAT, YOU OLD COOT!
プリ
プリ

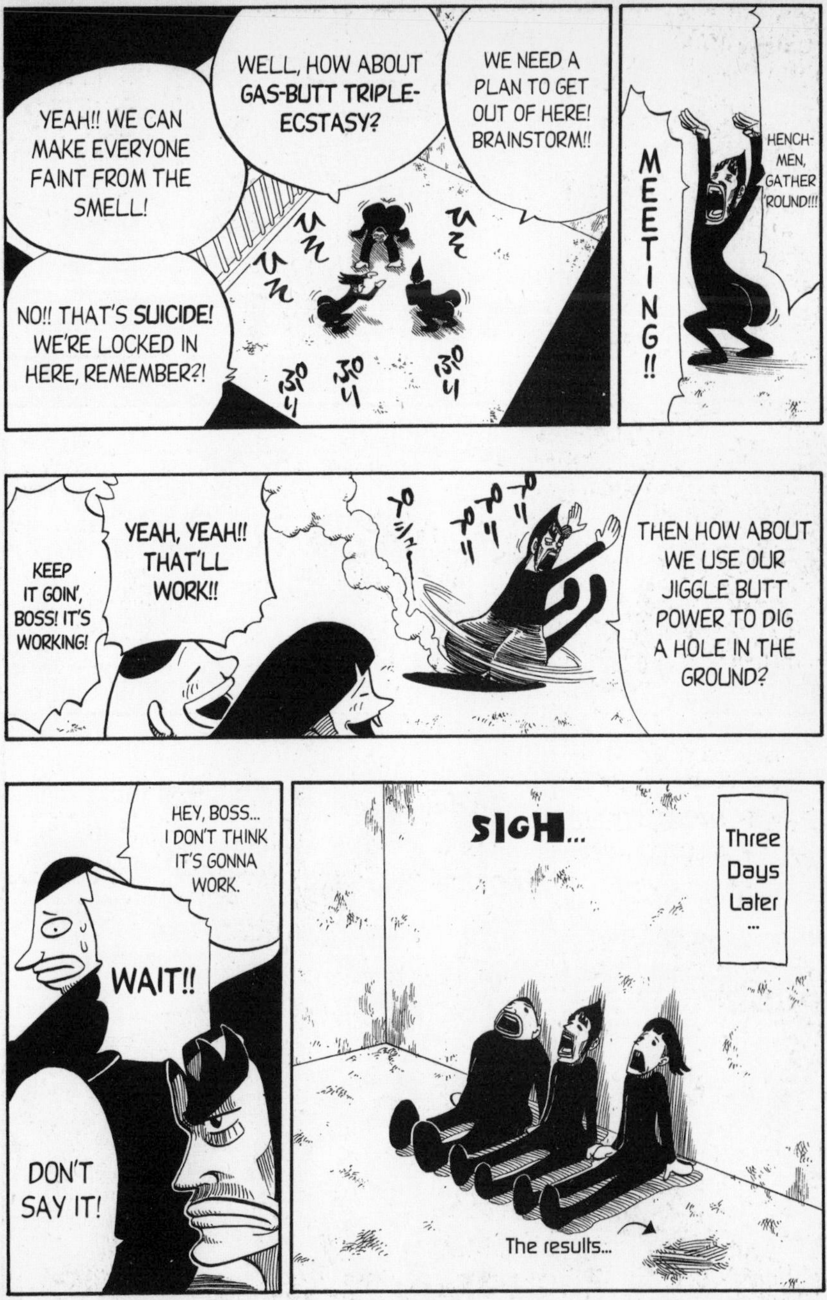
MEETING!!
HENCH-MEN, GATHER 'ROUND!!!
WE NEED A PLAN TO GET OUT OF HERE! BRAINSTORM!!
WELL, HOW ABOUT GAS-BUTT TRIPLE-ECSTASY?
YEAH!! WE CAN MAKE EVERYONE FAINT FROM THE SMELL!
NO!! THAT'S SUICIDE! WE'RE LOCKED IN HERE, REMEMBER?!
THEN HOW ABOUT WE USE OUR JIGGLE BUTT POWER TO DIG A HOLE IN THE GROUND?
YEAH, YEAH!! THAT'LL WORK!!
KEEP IT GOIN', BOSS! IT'S WORKING!
Three Days Later ...
SIGH...
The results...
HEY, BOSS... I DON'T THINK IT'S GONNA WORK.
WAIT!!
DON'T SAY IT!

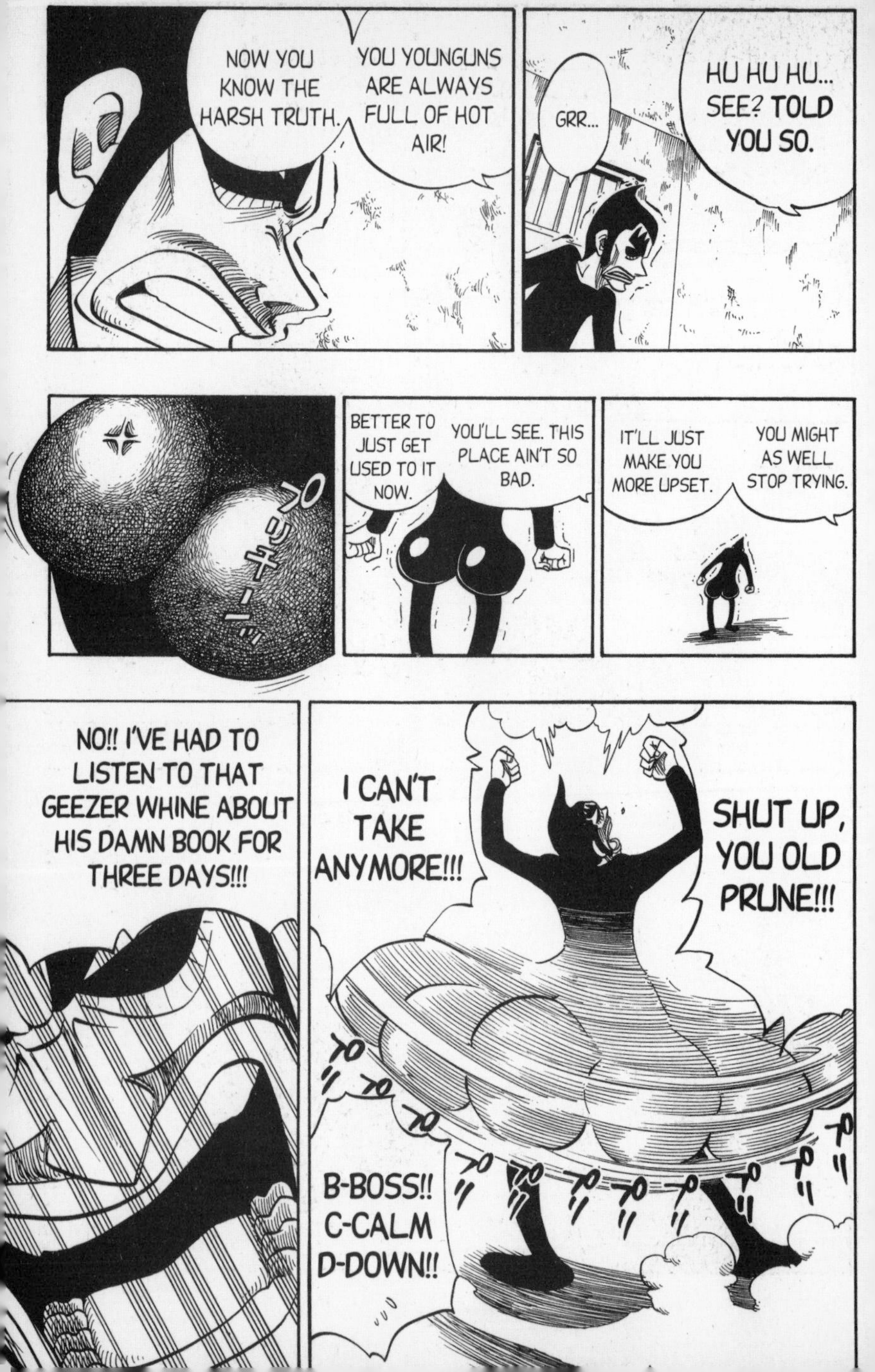
HU HU HU... SEE? TOLD YOU SO.
GRR...
YOU YOUNGUNS ARE ALWAYS FULL OF HOT AIR!
NOW YOU KNOW THE HARSH TRUTH.
YOU MIGHT AS WELL STOP TRYING.
IT'LL JUST MAKE YOU MORE UPSET.
YOU'LL SEE. THIS PLACE AIN'T SO BAD.
BETTER TO JUST GET USED TO IT NOW.
SHUT UP, YOU OLD PRUNE!!!
I CAN'T TAKE ANYMORE!!!
B-BOSS!! C-CALM D-DOWN!!
NO!! I'VE HAD TO LISTEN TO THAT GEEZER WHINE ABOUT HIS DAMN BOOK FOR THREE DAYS!!!

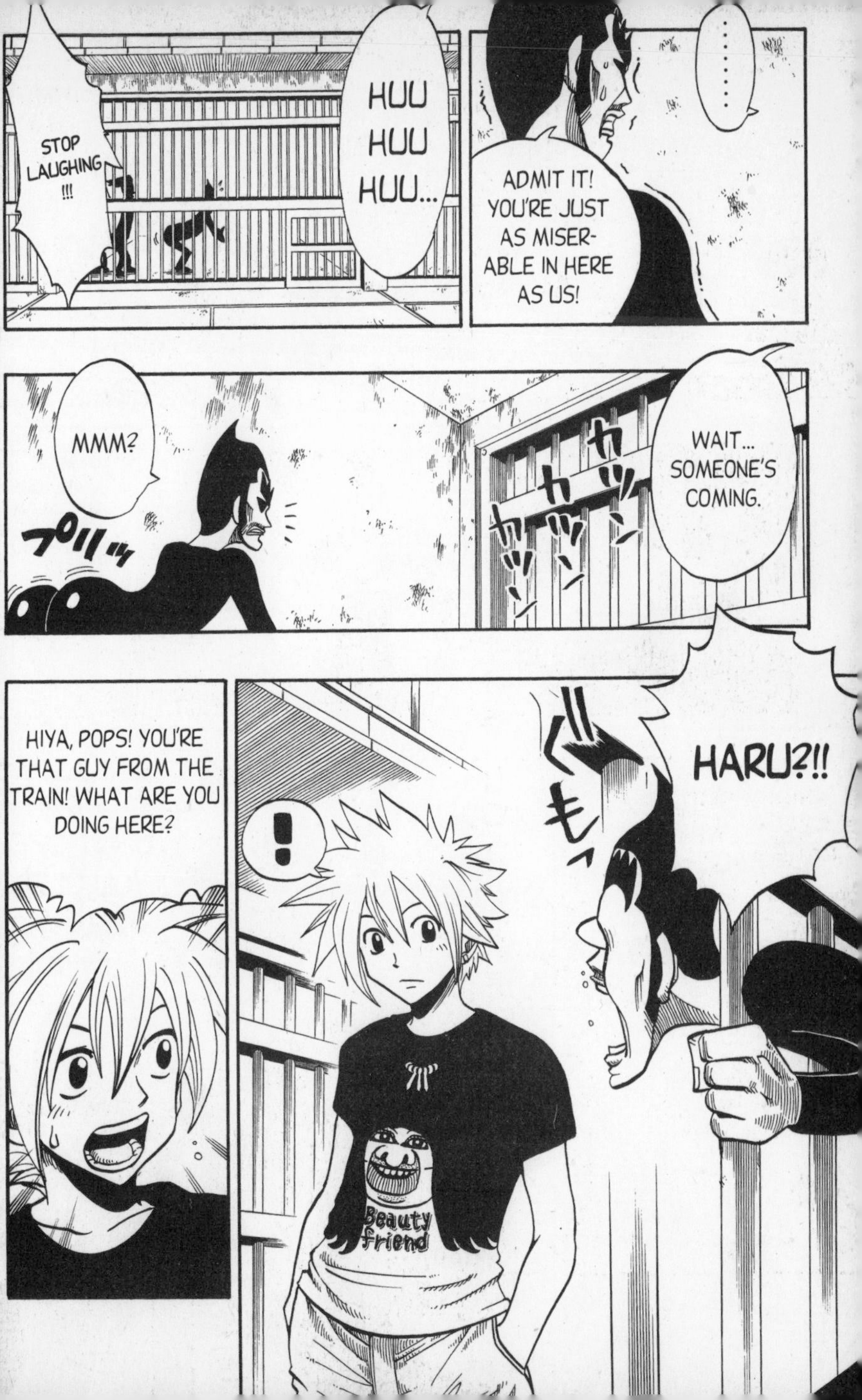

......
ADMIT IT! YOU'RE JUST AS MISER-ABLE IN HERE AS US!
HUU HUU HUU...
STOP LAUGHING !!!
WAIT... SOMEONE'S COMING.
MMM?
HARU?!!
!
HIYA, POPS! YOU'RE THAT GUY FROM THE TRAIN! WHAT ARE YOU DOING HERE?
Beauty friend

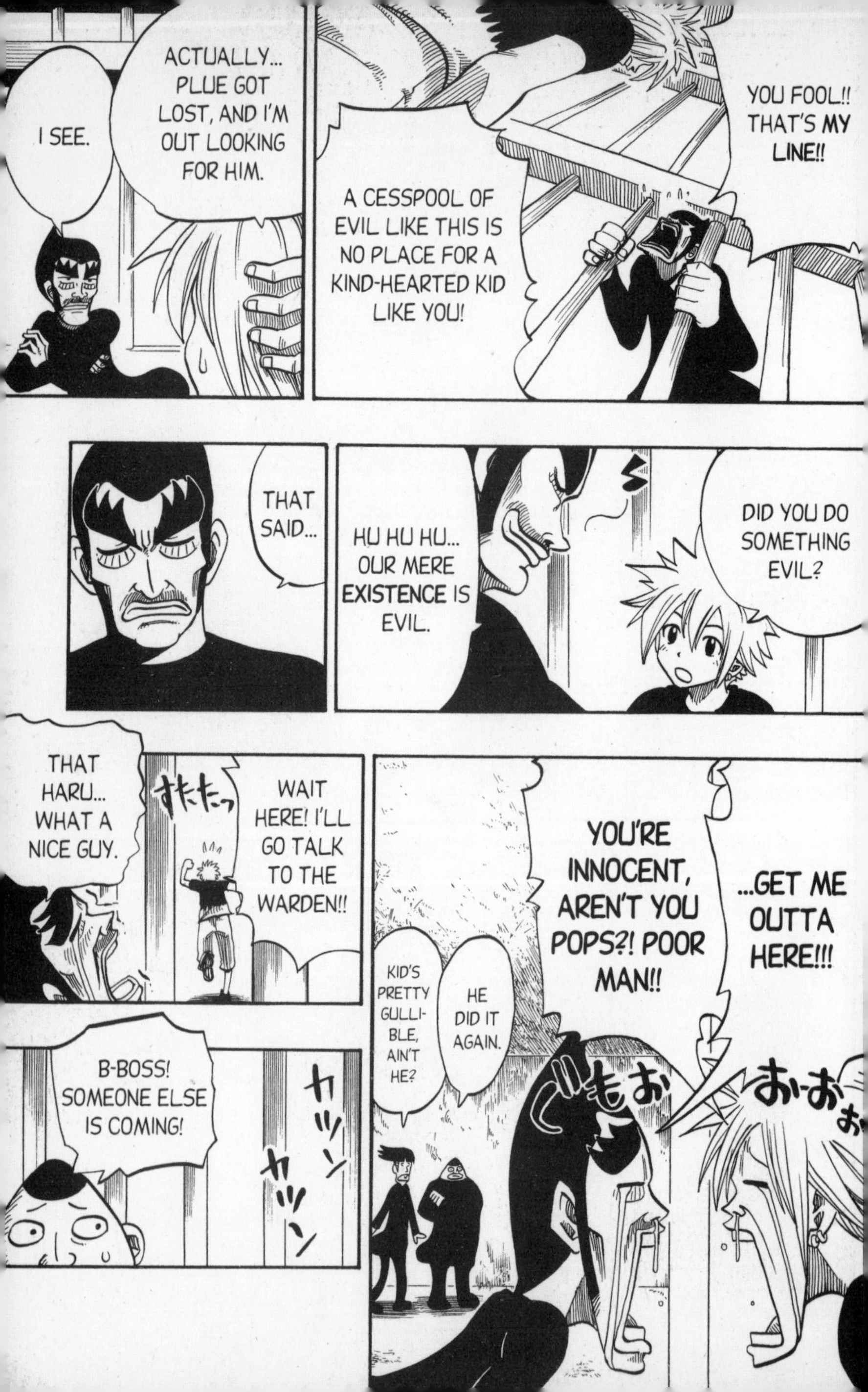
YOU FOOL!! THAT'S MY LINE!!
A CESSPOOL OF EVIL LIKE THIS IS NO PLACE FOR A KIND-HEARTED KID LIKE YOU!
ACTUALLY... PLUE GOT LOST, AND I'M OUT LOOKING FOR HIM.
I SEE.
DID YOU DO SOMETHING EVIL?
HU HU HU... OUR MERE EXISTENCE IS EVIL.
THAT SAID...
...GET ME OUTTA HERE!!!
YOU'RE INNOCENT, AREN'T YOU POPS?! POOR MAN!!
おーおぉ
ぐもぉ
HE DID IT AGAIN.
KID'S PRETTY GULLI-BLE, AIN'T HE?
WAIT HERE! I'LL GO TALK TO THE WARDEN!!
すたたっ
THAT HARU... WHAT A NICE GUY.
カッン
カッン
B-BOSS! SOMEONE ELSE IS COMING!

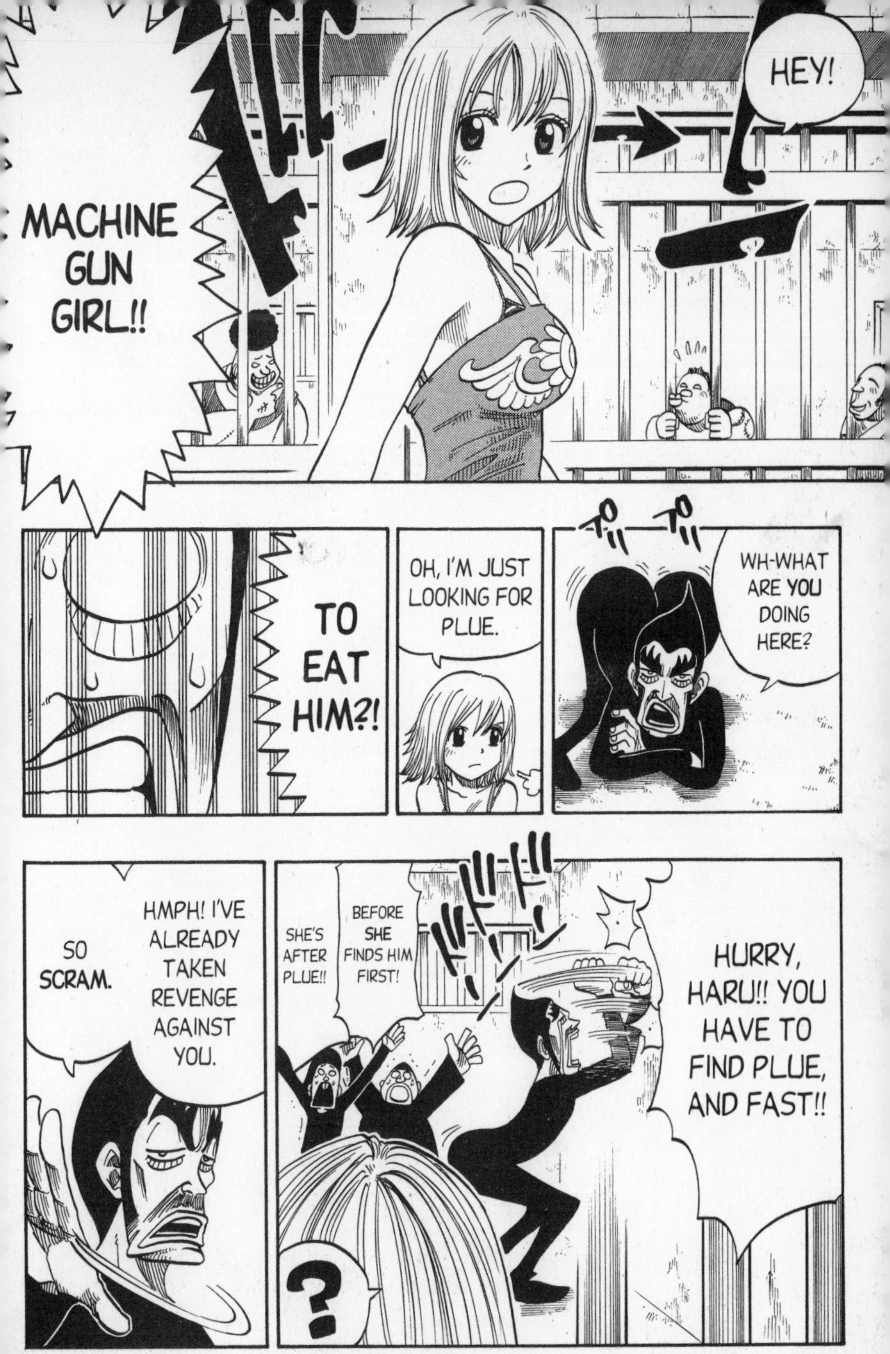
HEY!
MACHINE GUN GIRL!!
WH-WHAT ARE YOU DOING HERE?
OH, I'M JUST LOOKING FOR PLUE.
TO EAT HIM?!
HURRY, HARU!! YOU HAVE TO FIND PLUE, AND FAST!!
BEFORE SHE FINDS HIM FIRST!
SHE'S AFTER PLUE!!
?
HMPH! I'VE ALREADY TAKEN REVENGE AGAINST YOU.
SO SCRAM.

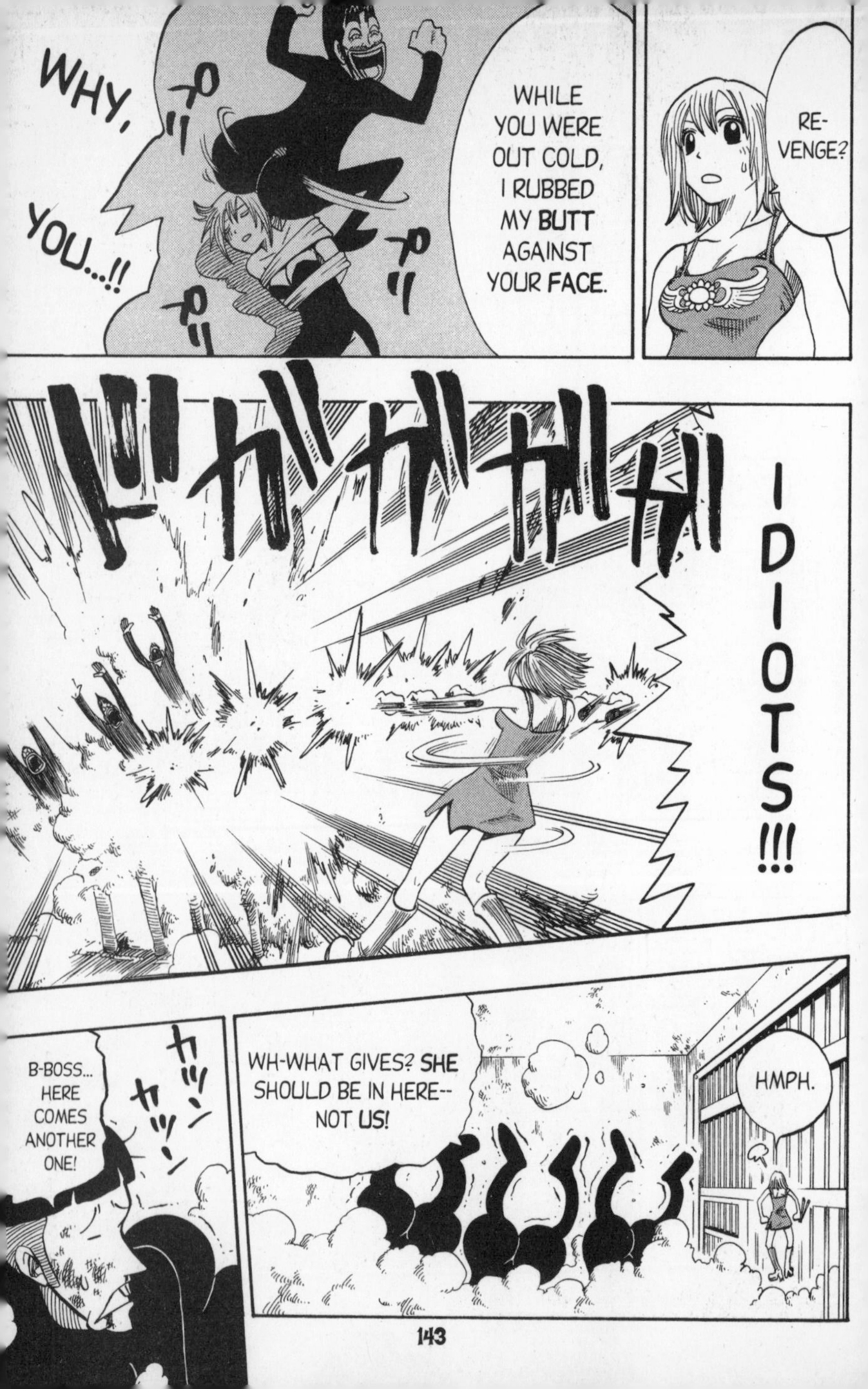
RE-
VENGE?
WHILE YOU WERE OUT COLD, I RUBBED MY BUTT AGAINST YOUR FACE.
プリ
プリ
プリ
WHY, YOU...!!
ドガガガガ
IDIOTS!!!
HMPH.
WH-WHAT GIVES? SHE SHOULD BE IN HERE-- NOT US!
カッ
カッ
B-BOSS... HERE COMES ANOTHER ONE!

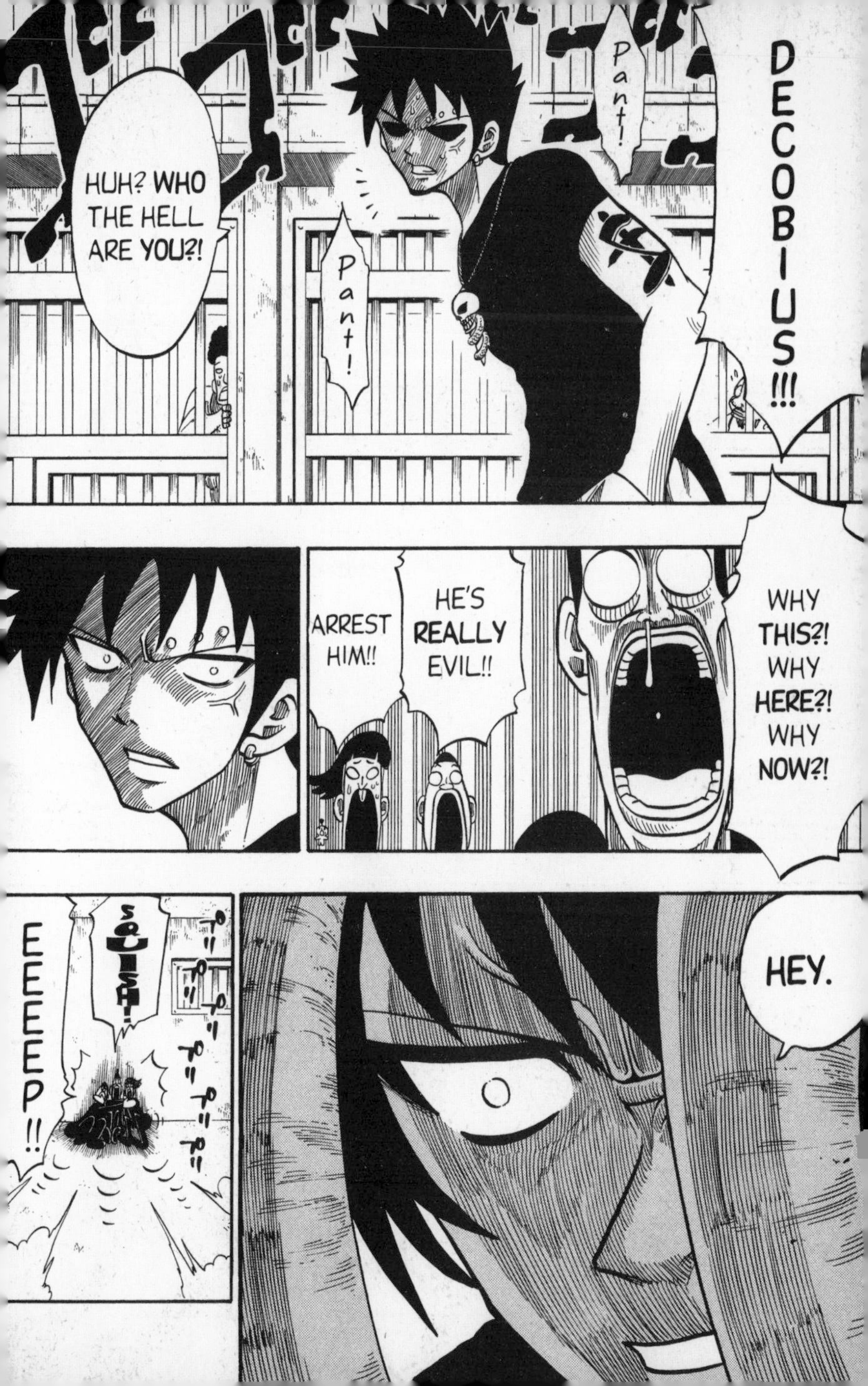
DECOBIUS!!!
Pant!
Pant!
HUH? WHO THE HELL ARE YOU?!
WHY THIS?! WHY HERE?! WHY NOW?!
HE'S REALLY EVIL!!
ARREST HIM!!
HEY.
SQUISH!
EEEEP!!

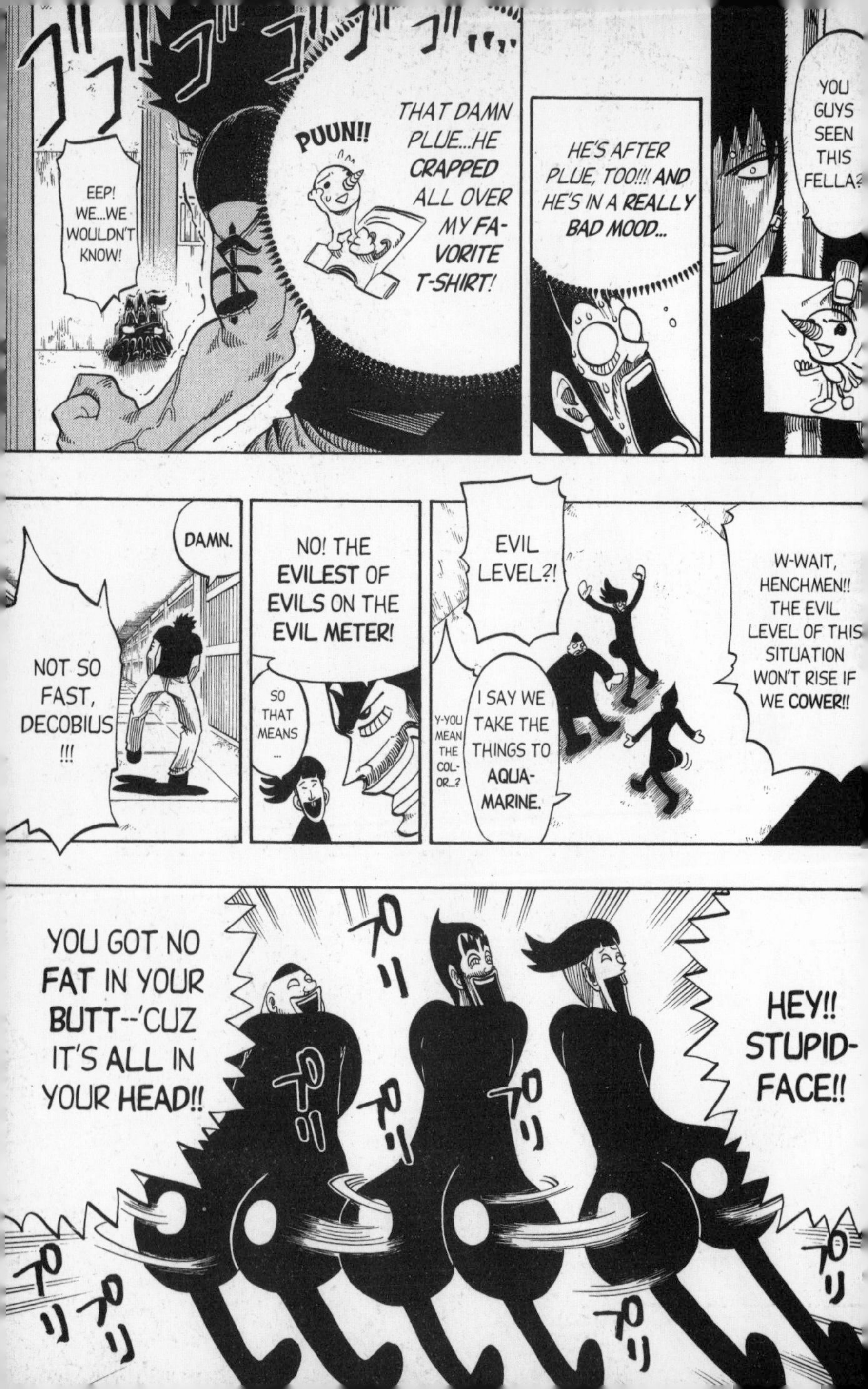

YOU GUYS SEEN THIS FELLA?
HE'S AFTER PLUE, TOO!!! AND HE'S IN A REALLY BAD MOOD...
THAT DAMN PLUE...HE CRAPPED ALL OVER MY FAVORITE T-SHIRT!
PUUN!!
EEP! WE...WE WOULDN'T KNOW!
W-WAIT, HENCHMEN!! THE EVIL LEVEL OF THIS SITUATION WON'T RISE IF WE COWER!!
EVIL LEVEL?!
I SAY WE TAKE THE THINGS TO AQUAMARINE.
Y-YOU MEAN THE COLOR...?
NO! THE EVILEST OF EVILS ON THE EVIL METER!
SO THAT MEANS ...
DAMN.
NOT SO FAST, DECOBIUS!!!
HEY!! STUPID-FACE!!
YOU GOT NO FAT IN YOUR BUTT--'CUZ IT'S ALL IN YOUR HEAD!!

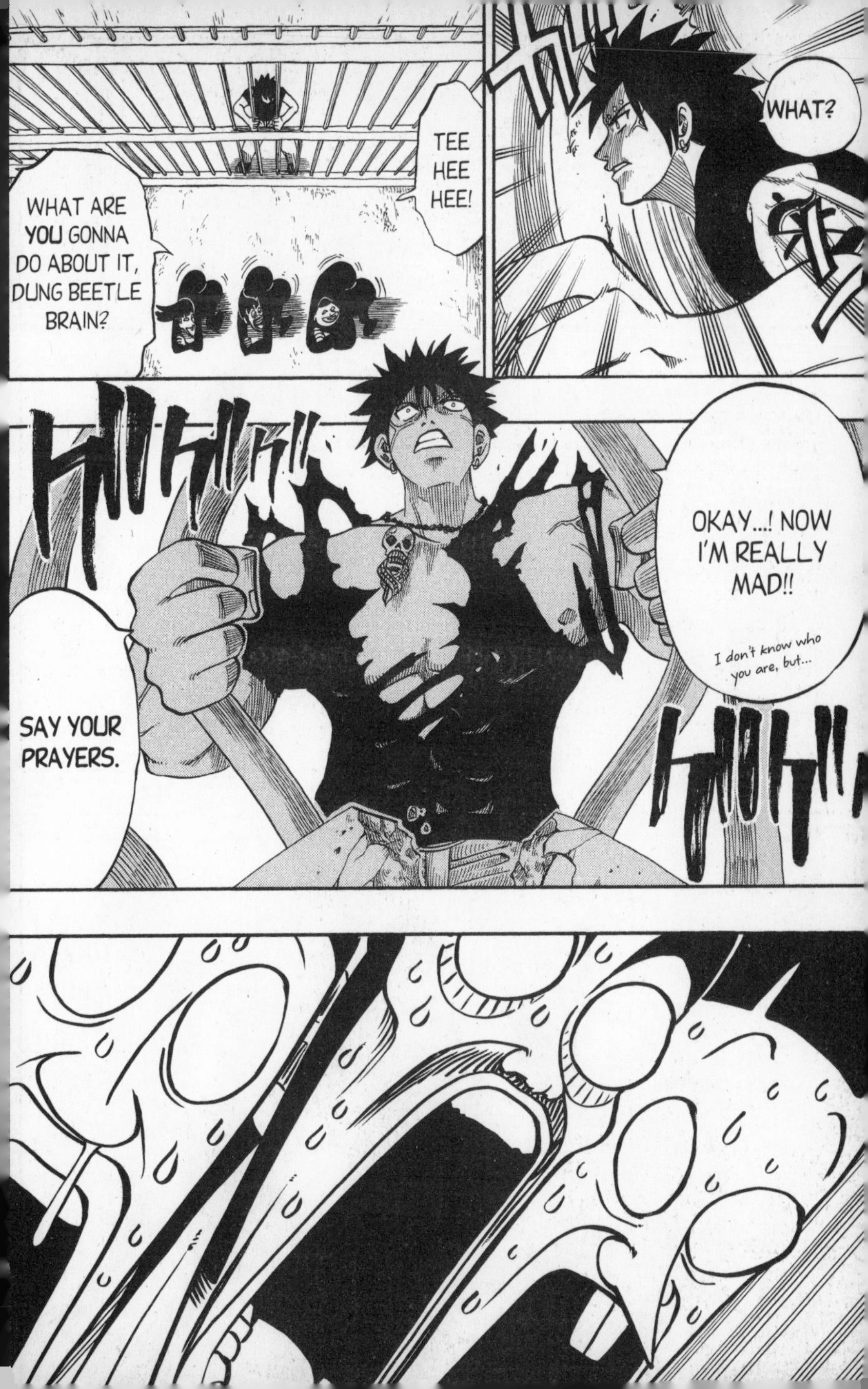
WHAT?
TEE HEE HEE!
WHAT ARE YOU GONNA DO ABOUT IT, DUNG BEETLE BRAIN?
OKAY...! NOW I'M REALLY MAD!!
I don't know who you are, but...
SAY YOUR PRAYERS.

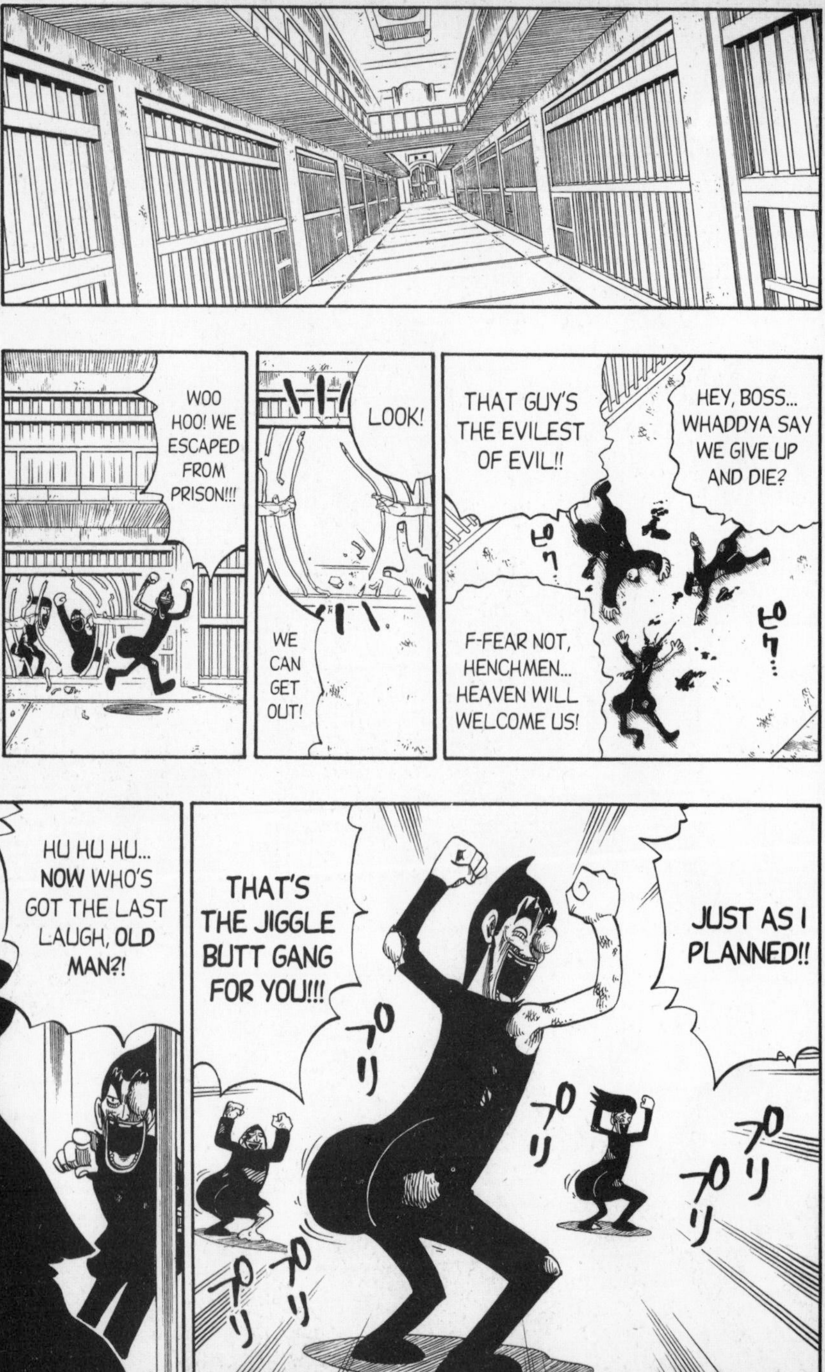
HEY, BOSS... WHADDYA SAY WE GIVE UP AND DIE?
THAT GUY'S THE EVILEST OF EVIL!!
ピク
ピク…
F-FEAR NOT, HENCHMEN... HEAVEN WILL WELCOME US!
LOOK!
WE CAN GET OUT!
WOO HOO! WE ESCAPED FROM PRISON!!!
JUST AS I PLANNED!!
THAT'S THE JIGGLE BUTT GANG FOR YOU!!!
プリ
プリ
プリ
プリ
プリ
プリ
HU HU HU... NOW WHO'S GOT THE LAST LAUGH, OLD MAN?!

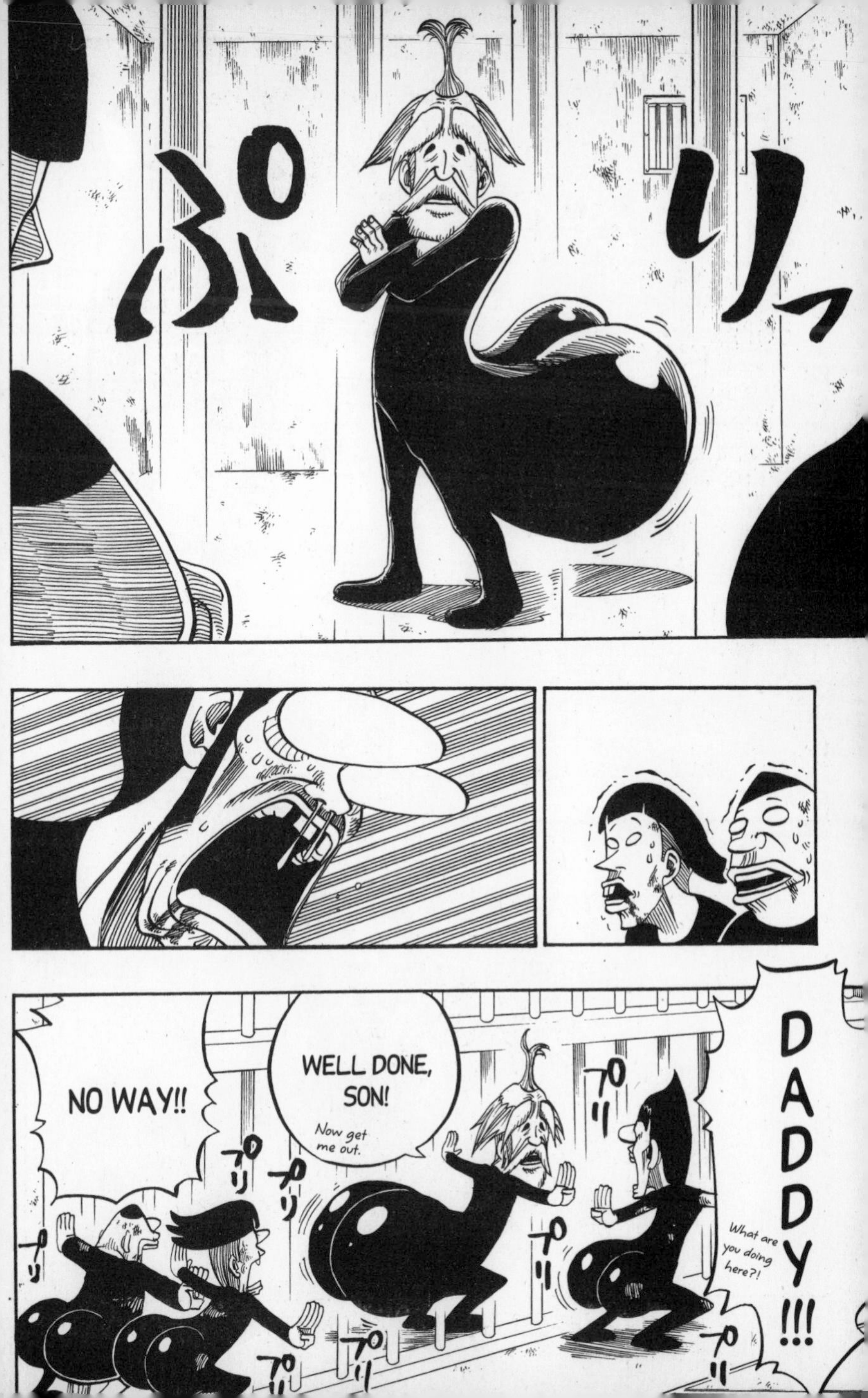
ぷりっ
DADDY!!!
What are you doing here?!
WELL DONE, SON!
Now get me out.
NO WAY!!
プリ
プリ
プリ
プリ
プリ
プリ
プリ
プリ

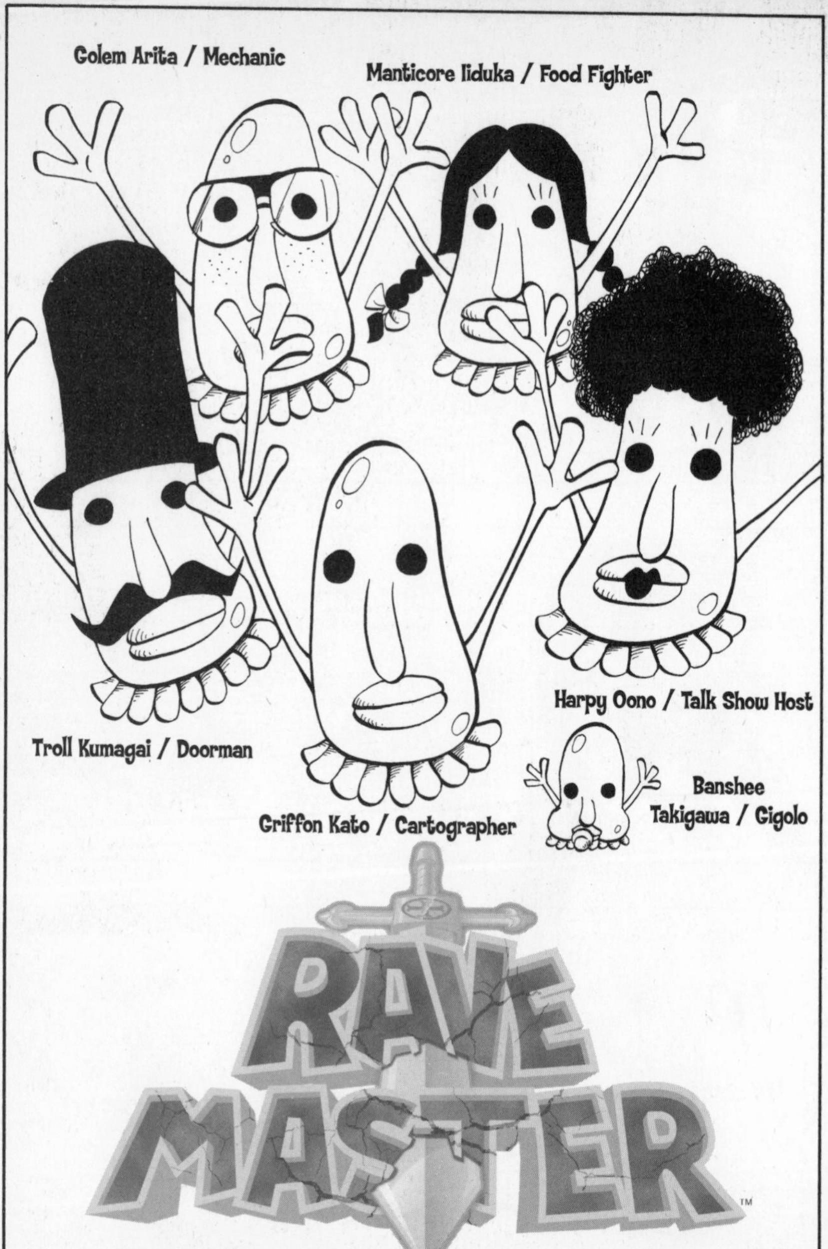
Golem Arita / Mechanic
Manticore Iiduka / Food Fighter
Harpy Oono / Talk Show Host
Troll Kumagai / Doorman
Banshee Takigawa / Gigolo
Griffon Kato / Cartographer
RAVE MASTER™

RAVE:145 ✠ INSPECTING THE HORROR

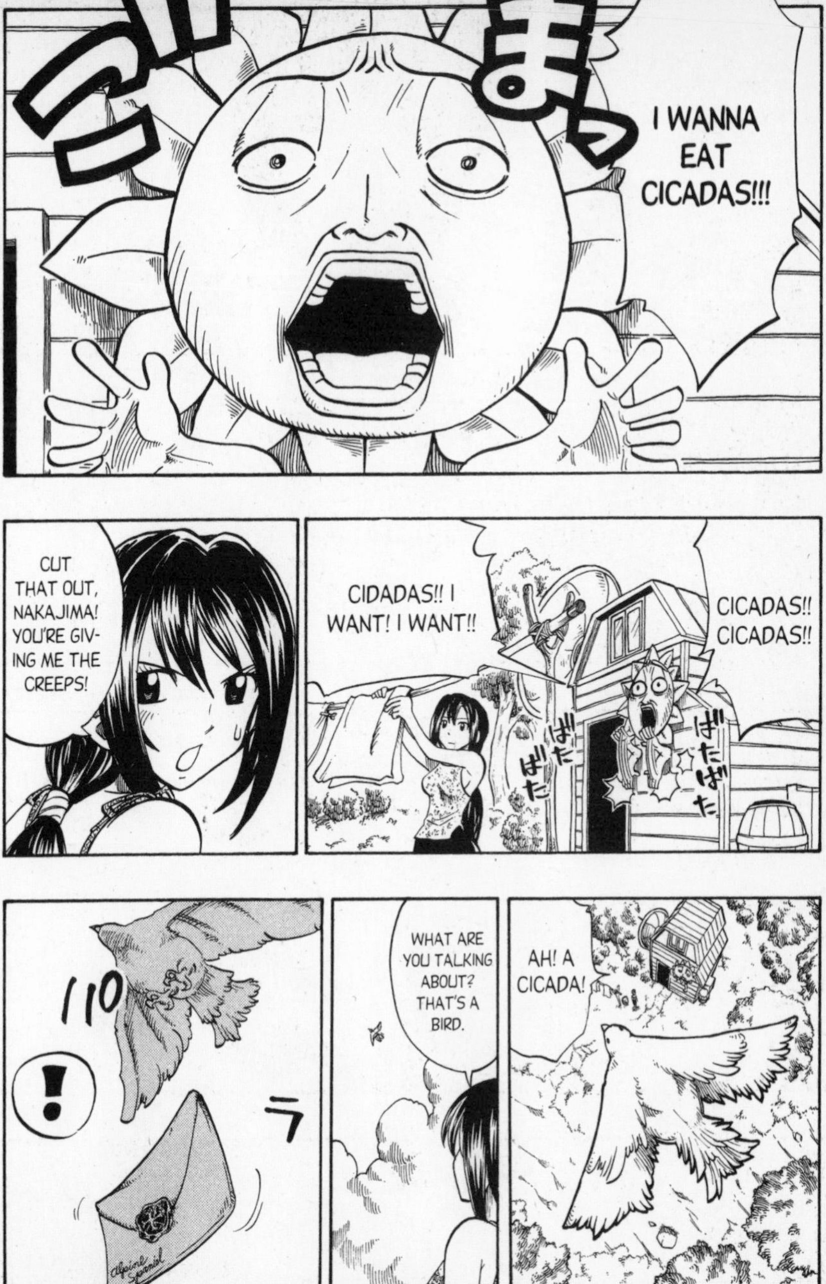
I WANNA EAT CICADAS!!!
CICADAS!! CICADAS!!
CIDADAS!! I WANT! I WANT!!
ばたばた
ばたばた
CUT THAT OUT, NAKAJIMA! YOU'RE GIVING ME THE CREEPS!
AH! A CICADA!
WHAT ARE YOU TALKING ABOUT? THAT'S A BIRD.
!

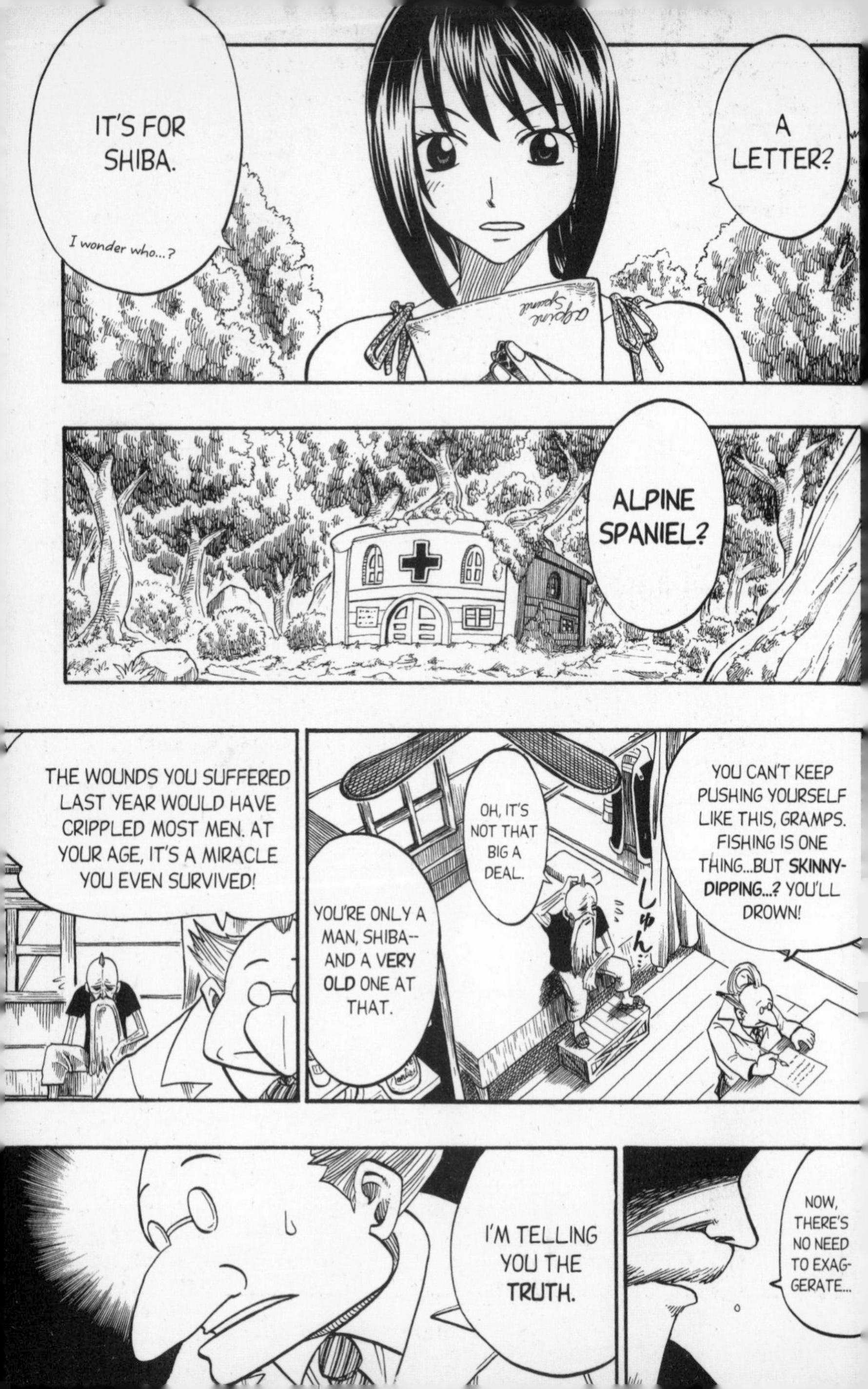
A LETTER?
IT'S FOR SHIBA.
I wonder who...?
ALPINE SPANIEL?
YOU CAN'T KEEP PUSHING YOURSELF LIKE THIS, GRAMPS. FISHING IS ONE THING...BUT SKINNY-DIPPING...? YOU'LL DROWN!
OH, IT'S NOT THAT BIG A DEAL.
しゅん...
YOU'RE ONLY A MAN, SHIBA-- AND A VERY OLD ONE AT THAT.
THE WOUNDS YOU SUFFERED LAST YEAR WOULD HAVE CRIPPLED MOST MEN. AT YOUR AGE, IT'S A MIRACLE YOU EVEN SURVIVED!
NOW, THERE'S NO NEED TO EXAG-GERATE...
I'M TELLING YOU THE TRUTH.

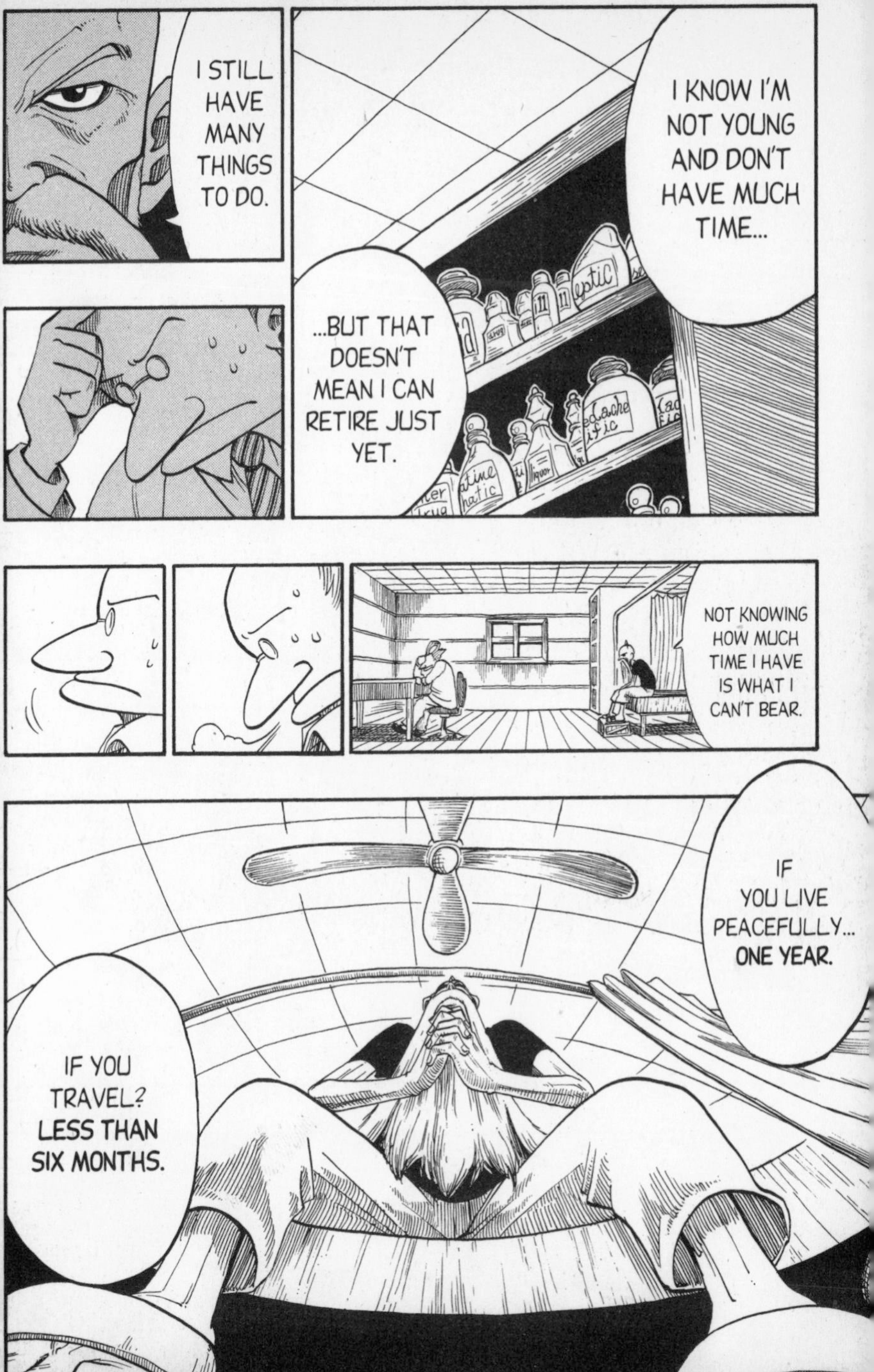
I KNOW I'M NOT YOUNG AND DON'T HAVE MUCH TIME...
...BUT THAT DOESN'T MEAN I CAN RETIRE JUST YET.
I STILL HAVE MANY THINGS TO DO.
NOT KNOWING HOW MUCH TIME I HAVE IS WHAT I CAN'T BEAR.
IF YOU LIVE PEACEFULLY... **ONE YEAR.**
IF YOU TRAVEL? **LESS THAN SIX MONTHS.**

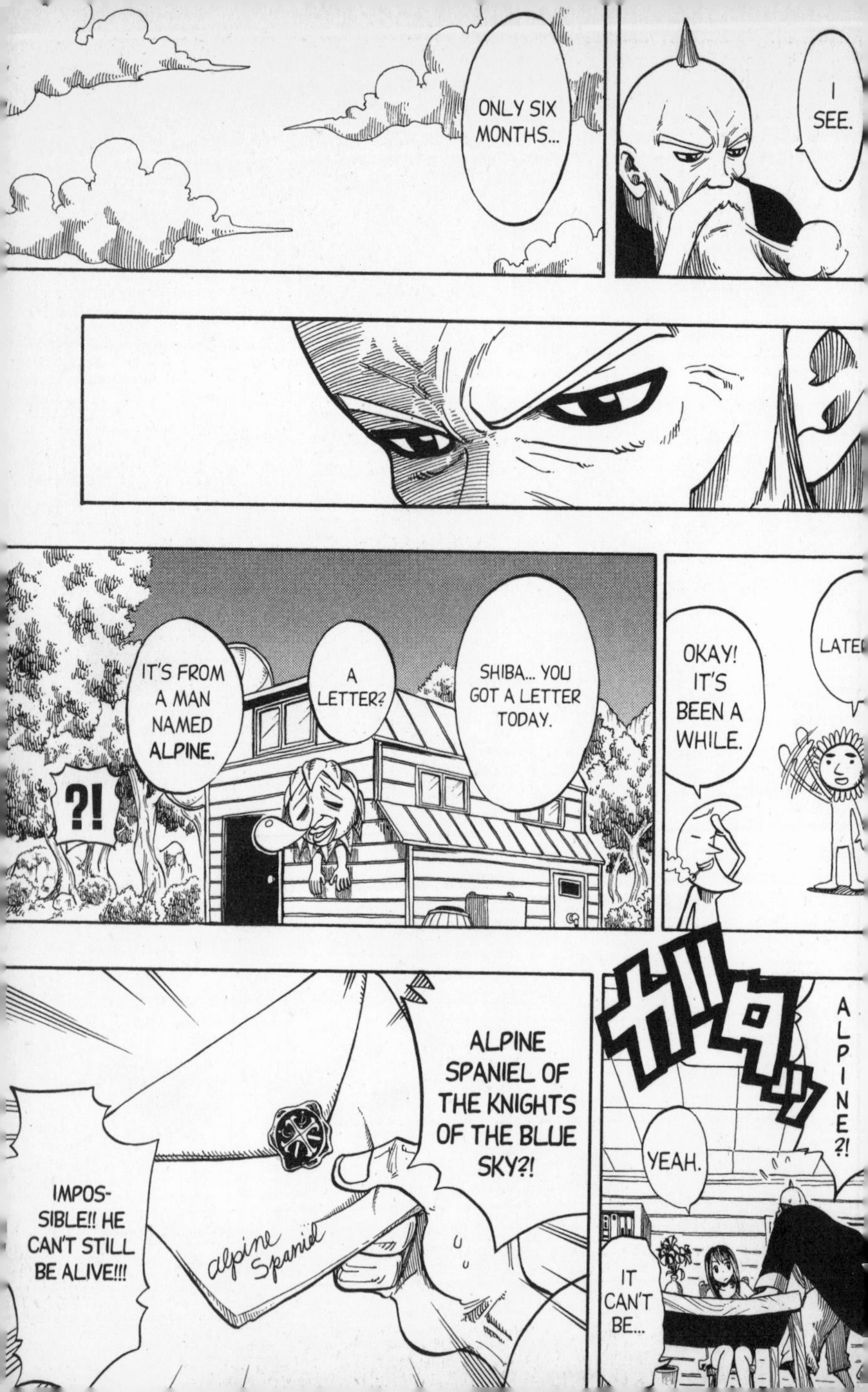
I SEE.
ONLY SIX MONTHS...
LATE
OKAY! IT'S BEEN A WHILE.
SHIBA... YOU GOT A LETTER TODAY.
A LETTER?
IT'S FROM A MAN NAMED ALPINE.
?!
ALPINE?!
ガタッ
YEAH.
IT CAN'T BE...
ALPINE SPANIEL OF THE KNIGHTS OF THE BLUE SKY?!
alpine Spaniel
IMPOSSIBLE!! HE CAN'T STILL BE ALIVE!!!

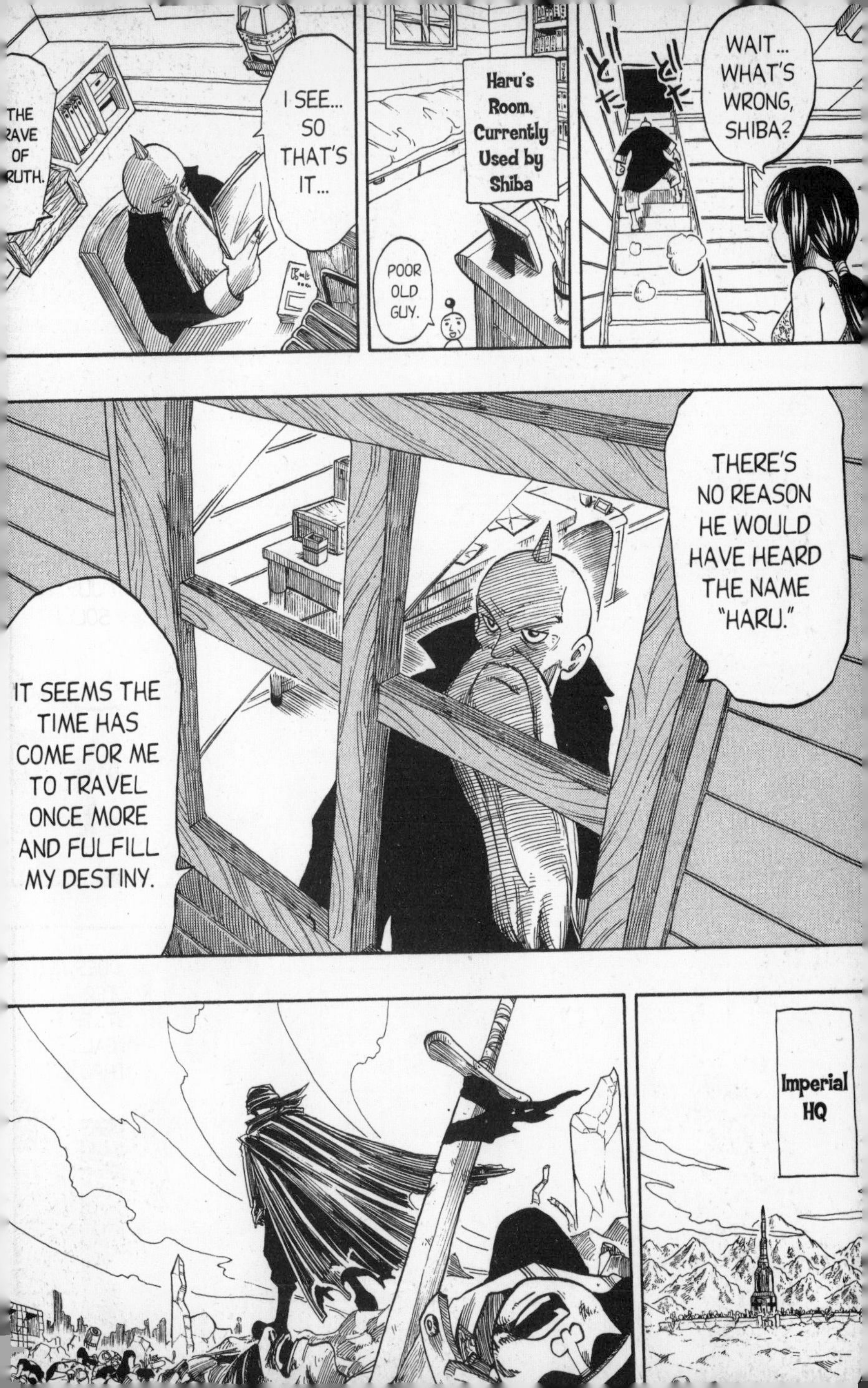
どた どた
WAIT... WHAT'S WRONG, SHIBA?
Haru's Room, Currently Used by Shiba
POOR OLD GUY.
I SEE... SO THAT'S IT...
THE RAVE OF RUTH.
THERE'S NO REASON HE WOULD HAVE HEARD THE NAME "HARU."
IT SEEMS THE TIME HAS COME FOR ME TO TRAVEL ONCE MORE AND FULFILL MY DESTINY.
Imperial HQ

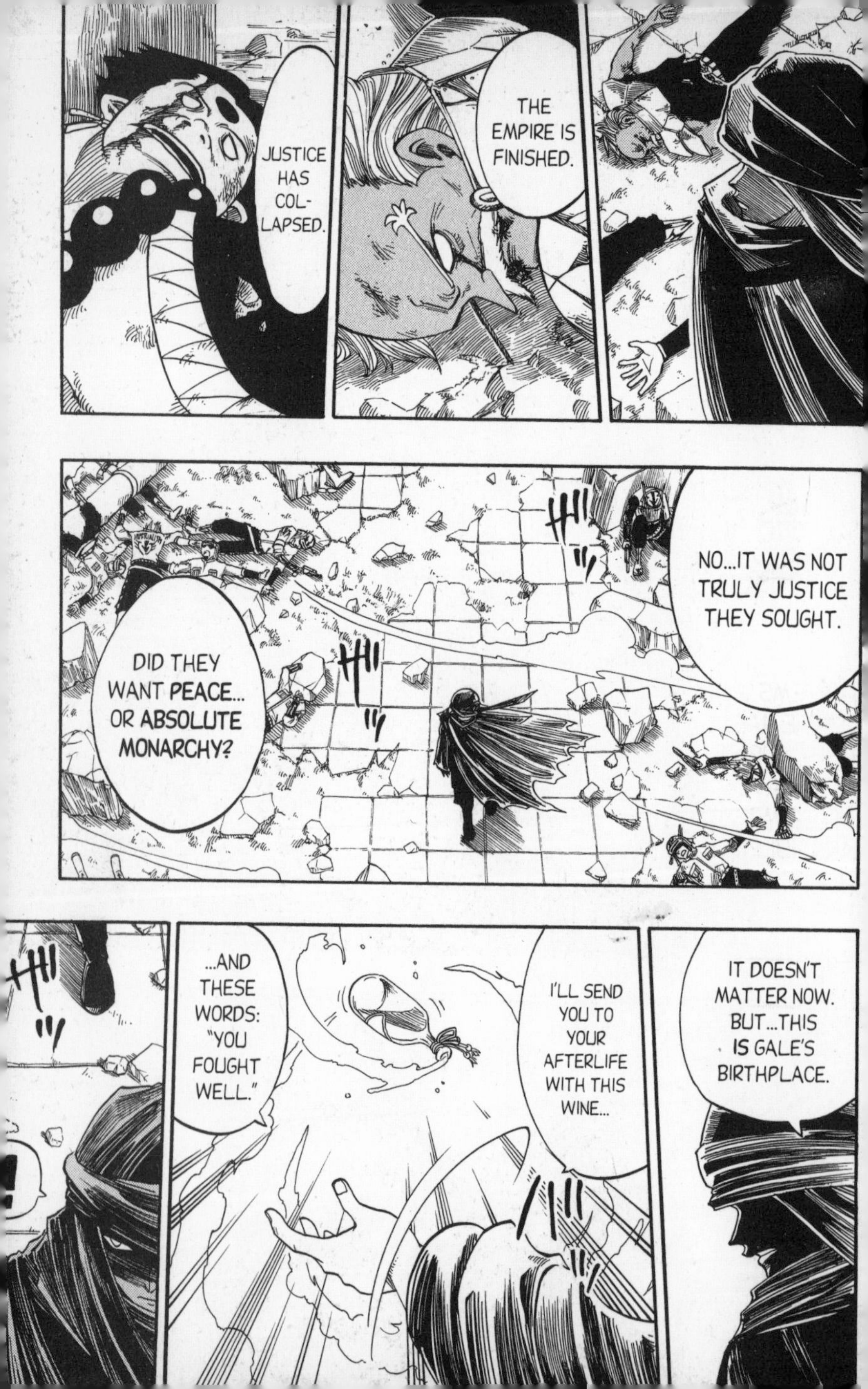
THE EMPIRE IS FINISHED.
JUSTICE HAS COL-LAPSED.
NO...IT WAS NOT TRULY JUSTICE THEY SOUGHT.
DID THEY WANT **PEACE**... OR **ABSOLUTE MONARCHY**?
IT DOESN'T MATTER NOW. BUT...THIS **IS** GALE'S BIRTHPLACE.
I'LL SEND YOU TO YOUR AFTERLIFE WITH THIS WINE...
...AND THESE WORDS: "YOU FOUGHT WELL."

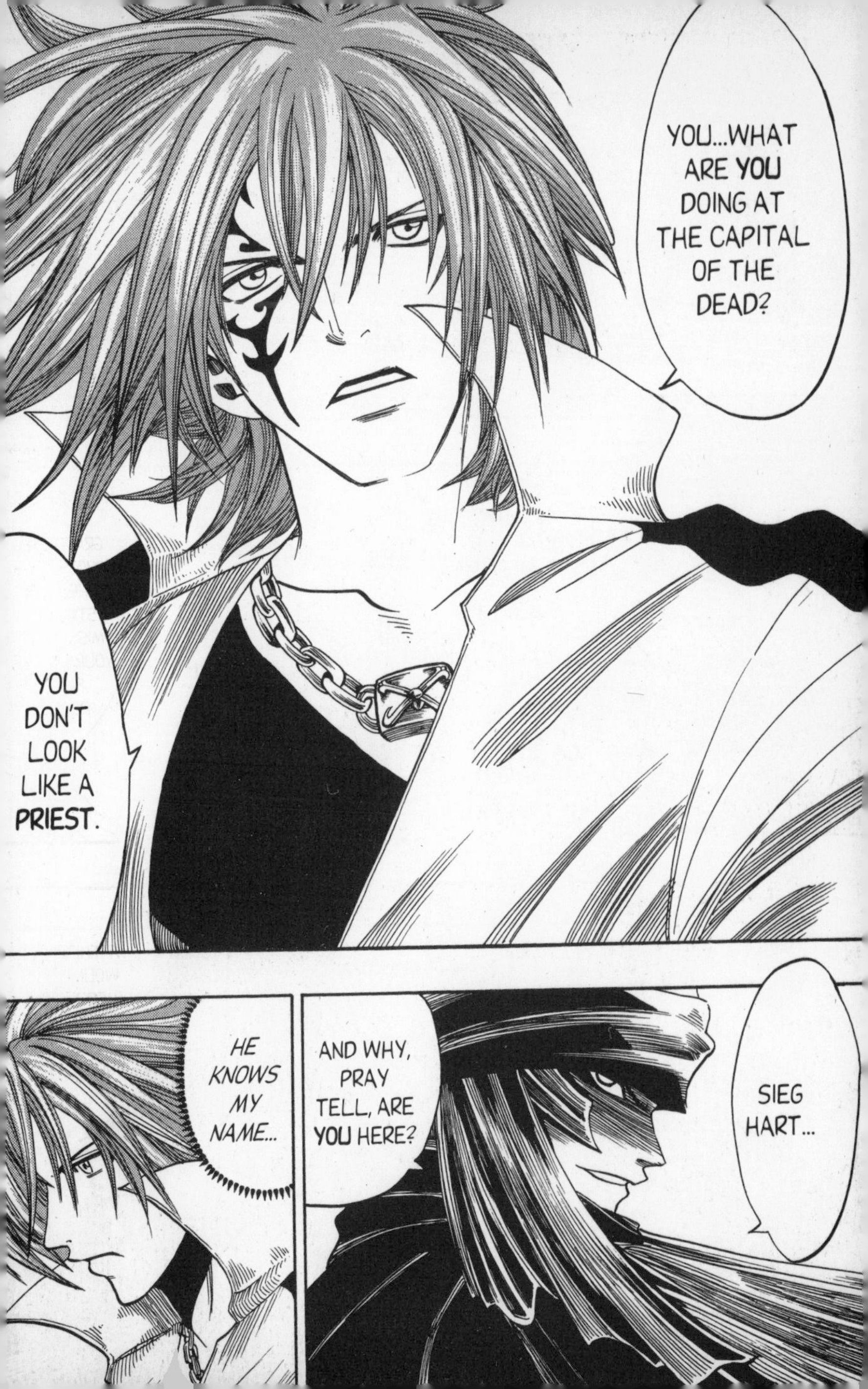
YOU...WHAT ARE YOU DOING AT THE CAPITAL OF THE DEAD?
YOU DON'T LOOK LIKE A PRIEST.
SIEG HART...
AND WHY, PRAY TELL, ARE YOU HERE?
HE KNOWS MY NAME...

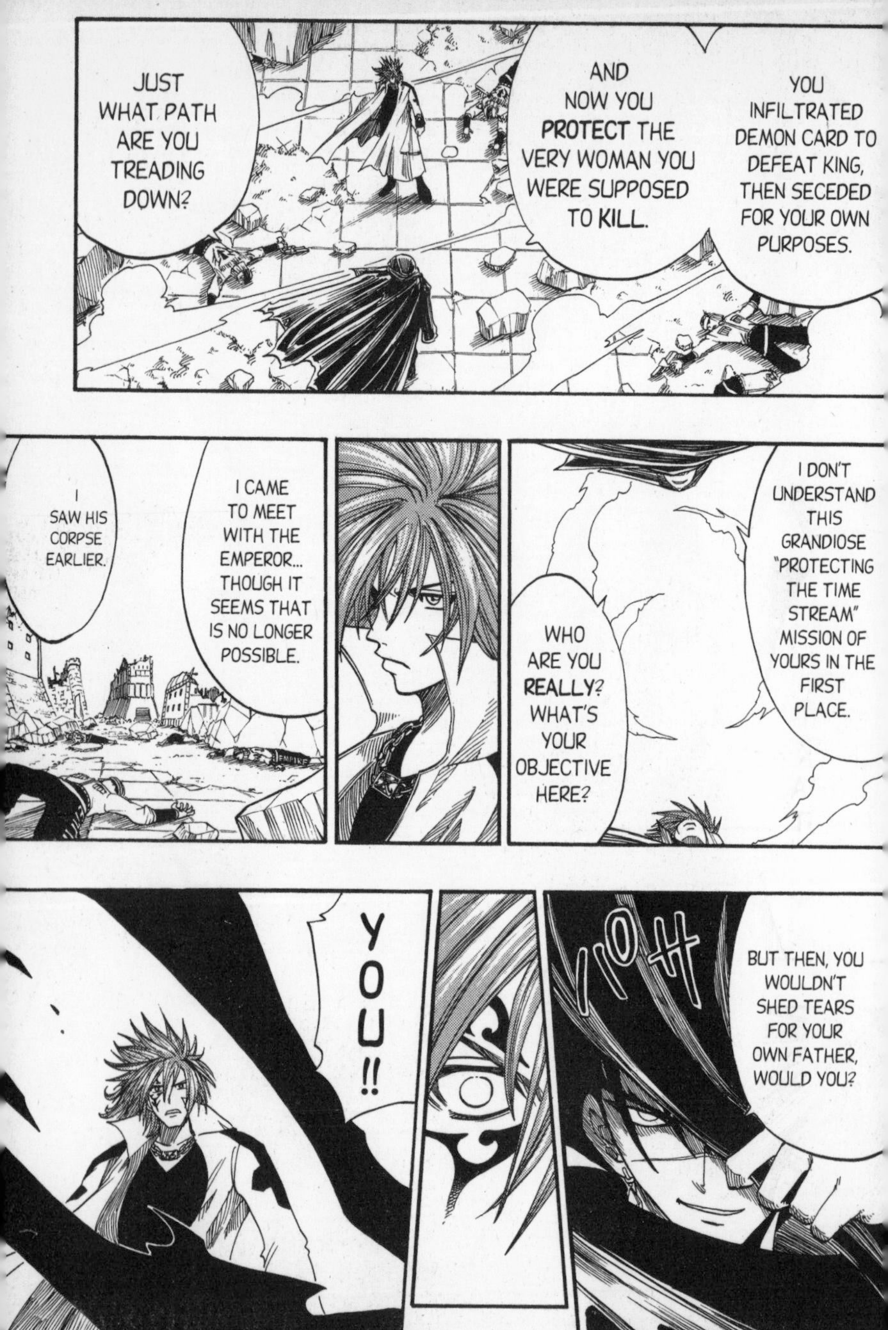
YOU INFILTRATED DEMON CARD TO DEFEAT KING, THEN SECEDED FOR YOUR OWN PURPOSES.
AND NOW YOU PROTECT THE VERY WOMAN YOU WERE SUPPOSED TO KILL.
JUST WHAT PATH ARE YOU TREADING DOWN?
I DON'T UNDERSTAND THIS GRANDIOSE "PROTECTING THE TIME STREAM" MISSION OF YOURS IN THE FIRST PLACE.
WHO ARE YOU REALLY? WHAT'S YOUR OBJECTIVE HERE?
I CAME TO MEET WITH THE EMPEROR... THOUGH IT SEEMS THAT IS NO LONGER POSSIBLE.
I SAW HIS CORPSE EARLIER.
BUT THEN, YOU WOULDN'T SHED TEARS FOR YOUR OWN FATHER, WOULD YOU?
YOU!!

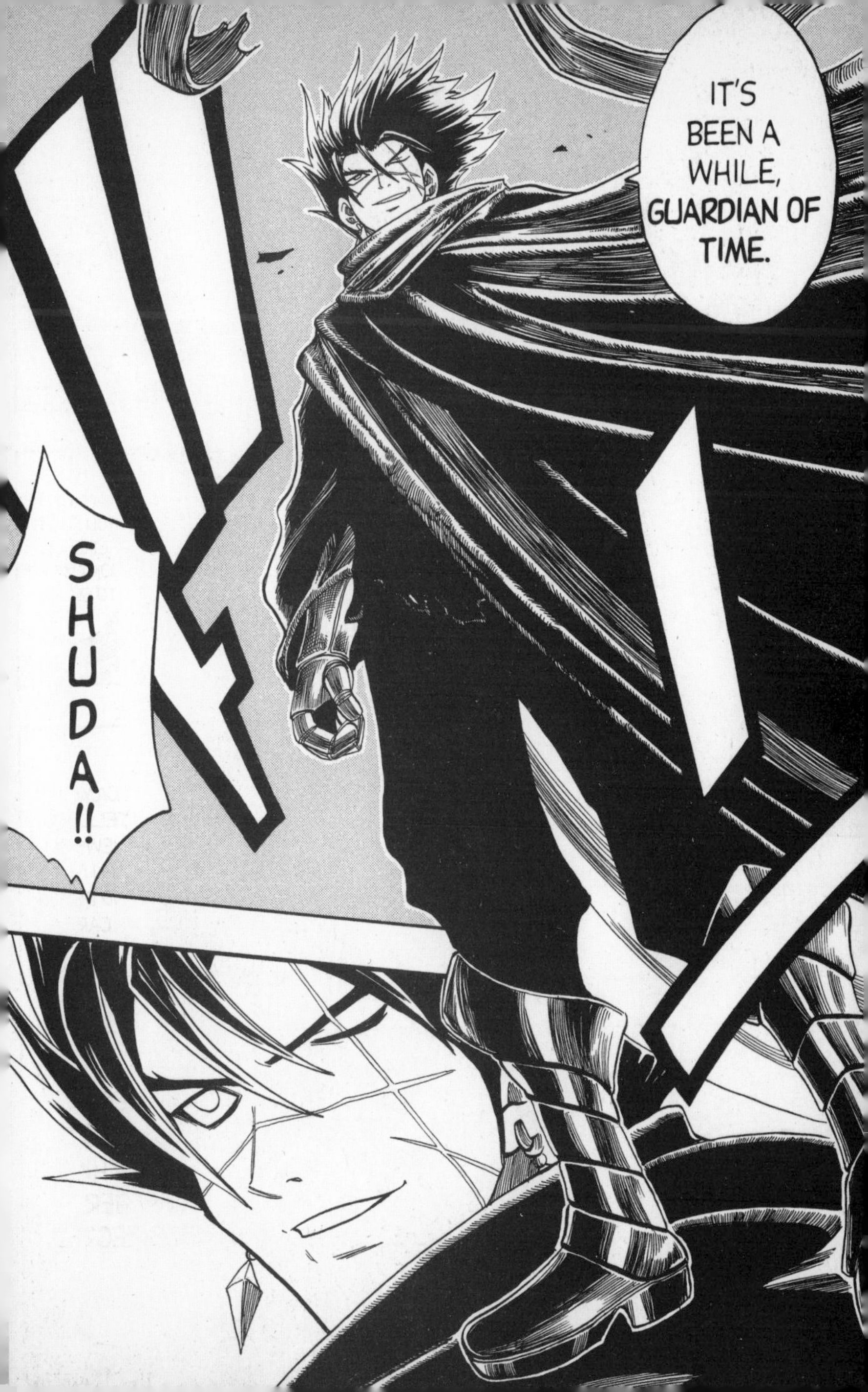
IT'S BEEN A WHILE, GUARDIAN OF TIME.
SHUDA!!

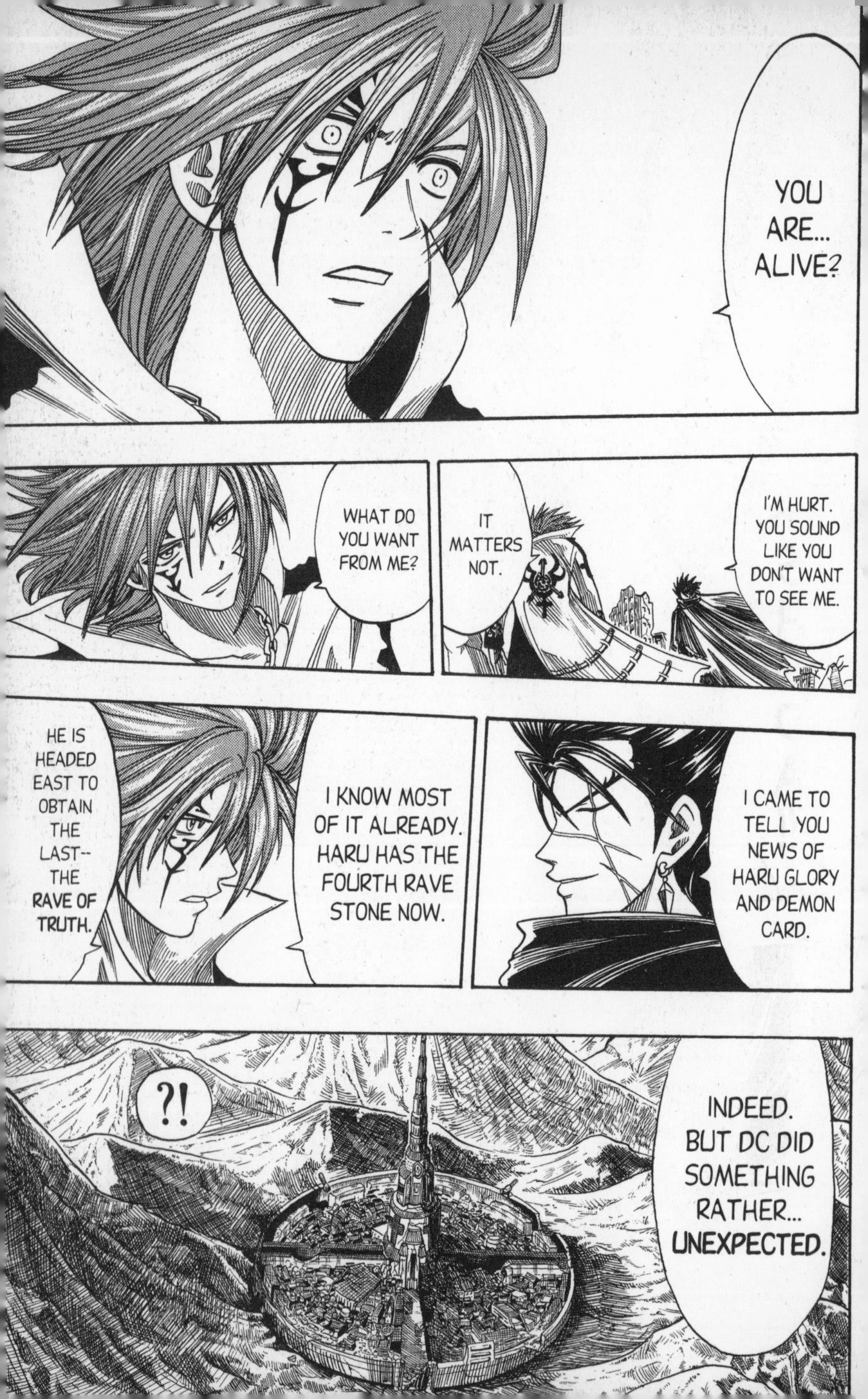
YOU ARE... ALIVE?
I'M HURT. YOU SOUND LIKE YOU DON'T WANT TO SEE ME.
IT MATTERS NOT.
WHAT DO YOU WANT FROM ME?
I CAME TO TELL YOU NEWS OF HARU GLORY AND DEMON CARD.
I KNOW MOST OF IT ALREADY. HARU HAS THE FOURTH RAVE STONE NOW.
HE IS HEADED EAST TO OBTAIN THE LAST-- THE RAVE OF TRUTH.
INDEED. BUT DC DID SOMETHING RATHER... UNEXPECTED.
?!

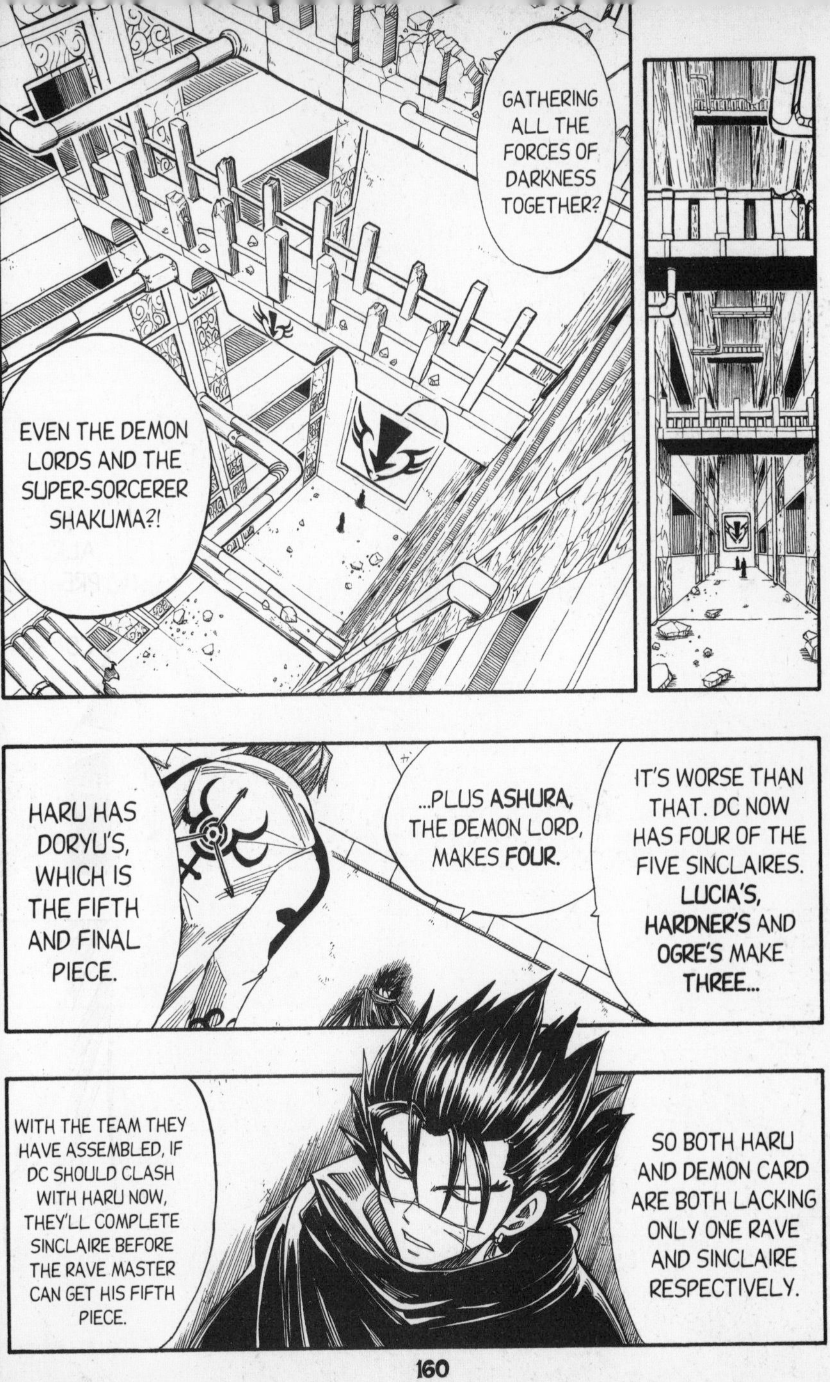
GATHERING ALL THE FORCES OF DARKNESS TOGETHER?
EVEN THE DEMON LORDS AND THE SUPER-SORCERER SHAKUMA?!
IT'S WORSE THAN THAT. DC NOW HAS FOUR OF THE FIVE SINCLAIRES. LUCIA'S, HARDNER'S AND OGRE'S MAKE THREE...
...PLUS ASHURA, THE DEMON LORD, MAKES FOUR.
HARU HAS DORYU'S, WHICH IS THE FIFTH AND FINAL PIECE.
SO BOTH HARU AND DEMON CARD ARE BOTH LACKING ONLY ONE RAVE AND SINCLAIRE RESPECTIVELY.
WITH THE TEAM THEY HAVE ASSEMBLED, IF DC SHOULD CLASH WITH HARU NOW, THEY'LL COMPLETE SINCLAIRE BEFORE THE RAVE MASTER CAN GET HIS FIFTH PIECE.

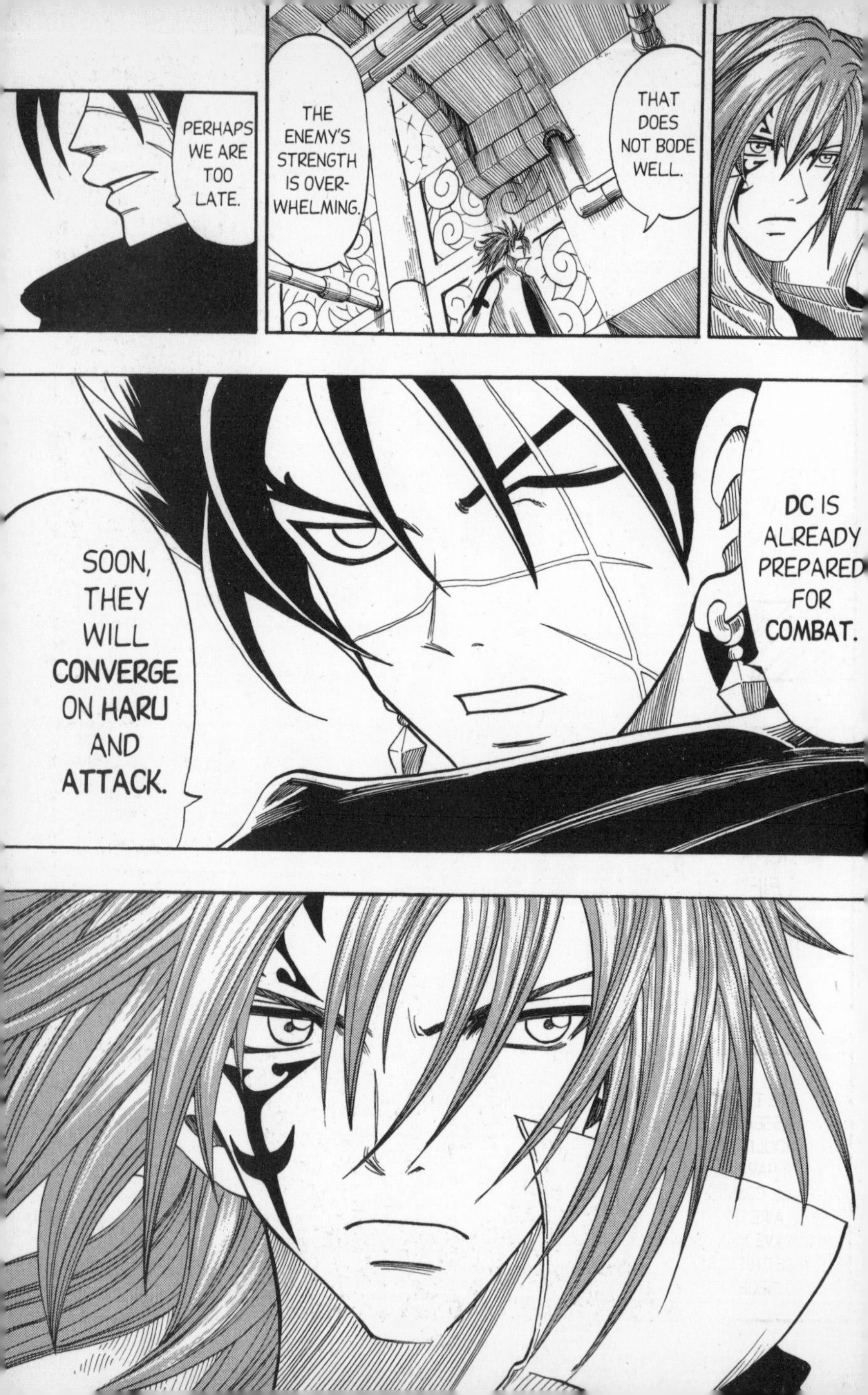
THAT DOES NOT BODE WELL.
THE ENEMY'S STRENGTH IS OVER-WHELMING.
PERHAPS WE ARE TOO LATE.
DC IS ALREADY PREPARED FOR COMBAT.
SOON, THEY WILL CONVERGE ON HARU AND ATTACK.

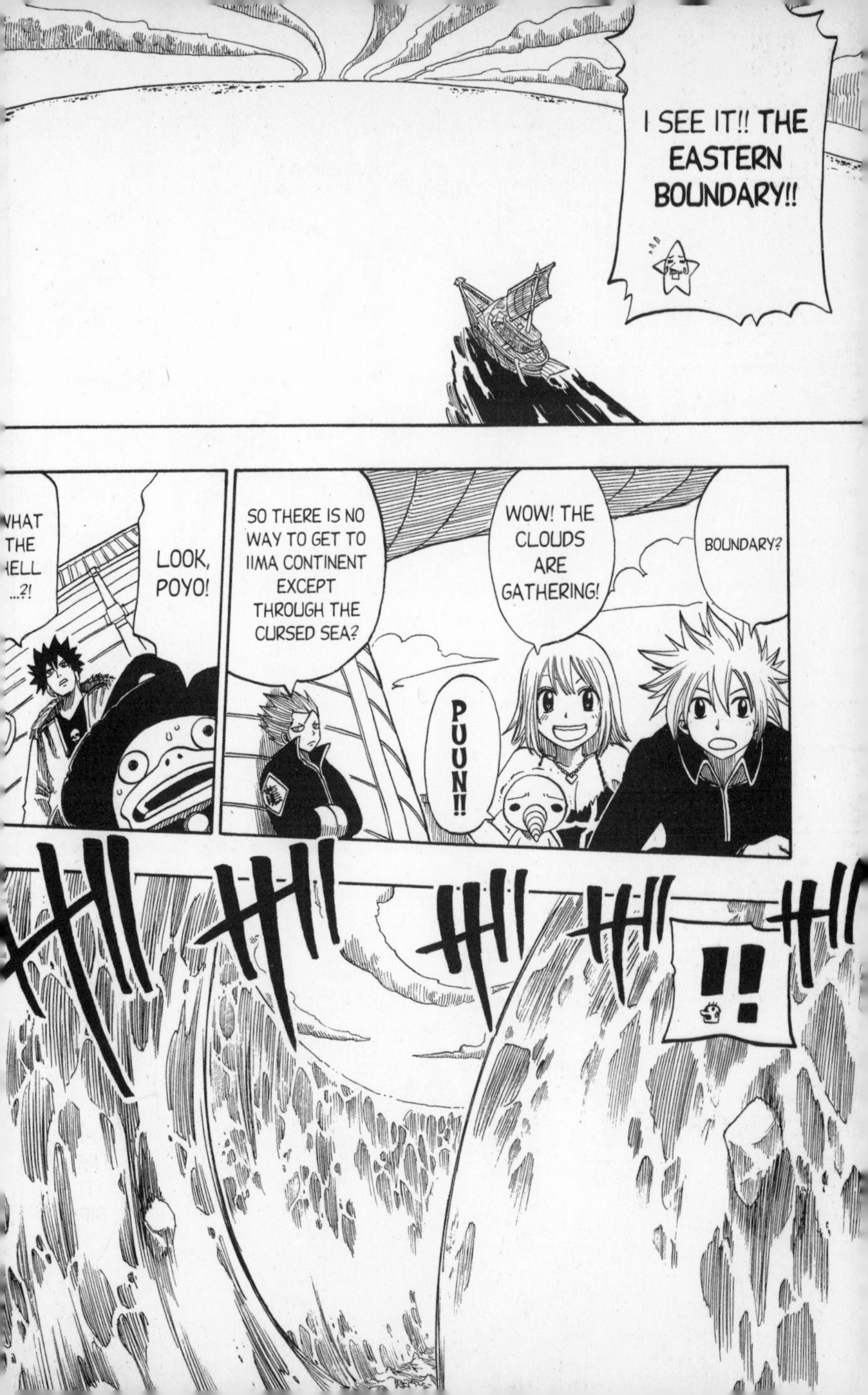
I SEE IT!! THE EASTERN BOUNDARY!!
BOUNDARY?
WOW! THE CLOUDS ARE GATHERING!
SO THERE IS NO WAY TO GET TO IIMA CONTINENT EXCEPT THROUGH THE CURSED SEA?
PUUN!!
LOOK, POYO!
WHAT THE HELL ...?!
!!

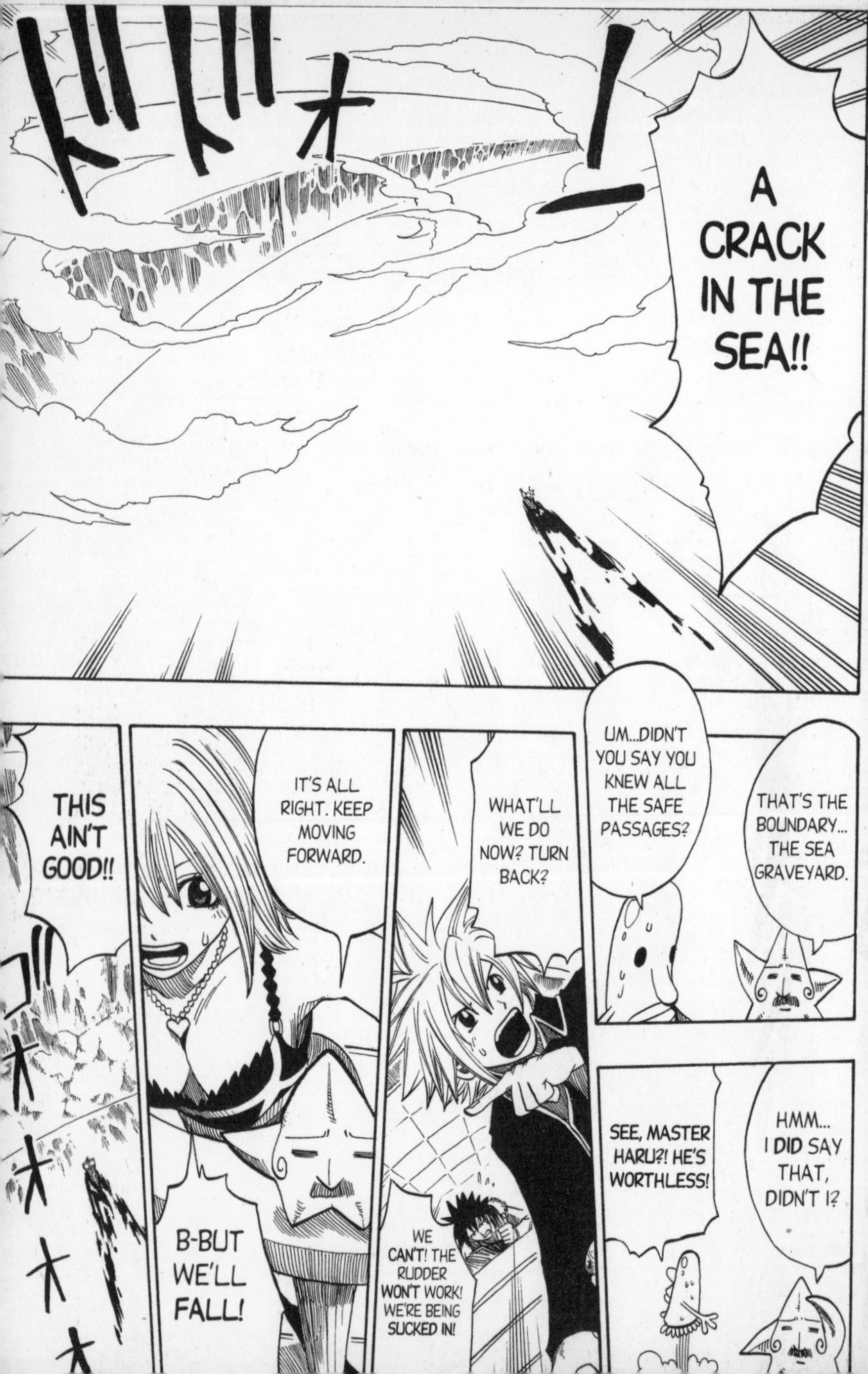
A CRACK IN THE SEA!!
THAT'S THE BOUNDARY... THE SEA GRAVEYARD.
UM...DIDN'T YOU SAY YOU KNEW ALL THE SAFE PASSAGES?
HMM... I DID SAY THAT, DIDN'T I?
SEE, MASTER HARU?! HE'S WORTHLESS!
WHAT'LL WE DO NOW? TURN BACK?
WE CAN'T! THE RUDDER WON'T WORK! WE'RE BEING SUCKED IN!
IT'S ALL RIGHT. KEEP MOVING FORWARD.
B-BUT WE'LL FALL!
THIS AIN'T GOOD!!

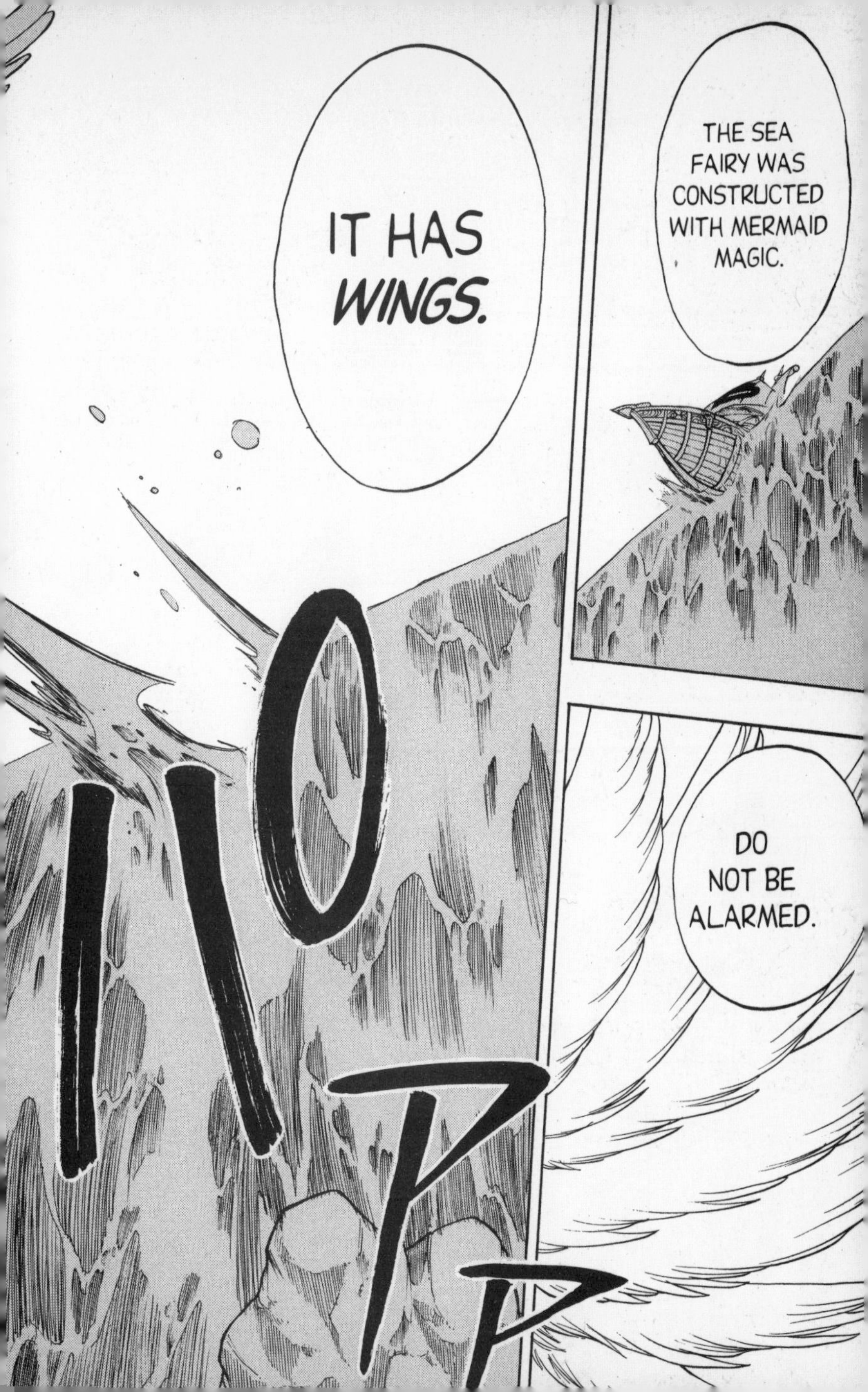
THE SEA FAIRY WAS CONSTRUCTED WITH MERMAID MAGIC.
DO NOT BE ALARMED.
IT HAS *WINGS.*

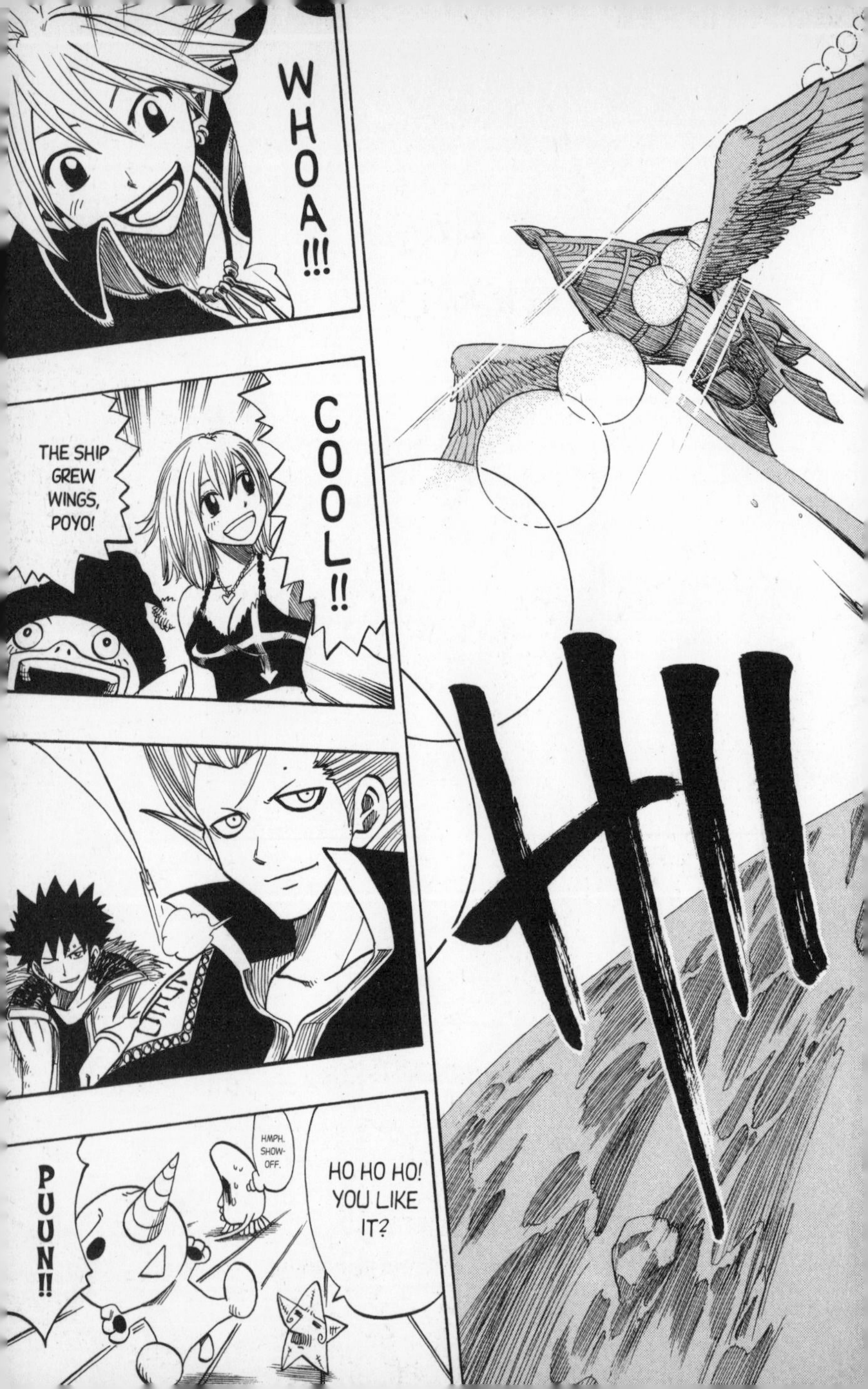
WHOA!!!
COOL!!
THE SHIP GREW WINGS, POYO!
HO HO HO! YOU LIKE IT?
HMPH. SHOW-OFF.
PUUN!!

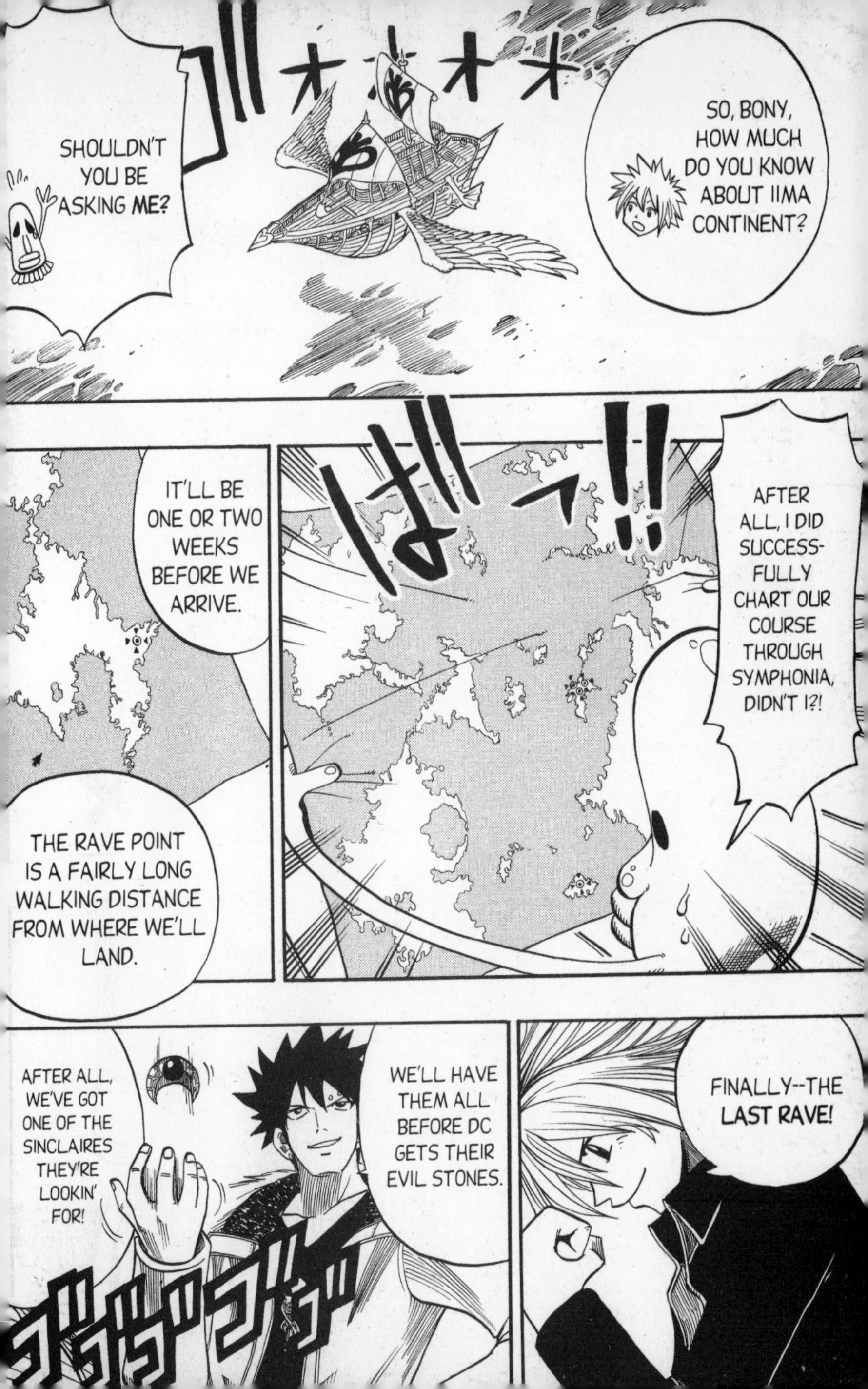
SO, BONY, HOW MUCH DO YOU KNOW ABOUT IIMA CONTINENT?
SHOULDN'T YOU BE ASKING **ME**?
AFTER ALL, I DID SUCCESSFULLY CHART OUR COURSE THROUGH SYMPHONIA, DIDN'T I?!
ばっ!!
IT'LL BE ONE OR TWO WEEKS BEFORE WE ARRIVE.
THE RAVE POINT IS A FAIRLY LONG WALKING DISTANCE FROM WHERE WE'LL LAND.
FINALLY--THE **LAST RAVE**!
WE'LL HAVE THEM ALL BEFORE DC GETS THEIR EVIL STONES.
AFTER ALL, WE'VE GOT ONE OF THE SINCLAIRES THEY'RE LOOKIN' FOR!

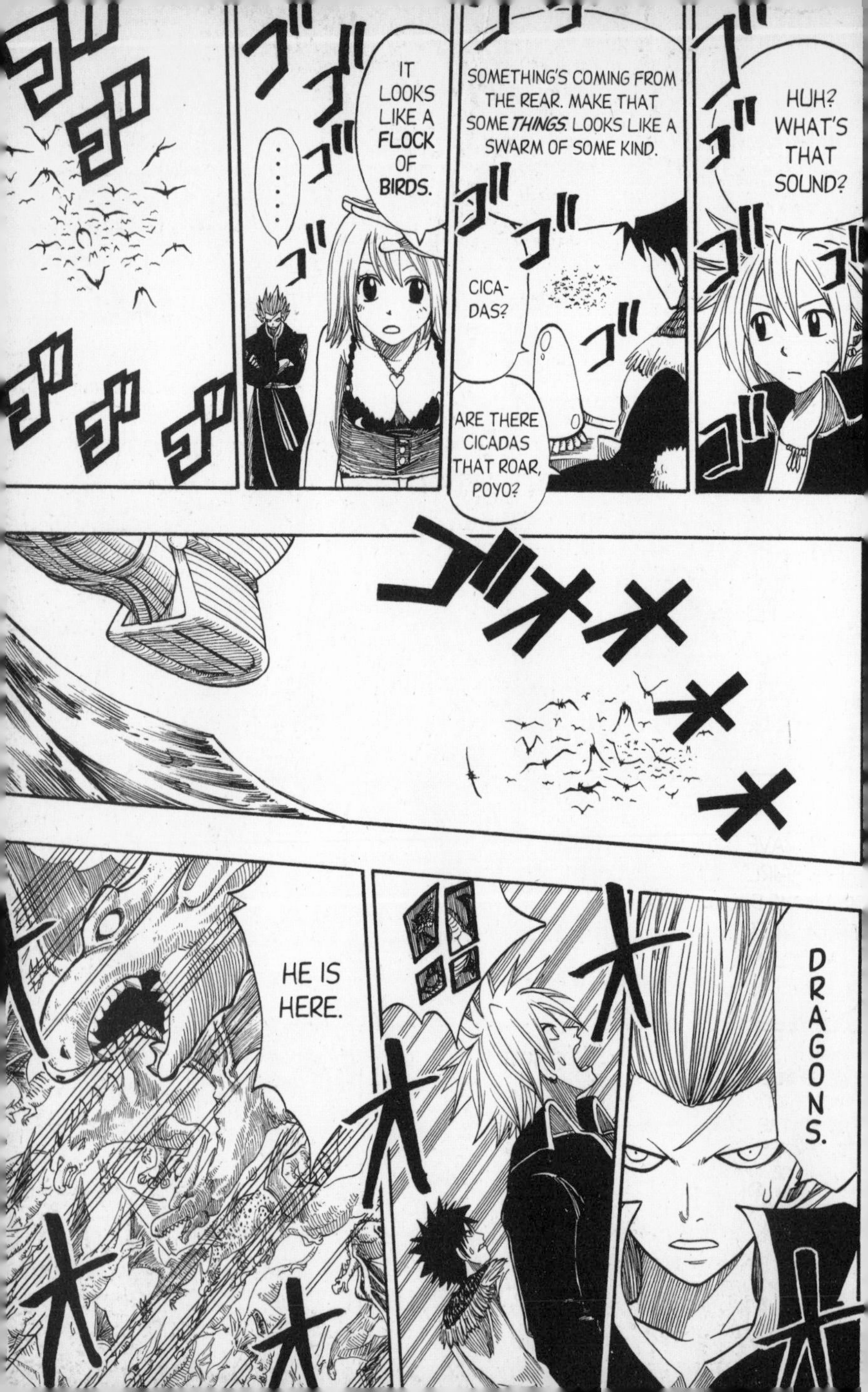
HUH? WHAT'S THAT SOUND?
SOMETHING'S COMING FROM THE REAR. MAKE THAT SOME *THINGS*. LOOKS LIKE A SWARM OF SOME KIND.
CICADAS?
ARE THERE CICADAS THAT ROAR, POYO?
IT LOOKS LIKE A **FLOCK** OF **BIRDS.**
......
DRAGONS.
HE IS HERE.

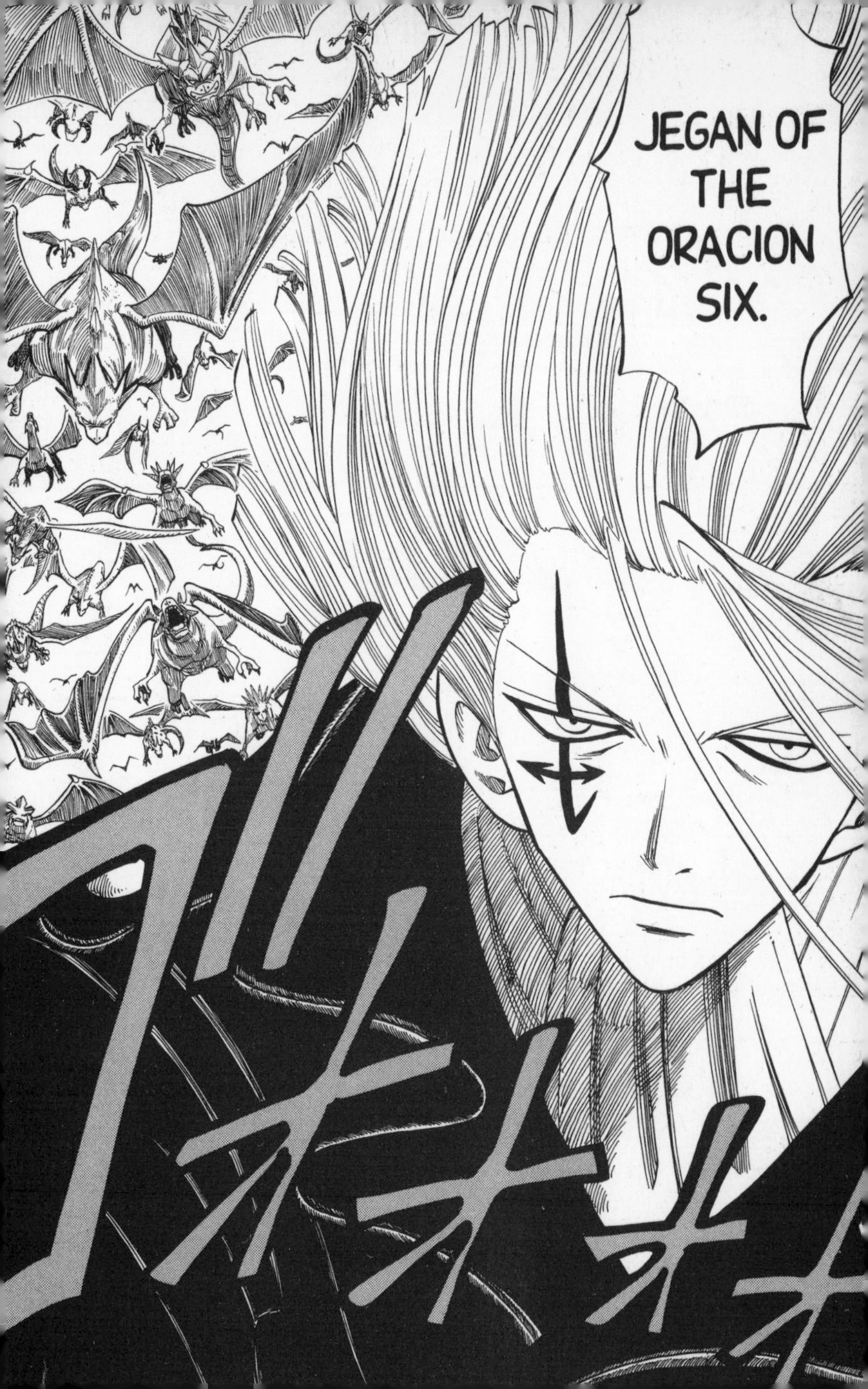
JEGAN OF THE ORACION SIX.

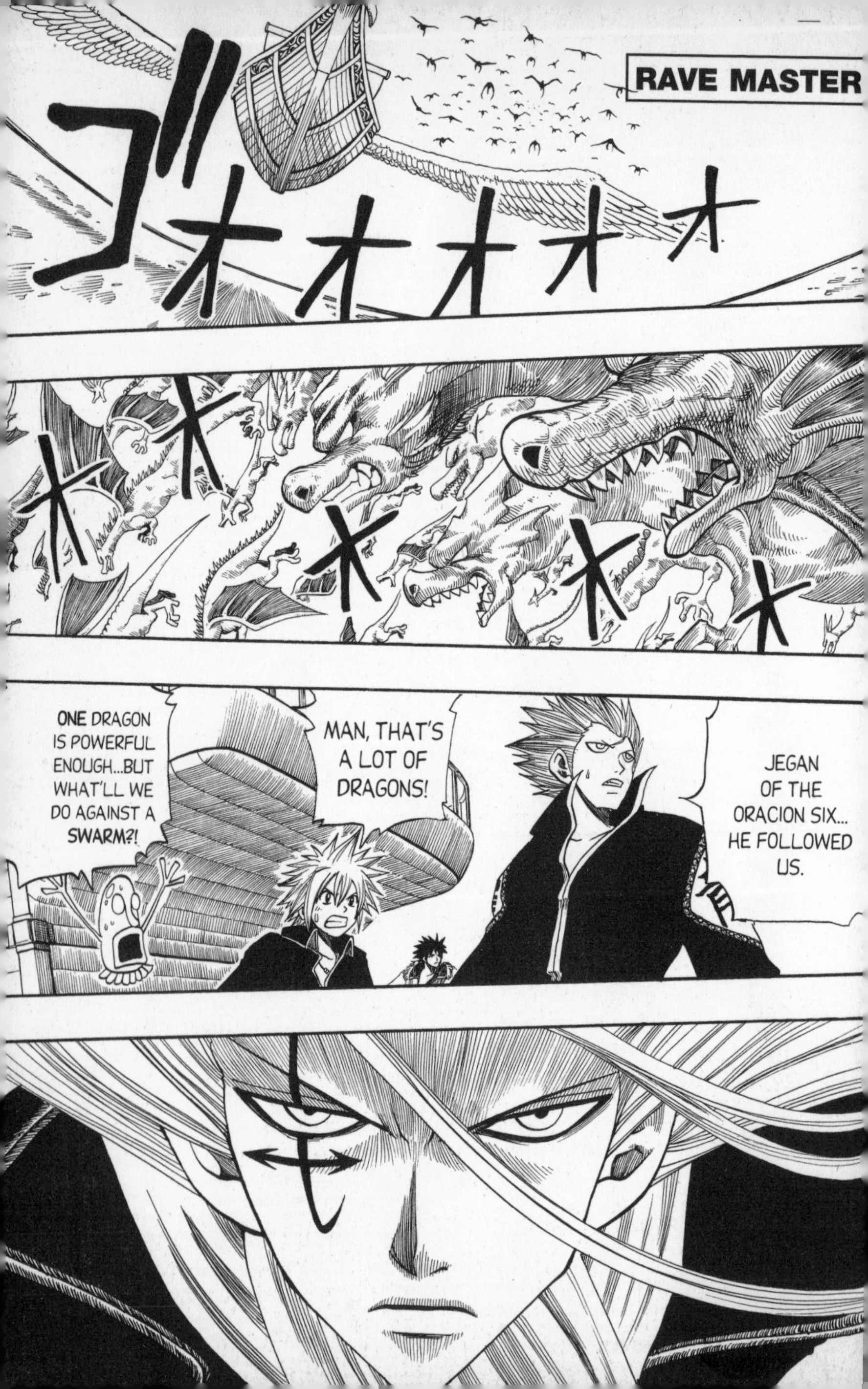
ゴオオオオオ
JEGAN OF THE ORACION SIX... HE FOLLOWED US.
MAN, THAT'S A LOT OF DRAGONS!
ONE DRAGON IS POWERFUL ENOUGH...BUT WHAT'LL WE DO AGAINST A SWARM?!

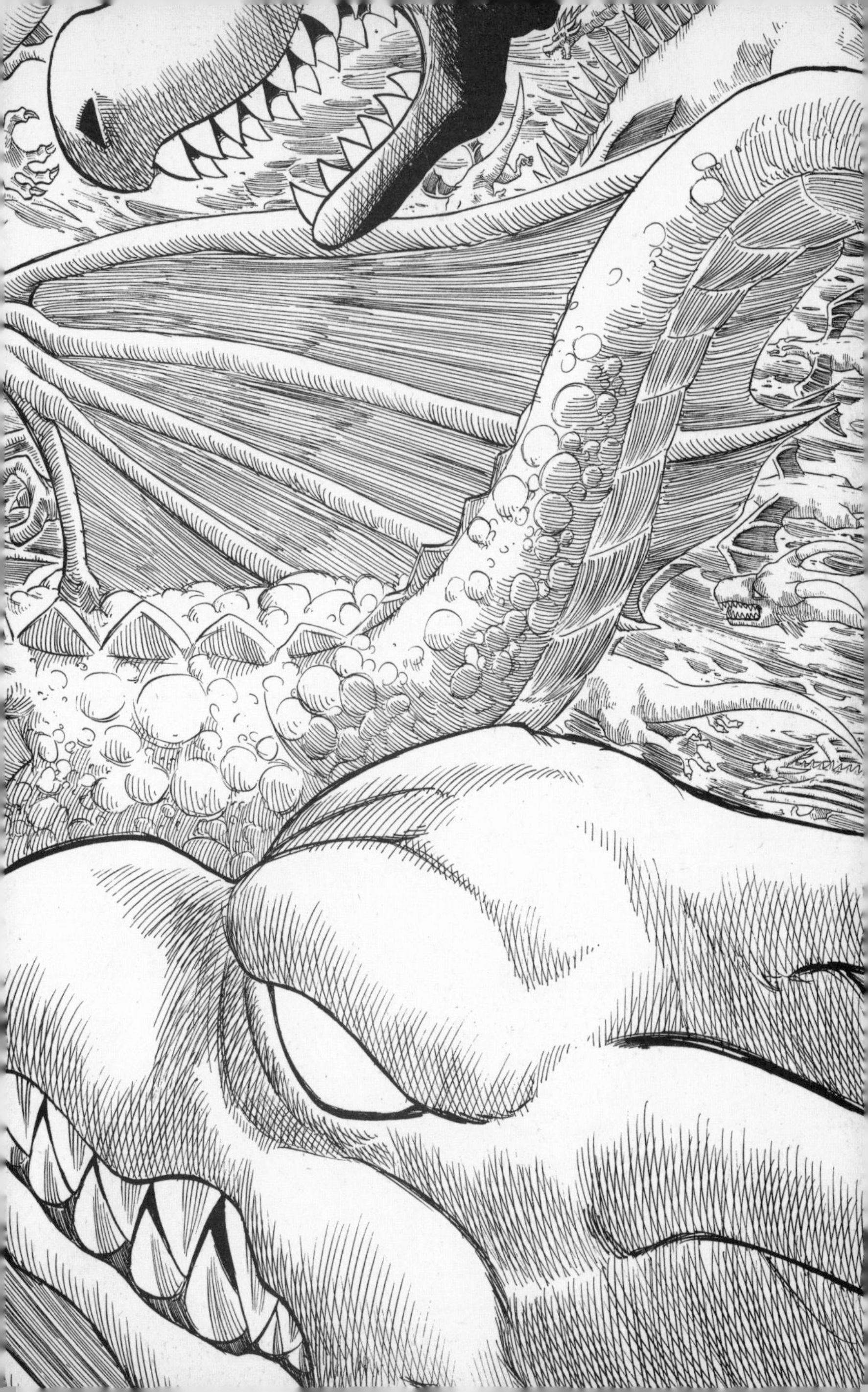

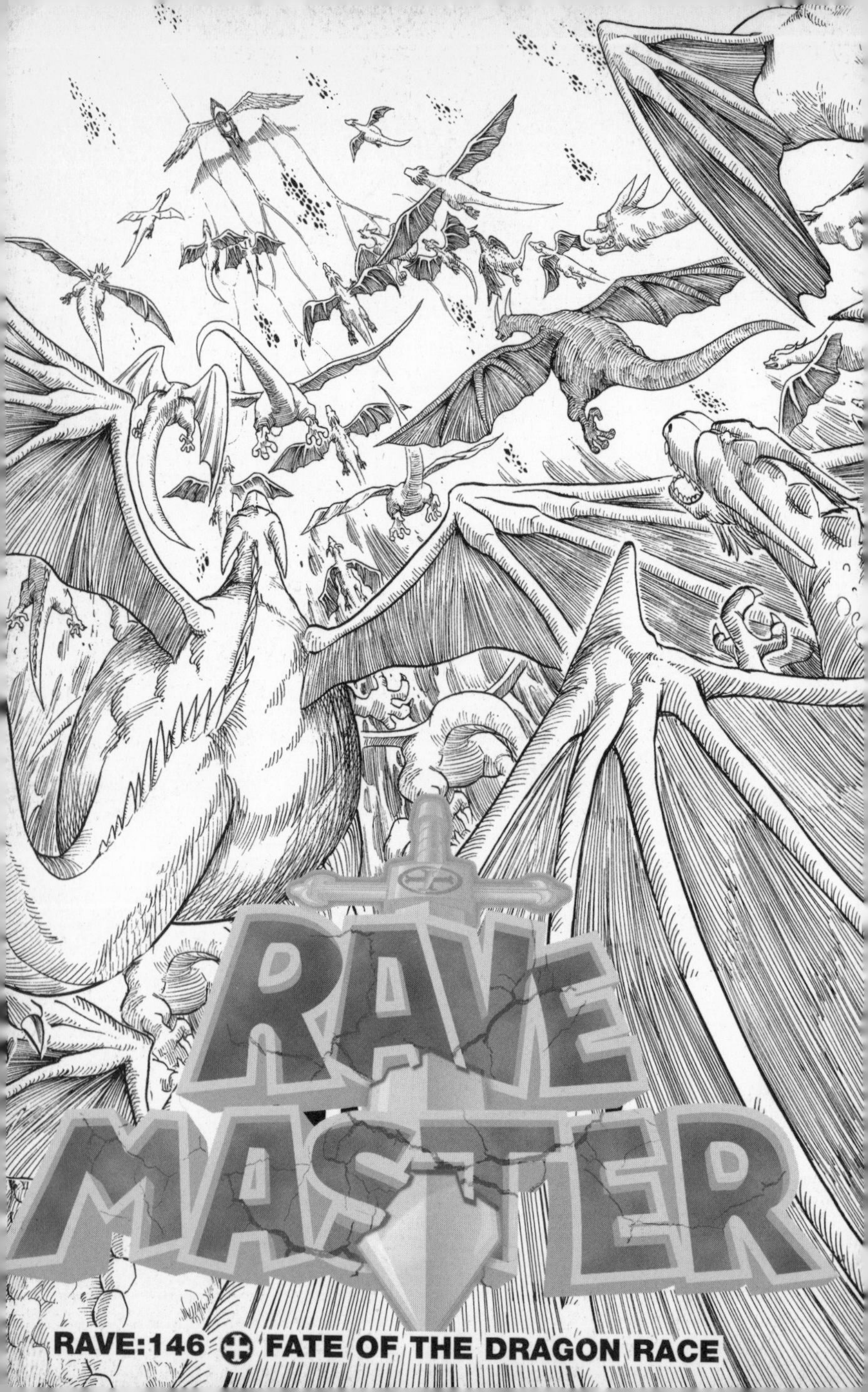
RAVE MASTER
RAVE:146 FATE OF THE DRAGON RACE

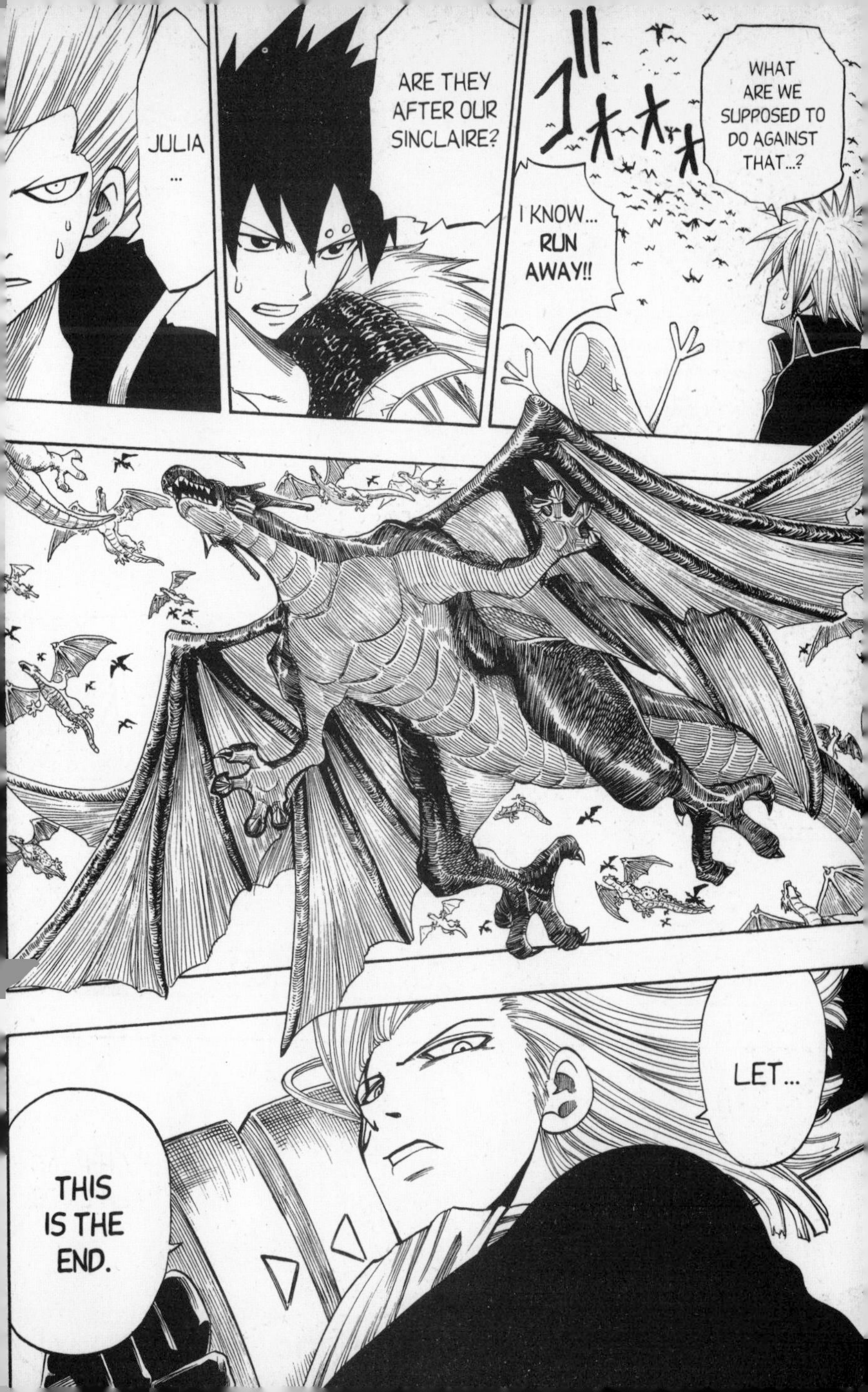
WHAT ARE WE SUPPOSED TO DO AGAINST THAT...?
ゴォォォ
I KNOW... RUN AWAY!!
ARE THEY AFTER OUR SINCLAIRE?
JULIA ...
LET...
THIS IS THE END.

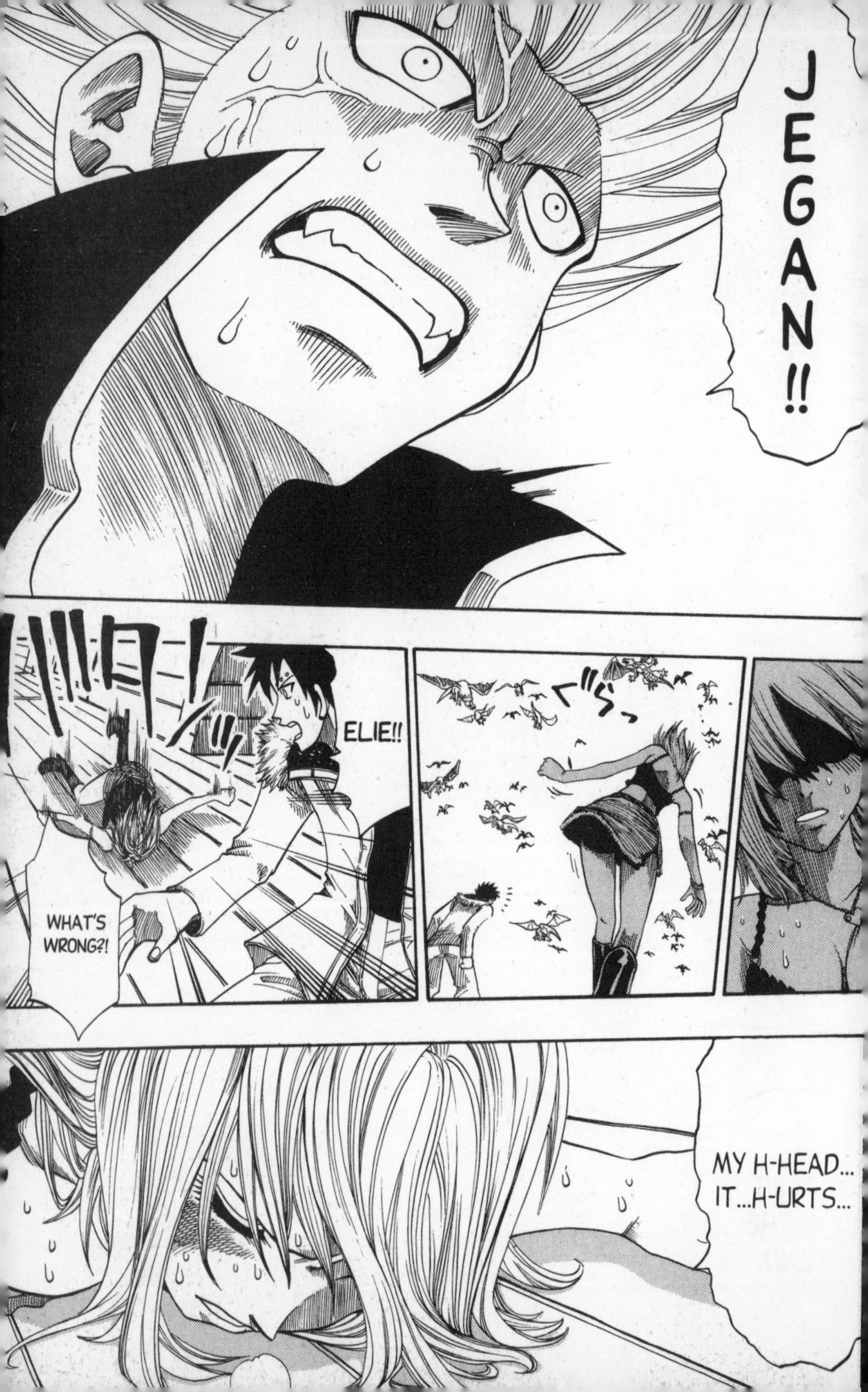
JEGAN!!
ぐらっ
ELIE!!
WHAT'S WRONG?!
MY H-HEAD... IT...H-URTS...

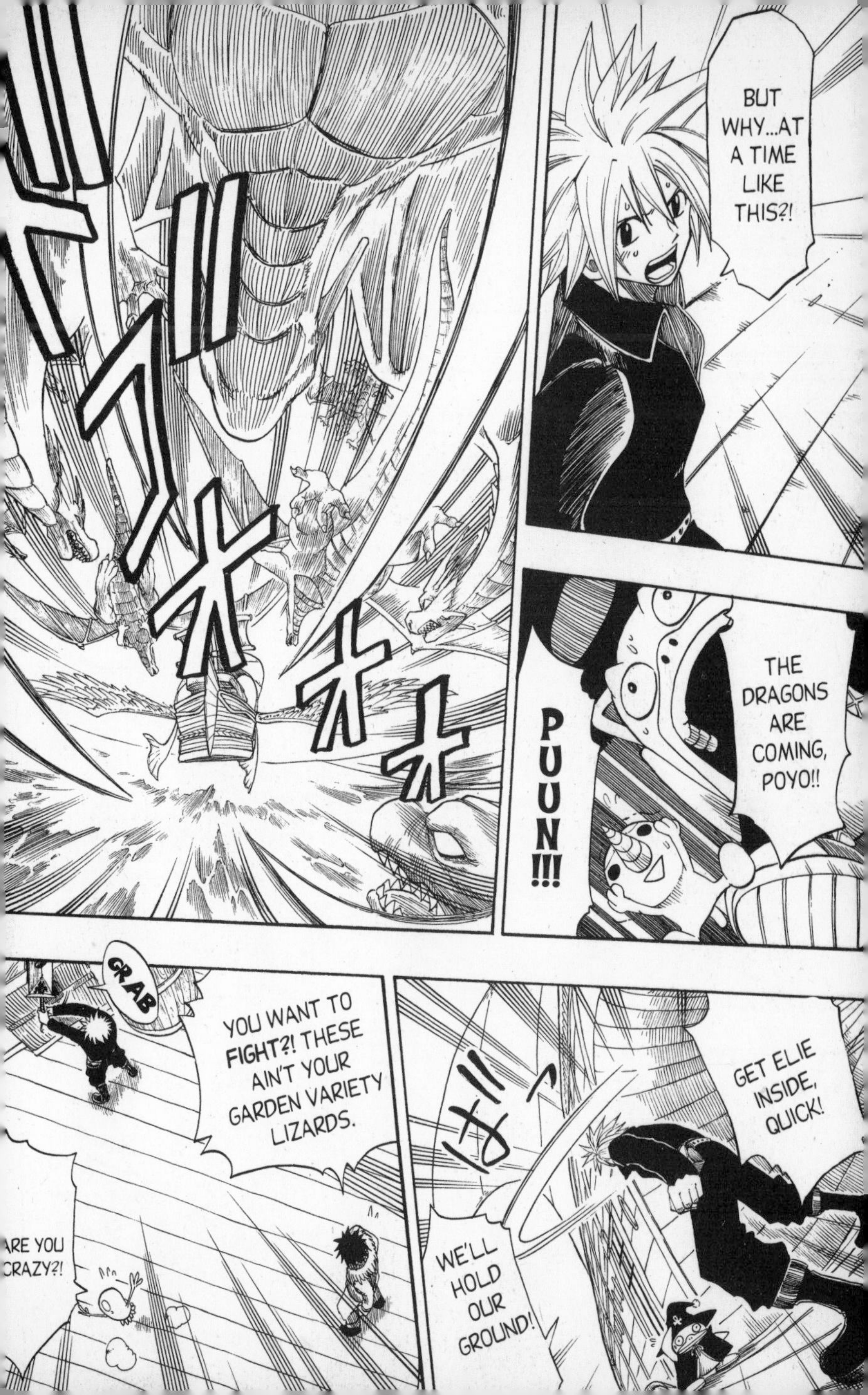
BUT WHY...AT A TIME LIKE THIS?!
PUUN!!!
THE DRAGONS ARE COMING, POYO!!
GET ELIE INSIDE, QUICK!
WE'LL HOLD OUR GROUND!
GRAB
YOU WANT TO FIGHT?! THESE AIN'T YOUR GARDEN VARIETY LIZARDS.
ARE YOU CRAZY?!

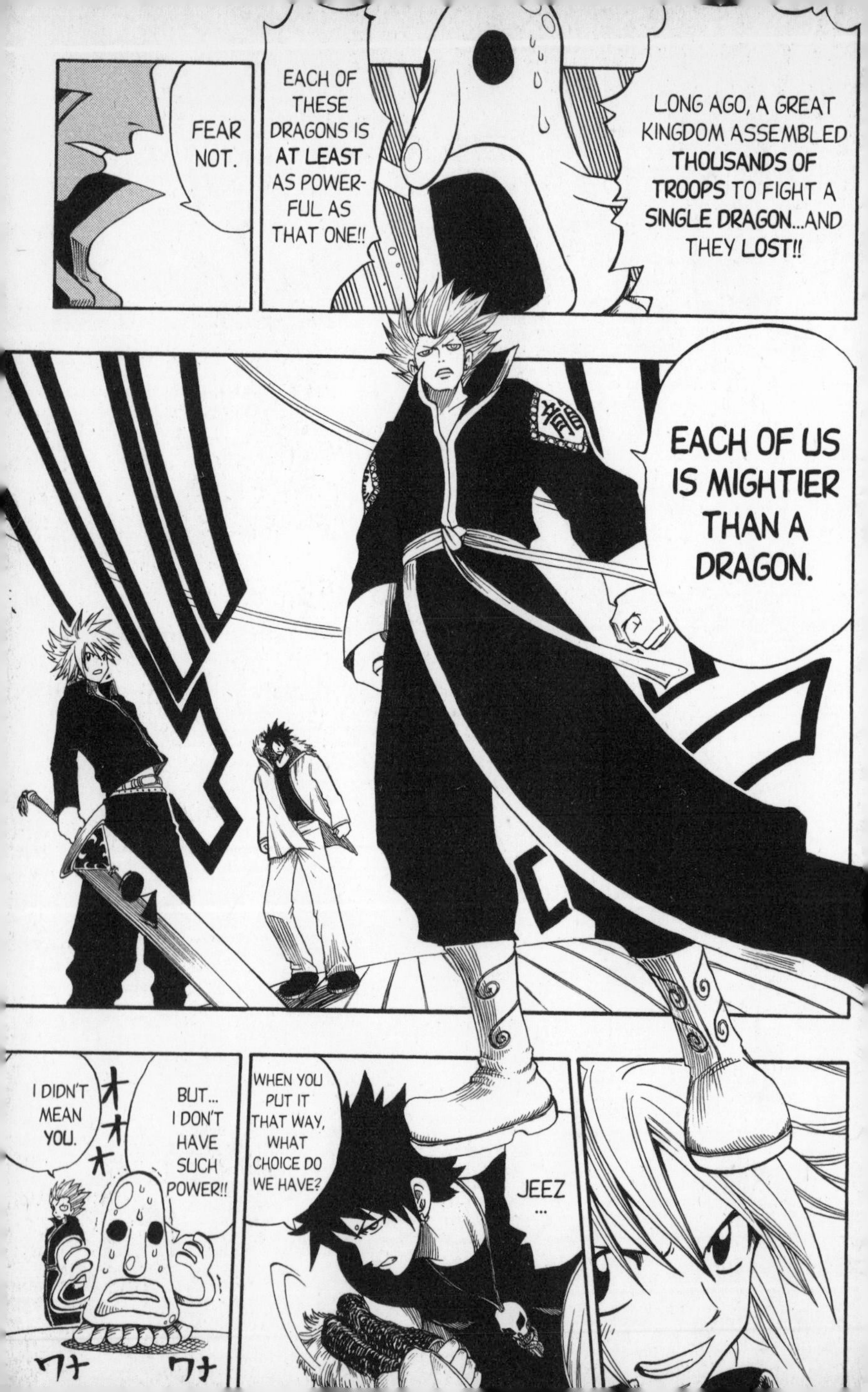

LONG AGO, A GREAT KINGDOM ASSEMBLED THOUSANDS OF TROOPS TO FIGHT A SINGLE DRAGON...AND THEY LOST!!
EACH OF THESE DRAGONS IS AT LEAST AS POWERFUL AS THAT ONE!!
FEAR NOT.
EACH OF US IS MIGHTIER THAN A DRAGON.
JEEZ...
WHEN YOU PUT IT THAT WAY, WHAT CHOICE DO WE HAVE?
BUT... I DON'T HAVE SUCH POWER!!
オオオ
I DIDN'T MEAN YOU.
ワナ ワナ

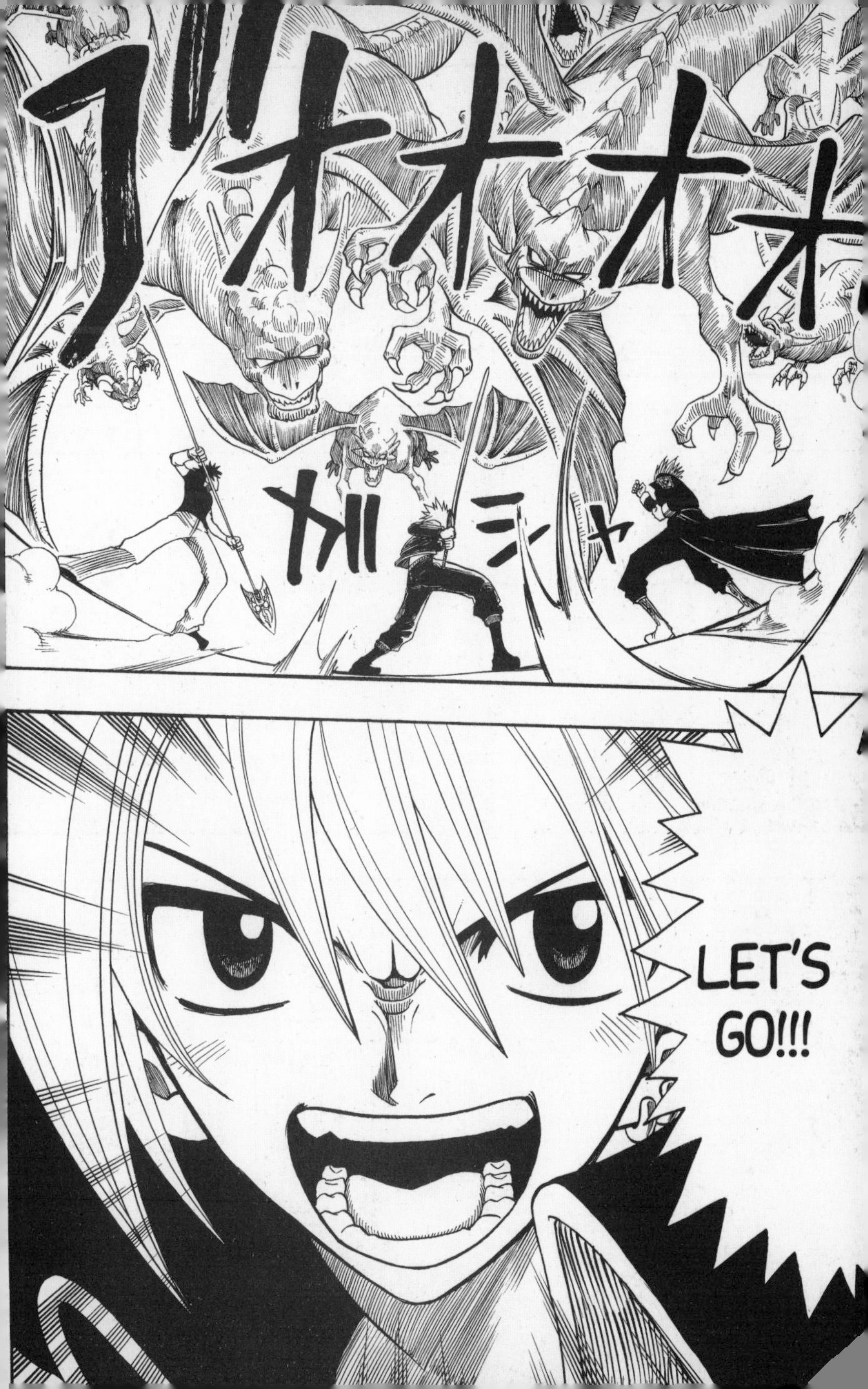
ブオオオオ
ガシャ
LET'S GO!!!

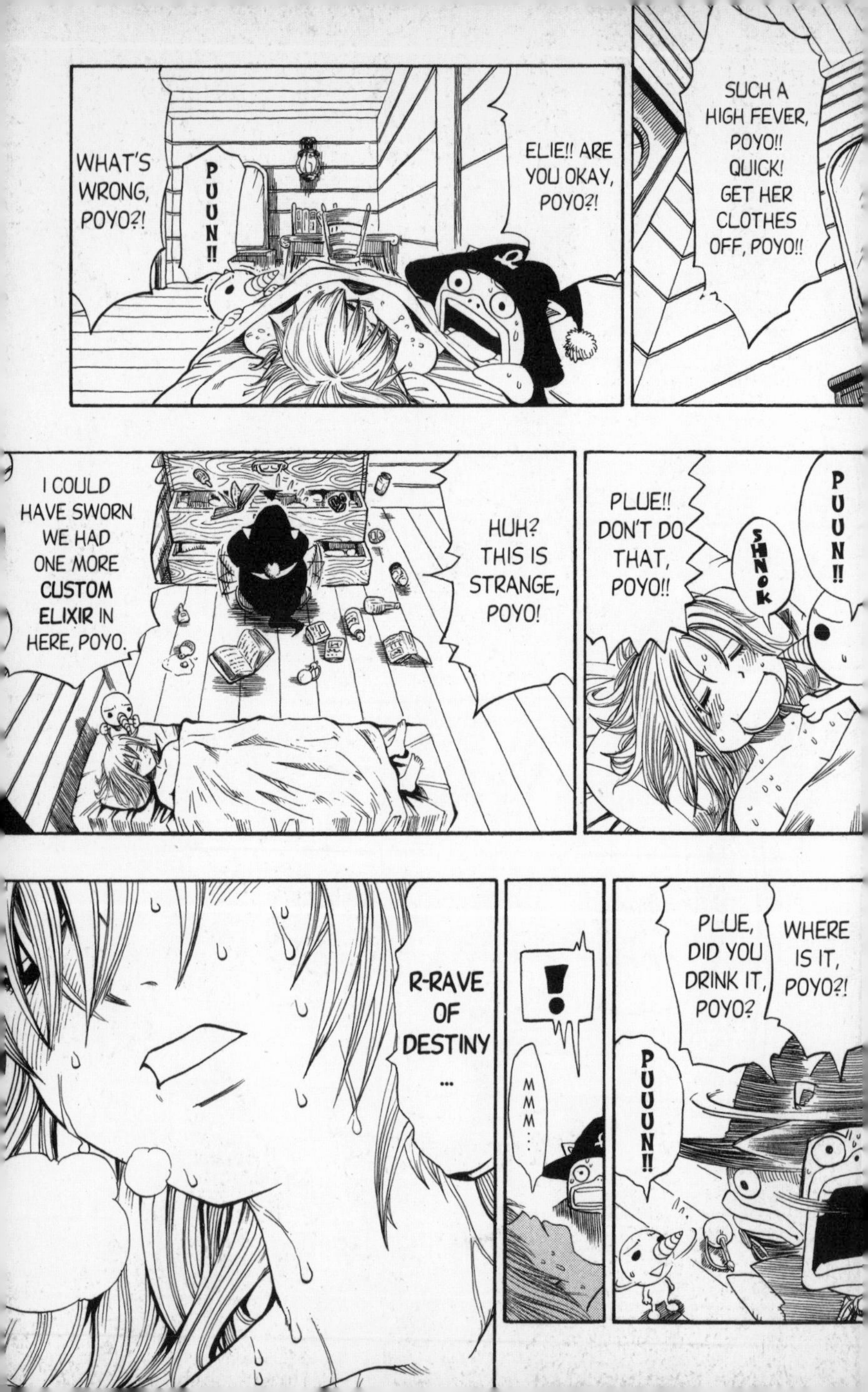
SUCH A HIGH FEVER, POYO!! QUICK! GET HER CLOTHES OFF, POYO!!
ELIE!! ARE YOU OKAY, POYO?!
PUUN!!
WHAT'S WRONG, POYO?!
PUUN!!
SHNOK
PLUE!! DON'T DO THAT, POYO!!
HUH? THIS IS STRANGE, POYO!
I COULD HAVE SWORN WE HAD ONE MORE CUSTOM ELIXIR IN HERE, POYO.
WHERE IS IT, POYO?!
PLUE, DID YOU DRINK IT, POYO?
PUUUN!!
!
MMM...
R-RAVE OF DESTINY ...

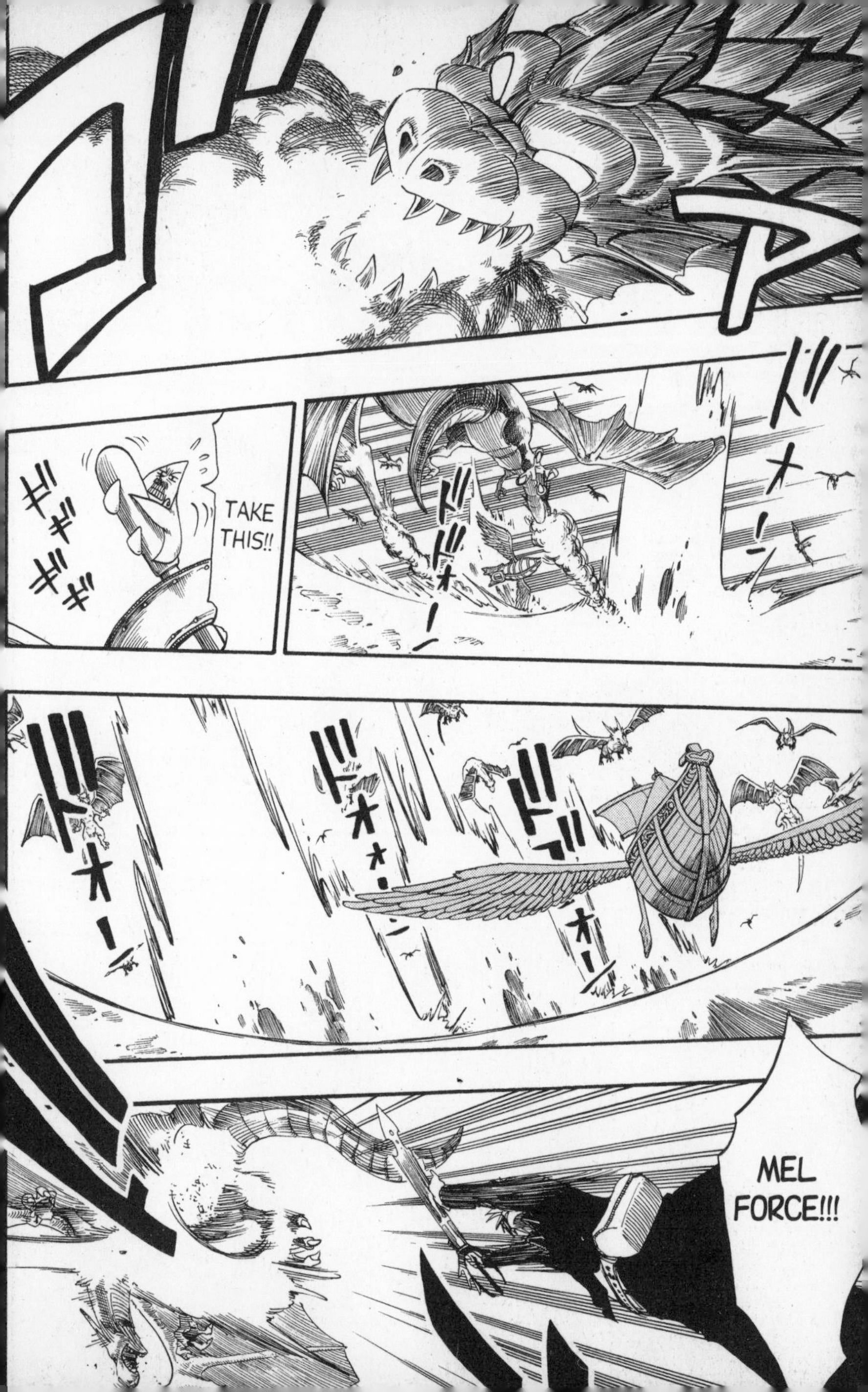
TAKE THIS!!
MEL FORCE!!!

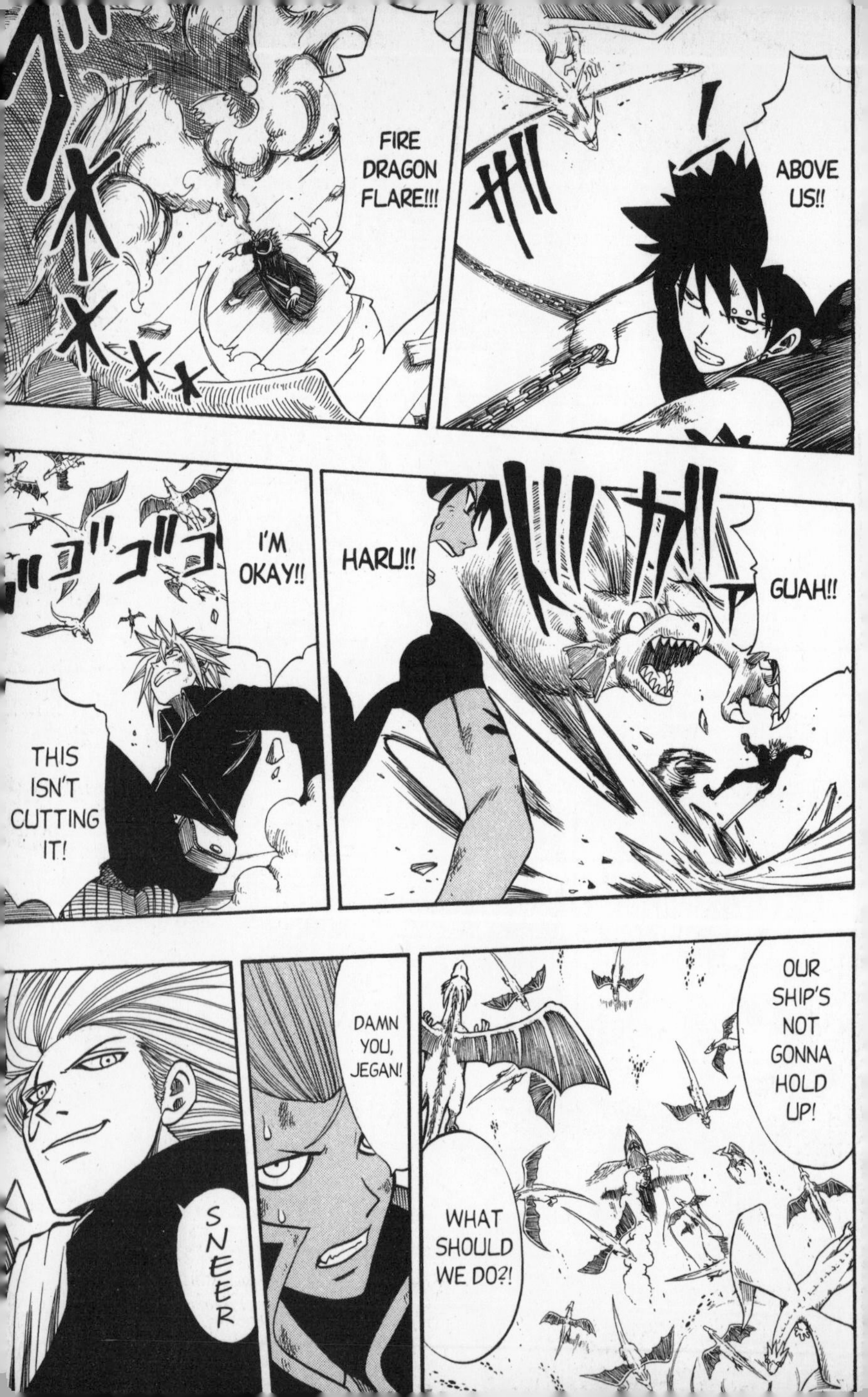
ABOVE US!!
FIRE DRAGON FLARE!!!
GUAH!!
HARU!!
I'M OKAY!!
THIS ISN'T CUTTING IT!
OUR SHIP'S NOT GONNA HOLD UP!
WHAT SHOULD WE DO?!
DAMN YOU, JEGAN!
SNEER

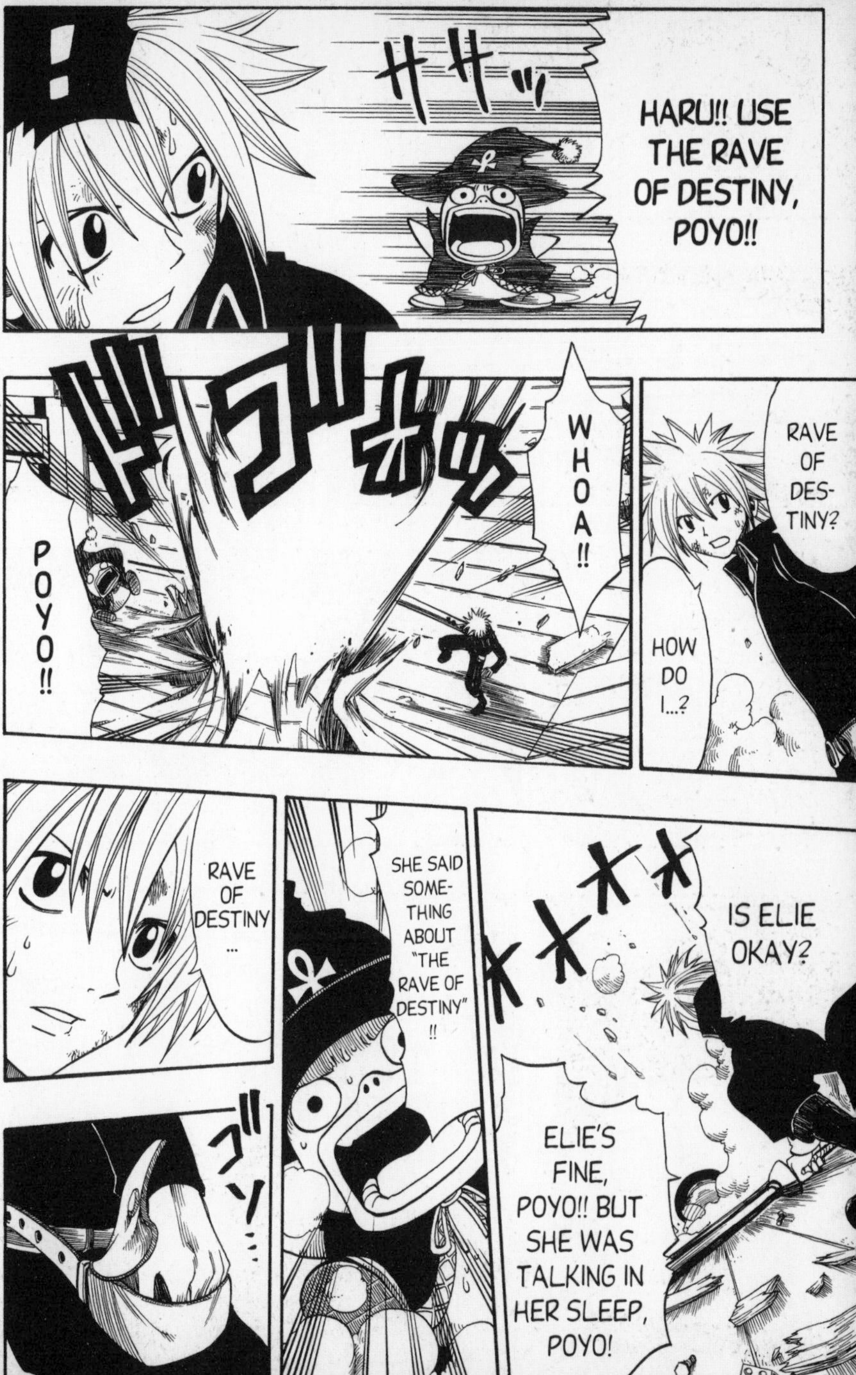
HARU!! USE THE RAVE OF DESTINY, POYO!!
RAVE OF DES-TINY?
HOW DO I...?
WHOA!!
POYO!!
IS ELIE OKAY?
ELIE'S FINE, POYO!! BUT SHE WAS TALKING IN HER SLEEP, POYO!
SHE SAID SOME-THING ABOUT "THE RAVE OF DESTINY"!!
RAVE OF DESTINY ...

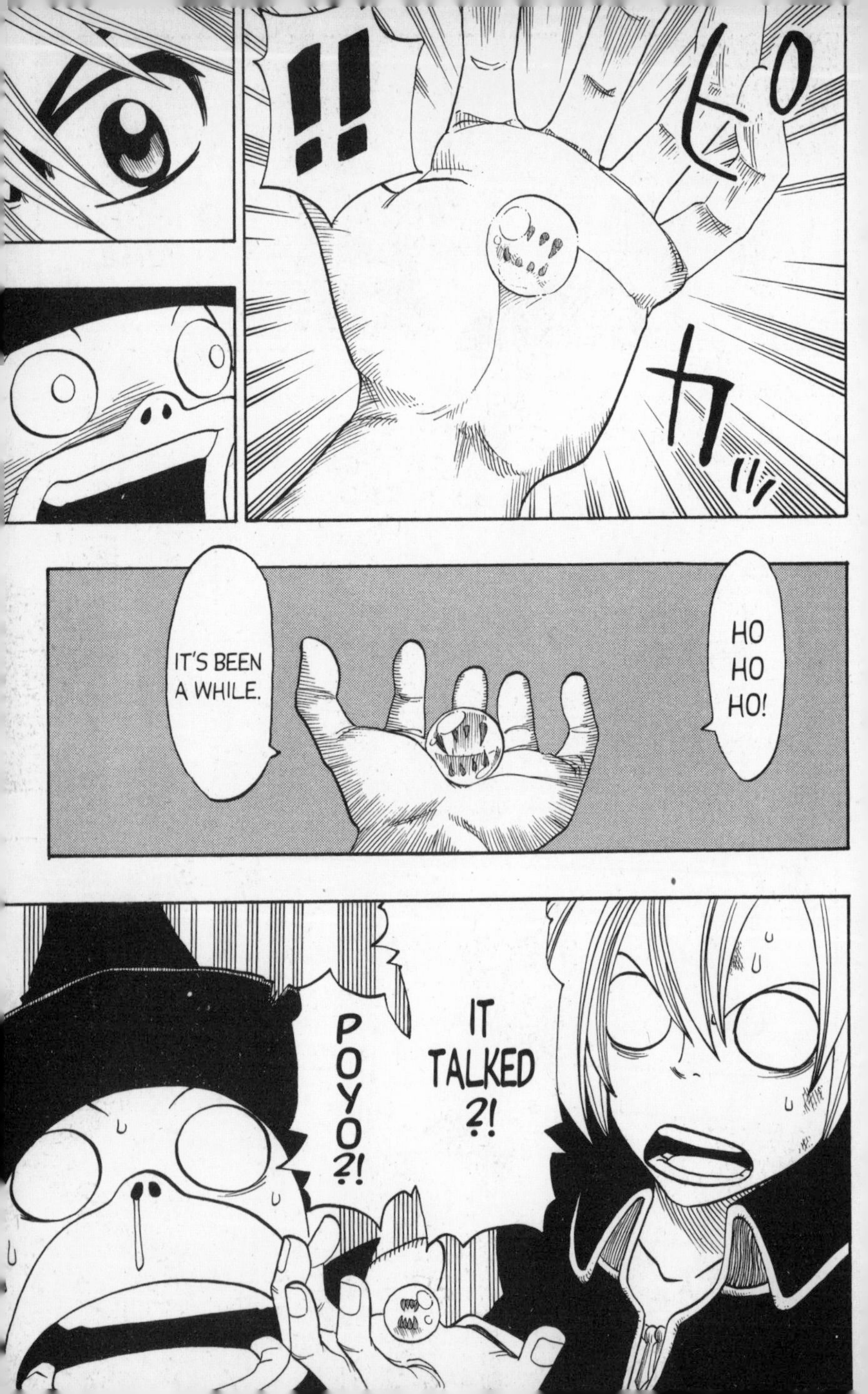
!!
HO HO HO!
IT'S BEEN A WHILE.
IT TALKED ?!
POYOO?!

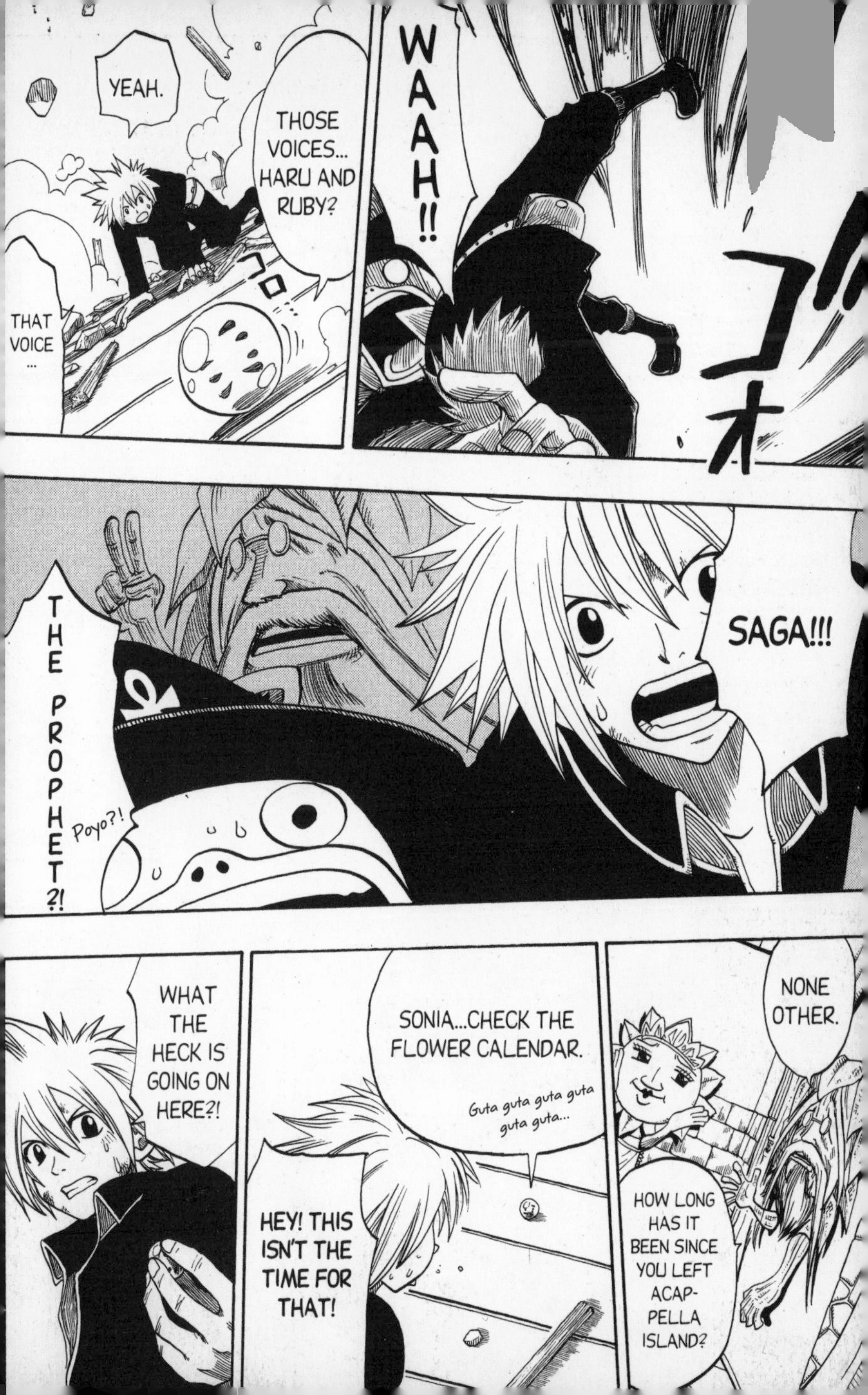
WAAH!!
THOSE VOICES... HARU AND RUBY?
YEAH.
THAT VOICE ...
SAGA!!!
THE PROPHET?!
Poyo?!
NONE OTHER.
HOW LONG HAS IT BEEN SINCE YOU LEFT ACAP-PELLA ISLAND?
SONIA...CHECK THE FLOWER CALENDAR.
Guta guta guta guta guta guta...
HEY! THIS ISN'T THE TIME FOR THAT!
WHAT THE HECK IS GOING ON HERE?!

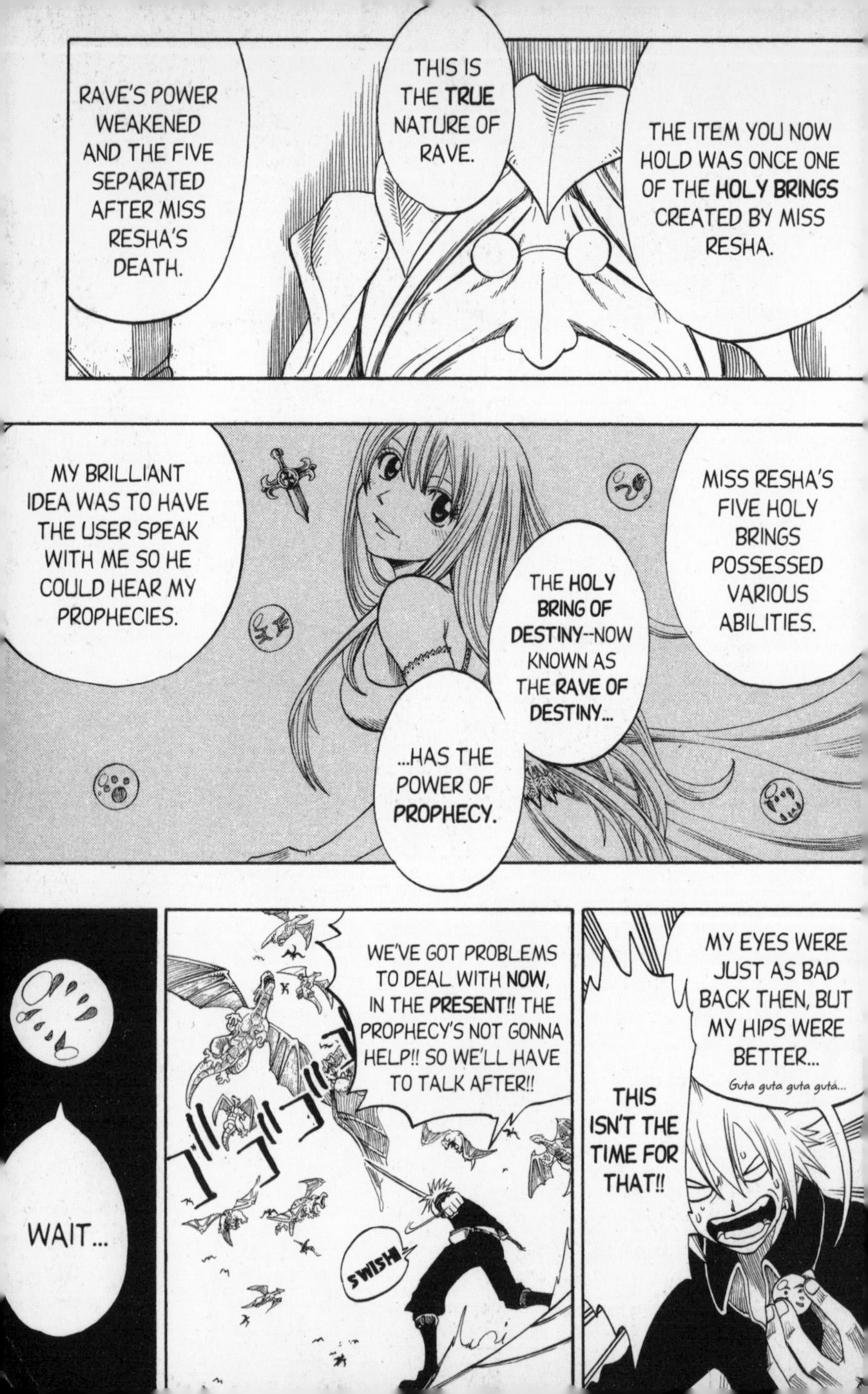
THE ITEM YOU NOW HOLD WAS ONCE ONE OF THE HOLY BRINGS CREATED BY MISS RESHA.
THIS IS THE TRUE NATURE OF RAVE.
RAVE'S POWER WEAKENED AND THE FIVE SEPARATED AFTER MISS RESHA'S DEATH.
MISS RESHA'S FIVE HOLY BRINGS POSSESSED VARIOUS ABILITIES.
THE HOLY BRING OF DESTINY--NOW KNOWN AS THE RAVE OF DESTINY...
...HAS THE POWER OF PROPHECY.
MY BRILLIANT IDEA WAS TO HAVE THE USER SPEAK WITH ME SO HE COULD HEAR MY PROPHECIES.
MY EYES WERE JUST AS BAD BACK THEN, BUT MY HIPS WERE BETTER...
Guta guta guta gutá...
THIS ISN'T THE TIME FOR THAT!!
WE'VE GOT PROBLEMS TO DEAL WITH NOW, IN THE PRESENT!! THE PROPHECY'S NOT GONNA HELP!! SO WE'LL HAVE TO TALK AFTER!!
SWISH
WAIT...

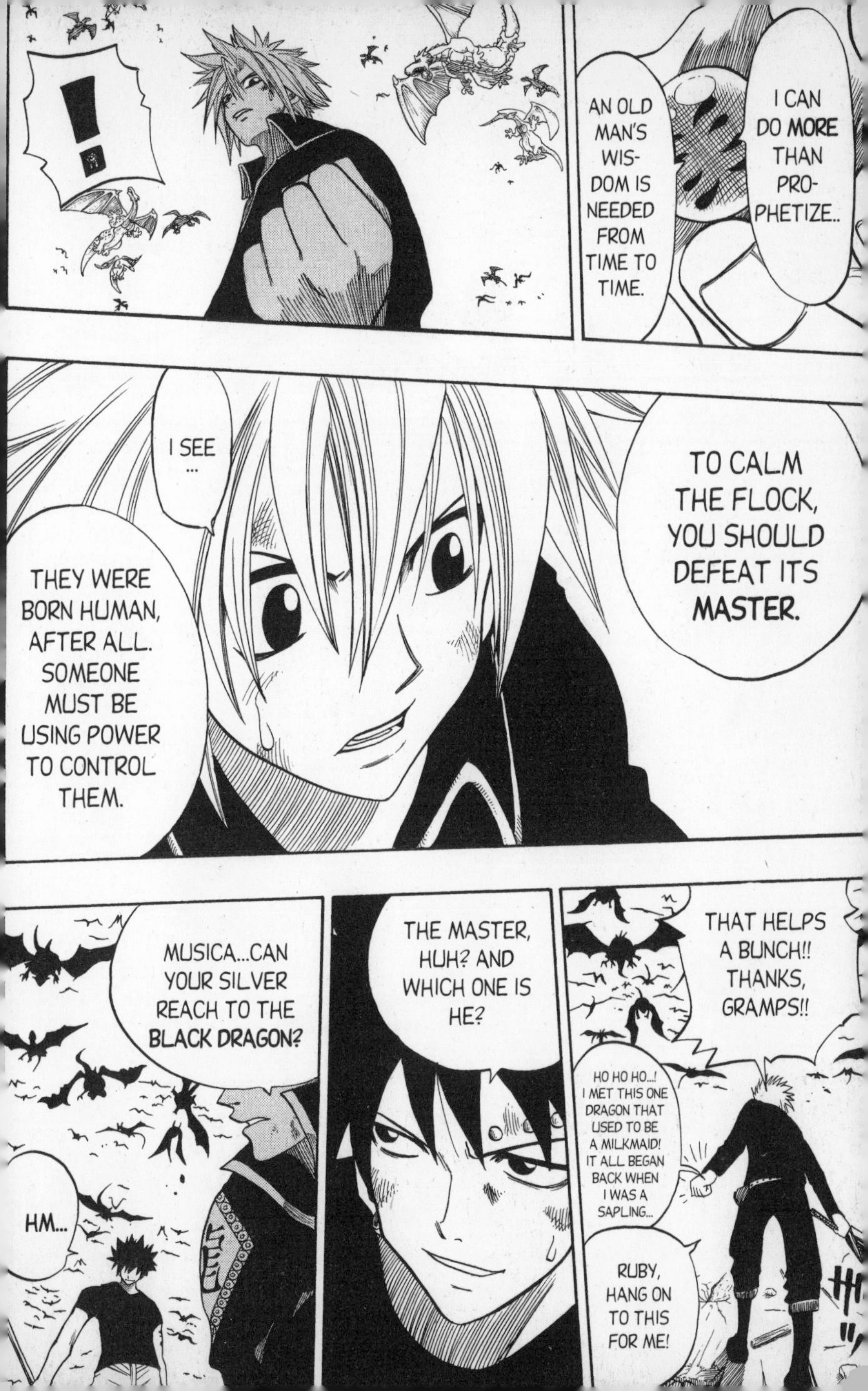
I CAN DO MORE THAN PROPHETIZE..
AN OLD MAN'S WISDOM IS NEEDED FROM TIME TO TIME.
!
TO CALM THE FLOCK, YOU SHOULD DEFEAT ITS MASTER.
I SEE ...
THEY WERE BORN HUMAN, AFTER ALL. SOMEONE MUST BE USING POWER TO CONTROL THEM.
THAT HELPS A BUNCH!! THANKS, GRAMPS!!
HO HO HO...! I MET THIS ONE DRAGON THAT USED TO BE A MILKMAID! IT ALL BEGAN BACK WHEN I WAS A SAPLING...
RUBY, HANG ON TO THIS FOR ME!
THE MASTER, HUH? AND WHICH ONE IS HE?
MUSICA...CAN YOUR SILVER REACH TO THE BLACK DRAGON?
HM...

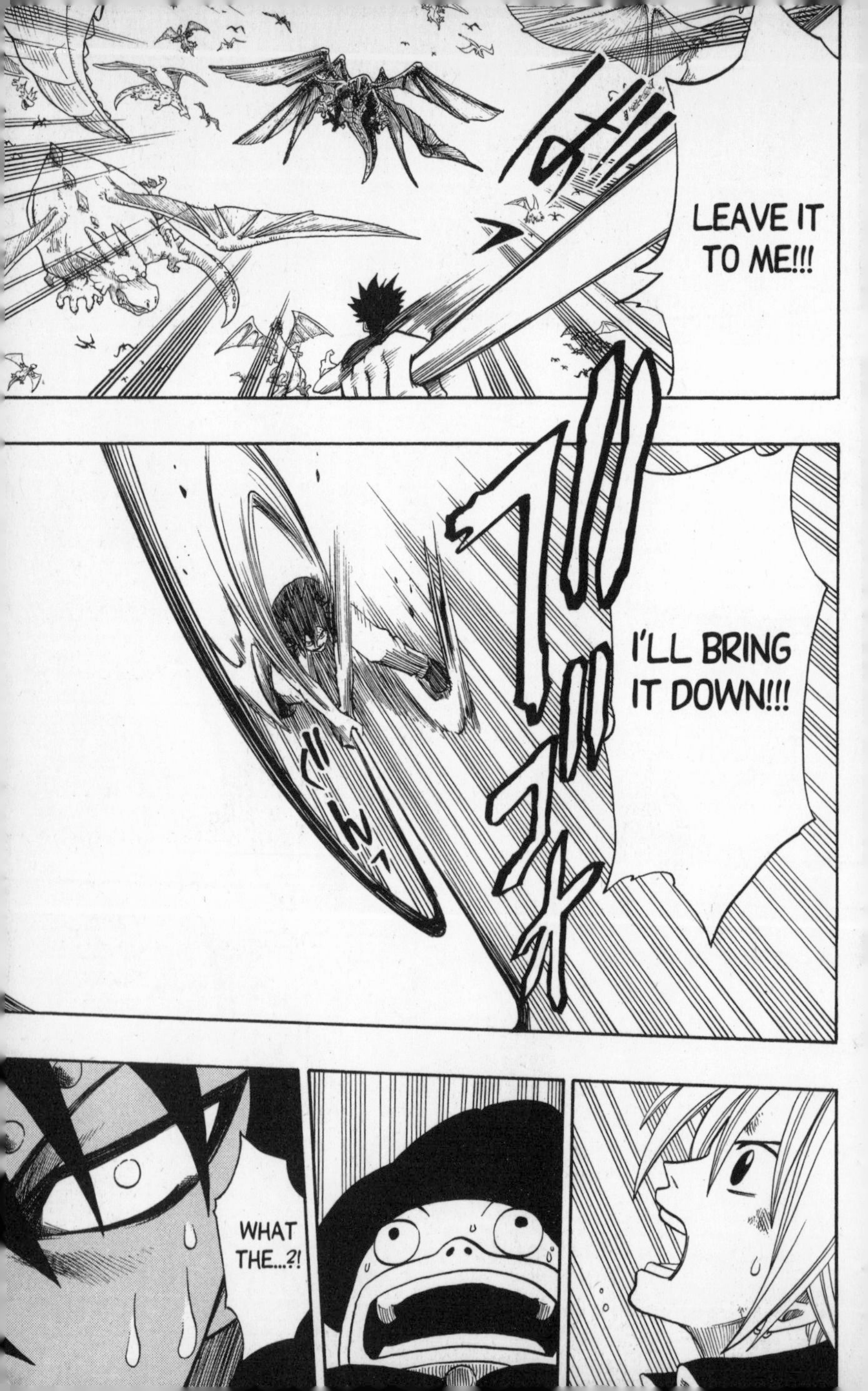
LEAVE IT TO ME!!!
I'LL BRING IT DOWN!!!
WHAT THE...?!

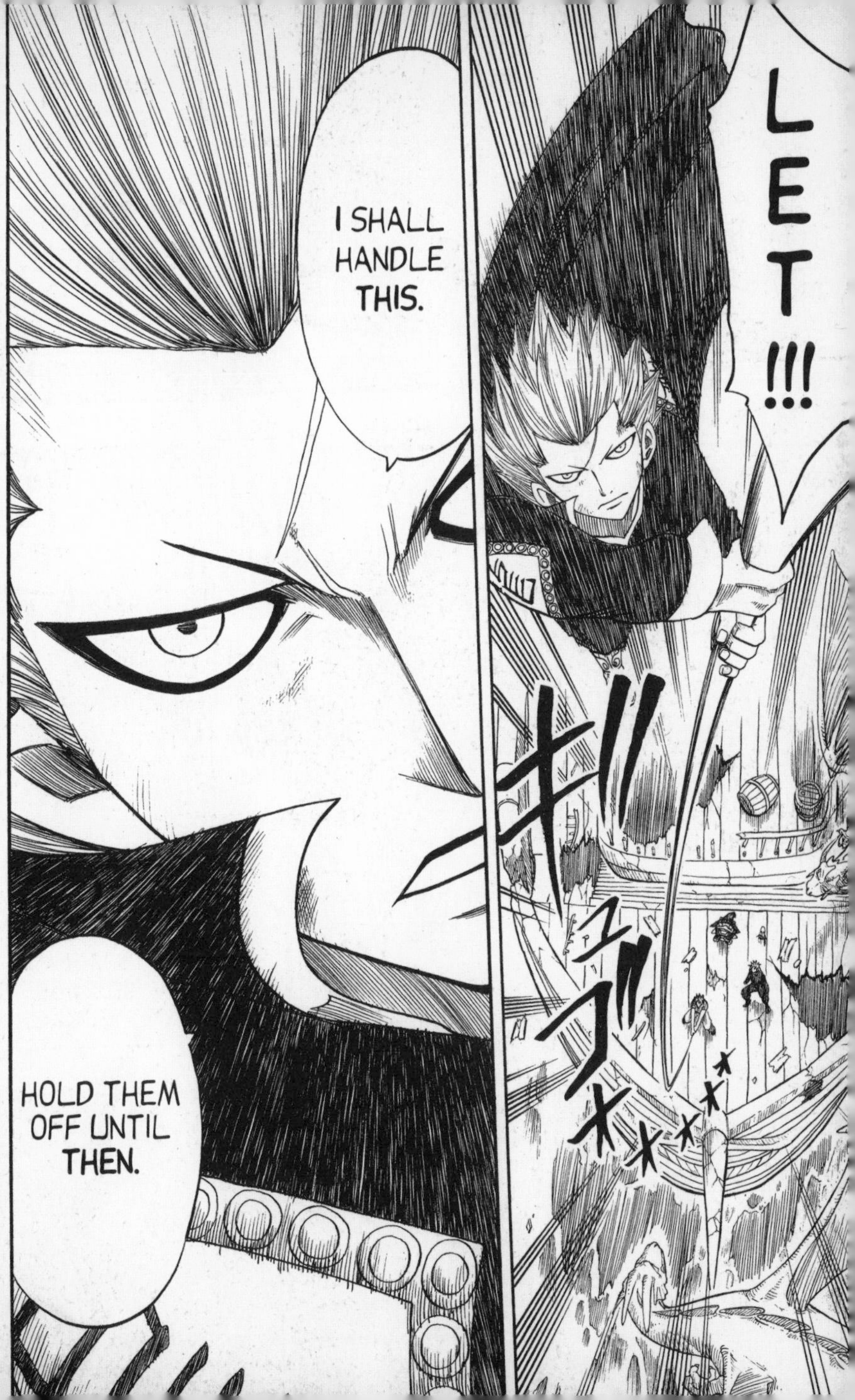
LET!!!
I SHALL HANDLE THIS.
HOLD THEM OFF UNTIL THEN.

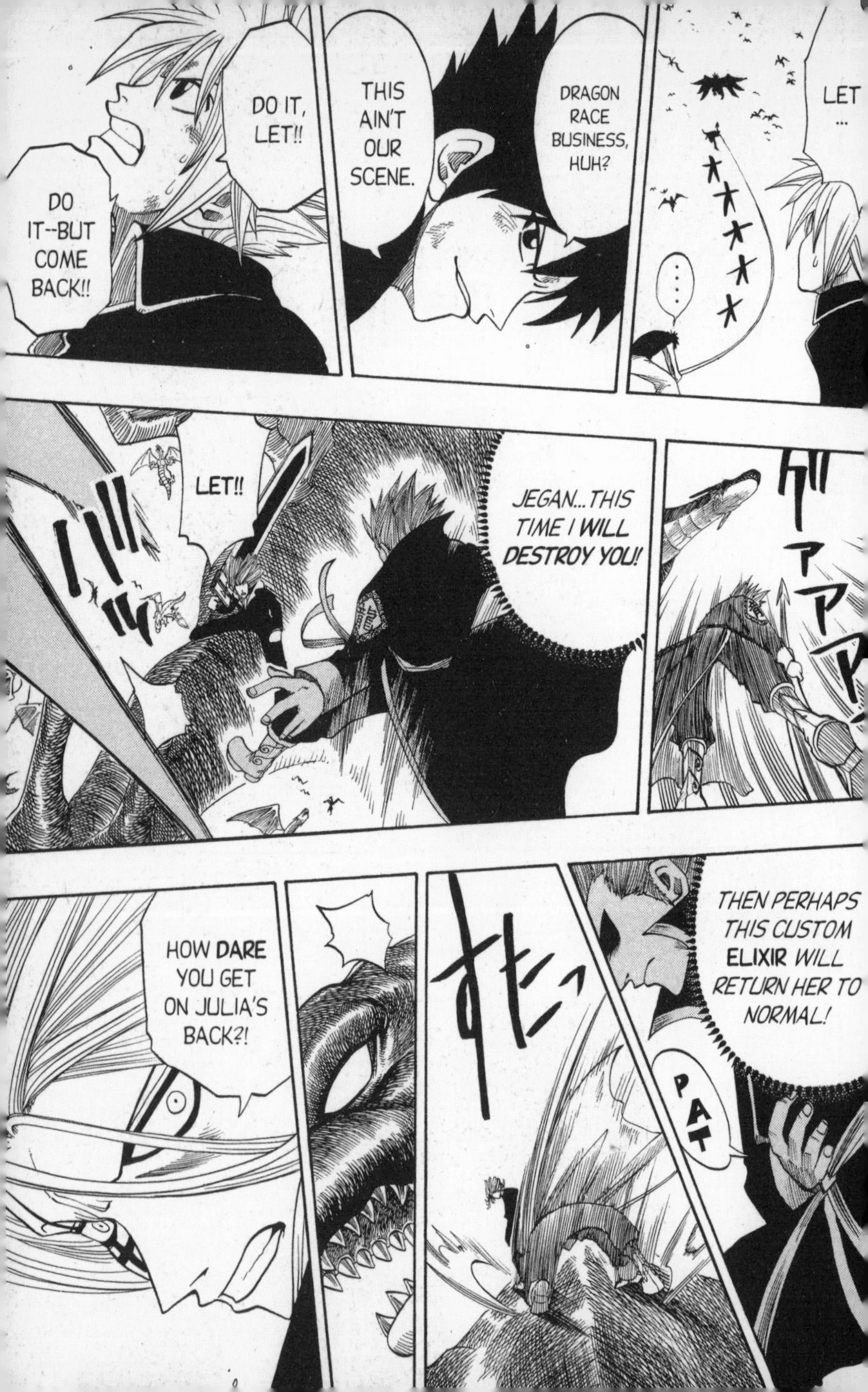
LET ...
.....
DRAGON RACE BUSINESS, HUH?
THIS AIN'T OUR SCENE.
DO IT, LET!!
DO IT--BUT COME BACK!!
JEGAN...THIS TIME I **WILL** DESTROY YOU!
LET!!
THEN PERHAPS THIS CUSTOM **ELIXIR** WILL RETURN HER TO NORMAL!
PAT
HOW **DARE** YOU GET ON JULIA'S BACK?!

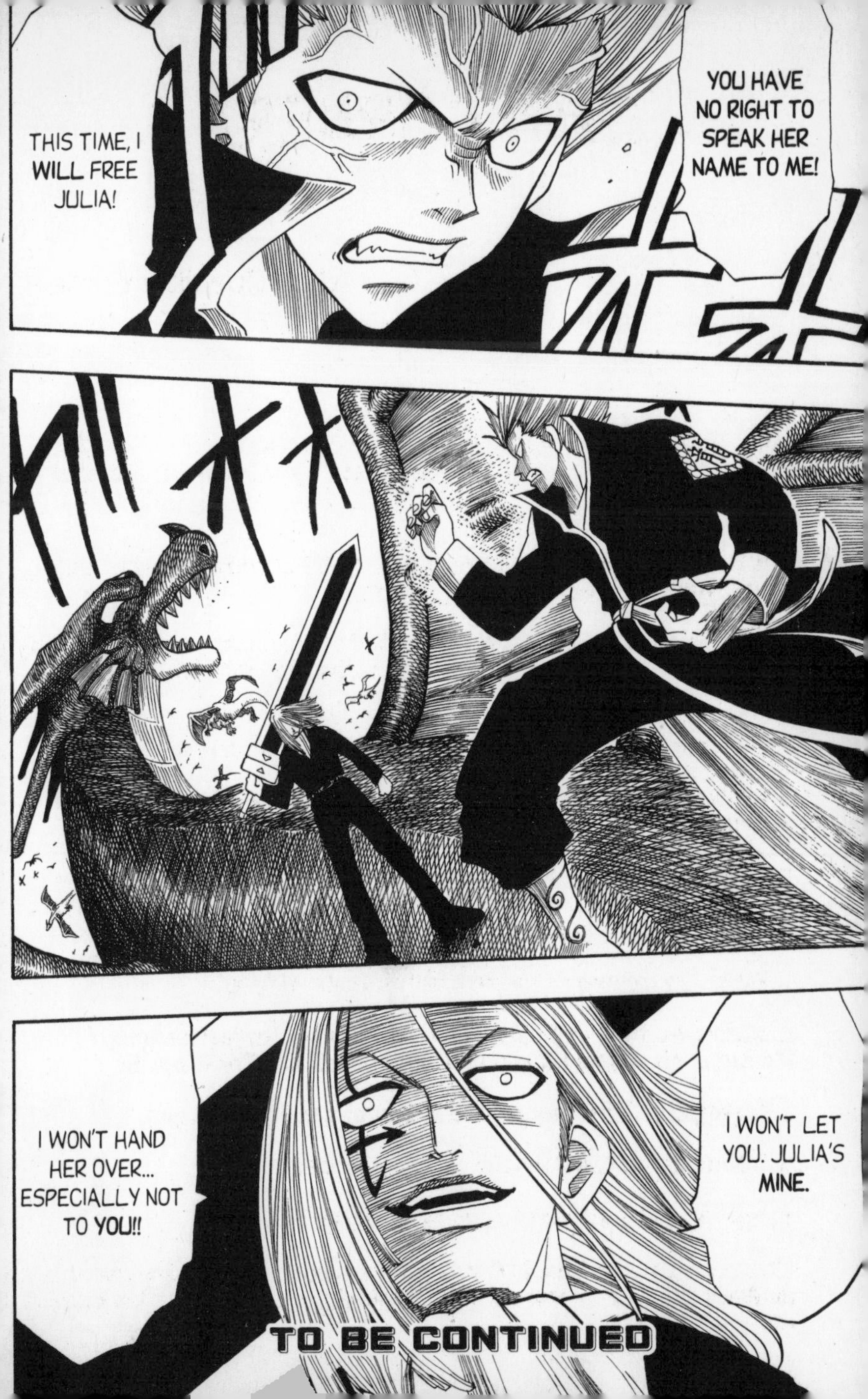
YOU HAVE NO RIGHT TO SPEAK HER NAME TO ME!
THIS TIME, I WILL FREE JULIA!
I WON'T LET YOU. JULIA'S MINE.
I WON'T HAND HER OVER... ESPECIALLY NOT TO YOU!!
TO BE CONTINUED

Q&A CORNER!!

Q. What are the origins of all the Ten Powers' names?
(Foot Monkey - Miyagi Prefecture)

A. Hmm, not that the origins are such a huge thing...well, I'd written some down. So let's give this a shot!

1. First, Ten Powers. This is a variation of "Ten Commandments," which are the commandments given by God in the Old Testament. No relation beyond the name.

2. Explosion is exactly what it sounds like. Sword go boom.

3. Silfarion is a play on a word usually associated with wind and speed (Sylph).

4. Rune Save. Well, runes come up a lot in fantasy novels in relation to magic and mythology. "Save" was meant to stand for "restraint" and "magic defense," so you get the point.

5. Blue Crimson stands for ice and fire. Pretty simple.

6. Mel Force. Hee hee! I just made that one up. No real meaning to it. It's like a mix of Mel Gibson and The Force (from *Star Wars*). (^_^)

7. Gravity Core. That means "the center of gravity," basically.

8. Million Suns means what it sounds like, too.

9. Eisenmeteor basically means "Iron Meteorite."

10. Lucia's Demon Sword "Decalogue" is named after another word meaning the Ten Commandments. Basically, it means it has ten powers.

AFTERWORDS

HUMAN GENOME!! MASHIMA HERE. I WAS IN TOKYO THIS JULY AND I'LL BE IN OSAKA IN AUGUST FOR BOOK SIGNINGS. HAVING SAID THAT, I DON'T KNOW WHEN I'LL DO MORE WITH ALL THE WORK I'VE GOT ON MY PLATE!

BY THE WAY, AT KODANSHA'S **SUPER CHARACTER** FESTIVAL EVENT, SOMEHOW PLUE GOT IN AS A SUPER CHARACTER, TOO! HE HUNG OUT AT THE MASHIMA SIGNING EVENT. DOING EVENTS LIKE THAT IS LIKE RUNNING ERRANDS. IT KEEPS ME SO BUSY!

THERE WAS AN INTERESTING GIRL AT THE HALL WHO HANDED ME A PAMPHLET SAYING, "THERE'LL BE A SIGNING EVENT WITH HIRO MASHIMA-SENSEI." AND I'M LIKE, "BWA HA HA HA HA!! **I'M MASHI-MA!!**"

HA HA...! SERIOUSLY, THANKS TO EVERYONE WHO CAME. I WAS THINKING "WHAT'LL I DO IF **NO ONE** COMES?" AT BOTH SIGNING EVENTS. I WAS REALLY HAPPY TO SEE EVERY LAST TICKET GET SNAPPED UP LIKE THEY DID. I'M REALLY SORRY FOR EVERYONE WHO COULDN'T GET ONE. I'D LOVE TO SIGN STUFF FOR EVERYONE, BUT HUMAN BEINGS DO HAVE LIMITS...

WHEN I TALKED TO THE EVENT MANAGER AFTER THE SIGNING, HE THOUGHT THERE WERE A LOT OF NEW *RAVE MASTER* FANS. IT WASN'T ANY TROUBLE AND THERE WERE WARM FEELINGS ALL AROUND. MEETING SO MANY FANS FACE-TO-FACE HAS GIVEN ME MORE COURAGE. OKAY, THEN! I'LL DO MY BEST AT OSAKA!! WAIT... ACTUALLY, BY THE TIME YOU READ THIS, THE OSAKA EVENT WILL BE OVER. BET YOU WISH BOOKS WERE PUBLISHED IN REAL-TIME NOW, HUH? (^_^)

HIRO MASHIMA

To save his friends, Let must perform the ultimate sacrifice!

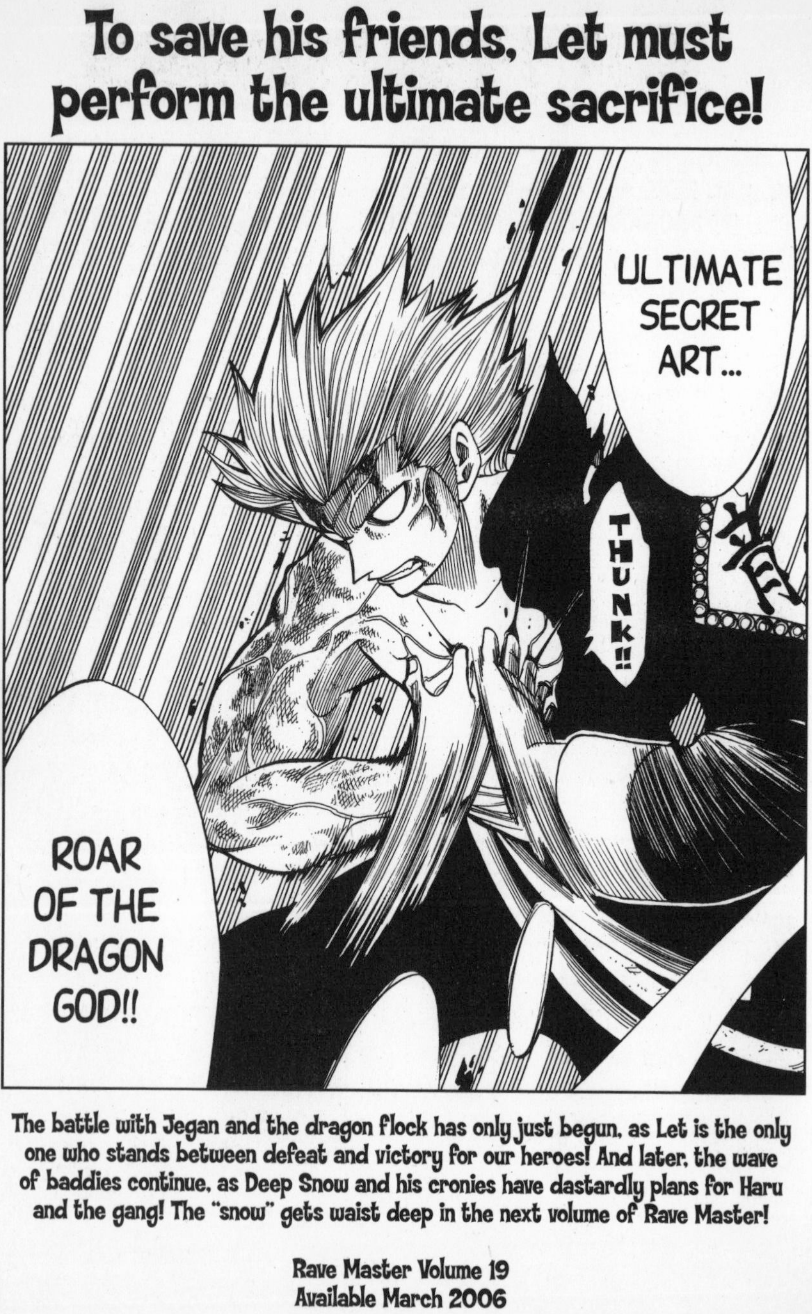
ULTIMATE SECRET ART...
THUNK!!
ROAR OF THE DRAGON GOD!!

The battle with Jegan and the dragon flock has only just begun, as Let is the only one who stands between defeat and victory for our heroes! And later, the wave of baddies continue, as Deep Snow and his cronies have dastardly plans for Haru and the gang! The "snow" gets waist deep in the next volume of Rave Master!

Rave Master Volume 19
Available March 2006

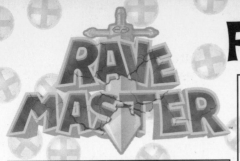

Fan Art

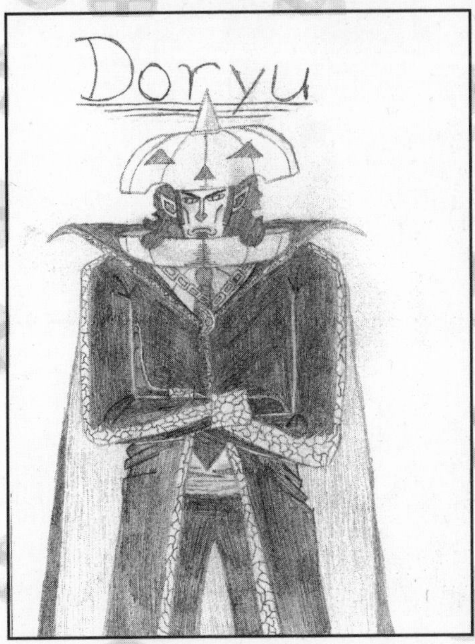
Doryu

IN KEEPING WITH THE DORYU-CENTRIC SPIRIT OF THE PREVIOUS VOLUMES, WE THOUGHT WE'D FEATURE OL' PUMPKIN HEAD ONE MORE TIME. NICE JOB, MARK! NOW IF ONLY WE COULD FIND A HAT LIKE THAT...

MARK S.
AGE 12
WINCHESTER, MA

HEY, ASPIRING MANGA ARTISTS! WANT TO SEE YOUR PICTURES IN PRINT? WELL, IF YOU THINK YOU CAN DRAW A COOL-LOOKING HARU, A SEXY ELIE OR A FUNNY PLUE, SEND 'EM THIS WAY! WHAT DO YOU HAVE TO LOSE? NOTHING!

HOW TO SUBMIT:

1) SEND YOUR WORK VIA REGULAR MAIL (NOT E-MAIL) TO:

RAVE MASTER FAN ART
C/O TOKYOPOP
5900 WILSHIRE BLVD.
SUITE 2000
LOS ANGELES, CA 90036

2) ALL WORK SUBMITTED SHOULD BE IN BLACK-AND-WHITE AND NO LARGER THAN 8.5" X 11". (AND TRY NOT TO FOLD IT TOO MANY TIMES!)

3) ANYTHING YOU SEND WILL NOT BE RETURNED. IF YOU WANT TO KEEP YOUR ORIGINAL, IT'S FINE TO SEND US A COPY.

4) PLEASE INCLUDE YOUR FULL NAME, AGE, CITY AND STATE FOR US TO PRINT WITH YOUR WORK. IF YOU'D RATHER WE USE A PEN NAME, PLEASE INCLUDE THAT, TOO.

5) IMPORTANT: IF YOU'RE UNDER THE AGE OF 18, YOU MUST HAVE YOUR PARENT'S PERMISSION IN ORDER FOR US TO PRINT YOUR WORK. ANY SUBMISSIONS WITHOUT A SIGNED NOTE OF PARENTAL CONSENT CANNOT BE USED.

6) FOR FULL DETAILS, PLEASE CHECK OUT HTTP://WWW.TOKYOPOP.COM/ABOUTUS/FANART.PHP

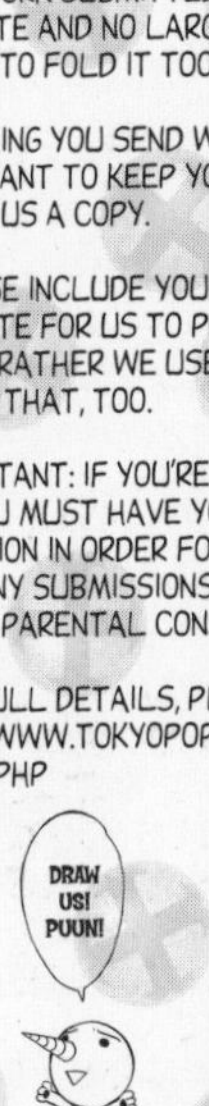
DRAW US! PUUN!

DISCLAIMER: ANYTHING YOU SEND TO US BECOMES THE PROPERTY OF TOKYOPOP INC. AND, AS WE SAID BEFORE, WILL NOT BE RETURNED TO YOU. WE WILL HAVE THE RIGHT TO PRINT, REPRODUCE, DISTRIBUTE OR MODIFY THE ARTWORK FOR USE IN FUTURE VOLUMES OF *RAVE MASTER* OR ON THE WEB WITHOUT PAYMENT TO YOU.

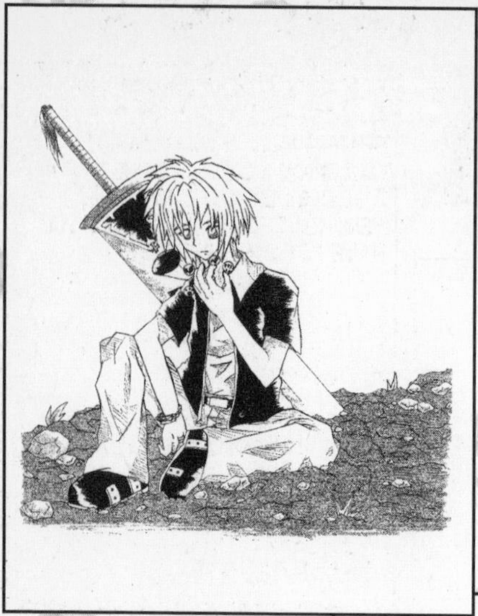

HERE'S A WONDERFUL PICTURE OF HARU IN A REFLECTIVE MOMENT. WE JUST LOVE THE CLEAN, CONFIDENT LINES IN THIS, LINDSAY!

LINDSAY C.
AGE 14
SOUTH SAN FRANCISCO, CA

HERE WE HAVE HARU, ELIE AND PLUE IN A NICE GROUP PICTURE. LOOKS LIKE THEY'RE HAVING A BLAST...THOUGH PLUE SEEMS TO BE A LITTLE WARY ABOUT THE HEIGHT. FANTASTIC WORK, ANNIE!

ANNIE W.
AGE 11
FOREST HILLS, NY

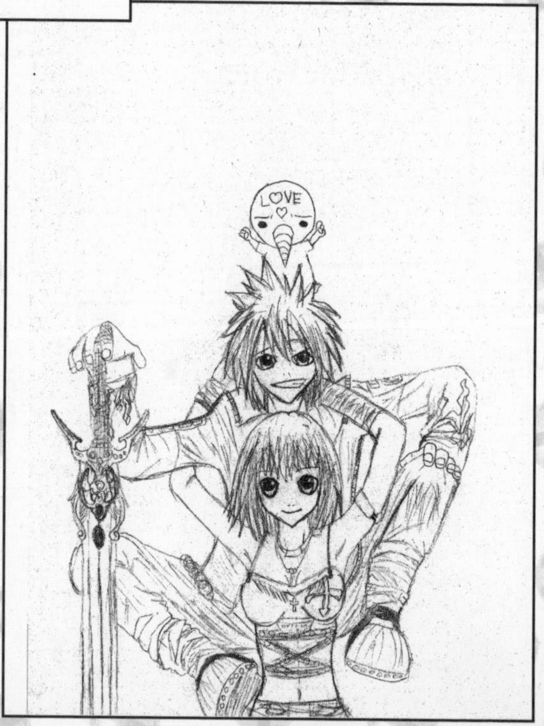
LOVE

SPEAKING OF PLUE...THIS PICTURE IS HILARIOUS! WE ESPECIALLY LOVE HIRO MASHIMA PLUE! AND HIS HAIR IS JUST LIKE THIS! THANKS FOR TICKLING OUR FUNNY BONES, JAMES!

JAMES D.
AGE 13
SHAKOPEE, MN

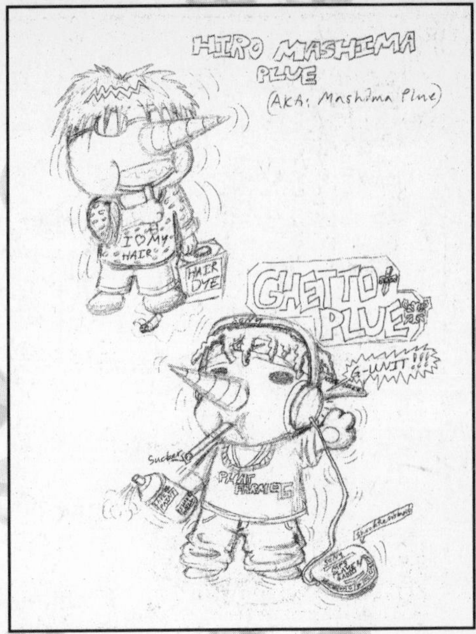
HIRO MASHIMA PLUE
(AKA: Mashima Plue)
I ♥ My HAIR
HAIR DYE
GHETTO PLUE
G-UNIT!!!
Sucker

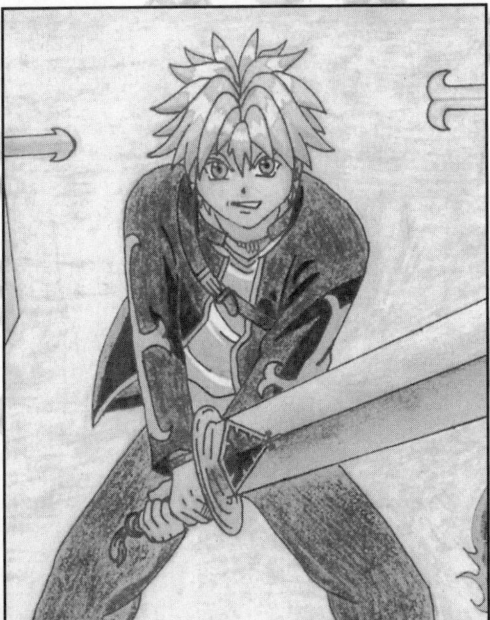

HERE'S HARU AGAIN, IN A "COME GET SOME!" POSE. THE SHADING IN THIS IS SPOT ON, ATHENA!

ATHENA A.
AGE 17
VICTORVILLE, CA

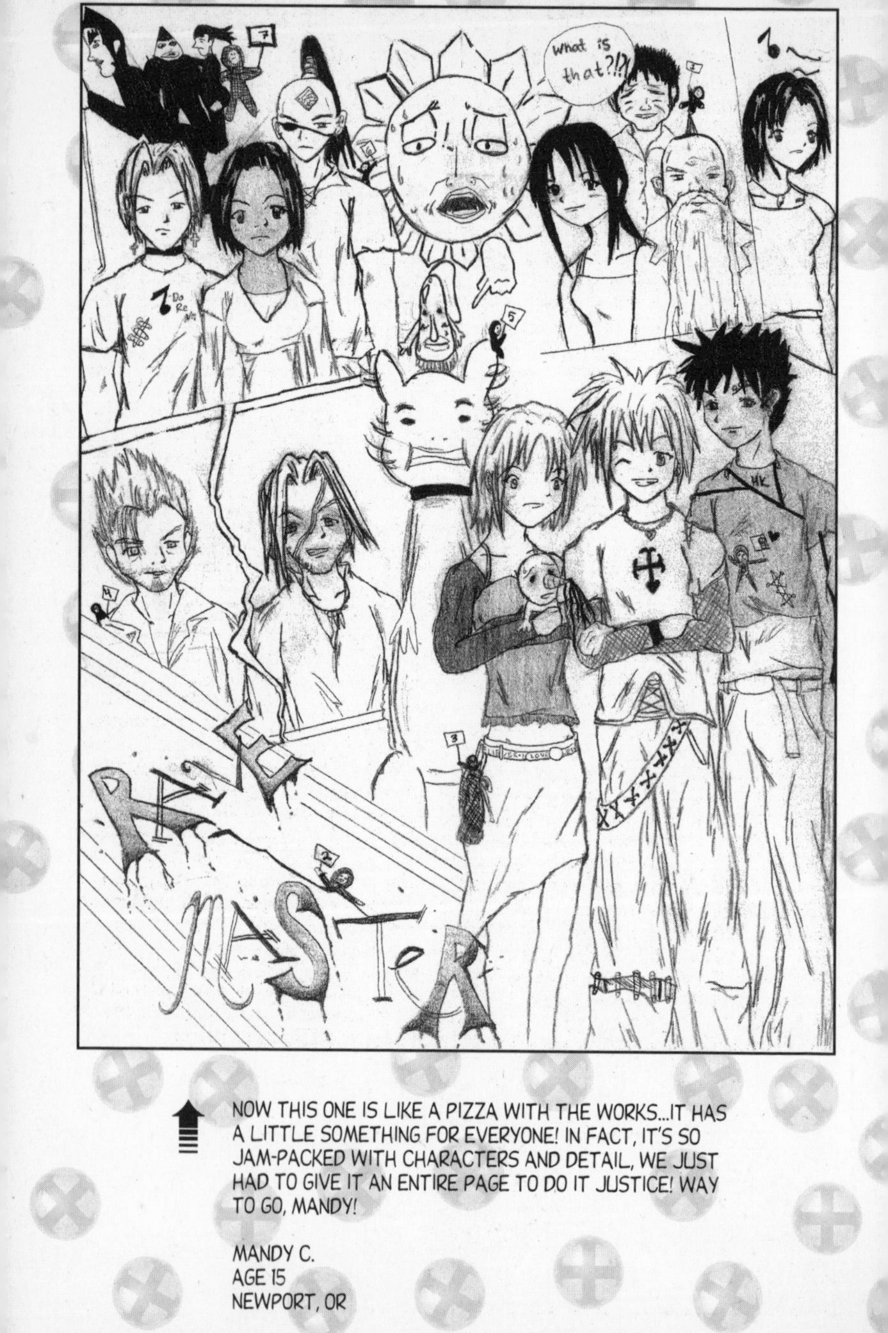
What is that?!?!
RAVE MASTeR

NOW THIS ONE IS LIKE A PIZZA WITH THE WORKS...IT HAS A LITTLE SOMETHING FOR EVERYONE! IN FACT, IT'S SO JAM-PACKED WITH CHARACTERS AND DETAIL, WE JUST HAD TO GIVE IT AN ENTIRE PAGE TO DO IT JUSTICE! WAY TO GO, MANDY!

MANDY C.
AGE 15
NEWPORT, OR

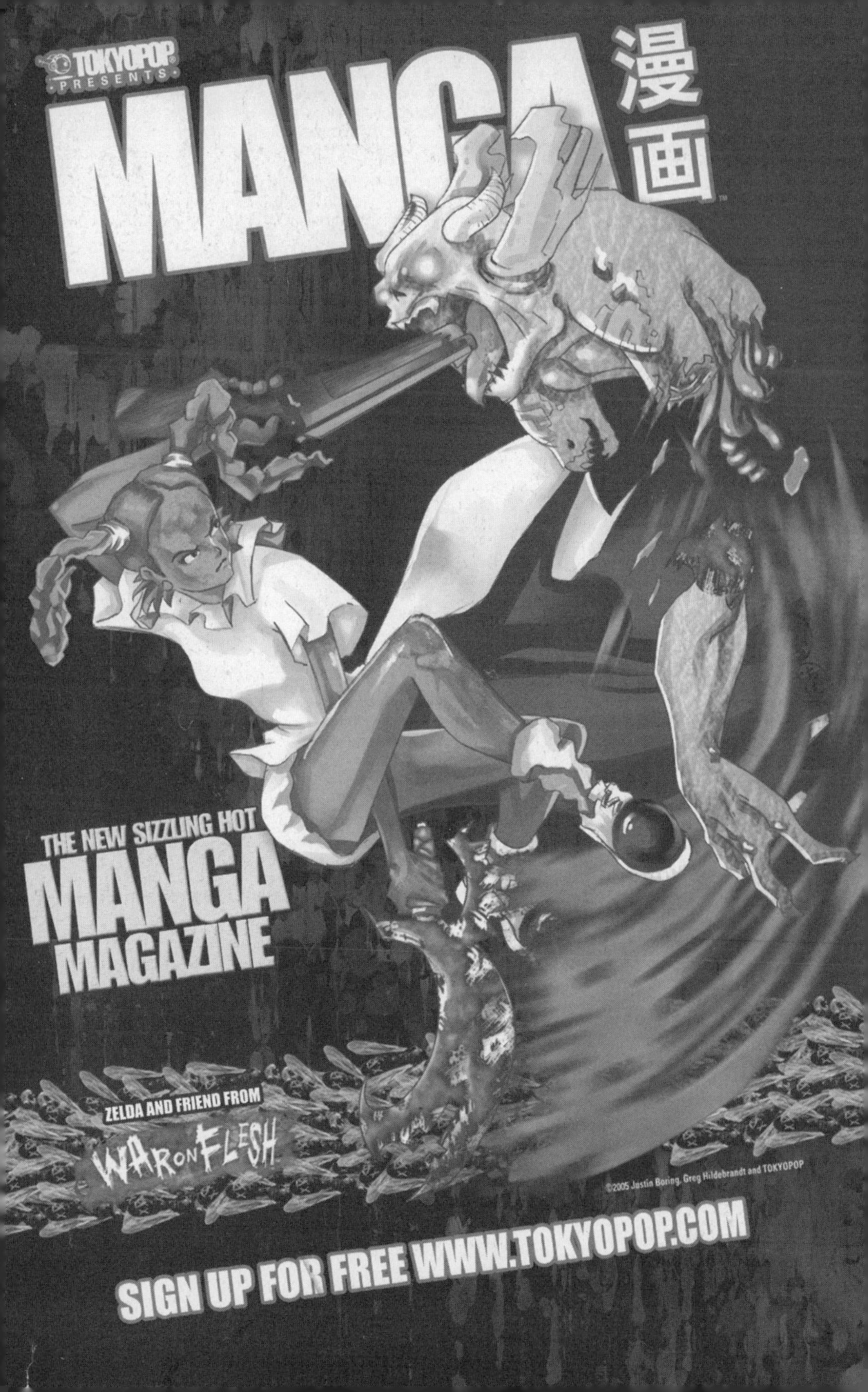

TOKYOPOP PRESENTS
MANGA 漫画
THE NEW SIZZLING HOT
MANGA
MAGAZINE
ZELDA AND FRIEND FROM
WAR ON FLESH
©2005 Justin Boring, Greg Hildebrandt and TOKYOPOP
SIGN UP FOR FREE WWW.TOKYOPOP.COM

TOKYOPOP SHOP

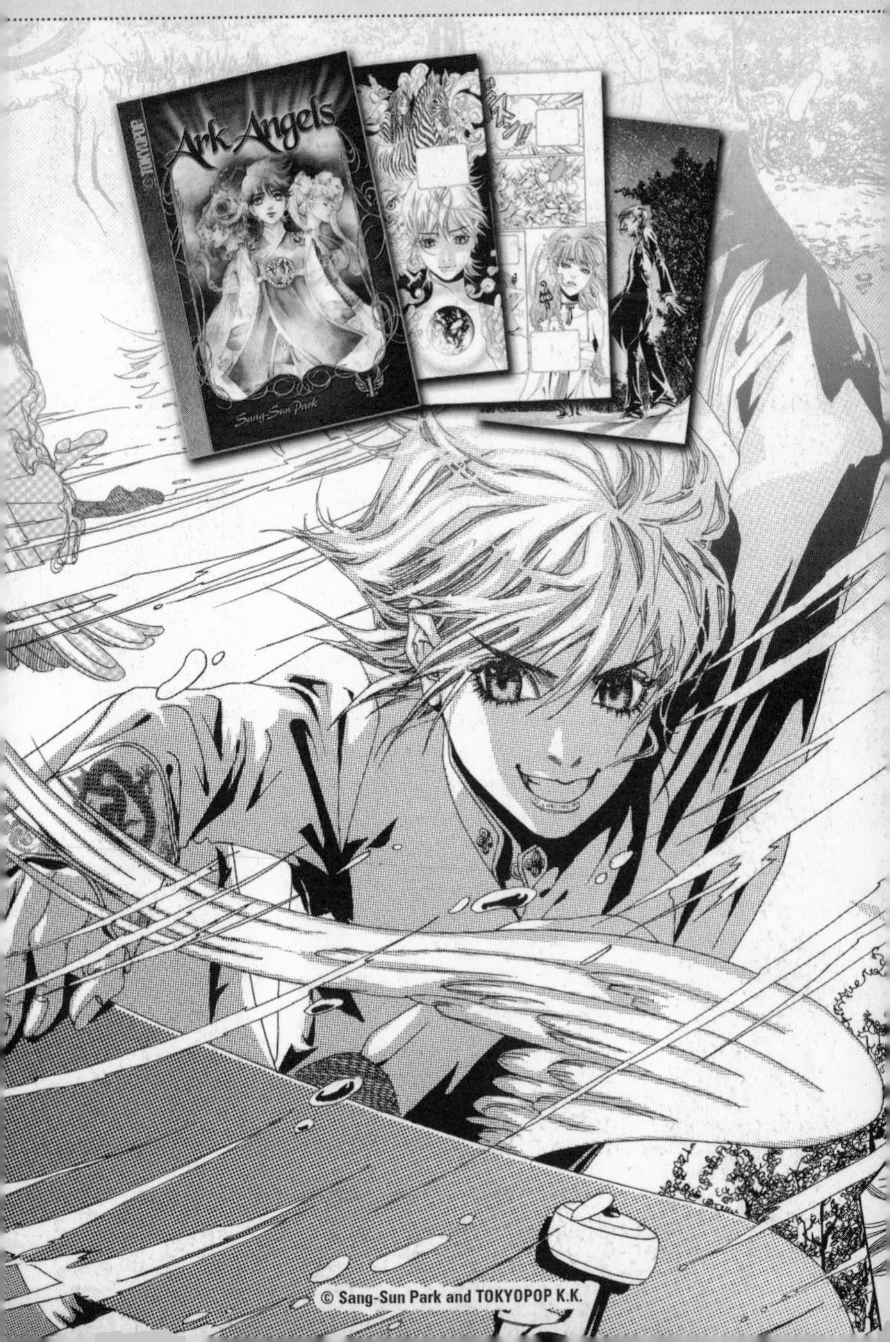
Ark Angels
TOKYOPOP
Sang-Sun Park

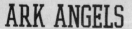

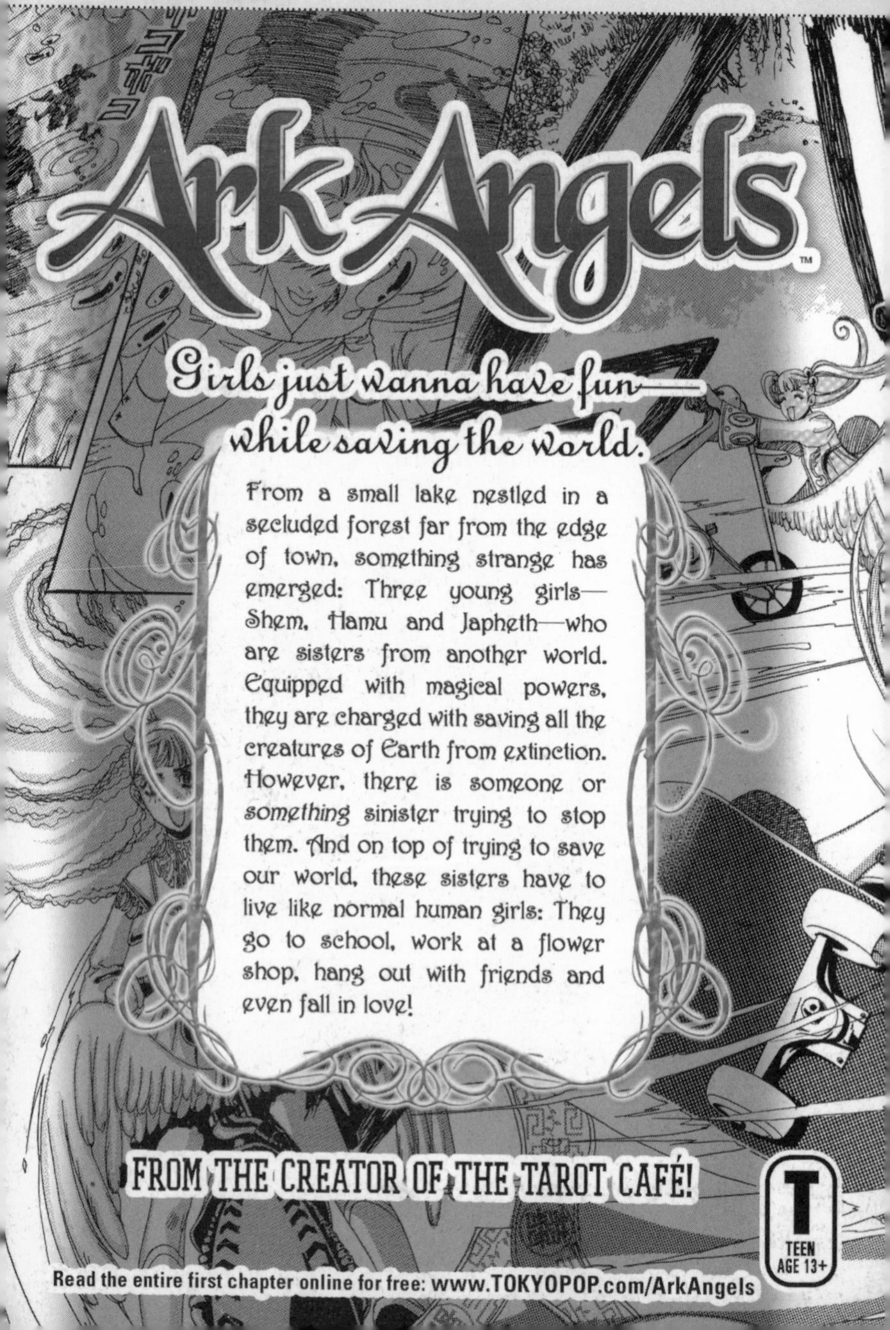
Ark Angels™
Girls just wanna have fun—
while saving the world.
From a small lake nestled in a secluded forest far from the edge of town, something strange has emerged: Three young girls—Shem, Hamu and Japheth—who are sisters from another world. Equipped with magical powers, they are charged with saving all the creatures of Earth from extinction. However, there is someone or *something* sinister trying to stop them. And on top of trying to save our world, these sisters have to live like normal human girls: They go to school, work at a flower shop, hang out with friends and even fall in love!
FROM THE CREATOR OF THE TAROT CAFÉ!
T TEEN AGE 13+
Read the entire first chapter online for free: www.TOKYOPOP.com/ArkAngels

STOP!

This is the back of the book.
You wouldn't want to spoil a great ending!

This book is printed "manga-style," in the authentic Japanese right-to-left format. Since none of the artwork has been flipped or altered, readers get to experience the story just as the creator intended. You've been asking for it, so TOKYOPOP® delivered: authentic, hot-off-the-press, and far more fun!

DIRECTIONS

1
2
3
4
5
6
7
8
9
10

If this is your first time reading manga-style, here's a quick guide to help you understand how it works.

It's easy... just start in the top right panel and follow the numbers. Have fun, and look for more 100% authentic manga from TOKYOPOP®!

100% AUTHENTIC MANGA
品質第一公式商品

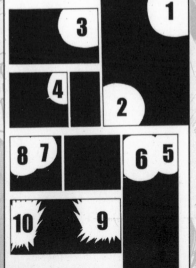

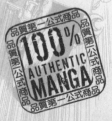